Liberating
Memory

Liberating Memory Our Work and Our Working-Class Consciousness

Edited
and with an
introduction by

Janet Zandy

Rutgers University Press
New Brunswick, New Jersey

Library of Congress Cataloging-in-Publication Data

Liberating memory : our work and our working-class consciousness / edited and
    with an introduction by Janet Zandy.
        p.   cm.
    Includes bibliographical references.
    ISBN 0-8135-2121-1 (cloth)—ISBN 0-8135-2122-X (pbk.)
    1. Working class—United States.   2. Class consciousness—United States.
I. Zandy, Janet, 1945–
HD8072.5.L53   1994
305.5′62′0973—dc20
                                                                      94-8042
                                                                      CIP

British Cataloging-in-Publication information available

In Loving Memory
of my father
Charles F. Ballotta
1915–1965

Contents

Part Five   The "We" Inside the "I"

Preface

What happens if you are born into a working-class family in the United States? How do you produce culture, engage in politics, acquire and construct knowledge? How do you keep and use the consciousness of class difference in the work that you do? How do you resist assimilation into bourgeois sensibilities and institutions? This is a collection that addresses these and other "hows" of working-class lived experience. It evolves out of the conviction that working-class identities are mobile, durable, and have democratic use-value.

In *Calling Home,* a collection of writing by working-class women I published with Rutgers in 1990, my purpose was to prove—by the collective weight of the material—that working-class women have a powerful writing tradition. It took ten years to collect the material and see the book to publication. The project was finished, but not finished; the process of recovery led to more complicated and difficult questions. I wanted to investigate further how working-class consciousness *acts* in the world. I realized that I was able to sustain my own cultural work *because*—not in spite of—my working-class roots. I also knew that this sense of connection was not unique to me.

How does this happen? It happens for many of us because of the physics of memory—not memory as weepy nostalgia, but memory as lever, a physical force—rough and beautiful—that multiplies our power to act in the world. To be sure, it is not a soothing, secure, or easy tool. Memory is unsafe. There is the risk of releasing what others—perhaps our own families—would prefer were kept hidden.

When I put out my first call for contributors in 1991, I knew that I was asking for writing that was both compelling and dangerous. From the more than forty submissions of essays and proposals, I selected these twenty-five. I see them as strategic rather than representational. That is, they do not dissolve into one blended working-class essence. Rather, they show

how individual migrations and practiced cultural work loop back to human relationships in recognizable working-class circumstances. These narratives are about the usefulness of private memory to democratic political struggle. I hope they will be viewed as tools rather than as testimonials or trophies.

The divisions of this book underscore certain patterns in the development of working-class consciousness and the creation of cultural work. Obviously, they are not fixed or exclusive, but shifting theoretical categories of location, language, and multiple and fragmented identities. All but three of these essays were written expressly for this collection. Seven of the contributors are not academics. My original intent was to pair each memoir with some example or artifact of the writer's cultural work. However, in some cases, the two were not separate things; instead, the cultural work was an expression of the writer's current professional and working identity. In one instance, the autobiography is missing because this writer, Wilma Elizabeth McDaniel, wanted her poetry to stand on its own. Her individual identity—she made clear to me—was not particularly important.

I regret that I have not been able to include everyone who submitted essays for this collection. The problems of space and the peculiar dynamics of any collection where the pieces must cohere as parts of a whole prevented me from using the work of many fine writers. Especially to those who were willing revisers but could not be included, my apologies.

The photographs—how the subjects are posed, their context and occasion—are both familiar and distinct. I asked each contributor for pictures of emergence—not specifying a particular age. Some were able to locate clusters of images from certain time periods, but found virtually no visual documentation for long periods of time. Locating any suitable image at all was a challenge for those writers whose family pictures are all but lost because of deaths, or moves, or natural disasters, or the unexpected upheavals of working-class life. Some have no early pictures; others were able to draw on a rich but selective record of vacations, holidays, graduations, and shared meals. Images of people at work or the struggle inherent to working-class life are rarer.

As was true with *Calling Home,* the evocative and varied quality of the submitted work suggests to me a living working-class culture in the United States, often practiced outside the academy, and usually unrecognized and unnamed by the media. We do not yet have institutionalized "working-class studies." Perhaps it awaits the pressure of a larger, political, workers' movement comparable to earlier labor struggles or the Civil Rights or women's liberation movements. In the meantime, we have these voices.

Acknowledgments

Although the notion of literary inheritance has rightly been scrutinized and criticized for its patriarchal foundation, I think it is a mistake to abandon the word "inheritance" completely. It is certainly as much a process as it is a thing. This book is about another kind of inheritance—hidden, unnamed, unpropertied, perhaps—but, nonetheless, alive in us. Here I acknowledge some small part of that gift.

First, I wish to thank these writers, for their patience and work, for the risks they've taken, and for the voices inherent in their work. I want to acknowledge my debt to the intellectual work of Raymond Williams and to Tillie Olsen for showing the way, for her language and sustaining love. I thank the friends and colleagues who responded to this manuscript in its many phases, in particular: Joseph Nassar, Sandra Saari, Thomas Cornell, Lawrence Chisolm, Michael Frisch, Masani Alexis DeVeaux, Constance Coiner, Paul Lauter, Manning Marable, Chojy Schroeder, Florence Howe, Dolores L. Kleinberg, and Carol Ann Bamdad. My gratitude to Stuart Mitchner for his expert copyediting, and to Margaret Evans who meticulously reprinted precious family photographs. I thank the editors and staff at Rutgers University Press for the respect and care they give to working-class voices. Especially, I thank Leslie Mitchner, editor and friend, whose intellect and insight I deeply cherish.

To my family, my husband, William Zandy, and my children, Anna and Victor, my love and thanks for affirming my work life. To my father who taught me that learning and books are more important than money, I dedicate this book.

Liberating Memory

Academic Career
of Orville Kincaid

Back in the old neighborhood
some will remember him if
you prod them. The boy who didn't
wear socks until he was past thirteen.
All will remember his love of books,
reading while he stood in line for his
family's welfare butter and flour.

But they lose him for his scholarship
years at Oxford University, trying to
erase who he was. Eating watercress
sandwiches
when he really wanted grits and gravy.

And none of them had read of a man
who walked out of a ten-story window
wearing a velvet robe
with a copy of Yeats in the pocket.
                    —Wilma Elizabeth McDaniel

"The most uneventful life would take a library of books to transcribe."
                    —Raymond Williams

Introduction

A working-class identity is an ambiguous gift. To develop that identity, to recognize its potential in a society where the working class is denied its own name, is to claim a responsibility that goes beyond the individual self. That is why this is a collection and not just my own story. The intent of this book is not to lament exclusion, but to illustrate agency. The contributors to *Liberating Memory* are cultural workers who trace the inscription of class on their lives and on their work. They have found ways to resist class amnesia, and to use their working-class identity and consciousness as tools to shape culture. This interplay of class, culture, and memory is the subject of *Liberating Memory.*

Identity, Consciousness, and the Problem of Measurement

According to the book of success, a working-class identity is intended for disposal. In order to "make it" into the dominant society, one "overcomes" the class circumstances of birth, and moves into the middle and then upper class. Not only is this projected trajectory becoming economically *less* feasible as job opportunities shrink and downward mobility increases, but it is an assumption that reduces human interaction and potential to mere commodity exchange and personal enhancement.[1]

We are not concerned here with the conventional American Dream version of upward mobility nor are we offering a romantic reconceptualization of working-class life. We are engaged, instead, with a rarely articulated alternative movement: with reconstructing the ways in which working-class identity moves in time, with change and continuity, and with the concomitant development of a critical class consciousness that recognizes the value of this identity to collective struggle.

My parents, like most working-class parents, wanted a better life for their children. This kind of "better" meant safe, justly compensated work, work with possibility for autonomy and craft, work that does not exhaust or dehumanize. But, they did not wish a better life that extracted as its cost familial and historic memory. The voices in this collection argue for the

1

power and fluidity of memory as a force against a false and paradoxically static private mobility. In liberating memory that is both personal and historic we trace the dynamic between working-class identity, with all its ambiguity and fragmentation, and working-class consciousness, with its myriad possibilities for acting on and in the worlds we inherit.[2]

A critical, working-class consciousness is both expansive and grounded. Individual and collective. It is an alternative to the bifurcation of politics and culture, work and home. It recognizes ambiguity and contradiction without excusing the damage that one individual can do to another. It is multigenerational and historically situated, but, paradoxically, not dependent on linear time. This consciousness is not "success." It is not a safe harbor. It does not deny death. Nor is it bourgeois cynicism or despair. Working-class consciousness includes identity, but it is not fixed on identity. It is an aperture. A radical, portable alternative to the individualistic way out. It is that crucial attentiveness to others that fuels and enables resistance to injustice.

Marking the dialectical, changing movement between individual working-class identity and class consciousness is the ambitious and fragile course these writings attempt to explore. It is dangerous work because dominant bourgeois culture is hostile to working-class identities. They are perceived as too rough, too loud, too dirty, too direct, too "uneducated." They are valued—if at all—as requisite labor and service, but not valued as intelligence and knowledge.[3] The lived experience of working-class people encodes a kind of knowledge—especially of the body—that is absent in bourgeois academic institutions.[4] To a degree, class is theorized in the academy (and here I am not addressing questions of theoretical efficacy), but the language of theory trickles down to the many layers of institutional education slowly. Children learn class difference—just as they learn gender and race difference—early—in schools that are constructed from unspoken, masked, aspiring, bourgeois, and, more recently, corporate perspectives. Those contributors to *Liberating Memory* who are of the fortunate generation that secured a college education all acknowledge the schism between their working-class lived experience and their educations.[5] But, that is not where their stories end. Their voices attest to the possibilities not of going back home in a literal sense, but of using working-class knowledge of home to do their valuable work in the world. We all face a problem of the means of measurement, of distance, of getting the story right.

In his novel *Border Country*, Raymond Williams tells the paradigmatic story of the scholarship student who leaves his working-class village and becomes a university lecturer. The son is called "home," back to the village, because of his father's stroke. This return necessitates adjustments of language, recalls old, daily rhythms, and elicits the following conversation between father and son. The father says:

> "Yes, the work is changing but that isn't the heart of it. There's no virtue in the work, but that men [sic] should stand as they are."
> "Stand equal?" [The son replies.]
> "Stand as they are, with nothing bearing them down. For you that was made quick."
> "Part of it was made quick."
> "Only it isn't solved, when it's made quick for you. The rest of us need it, remember."[6]

The father's language only hints at the depth of his feelings. There isn't an easy language that fits the feelings. The father is not asking the son to come back or to replicate his life; he does not deny the son his distance. What he asks the son to do is to measure the distance well, and to bring the world of the village back to the university. What he wants of his son is something larger than individual accomplishment.

The son, an economic historian whose research in recent years has gone flat, comes to realize in his journey through the border country between two homes, that he has mismeasured, or rather, that he has not found the right means of measurement. He has focused on the wrong things, on the numbers—tracing Welsh population patterns—rather than on the people. His task is to recognize the problem of measurement, which is the problem of knowledge and how it is used.[7] His job is to measure the distance right by using memory as a tool. The son "watches memory move, across the wide valley. That was the sense of it: to watch, to interpret, to try to get clear."[8]

Memory, Not Nostalgia

To try to get clear. To watch memory move. The kind of memory that concerns us is not an accumulation of data, a taking in and returning without mediation.[9] Nor is it nostalgia, a sweetening of reflection, an easy sell, a boon to politicians and advertisers. It is not quantifiably measurable or linear. Liberating this kind of memory involves the reconstruction of a set of relationships, not the exactitude of specific events.[10] These are historically grounded, private memories with shifting public markers: the factory is shut down or leveled, or the people of the old neighborhood speak a different language. These memories attest to change, but also to continuity, noticeable resemblances, and familiar patterns situated in differing geographies and generations. Memory is a catalyst for engagement with the present and the future as much as for reconstructing the past. This work resists the message of the dominant culture which says suppress, sever, and "get on with it" without ever examining what "it" is.

Working-class life is hard, dominated by work or the lack of it. Often that work is unsafe, unreliable, oppressive, and exhausting. When working-class people stick together, they do so not because of an inherent nobility, but because that is the way they survive. These memories recall pain and oppression, but also possibilities and models for resistance. Working-class historical memory includes episodes of resiliency and courage as well as defeat and despair.

Memory has purpose. It is a bridge between the subjective and intersubjective—the private and unprivileged circumstances of individual lives—and the objective—the collective history of class oppression.[11] It is a way of moving from personal pain to public and cultural work. The "stuff" of one's life can be transformed into fruitful practices. Even grief can be put to good use.

Writing about the formation of teachers as "transformative intellectuals," Henry Giroux says "the most important referent for such a position is 'liberating memory'—the recognition of those instances of public and private suffering whose causes and manifestations require understanding and compassion.... Liberating memory does more than recover dangerous instances of the past, it also focuses on the subject of suffering and the reality of those treated as 'the other.' Then we can begin to understand the reality of human existence and the need for all members of a democratic society to transform existing social conditions so as to eliminate such suffering in the present."[12] I have extended Henry Giroux's setting for the liberation of memory from the classroom to a larger cultural context and practice. The memories that are retold here reside inside the multiple realities of working-class experience, and as they are released, we see hints of what Giroux envisions as communities developed around an "alternative horizon of human possibilities."

Each individual and particular "I" in this book struggles to rescue and "get clear" about the historic multiplicity of the autobiographical act. These writers face the risk and responsibility of giving voice to the many "we's" inside the "I." Time is a multigenerational layering, not neatly segmented historical moments. Memories about the old neighborhood, the laughter at the kitchen table, the visit to a parent's workplace lead out to a more expansive understanding of class identity—practiced in the classroom, in political activism, in the shaping of culture—not back onto themselves. Working-class consciousness is not just about family lore. It is a larger inheritance. These are historic, not narcissistic, memories. That is why they are dangerous.[13] They insist that reality is not merely a text.

Language and Class

Memory relies on language, but it is also *about* language. Oral language (vocabulary, syntax, inflection, pronunciation, diction, exclamations, blessings, curses) is a giveaway class identity marker.[14] A middle-class child goes from the language of home to the language of school without disruption. She does not have to hesitate, relearn, or adapt because she does not need to switch linguistic codes. Working-class children wherever they grow up—unless at least one parent has had access to a formal education—will not be able to move from the language of home to the language of school without disruption.[15] In school, I remember corrections, many probably well intended: "Say SATURDAY not saddiday; use Yes not yeah." At home, I remember saying, "Momma, don't say 'ain't.'" I learned early that school involved another language system; I learned later how language could be a weapon to demolish and oppress; and still later, I recognized language as a tool to reconstruct and reclaim.

Class marks not only our tongues, but also our bodies. Working-class people practice a language of the body that eludes theoretical textual studies. Working-class people do not have the quiet hands or the neutral faces of the privileged classes—especially when they are within their own communities. The physicality of class difference, the use of the body for expression, communication, and as a substitute for abstract language, is evident in the literature produced by working-class writers, but is rarely recognized, never mind theorized, as a language system.[16] The writers in this collection share this inheritance of a physical language in the same way others might inherit the family library.

What we call "English" has many accents in this collection, including Portuguese, Northern and Southern African-American, West Virginian, Greek, Polish, Yiddish, Italian, as well as a version of American Sign Language. The working-class intellectual must decide how to negotiate the linguistic border between these languages of home and the official language of the academy and publishing institutions. She or he could take speech lessons and attempt to pass linguistically. Or they could "cube" their writing for certain professional audiences. (This is a drill I learned in art class. The task is to begin by sketching a realistic still life, and then—à la Picasso—progressively abstract or "cube" each form in sketch after sketch. In academic writing it means being clear about what you want to say and then revising for academic interlocution and discourse.)

What is at risk with this assimilationist approach is the loss of contact with the mother tongue and the concomitant loss of the special knowledges and experiences of the people who speak it. For working-class academicians, monologism is not an option. We speak a hybrid language and find linguistic virtue in fragmentation. Paradoxically, it is class consciousness that liberates our multiple tongues.[17]

Conversations with Silences

Tillie Olsen's *Silences,* written to "re-dedicate and encourage," is a crucial antecedent for this book. By affirming not only what is not spoken, but how and why it is not spoken, Olsen points the way to those conditions where public sounds can replace private silences. Nothing is wasted in Tillie Olsen's use of language. Even the Dedication in *Silences* encapsulates the "we" inside the "I," the past and future within the present, the heart of working-class consciousness:

> For our silenced people, century after century their beings consumed in the hard, everyday, essential work of maintaining human life. Their art, which still they made—as their other contributions—anonymous; refused respect, recognition; lost.

> For those of us (few yet in number, for the way is punishing), their kin and descendants, who begin to emerge into more flowered and rewarded use of our selves in ways denied to them;—and by our achievement bearing witness to what was (and still is) being lost, silenced.[18]

The contributors to *Liberating Memory* are "those of us few" who were fortunate or steadfast or privileged enough to break silence. Although these are autobiographical accounts, this project is not so much a presentation of the *formation* of class identities as it is of the *emergence* of those identities out and into the dominant culture.[19] My own concern is less with origins and more with continuities, affinities, and processes.

Before introducing these voices more specifically, I want to speak directly about the underpinnings of my labor, the thoughts and feelings inherent in this theoretical narrative. First, it is impossible to sever the intellectuality of this work from its emotional pulse. My dialogue is as much with the actual inhabitants—living and dead—of my lived experiences as it is with any critical or theoretical practice. I am suspicious of the bossy tendencies in any theory. I will not clap on in a top-down fashion any theoretical apparatus to working-class lived experience—my own or anyone else's. On the other hand, it would be disingenuous to suggest that this book just emotionally sprung up and was not the work of years of careful study. I do not want so much to untangle the knot of theory and practice, but to make praxis visible—in the broad strokes of a "general consciousness" and then more specifically in resemblances shared by the contributors.[20]

Those of us in academic life are accustomed to seeing finished cultural products—the poem in the anthology, the staged play, the book. The process of cultural production is no more immediately visible than is the process of material production of the cars we drive or the food we eat. Exposing the process of forming culture is one of the underlying impulses of this collection. But I want to be specific about the kind of culture I have in mind. I begin with Raymond Williams's simple statement and admonition: "Culture is ordinary." By culture he means two things: "A whole way of life—the common meanings; [and] the arts and learning—the special processes of discovery and creative effort."[21] *Liberating Memory* seeks to illuminate both aspects of culture—a whole way of working-class lives, as told through autobiographical memories, and those specific cultural efforts and expressions which result from an engagement with that "whole way of life." That is, we make a case here for working-class lived experience as a vital, *usable* past.[22]

The experience itself—it must be emphasized and repeated—is not idealized; working-class life is not bucolic. We make this case to the next generation of working-class cultural workers, and we also make it to the academy. No one can get it right; no one can speak authoritatively about what constitutes culture or knowledge or gender or race without including working-class epistemology. Unacknowledged bourgeois sensibilities permeate academic life—class consciousness does not.[23]

I want the reader who is of the next generation of working-class intellectuals to know that it is possible to engage in a process of self-creation that resists the denial of working-class identity and consciousness, indeed, uses working-class knowledge to produce culture and to claim a place as a public intellectual. Although it is not easy, it does not have to be isolating work.

We write out of a sensibility of community. For some of us this sense of community is inherent in the dailiness of our existence—in the mutual support we find in the family or through the job or out of our political commitments. For others, particularly those who have spent much of their adult lives in academe, this communal sense has to be retrieved. For all of us it is more than just being connected to a community—however immediate or distant—we are also in conversation with that community.

As writers, the contributors are engaged in what I call the *aesthetics of relationality*. Their autobiographical acts illuminate the process of sustaining and negotiating relationships which are often complex, knotted, and thorny as well as sometimes beautiful and poignant. They cannot be "straightened out" in any ultimate "ur" narrative, nor should they be. The aesthetics of these relationships lies not in exquisite form or perfection, but in the patient labor and craft involved in sustaining them in a struggle for a reliable truth. Power lies not in mastery, but in persistence and endurance—not in domesticated working-class nostalgia or in colonized academic posturing, but in the courage to confront painful memories.

Many of us are able to speak at all because we got lucky. We have had more control over our bodies. We were not killed or severely disabled on the job. We haven't given birth to children year after year and watched some of them die. We haven't been so exhausted from work day after day that we were robbed of the right to develop our humanity. A few of us have come from families where there was a bit more job security or where the family had an emotional base not destroyed by violence or alcohol. And many of us have not had to face the multiple pressures and historic sediment of race superiority, gender bias, and homophobia.

On the other hand, most of us did not come into adulthood with given assurances and expectations. The dominant culture has not valued our history. We did not have easy, accessible paradigms or outlets for our creative work. We did not have much money. Some of us have left home looking for work, looking for a way of finding a place in the world without invalidating self or home. For most of us, work is school; school is a way out of another kind of work. There is no way to return home the same after this disruption. "Home" here is a metaphor for working-class lived experience as a complex body of knowledge that is not part of bourgeois educational practices. Home can be a sacred, safe place or a living hell. This book is not about nostalgia for another world. It is not a sentimentalized remembrance of home—but home in its complexities and contradictions carried with and in us out to the world. We are *not* at home in the bourgeois world; that is our strength. We are insisting here on a risky exposure, a view that the bourgeois world would rather not see. We resist permanent exile as we cross the borders of class difference and make our own places in the world.[24]

One of the problems of cultural representation that is textual rather than oral is that it can become a static, ahistorical thing—a book in the hands of a disengaged reader. A commodity rather than a tool. My concern is with the historic fluidity of all the voices in this book. We and our work are in no sense *finished.* The past is alive in our present. This sensibility about time comes out of an epistemology that is not grounded in academic ordering, sequencing, and fixing forms. There are different priorities involved here. Locating and situating these particular cultural patterns in *Liberating Memory* is a way of identifying what Raymond Williams calls "structures of feeling":

> We are talking about characteristic elements of impulse, restraint, and tone; specifically affective elements of consciousness and relationships: not feeling against thought, but thought as felt and feeling as thought: practical consciousness of a present kind, in a living and interrelating continuity. We are then defining these elements as a 'structure': as a set, with specific internal relations, at once interlocking and in tension.[25]

What is implicit in Williams's concept and may be overlooked because of his use of the powerfully evocative word "feeling" is his understanding of cultural time as *active.* We see this embodied in the cultural forms included here. Our resistance to a "fixed past" is evident in our cultural work. This book is just one artifact. We are concerned that memory or the interpretation of memory might be flattened into working-class reductivity. To attempt to "total it up" (so clearly understood by Tillie Olsen, especially in "I Stand Here Ironing"[26]) is just the problem of measurement that Raymond Williams explores in *Border Country.* The point of *Liberating Memory* is exactly that: we can never "total it up."

Our Common Work

One third of the wealth in the United States is controlled and owned by one percent of the people.[27] The voices in this book are not that one percent. We are a minuscule representation of another economic reality. We come from a long line of unpropertied people. True, we've been told that home ownership means arrival into the owning class. This is a specious message, not only because it depends on the mortgage and the kind of home one "owns," but because it is an economic measurement trap. This reduction masks real wealth, control, and autonomy. There is also the trap of willed ignorance, of simplifying the class argument and ignoring race and gender oppression.[28] "The white worker" as a category of race superiority has been, historically, an effective device of capitalist control. This is the race card, the promise of individual race superiority instead of collective economic equity, the push for competition instead of solidarity. Desiring to define themselves against the "other," white workers have too often accepted what David Roediger calls the "wages of whiteness" in lieu of real economic and democratic gains for all workers.[29] Under capitalism everyone is not equally human, not certain ethnicities and races, and not women. The acquiescence to the ideology of male gender superiority, the false opposition between wage labor and domestic labor, and the definitions of womanhood as white and middle class have blocked the development of a multiplicitous working-class consciousness and a liberatory politics.

For our common work to continue we need a mutuality of vision that is historically grounded. Without the capacity to see each other's history we cannot construct a viable paradigm that addresses multiple oppressions. We focus on class here—not because it is the predominant identity but because in recent scholarship it is, in practical terms and use, the missing identifying principle. Like a ghost, it is there but not there, mentioned but not really welcomed into the multicultural conversation. These voices suggest a more complicated paradigm. Through memoir, poetry, and visual images we can see the historic markings of class on present circumstances.

What about the common work of this collection? We have a range of working-class identities. The youngest contributor was born in 1959 and the oldest in 1912. A few writers were born in the 1930s, but most were born when the soldiers came home—in the mid to late 1940s. Many of this particular generation were able to take advantage in the 1960s of low-cost, quality educations in state university systems that may not be as economically available to their own children today. One writer experienced dramatic class and geographic change, a few were of mixed class parentage, a number downright poor, but most grew up in the uncertain, but not destitute, economic rhythms of working-class life.

There is a cluster of voices from the New York metropolitan area (three from the Bronx), Harlem, Queens, New Rochelle, Brooklyn, Union City, New Jersey; others come from a scattering of locations across the country: Lynn, Massachusetts; Detroit; Oklahoma; Toledo and Garrettsville, Ohio; Los Angeles; San Diego; Omaha; Washington, D.C.; and Milwaukee. Their identities within working-class families were largely shaped by their parents' occupations, particularly their fathers'. Their mothers were of the generation where women were supposed to be able to stay home while their men earned a living wage. The lived reality does not quite fit the sociological model. Many of these writers' mothers worked part- or full-time or were in or out of the workforce depending on family responsibilities, or were the sole support of their children because of divorce or widowhood, or forced separation, or alcoholism. Some of the parents' occupations were: seamstress, short order cook, chemical factory worker, auto line worker, welder, rubber plant worker, bookkeeper, small shopkeeper, tenant farmer, truck driver, clerical worker, riveter, millwright, pipefitter, cab driver, schoolteacher, waitress, meat wrapper, domestic, and housewife.

In our common work we share certain discernible characteristics as working-class intellectuals and cultural workers:

> We bring the knowledge of physical labor (either from personal experience or through the lives of our parents or both) into the cultural work of organizing, teaching, painting, photographing, writing poetry, and publishing.

> We oppose the dehumanization of workers—of turning human beings who do not own and control their own labor into *things.* Our desire is for the democratization of work and culture.

> We resist working-class identity as negation, but do not gloss over the contradictions, ambivalences, and paradoxes. We use these complexities by engaging in dialogue with them and by recognizing our own place in larger historical patterns. At the same time, we struggle to resist the colonizing capacities of the dominant culture—of succumbing to the lure of the master codes or being trapped as gatekeepers for the owning class.

> We see risk taking as necessary for strategic political and cultural work, not because we are more heroic than anyone else. We look for opportunities for rejecting the modalities of bourgeois society and acting in behalf of our own class interests. We are still capable of imagining alternatives to capitalism.

> We know what it feels like to be cut out of the action, even though we are of the majority class, the working class.

> We love books.

Organic Intellectuals?

On the day of my mother's funeral one of her neighbors stopped by the house. It had been twenty years since I lived in that house and in that neighborhood. I would not have recognized this neighbor, but he recognized me—not only from the family pictures on the walls, but through my mother. He visited quickly, would not take coffee. When he left he shook my hand and slipped something into my palm. As the door closed I saw the crumpled bills in my hand—$35.00 in five's and ten's. No card, no check, just cash. As a working-class person he understood about out-of-pocket expenses and how awful it would be to be "caught short" on the day of your mother's funeral.

Editing this collection is a small way of acknowledging that gift and the many others—less tangible perhaps—that have unexpectedly, but appropriately, come out of the best of working-class experience, that is, out of a mutuality, an adherence and allegiance, a kinship welded from common work and in the face of a system that calls for distrust and self-interest.[30]

Antonio Gramsci has said "All men [sic] are intellectuals, . . . but not all men have in society the function of intellectuals."[31] The function of intellectuals, the historical value of their work, seems to be a much more vital and useful concern than the taxonomy of categorizing, a priori, various dimensions of organic or traditional intellectuality. Whether these voices are labeled as "organic intellectuals" is less important than how they use intellectual space in their own work and how they make room for other democratic intellectuals, especially those outside the academy.

Beneath Theory

April 28 is Workers Memorial Day. For the last five years, hundreds of communities across the country have held memorial services on this day to remember dead and injured workers. In Rochester, New York, we meet late in the afternoon on a windy knoll in Highland Park. The setting is landscaped with junipers and white and yellow daffodils. Nesting in the grass is a small memorial plaque inscribed with Mother Jones's feisty injunction to "Pray for the dead, but fight like hell for the living."

The service is organized by the local labor council. Dignitaries, public officials, politicians, and the media often show up—though how many depends on whether or not it is an election year. The crowd is mostly a mixture of activists, union leaders, and working people—not mutually exclusive categories. Some are retired; some were able to get off early from work; some are children. We don't necessarily know each other, but faces are familiar and recognizable year after year. Many wear union buttons, jackets, and caps. We hold red carnations and carry cards with the names of fallen workers. We are the majority class—the working class—and we have come to honor our own.[32]

The ceremony begins. After the speeches, the display of public language, comes the remembrance. One by one we walk to the podium and read the name of a worker who has died or been injured in the Rochester area, and place a carnation on the memorial. Sometimes, people use their moment at the podium to remember special friends, co-workers, heroes of the labor movement. This year César Chávez was remembered along with the three women social service workers who were gunned down in their offices by a man who refused to pay child support. One by one the names are read, and the blood-red carnations accumulate on the Mother Jones memorial.

The reading of the names opens us to each other. Not just the names, but the experience of unsafe work behind the names. A shift occurs. We are no longer an assemblage of strangers, but a community who share a special knowledge about work and struggle. Two local men died this year. In accidents that didn't have to happen. One was digging a tunnel, laying the foundation for a new Taco Bell. Perhaps because of the heavy spring rains, or because of inadequate shoring, the earth gave way, and he was buried alive. The other was a young carpenter. He was injured on the job and died within a week. There were many blue carpenters' union caps this year, and the man's family was there, his wife and two young sons. The look on the wife's face was familiar—the flat stare of shock. It is the body's way of absorbing the knowledge of loss. Then shock wears off and grief permeates the body.

Grief is physical. I saw that same stare on my mother's face the spring my father died so unexpectedly. This is knowledge. It cannot be taught and I am not sure any text can fully convey it. It is the awareness of sudden and swift loss coupled by economic uncertainty. How to live with this knowledge is a personal question. How to put this knowledge to good use is a public and cultural question. *Liberating Memory* is an attempt to respond to that question.

Notes

1. See Gregory Mantsios, "Rewards and Opportunities: The Politics and Economics of Class in the U.S." in *Race, Class and Gender in the U.S.: An Integrated Study,* edited by Paula Rothenberg (New York: St. Martin's Press, 1992). Also, Donald L. Barlett and James B. Steele, *America: What Went Wrong?* (Kansas City: Andrews and McMeel, 1992). For subjective testimony to this economic data, see *Portraits in Steel,* photographs by Milton Rogovin, interviews by Michael Frisch (Ithaca: Cornell University Press, 1993), oral histories of displaced steelworkers in Western New York. One of the most consistent concerns of these former steelworkers was whether or not their own children would have access to a steady, living wage.

2. My thinking on the multiple voicings of *consciousness* is informed by the work of Raymond Williams—especially *Resources of Hope,* edited by Robin Gable (London: Verso, 1989), and *Marxism and Literature* (New York: Oxford University Press, 1977). Also Bertell Ollman, *Dialectical Investigations* (New York: Routledge, 1993); Paulo Freire, *Pedagogy of the Oppressed* (New York: The Seabury Press, 1973) and Antonio Gramsci—especially *An Antonio Gramsci Reader,* edited by David Forgacs (rpt.; New York: Schocken, 1988). See also the merging of political consciousness and moral conscience in Alessandro Portelli, *The Death of Luigi Trastulli and Other Stories* (Albany: State University of New York Press, 1991), p. 126. For the narrative fiber essential to these theoretical writings see the work of Tillie Olsen.

3. If anything, this preference for machines and prejudice against human beings is heightened in the technical economy. See Barbara Garson, *The Electronic Sweatshop* (New York: Penguin, 1988).

4. My concern is with the individual human body and the collective experience of using one's body in a demanding, physical way. See M. M. Bakhtin's use of "body" as "material bearers of meaning" in *Speech Genres and Other Late Essays,* translated by Vern W. McGee, edited by Caryl Emerson and Michael Holquist (Austin: University of Texas Press, 1986), p. xii.

5. Here I am reminded of Tillie Olsen's frequent question to academic audiences: "How many of you are the first in your family to graduate from college?"

6. Raymond Williams, *Border Country* (London: Chatto and Windus, 1960), pp. 311–312. Conceptually, "the border" is both a highly specific epistemological location and a traveling theory that allows us to study parallel situations across cultural, gender, and geographic differences. See Gloria Anzaldúa, *Borderlands/La Frontera* (San Francisco: Aunt Lute, 1987).

7. To ask the question, "In whose interests am I working?" See Paulo Freire's distinctions between knowledge as commerce and knowledge as critical liberation in *The Pedagogy of the Oppressed* (New York: Seabury, 1973) and in *The Politics of Education: Culture, Power and Liberation* (Granby, Massachusetts: Bergin and Garvey, 1985).

8. *Border Country,* p. 293. In his essay "Methodology for the Human Science," M. M. Bakhtin writes: "The exact sciences constitute a monologic form of knowledge: the intellect contemplates a *thing* and expounds upon it. There is only one subject here—cognizing (contemplating) and speaking (expounding). In opposition to the subject there is only a *voiceless thing.* Any object of knowledge (including man [sic]) can be perceived and cognized as a thing. But a subject as such cannot be perceived and studied as a thing, for as a subject it cannot, while remaining a subject, become voiceless, and, consequently, cognition of it can only be *dialogic." Speech Genres and Other Late Essays,* p. 161.

9. A useful rethinking of how memory works is Michael M. J. Fischer's "Ethnicity and the Post-Modern Arts of Memory," 194–233 in *Writing Culture,* edited by James Clifford and George F. Marcus (Berkeley: University of California Press, 1986). For an interesting contrast to my use of memory see A. R. Luria's *The Mind of a Mnemonist: A Little Book About a Vast Memory,* trans. Lynn Solotaroff (Cambridge: Harvard University Press, 1968).

10. The zigzag, nonlinear quality of memory of working-class events is evident in the oral narratives in Alessandro Portelli's *The Death of Luigi Trastulli and Other Stories.* See "Memory and the Event" for Portelli's description of "subjective working-class chronology" (p. 25), and narrative time described as "shuttlework": "I go back and forth [in time] like a shuttle. . . ." (p. 65).

11. I am largely in agreement with the postmodern contention that categories of subjectivity and objectivity are blurred. However, to abandon all distinctions reduces reality to a text and I am arguing here that working-class lived experience is more than a discourse or a text. See Bertell Ollman, "How to Study Class Consciousness . . . and Why We Should" in *Dialectical Investigations* (New York: Routledge, 1993), p. 155.

12. Henry Giroux, *Teachers as Intellectuals* (Granby, Massachusetts: Bergin and Garvey, 1988), p. xxxiv. Giroux has in mind all oppressed, subaltern groups. The practice of an emancipatory cultural politics pedagogy involves unmasking the complications of class difference, especially as oppressions are viewed as multiple and cumulative.

13. Sharon D. Welch uses Foucault's concept of "subjugated knowledges" and "dangerous memories" to construct possibilities for a new, theological episteme. Sharon D. Welch, *Communities of Resistance and Solidarity* (Maryknoll, New York: Orbis, 1985) and *A Feminist Ethic of Risk* (Minneapolis: Fortress Press, 1990).

14. See Bakhtin's *Speech Genres and Other Late Essays.*

15. I want to emphasize a continuum of language differences among and within working-

class communities which includes pronounced and prolonged silences as well as bilingualism and multiple dialects.

16. See the poetic language of the body in Tillie Olsen's *Yonnondio* (New York: Dell, 1971).

17. For theoretical work on class and language see Richard Ohmann, especially, "Reflections on Class and Language," *College English* 44 (Jan. 1982): 1–17; also, scholars in the emerging field of working-class studies need to reconsider the implications of the widely cited research by Basil Bernstein in Britain on "restricted" and "elaborated" language codes—*Class, Codes and Control* (London: Routledge and Kegan Paul, 1971), vol. 1.

18. Tillie Olsen, *Silences* (New York, Dell, 1978).

19. Although the contributors are mostly strangers to each other, there are a few exceptions—a married couple, professional colleagues, a mother and daughter. Despite our differences, however, our experiences are familiar, recognizable patterns emerging from many generations of working-class life. The classic British study of the formation of working-class culture is E. P. Thompson's *The Making of the English Working Class,* and, equally worthy, Herbert Gutman's study of United States working-class culture, *Power and Culture: Essays on the American Working Class,* edited by Ira Berlin (New York: Pantheon, 1987). For his critical cultural analysis of *emergence* see Raymond Williams, *Marxism and Literature* (New York: Oxford University Press, 1977).

20. Raymond Williams, *The Politics of Modernism* (London: Verso, 1989).

21. Raymond Williams, "Culture is Ordinary" in *Resources of Hope* (London: Verso, 1989).

22. The concept of a usable past has been richly informed by feminist and African-American scholars. See, particularly, bell hooks, *Feminist Theory: From Margin to Center* (Boston: South End Press, 1984), and Gerda Lerner, *The Majority Finds Its Past: Placing Women in History* (New York: Oxford University Press, 1979).

23. For example, my recent efforts to petition the Program Committee of the Modern Language Association for a Discussion Group on "Working-Class Literature" have failed. The Program Committee decided that "a discussion group on the proposed topic was not needed" (Director of Convention Programs to Janet Zandy, June 1, 1993).

24. See John Berger and John Mohr's *A Seventh Man* (New York: Penguin, 1975).

25. Williams adds: "We are also defining a social experience which is still in process, often indeed not yet recognized as social but taken to be private, idiosyncratic, and even isolating. . . ." *Marxism and Literature,* p. 132.

26. Tillie Olsen, *Tell Me a Riddle* (New York: Dell, 1971).

27. Howard Zinn, *A People's History of the United States* (New York: Harper Perennial, 1980) is an accessible, comprehensive history of the effect of the capitalist system on ordinary lives.

28. See Manning Marable, *How Capitalism Underdeveloped Black America* (Boston: South End Press, 1983) for an interpretive analysis of the intersections of race and class. See Lise Vogel, *Marxism and the Oppression of Women* (New Brunswick: Rutgers University Press, 1983) for the intersection of class and gender.

29. David R. Roediger, *The Wages of Whiteness: Race and the Making of the American Working Class* (New York: Verso, 1991).

30. The practice of community is not without traps, as Williams noted: "There is, of course, a habit of mutual obligation which easily becomes the ground on which exploitation is possible. If you have the sense that you have this kind of native duty to others it can expose you very cruelly within a system of the conscious exploitation of labour" (*Resources of Hope,* p. 114).

31. *An Antonio Gramsci Reader,* edited by David Forgacs (New York: Schocken Books, 1988), p. 304.

32. My appreciation to Christopher Garlock, Coordinator of the Rochester, N.Y., and Vicinity Labor Council AFL–CIO, for his commentary on this section.

Part One

Memory, Not Nostalgia

Carol Tarlen

I was born on October 12, 1943, in San Diego, California. My grandparents were elementary school teachers and farmers. My father was a truck driver and member of the Teamsters Union. My mother was a riveter at Consolidated Airlines during World War II and was a member of the Machinists Union. I became a radical while in the womb when my mother filed a grievance against management after the company attempted to lay her off because of her pregnancy. She won the right of all women to work while pregnant, a political as well as personal victory. It enabled her to work long enough to earn vacation pay. After the war, she took care of children in her home. I moved continually through northern California and Nevada during my early years as my father attempted to find a steady job. Finally, my father got employment at Pacific Intermountain Express, driving diesel rigs from California to Chicago, and the family moved to Fremont, California. My father died in September 1993 and this essay is dedicated to him.

The photo on the garbage can was taken in 1960 in the backyard of the family house in Fremont. I was sixteen. Not pictured is the old mattress that sat on the front lawn. During summer evenings, my family would sit with neighbors on the mattress and gossip while kids played baseball in the streets and teenaged girls paraded up and down the sidewalks, waiting for cute guys in their '56 Chevies to pass by and whistle.

Carol Tarlen is a clerical worker at the University of California, San Francisco. Her poetry and prose have appeared in many literary and feminist journals and anthologies, including *Calling Home, The Berkeley Poetry Review, Cold Drill, Exquisite Corpse, Homeless Not Helpless,* and *Rain City Review.* She is the mother of two grown daughters and has two grandchildren. She works with peace, labor, and homeless advocacy groups and is active in the San Francisco poetry community. She is a member of AFSCME Local 3218. Presently, she lives on a sailboat in Sausalito, California.

Carol Tarlen

The Memory of Class and Intellectual Privilege

If memory is a past tense function, it plays no part in my working-class identity. If it produces nostalgia, then I have no use for it. If, on the other hand, memory enhances and informs the present, if it exists in a dialectical relationship to everyday life, then I can welcome it into my busy and activist working-class artist's life.

Although I have a Master of Arts degree (I earned both my college degrees by working full-time and going to night classes), I am now and always have been a member of the working class. Not only did I grow up poor, with a father who was a (frequently out-of-work) truck driver, I earn my living not as an academic with secretarial support, but as secretarial support for academics. I do not hire, fire, or review others' work performances—my work is evaluated, and if I do not live up to the expectations of my superiors, I'm canned. My labor is not prized for its intellectual content, but for its lack of typos. I may not get my clothes dirty (unless I am called upon to fix a jammed xerox machine or change the ink cartridge in my laser printer), but I work with my hands—and I have scars from surgery to correct carpal tunnel injury to prove it. I get as much respect for the way I earn my living as my father did earning his. I know what it is like to be sneered at because of your class. I also know how ignorant and insensitive middle- and upper-class people can be, and how they can ignore your feelings, no matter how loudly or frequently you articulate them.

My class background has deprived me of subtlety and nuance. When people use truck drivers as examples of ignorance and prejudice, or when they say that I am too intelligent to be a clerical worker, I tell them that they are bigots, and that my job is hard and I'm not ashamed of it. For some reason, these people continue to make offensive remarks, and then are surprised at my anger and bitterness.

I use my education in both my political and artistic work, but I especially use the anger that comes from my living in the working class. A healthy response to oppression is anger, and I use my mental health to enrich my creative life. Whenever I sit down to write, I remember—the pain of being humiliated because I was a skinny child who was teased at school for wearing too small dresses and living in a trailer; or a recent humiliation when one of the faculty I work for gave me a dirty look because I forgot to give her a message. I remember how the teenaged girls in my neighborhood were considered "cheap" because of our class and ethnicity. I remember sitting at my receptionist's desk as two female faculty carried on a conversation literally over my head, discussing the private schools their children were attending, oblivious to my presence. Yes, I have rage, and I use it, in my poetry, in public speaking, or in political actions. I am not afraid to take over the street, get arrested, or walk a picket line any more than I am afraid to face an audience at a poetry reading.

The motivation for my writing is very simple, and it's not nice. I write to get even with everyone who was mean to me in high school. I am motivated by the pain and anger that comes from being rejected because of my class background. I want to prove to all those girls whose parents had "professional" jobs and lived in Glenmore Gardens—the ones whose hair neatly curled into pageboys; who wore plaid knee-length pleated skirts and lambswool sweaters; the ones who quit associating with me when I said I lived in Stanley Davis, the housing tract notorious for its Latino and Okie inhabitants; and especially the ones who assumed that having an old mattress on your front lawn was a sign of intellectual inferiority and moral degeneration—I want to prove to that clique of middle-class "nice" girls that the tough girls from the other side of the highway can't be shoved to the back of the classroom anymore, that we have lives filled with love, honor, imagination, risk. See me, I want to say, acknowledge my talent and intelligence. You may have become a matron with a wealthy husband, an executive with an M.B.A. degree, or chairwoman of the Hillsborough Republican Party, but I am an in-your-face, unrepentant working-class writer.

When I was in high school, Diane, my best friend, called these girls "society." Diane was French Canadian and Indian, but because she was dark skinned, she was assumed to be "Mexican," and being "Mexican" meant that you went to boring classes taught by bored teachers who didn't bother to remember your name, that the "white" guys made nasty remarks as they passed you in the hallway and assumed that you were a "whore," someone the Glenmore Girls didn't speak to but were afraid of. That is, unless you were really Mexican, like our shy friend Dolores, a recent immigrant with a scar on her chest from a heart operation. Some of the Glenmore clique caught her alone in the bathroom, called her names like "dirty spic" and roughed her up. When Diane heard, she went after those Glen-

Memory, Not Nostalgia

21

more girls. Diane had a reputation, and they got scared, and started to cry. Diane didn't hurt them, just laughed, called them chickenshit, and walked away.

I feel privileged that my lowly address and my lack of middle-class finesse kept me out of the Glenmore Girls Clique. My experiences of racism and sexism have formed my politics and my writing. But I am more than just working class. Although my father was a truck driver who never finished high school, my mother has a B.A. degree in English literature. She comes from a long line of teachers and farmers. Although she embraced downward mobility, she couldn't erase all traces of her class. She wrote poetry and told us great, original stories. She gave my brother, sister, and me a love and respect for books, ideas, and the imagination. Because of my family's poverty—and because no one informed me, a buxom blonde from the wrong part of town, of available scholarships—I couldn't go to a prestigious university, but I was motivated to enter junior college and eventually a state university, where I earned both a B.A. degree and a Master's in Creative Writing. My literacy and white skin not only enabled me to complete my education, but it also enabled me to write about my working-class background.

My volunteer work with San Francisco Food Not Bombs, an organization that provides free food for the homeless community, made me face these contradictions. My personal values and my expectations were sometimes in conflict with those of homeless people. Having college degrees, even from publicly funded institutions, and particularly having white skin, are conditions that separate me from people forced onto the streets or into the jails of this nation.

The night I spent in jail because I defied the law and fed homeless people without a permit illuminated my own class privilege. My cellmates didn't have to worry about supervisors spying on them or faculty members evaluating their job performance. They had guards with keys who could take away simple privileges like television. There was no sense of real time in San Francisco's women's jail because there were no windows to look out of to see if it was day or night. The lights were continuously on—dark was a forbidden luxury, as was privacy. A shower was a privilege doled out by the guards. I learned something that night without having to write an NIH grant to fund a demographic study. The vast majority of women in prison are African American, although Latinas, Native Americans, and white working-class women without college degrees and jobs also make up the population.

My education and class were apparent the moment I stepped into the cell, dragging my mattress behind me. I was treated very nicely by the other incarcerated women, I think because my crime was feeding people like themselves. They did not have much respect for most forms of civil disobedience, and made disparaging remarks about arrestees from a recent action against U.S. intervention in Central America. "They should care about Americans," was the standard remark. I didn't mention that I have also been arrested for those issues. Food Not Bombs is a popular organization in the city's prison, but the majority of us who are jailed are white and considered middle class, no matter what our backgrounds.

Despite the class contradictions that I have to face in both my political and "intellectual" work, my creative writing does not contain nostalgia or guilt. Having never left the working class, I do not feel a necessity to sentimentalize it. In a recent anthology of poetry about factory workers, the vast majority of the poets published in it are university professors whose educations were paid for by the broken bodies and spirits of blue-collar parents. The poems are often tinged with guilt and relief at having escaped the fate of their fathers by entering academia. While wanting to flee the assembly line is understandable, it isn't necessarily heroic, and the poets sense this. I find this emotional ambiguity problematic. The writers seem to feel that they have failed their parents, and that nobility is reserved for those who stay and suffer. Well, my heroines are those who stay and try to change the working conditions at their jobs.

I understand that people have limited choices. We all do what we have to do to personally survive. What is surprising is how many working-class people have escaped into academia and the rather constricted arms of the intelligentsia. Holocaust survivors say they feel alienated from those who didn't experience their horror. I think working-class refugees also feel alienated. And lonely. The slights I receive because of my parents' or my work aren't imagined, and I am sure that professors, journalists, and editors from my background also are insulted. The difference is, I have nothing to lose, so I fight back.

If intellectualism means critical thinking, skepticism, and risk-taking, then I qualify as an intellectual. However, I doubt that many so-called academics are worthy of the term "intellectual." I share Gramsci's suspicion of the intelligentsia. I have read polls demonstrating that a majority of college graduates support Republican presidents and their policies (including financial and military aid to the Contras in Nicaragua), while the majority of high school dropouts support Democratic presidential candidates (and were against support for the Contras). I think the intelligentsia realize that their economic interests lie with conservatives, and high school dropouts would like U.S. tax dollars spent at home on their needs. Most of the neo-conservative intellectuals I read in the *New York Review of Books* or the *New York Times* are self-serving and use isolated facts to justify preconceived ideology. Furthermore, they frequently indulge in purple-prosed smear tactics. Then there are left-wing intellectuals who have graduate degrees in semiotics or deconstructionism who bore you to death with obscure language that bears no relationship to people's actual experiences with the written word, advertising, or just living in a modern city. I get a real kick out of reading "culture studies" about who "owns" Madonna or rap. These academicians are engaging in an economic battle about who gets tenured faculty positions in universities or employment in "think tanks" funded by corporations, who gets published in academic reviews, who gets grants—or, in the case of Camille Paglia, who gets on T.V. talk shows.

Recently I had to make an emergency visit to my parents, who live in a suburb of Denver. My mother, who is recovering from a mastectomy, had discovered a lump in her remaining healthy breast, and needed a biopsy. The message she left on my answering machine sounded scared, and I was worried that if the lump was malignant, it would mean that the medication she is presently taking isn't working and she would have to undergo chemotherapy. At age seventy-five, I didn't think she would be able to handle that ordeal. Although I was broke, my husband out of work, and my credit cards bulging, I decided to charge the airfare and see my parents for what might be the last time. That trip brought me closer to my class origins than all the political and artistic work I have done over the last ten years.

It was my father who seemed hungriest for conversation, particularly political talk. For decades, he had complained about foreign aid, and his reasons were similar to my cellmates' in the San Francisco jail. The United States should take care of its own. But now he has a sophisticated, leftist analysis, one I wholeheartedly agree with. Our tax dollars are spent to keep corrupt dictators in power, and many individuals from this country, as well as private relief agencies, also profit. He had read *America, What Went Wrong?* by Donald Barlett and James Steele, and the book convinced him that the United States needs a labor party. "The Democrats are elitist and are run by and for corporations just like the Republicans. We need a party run by workers," he said over and over.

Finally my mother, the loyal Democratic party worker, got upset. "Are you finished, Bob? I can't get a word in edgewise."

If one believes the media, these aren't the opinions of working-class white men, especially one who was raised on a farm in Kentucky during the Depression and who has a ninth grade education. He's not supposed to look toward women like Pat Schroeder or African Americans like Jesse Jackson for leadership, which he does. My mother was always the liberal of the family, but my father has become a radical.

I learned more about my parents than just politics. My father, the proud owner of several rifles and handguns, told me stories about hunting raccoons when he was young. "Coon skins were valuable then," he said. "I only killed animals for food or money, though. I always hated to hunt. How can anyone call that a sport? I could never shoot an animal now."

Religion has been a source of trouble between us since my parents became born-again Christians twenty years ago. This time we didn't argue. I refrained from loudly announcing my atheism, and they entertained me with stories about the church they belong to. The pastor and his followers have embraced the religious right, and my parents are outcasts because of their political opinions. Once Pastor Bob stood in front of the congregation and refused to offer them a blessing. The other Democrat in the church, Assistant Pastor Ed, was driven out, forced to preach to a congregation so poor it met in the living rooms of members' homes. Finally, in order to support himself, Pastor Ed began sticking up banks, and he now is a successful preacher with a large congregation made up of his fellow prison inmates. Daddy corresponds with Pastor Ed, who writes that he will be released soon. The thought of all these working people becoming Republicans just so they could be respectable Christians made me laugh, and my parents thought it was funny, too.

My parents have spent years trying to survive recessions, layoffs, strikes. They are now struggling with illness and its financial burden. Most of my father's Teamster's pension is spent on hospital and doctor bills, and medication. Medicare pays for little, and staying alive in a country with a for-profit health care system is exorbitant. But they survive together. Mother gives Daddy his insulin shots; Daddy bathes her three times a week because her cancer surgery has inhibited the use of her arms. I imagine him lifting the washcloth out of the water and slowly, gently scrubbing her naked back.

The morning that I left, Mother and I dressed together. She told me that she was embarrassed to be so vain at her age, but she missed her breast. I looked at the large, s-shaped scar, the nipple-less, puckered skin, the arm made frail from the stripping of muscle during surgery. I thought of how she had helped neighbors whose husbands were laid off or in jail, how sometimes they would have to borrow our bathroom because their water was turned off, how she taught me never to cross a picket line, and to respect the weak, the poor, the imprisoned, the uneducated. And especially, I remembered how my mother and daddy taught me to believe that if people struggled together, they could win not only better working conditions and higher wages, but justice. I learned that solidarity is more than just an ideology or a tactic, it is an everyday action. I am a product of my parents' long, hard lives, and their working-class ideals.

The working class is stereotyped by the middle-class white Protestant ideology of this country. I have attempted to use my writing to break down bigotry and stereotyping. I don't like to be dismissed because of my job or background, and I don't like it when my family, neighbors, and coworkers are sneered at, either. But what I have learned through many years of poetry readings and publications in small literary journals is that my audience isn't those Glenmore Girls now grown into yuppies, but intellectuals like myself, especially working-class intellectuals—and, surprisingly, my coworkers and union brothers and sisters, who are very receptive to poetry that portrays and celebrates their lives.

Looking at what remained of my mother's breast, I realized why I am an artist. Like the poets in the anthology about factory work, I write because I love my parents. It's that simple.

Carol Tarlen

Little Bit

"Look it her," a woman yells when I walk into the cell dragging my mattress behind me. "How old are you, forty?" Then she grins. "I'm Lurleen."

"I'm Carol," I answer.

"I'm Lurleen too," says a pregnant woman lying in the bunk below mine. She helps me lift my mattress to the top. "You got something to eat?" she asks. I give her a dollar to buy some cookies from one of the trustees,

"Little Bit" first appeared in *Hurricane Alice* 10 (Fall 1993): 13.

and then hand out more money until my pockets are empty save for bus fare home in the morning.

"We're in lock down," Lurleen #1 says. "We sang too loud last night and the guards got mad. That means we don't get to watch TV, but we can still sing. I sing real good."

"Here, sit by me." Lurleen #2 makes room for me on her bunk.

"I'm in for whoin'" says an angelic, curly-haired child who looks about twelve. "I'm called Little Bit."

"I'm in for feedin'," I say.

"Food Not Bombs!" says a blonde teenager in the top bunk along the far wall. "You guys fed me when I was pregnant."

"I used to see your truck parked along Eddy Street," the angel face says. "I ate your food sometimes. It was good. How come they arresting you?"

"The mayor hates us," I laugh.

"He don't like me neither," says Lurleen #1. "Hey Little Bit, you want me to cornrow your hair for court tomorrow?"

"I got five babies," says Lurleen #2. "They's in L.A."

"You remember me?" the blonde asks. "I hung out with this guy named Mad Dog last summer."

I try hard, but I don't. "Sorry," I say.

"My water broke while I was staying in the Civic Center. I walked all the way to General. It took me a long time 'cause I was in labor. I almost delivered in the street."

"Where's your baby?" Lurleen #2 asks.

"The court got him."

Little Bit dances between the bunks. "On the street," she says as her small hips swirl and bounce to Lurleen's sweet lilting rhythms, "I always wear a sweatshirt, jeans, and sneakers."

Someone shouts from the cell across the hall, "Girl, you wear *sneakers* to work?"

"I wear what I want, Corina." Her cupid's mouth forms a fake pout. "And if they don't like it, they can do without."

"I'll take 'em," Corina offers.

"Corina, you too *old*," Lurleen #1 laughs.

Sometimes I wear jeans to the office, I think, but that's a different kind of work environment, so I don't say anything about the nature of my job, just ask instead, "How much you make a night?" and she says "Sometimes

$300." Lois, whose pale yellowish face is scarred and tracks cover her arms says, "That's cause you got a babyface. Johns pay anything for that. I used to make a couple of hundred but now I'm lucky to get forty." Little Bit says "That's what I get a trick," and that's when I say, "You could get a lot more if you worked for an escort service."

Little Bit looks at me with pity, knowing I work for the man even if I only type. "I work for myself. I ain't got no pimp. I don't split my money with nobody."

"But," I say, not willing to admit my status, "you don't get any benefits. Not even sick leave or medical insurance," but Lois interrupts. "She's right. It's better not to have a boss and besides we got to feed our pleasures."

I have to agree about the bosses and remember but don't describe a nightmare I once had about sitting naked at my PC and being called into the head office and told to kneel and suck and I was only making $12 an hour but I guess even in my sleep I know what it means to have to work for a living.

San Francisco Food Not Bombs is an antimilitary and homeless advocacy group that feeds vegetarian food to homeless people (and anyone else who is hungry) in the parks and on the streets of San Francisco. Periodically, the city arrests those who are serving the food, which sometimes results in a night in jail and the subsequent dropping of charges. There have been over three hundred arrests, but only one Food Not Bombs member has been convicted of the crime of feeding the hungry without a permit. Food Not Bombs continues to feed hundreds of people on a daily basis.

Joseph Nassar

I was born on May 12, 1946, in Toledo, Ohio. Raised by my mother, Constance Matuszynski Nassar, I developed my understanding of self and community in the Polish, working-class neighborhood where I spent my childhood and adolescence. My maternal grandparents emigrated separately from Poznan just before the end of the nineteenth century. They met in Toledo, married, and raised seven children in their home on Avondale Avenue. My mother, the youngest, completed one year of high school, and then from her sixteenth to her sixty-seventh years worked in factories, in machine shops, and finally in a bank as a teller. She, her family, her neighborhood and its people, instilled in me the values and dreams I would take with me wherever I went: from St. Anthony's elementary school in my home parish to the middle-class Catholic high school where I often felt out of place; to West Berlin where I served for nearly three years as an Air Force Staff Sergeant; to the universities where I earned B.A., M.A., and Ph.D. degrees in literature; and to Rochester, New York, where I have lived and worked since 1977.

This photo was taken in late fall of 1965, just after I completed Basic Training at Lackland Air Force Base, San Antonio, Texas. As in most military photographs, whether official or informal, in a theater of war or in a place of peace, the subject is smiling.

The following essay pays tribute to the determination, dreams, and loyalty of the boys I grew up with, to the working-class men and women who have served in America's armed forces, and to my cousin, Danny Lipinski.

Joseph Nassar is chair of the Language, Literature, and Communication Division in the College of Liberal Arts at Rochester Institute of Technology. He has worked there since 1978 and has published essays and reviews on the teaching of writing and on the novels of Vladimir Nabokov and Saul Bellow. Dedicated to teaching, he delights in helping students to read and appreciate literature, particularly the insights such study offers to our understanding of what it means to be human. He lives in the city of Rochester with his wife, Gloria Farmer Nassar, whom he met when he was sixteen and married when he was twenty-two. They return annually to Toledo to see family and friends.

Cousin Danny
Comes Home

In 1950, on a Saturday in late November, I went with my mom to see my nineteen-year-old cousin Danny for the first time. With my hand in hers, we walked the five city blocks under gray clouds which absorbed the meager afternoon sunlight. I felt safe, and excited. Though only four, I knew of Danny's exploits. I had heard uncles and aunts and cousins recall with pride his athletic feats. Already devoted to fishing myself, I marveled that he had once caught forty perch in a single morning on Lake Erie. My greatest adventure thus far had been dipping my hand in the minnow bucket and trying to catch and hold a slippery darter!

From Aunt Mary's back door we passed through her kitchen, into the dining room where I released my mom's hand as someone took our coats. Free to wander through that forest of adult legs, I began my search for Danny. The frequent pictures I had seen of him—in Mom's, in all my aunts' and uncles' photo albums—had fixed his image sharply in my mind. Danny: tall and straight, light-haired with smiling, friendly eyes.

As I got closer to the living room, fewer grown-ups blocked my way. Then, beyond the pair of towering legs I saw him. There. In an alcove at the far end of the living room. Danny, between his two best friends, both in uniform. On his right, a sailor; on his left, a marine. Both of them straight and tall, both looking straight ahead. And Danny's face was the same as in the pictures Aunt Mary had lovingly shown me, unchanged by the years which had passed since he had gone to fight for his country in France.

Now he was finally home, years after he had stepped aboard that eastbound train, years after he had sailed to Europe, years after he had been killed on his first day of combat. Yes, Danny was home: a photo portrait of a young man with smiling, friendly eyes, set upon a sealed gleaming coffin. Still nineteen; nineteen forever.

As I turned back towards the dining room where the grown-ups had gathered around Uncle Eddie's radio, I heard a man tell of American troops fighting with Communist guerrillas in Korea. One war had just ended, another had begun, and more would follow.

For over forty years Danny lay silent among the sleeping giants of my

Cousin Danny.

past. Then, in 1991, the clash of armies in the Persian Gulf revived his memory and made me rethink my own military experiences. Nearly fifty years before, head held high, Danny had marched off to his war in Europe. And in the 1960s I had served proudly in mine, though a continent away from the fighting in Vietnam. We had taken our places in the unbroken ranks of American patriots, not descendants of Revolutionary War soldiers, but of poor folk who had left the old country in the 1890s for freedom and opportunity in a new land. Our grandfathers worked in factories; our grandmothers raised their children, saved their husbands' wages, and took care of the homes they were able to buy. Their younger brothers, sons, and grandsons fought America's wars, proclaimed the privilege of serving their new homeland.

As a small boy I saw the soldiers of the Great War, old men squeezed into uniforms smelling of camphor, proudly watching their younger comrades in Memorial and Veterans Day parades. Summers, they sat quietly on their front porches, sometimes in twos and threes, often alone. We children dared not ask how they had lost those fingers or that leg, and they never spoke to us of their soldiering. The younger men who had fought in a second great European war, in the Pacific, or in Korea lived routine, ordinary lives, except perhaps on the rare occasions when they donned their uniforms. In most of their homes, youthful photos of these Doughboys and GI's, swabbies and leathernecks were set out in special places.

Despite what we saw in our neighborhood, at the movies, and on TV, in 1965 my friends and I knew little of military service. We did know that we would surely be drafted, even in peace time, as our older brothers and cousins had been. We knew that we would go away for two or more years, return occasionally on leave, and that a portrait of us in uniform would take its expected place. Growing up, we paid scant attention to these certainties until our time grew near, until Vietnam became America's next war, our war.

My friends and I believed we had two options: to wait and be drafted, or to enlist. College and a deferment were unthinkable for the two who had finished the ninth grade and then caromed from one low-paying job to another for several years. In frustration over their meager wages and stultifying work, perhaps in desperation, they joined up. In 1964 the brighter one became a Marine; the other, rejected first by the Marines, then by the Navy and Air Force, landed in the Army. The four boys who had finished high school found good factory jobs and settled into them. I tried college for a year and concluded my life was with my friends. I dropped out and became a mail carrier.

For over a year after high school graduation the five of us spent most of our evenings and weekends together. We enjoyed the independence of being working men, and we silently dreaded the inevitable end of our brief freedom. When our two buddies who had enlisted came home on leave after basic training, we feted them and listened and laughed at the outrageous tales they brought to us. Beneath the comradery and exuberance, we hid our dread, they of their overseas assignments, we of the draft. In the fall of 1965, notices of our preinduction physicals came. After a bus ride and an overnight in a Cleveland hotel, each of us returned "1A." Our options were the same—be drafted or enlist—but our decisions were imminent. We believed we were free to choose the way we would fulfill our duty to our country.

We all enlisted: two in the Marines, two in the Navy. Leaving at different intervals, we celebrated the night before each departure and said good-bye at the bus station, the train station, and the airport. The last to go,

I left alone for San Antonio, Texas, and the Air Force. At first, our luck was exceptional: after basic training and before we went overseas, some of us came home at the same time. Then, we all left America, for historic West Berlin, or the exotic South Pacific, or the jungles of Vietnam.

At the end of 1969, I came home, the last to return. Miraculously, all had survived. During those years of service, two learned a trade which gave them job security and good pay, for a time. Four came home with permanent physical or psychological wounds, but got on with their lives nevertheless. None spoke bitterly of what they had lost, only of their joy to be home with family and friends. Welcomed by their neighborhoods and parishes, they reclaimed their jobs making spark plugs or operating heavy machinery. In the newspapers and on TV, however, they were called murderers and monsters, these gentle boys who had done only what their Uncle Sam had asked. So they stuck close together, worked and raised their families, and drank at the VFW Post, trying to forget the past, hoping for some sort of future.

In the succeeding years my boyhood friends and I gave our time to wives and children, to homes and jobs, and to new friends. Still, we kept in touch. Convinced that education meant success and freedom, I took advantage of the GI Bill and of my wife's patience and support. By 1977, after a seven-year compulsive learning spree, I had earned a B.A., an M.A., and a Ph.D. in English language and literature. Although my wife and I left our hometown in 1973, each year we were drawn back by a need to be with family and friends. I continued to see some of my buddies, to send them Christmas cards, and occasionally to speak with them over the phone. Stretched across miles and years, our bond would not break.

In January of 1991, when tens of thousands of U.S. troops were sent to the Persian Gulf and a new war drew near, my memories of Danny and of my boyhood friends forcefully returned. I heard President Bush proclaim our duty to restore "democracy" in Kuwait; I heard his supporters call for American solidarity and urge participation in this "just war"; I saw antiwar groups pray for peace. Though my days of soldiering were long past, this new war troubled me more than Vietnam had. In those days, as an Airman and later as a student, I was angered by the campus protests. In 1991 I was distressed by their scarcity. At my university, most students with whom I spoke said they trusted President Bush's judgment, and many even declared war with Iraq necessary. When a number of my colleagues decided to organize a "Teach-in on War and Peace," I agreed to help.

Being one of the organizers, I was also expected to speak, though I dreaded the responsibility. I could not approach it with the same distance which most of the others could. Few of them had served in the military—one even proclaimed that neither he nor any one of his peers had—and few saw soldiering as patriotic. They intellectualized the draft, military service, and going to war. They addressed these experiences from academic specialties such as philosophy, political science, history, or psychology. I tried but could not. The lesson I offered came from the gut. I spoke of boys like myself and my buddies who had told themselves and one another that they were willingly, even proudly serving our country. I spoke of Danny who had given his life. My concern was for the men and women who would fight and perhaps die in the Persian Gulf. My concern was that despite two world wars, despite Korea and Vietnam, America kept sending her soldiers into new battles, telling them it was their duty and privilege to serve. And many who went and many who stayed behind continued to believe.

During the twenty-two years since I had fulfilled my military obligation, I never spoke openly against the Vietnam War or, more significantly, against the obligation itself. In fact, I rarely even had negative thoughts, except perhaps for my draft-deferred colleagues who spoke so easily about experiences which were not their own. Instead, I conspicuously listed my military service on my resumé and spoke proudly of the four years I had given to my country. Preparing and delivering my "lesson" at the teach-in, then thinking about it afterwards, however, made me reassess my position, made me reconsider what my buddies and I—and Danny—had done, what we had believed.

Although most of us secretly dreaded military service, we also recognized that it was a duty, even a job option, and certainly unavoidable. Other, more privileged Americans grew up expecting to excel in high school, graduate from college, and embark on prosperous, personally satisfying careers. Few of them were ever "1A." Conversely, we of the working class couldn't wait to get out of high school, find a job, and earn a living. When Uncle Sam called, we couldn't be in college, and certainly not in Canada. Duty to our country and to our community required that we set aside self-interests, or so we believed. Our families and our neighbors frequently reinforced this belief: they celebrated our furloughs and our final homecomings (no matter what form the latter might take); they proudly displayed photos of us in uniform; and they frequently spoke to one another of our patriotism.

Military service itself offered us many rewards and benefits, such as the opportunity to learn a skilled trade which would lead to a good civilian job, or a bonus (often several thousand dollars) to reenlist and make the military a career. Under the GI Bill of Rights, we could receive education benefits, a guaranteed home loan, and in some states reduced property taxes. Our community honored us and our country rewarded us for merely doing what we ought to do.

Because my adult life has epitomized the fulfillment of America's promises to her people, and because compulsory military service seemed to end after Vietnam, I kept my old, traditional beliefs, at least outwardly. Thus at first, as I had with Vietnam, I hesitated to question the Gulf War. Perhaps middle age and the opportunity (and capacity) for introspection made me look beyond my own comfortable existence, made me reconsider the friends and community I had left behind.

In truth, my buddies and I did not enlist because we were patriots, but because we believed doing so was our best available option. In fact, we were willing to give up two, three, four years of freedom, to risk mutilation, even death, rather than be branded draft-dodgers, traitors, by our family, our friends, and our community. We did our military service because our grandfathers, fathers, uncles, and cousins had done so, probably for the very same reasons. Although I came home fit and well, four of my buddies did not. I left my community, worked hard and became successful; the other six stayed on, worked hard and were left behind by the good jobs they thought would be theirs for life.

And what of today's soldiers, those who would fight to restore "democracy" in Kuwait, end famine in Somalia, or reestablish peace in Bosnia? Are they truly members of an all-volunteer force? Or are they really ambitious, often desperate working-class or poor people for whom military service is the only acceptable alternative to underemployment, unemployment, and poverty? The sons and daughters of my buddies, they will not be drafted as their fathers were, but neither will they be offered those good jobs making spark plugs or operating a crane. A few may go to college and then find careers, but many will be left behind to hear stories about the wars that were won (and lost), about the factories that closed. They will scrape by in an America much unlike the one their fathers thought they knew.

Sue Doro

I was born on April 17, 1937, in Berlin, Wisconsin. I lived most of my life in Milwaukee. At the age of thirty-five, after years as a homemaker, I was compelled to make some challenging career decisions as a result of abandonment and divorce. I was left as a single parent with five children to raise without support. Following a family tradition of factory workers, I entered Milwaukee Area Technical School in 1972 and became the first female to graduate out of the machine shop class, as well as the first woman worker in the three factory jobs that I landed during the next thirteen years. At Allis Chalmers Tractor Plant I filed a sex discrimination lawsuit in order to be hired. In 1985, I "retired" as a machinist, along with thousands of others, because of the closure of the Milwaukee Road Railroad. At this time, with the children grown and on their own, I moved with my second husband to Oakland, California. I became the executive director of San Francisco's Tradeswomen, Inc., a ten-year-old "not for profit" national membership organization for women in blue-collar "new traditional" jobs. Since 1988 I have been poetry editor of this organization's quarterly, *Tradeswomen.* I began writing at the age of twelve.

Sue Doro is the author of three books of poetry and short stories about work and family life: *Of Birds and Factories* (self-published), *Heart, Home and Hard Hats* (Midwest Villages and Voices), and *Blue Collar Goodbyes* (Papier Mache Press). Her work has appeared in numerous union, women's, and "worker writer" publications and anthologies, including: *Calling Home* (ed. Janet Zandy, Rutgers University Press), *If I Had A Hammer* (ed. Sandra Martz, Papier Mache Press), *Paperwork* (ed. Tom Wayman, Harbour Publishing), *Women Brave in the Face of Danger* (ed. Margaret Randall, The Crossing Press), *Coffee Break Secrets* (ed. Susan Eisenberg, Word of Mouth Press). She is currently employed as an affirmative action/equal employment opportunity compliance officer for the Department of Labor's Office of Federal Contract Compliance Programs in Oakland, California.

Focus

write about it she
said the dream gray
red the man
his penis entering

his features
resembling
a movie star
suggesting
my father's face
was handsome

he was a sears roebuck
model some time
around 1920
before he traveled
to milwaukee to become a
factory worker

in between the small town
chicken and egg enterprise
when my mother was
not yet
his wife

she kept a
picture cut out of a
catalog page featuring
him dressed in a
knee length dark
overcoat buckled at
the waist

collar wide lapeled a
sears smile on his face
he was bare-headed one
hand at his side the
other tucked against
his chest like
napoleon the image
torn in
several pieces

one of the times
my mother
verified her anger

reattached like a puzzle
pasted on a piece of
yellowed cardboard
preserved in our
family album
before my child
eyes could see it all
happen

the handsome man
is talking now
requesting
the return of his penis

seems it got stuck
when I broke it off
at the root like
the fat gray stem
of one of those
strange sea plants
sticking up from
the ocean floor
blood red tipped

I couldn't feel
anything all
I knew was I
didn't want it in me

so I simply pinched it
off with my thumb and
index finger there
wasn't any physical pain
involved although the man
appeared concerned about
his penis

while
I was in turn
interested
in the fact that
it remained inside
now that I had
severed the organ from
its source

so with a casualness of
someone not myself I
plucked it out with
the same thumb and finger
and it felt
pleasant removing it
in fact I did enjoy
an orgasm at this point
returning the artifact

watching with
head tilted curiosity
while he attempted to
reconnect the thing
to the stump above
his testicles the entire
area favoring segmented
clay characters
in animated cartoons

it was indeed funny it
made me
laugh

My father had control of the family camera. It was a black box "Brownie," that he held against his stomach to steady, while he flicked the shutter switch with his right thumb. I was not supposed to touch the camera. In fact, I can't recall where it was kept in the house.

I don't remember much about the inside of that Milwaukee lower flat on 29th and Brown Street, even though I lived there the first ten years of my life.

There aren't many family photographs from my childhood in the old album I took from my father's place when I finally was able to leave him. It was my third attempt at "running away." The first two tries were aborted by him at ages fifteen and sixteen. I remember him grabbing my wrist and holding it painfully tight, so I couldn't move on the street in front of our house. I remember his frighteningly calm voice telling me that if I tried to run away again he'd send me to a girls' reformatory. I believed him.

I waited until I was eighteen, when he could no longer legally own me and quietly, purposefully closed the back door behind me one afternoon while he was at work. I went to stay at my best friend's house. Her mother understood. She knew my father. She let me live there until I found

June 1955—High School
graduation day.
Photo taken by my aunt Louise
in our living room before I ran
away.

a job in a dairy, printing route books for the milk delivery drivers. I left my friend's house after I'd saved enough money to rent a room in a boarding house a few blocks from where I worked.

I went back to his house only once more, a few days after I ran away. I had to climb in through the kitchen window because the locks had been changed. I wanted to retrieve some things from a white wicker doll trunk in my bedroom. The trunk was filled with stuffed animals that my grandmother had made for me, and two soft twin baby dolls that my mother made. Their faces had embroidered features . . . little blue eyes and pink cheeks. She sewed white dresses, with matching bonnets for them. I wanted to get the dolls and one of the stuffed animals. It was a bright red horse with a white yarn tail and mane with gray hooves. Its legs were attached with buttons so that it could stand by itself if you carefully positioned it. It felt weird to go back into his house. My bedroom door was open. The trunk was in front of the window. When I opened the trunk lid I found it empty. Then I heard someone opening the back door. I turned and there stood the upstairs landlady. I felt like a thief. I was embarrassed and frightened. She asked me what I was doing. I told her. She said that my father had burned the dolls in the furnace the day before. She said this factually without any feelings showing on her face. I can't remember what I felt. All I wanted to do was to get out of there. She asked me where I was living. I don't remember what I said back to her. I just flew out the door.

When I returned to my friend's house I went and got the family album that I had taken with me when I left my father. I ran my hands over its black leather covers and sat on the back porch slowly looking through the pictures. Most of the brownish tinted snapshots in the album came from a time before 1937, the year I was born. They were pre–Depression-era pictures taken in Berlin, Wisconsin, where my parents and grandparents were born and raised.

There are photos of my mother in a fur-trimmed coat and my brother, a smiling three-year-old in a winter snowsuit, straddling the barrel of a military cannon in the small town park square. My thirteen-year-old sister and my mother stand there, one on each side of the cannon, looking happier than I ever remember them together.

The album also included a photo of my father and me, standing in front of the entrance to a tourist attraction in western Wisconsin called The Cave of the Mounds. His arm is grasped tightly around my twelve-year-old shoulders. The whole top of my body is being held in place. It looks squashed like a half-opened accordion. There is what could be called a small smile on my father's face and a very small smile on mine.

Another picture, taken on the same trip, shows my father clutching my mother in the identical pose. They're not smiling.

The trip stands out in my mind as the only time I can remember the three of us doing anything like that together. It was shortly before my mother died. The car ride in my father's secondhand Ford was accomplished without one argument between my parents . . . also something that rarely happened.

I don't remember who took the pictures.

The day I ran away, I stuffed the album in a pillowcase filled with as many clothes as it could hold and my mother's jewelry box. Inside the box were a few pieces of what people who own real pearls and diamonds would call "costume jewelry." I thought they were beautiful and most of all, the box and her ivory bone hand mirror were two of the few things I had left of anything that belonged to her.

I remember sitting on my friend's back porch after I tried to reclaim the things from my doll trunk, holding the album and wishing it held pictures of my dolls.

I wasn't born in Milwaukee. I was taken there as an infant, a few months after my mother gave birth to me, along with my five-year-old brother. My mother and my sister, who was fifteen at the time, and my brother had been living in Berlin, while my father searched for work in Milwaukee. My sister didn't make the move with us. The story goes that she came home from school one day to find everything we owned packed in the back of a pickup truck. A small suitcase of her belongings stood on the sidewalk. She was dropped off at our grandmother's house on the outskirts of town, and that's where she lived for the next three years.

My father had found a job as a welder at Milwaukee's A. O. Smith's. It was the same factory that employed him until he retired in 1962.

A. O. Smith was a huge corporation, with more than ten thousand employees. The department my father worked in manufactured auto body frames and farm equipment. During World War II the plant made millions with its military contracts. One of my father's jobs was to weld the seams of "block buster" bombs from their insides. I remember him explaining how he would crawl into the shell head first, in a space just wide enough to admit his body. He'd hold the welding torch in front of him, wiggling out backwards as he worked. A. O. Smith didn't "waste" any of its profits on safety and better working conditions, either before, during, or after the production speed of the "war effort" years. He eventually lost a lung to the toxic fumes. He developed asthma, arthritis, and a heart condition.

My father drank excessively as long as I can remember. He claimed it helped "cut the phlegm." He also became a drug abuser. He had the help of industrial clinic doctors and most of his personal physicians who apparently never cared or checked to see if he was becoming addicted to the various narcotics they prescribed for his constant pain. My father was a number sitting in their waiting rooms, and if another prescription could move him out the door faster that's all they cared about. And evidently as long as our neighborhood pharmacist got his money, he didn't question the amount of pain prescriptions dispensed to Joe Doro either.

Since I was the usual pickup and delivery person, I argued with my father about these weekly trips every time I was ordered to go. There were crowds of boys who would "hang out" at the drug store teasing and trying to kiss me as I ran in. I never told my parents why I hated going, I just stubbornly fought against the ordeal regularly, all the while knowing I would lose the battle.

When my mother was still alive, she'd open up the capsules as soon as I got home, pouring their contents down the kitchen drain and carefully refilling them with sugar before giving the pill bottle to her husband. After her death, I inherited the job. Her reason for "doctoring" the medication was that she feared he would "take too many" and "something bad would happen to him."

My father was a union member and he talked about voting for Democrats. He also was a racist, a wife-beater and a child-abuser. At the age of sixty-two, shortly after retiring, he died of heart failure from washing down too many real pain pills with half pints of Coronet brandy.

"Focus" is the second poem I've written that included him. The first was called, simply, "The Father Poem." It concerned living and dying in the working class in this country. People who had problems dealing with memories of their fathers related to it. They'd come to me after readings with tears in their eyes, thanking me for giving them some words to connect with their own unspoken thoughts.

Then about four years ago, I stopped reciting it in public. The events were historically intact, but there were whole sections of the poem I couldn't live with. I knew that I was lying to myself.

To understand the importance of this choice, I have to say that the poem was considered to be my "best" work by many people. There continued to be requests to publish it. I felt torn, and confused. On the one hand, the poem was technically good, and, in fact, some people seemed to be "helped" by it. I should have been proud and anxious for an editor to want to publish any of my poems. I ended up telling myself that it was a poem about someone else's father, and let it go at that. *I* just wouldn't read it anymore. But the poem followed me. It wouldn't let me alone. I decided that I had to face it. I had to take control of the poem.

In the original version, I spoke about what I think I *should* have done as my father's daughter. Things like sticking by him and fighting side by side against "the rich men who caused my father to . . . ."

"The Father Poem" was written in 1972. My political awareness based on working-class, Franklin D. Roosevelt Democrat background, tilted noticeably leftward during the late sixties. I had been forced into the role of a single parent after a thirteen-year "perfect" high school marriage ended abruptly in abandonment. I was trying to figure out how to survive and raise five kids without the financial (or any other) support of an ex-husband. The Vietnam War, women's movement, and poor people's struggles had touched Milwaukee's south side and the idea of female oppression, war, and economic suffering seemed to fit me perfectly. I was angry at my "X" and at the "system," but not at a dead father.

It seemed that I just couldn't let the rich and powerful win yet another victory. Screwed up as my father was, I felt if I allowed even a bit of blame to rest at his feet, millionaires all over the world would smile gleefully, relishing the idea that they were being released of any blame. I had it figured out. It seemed plain to me that the pain he dished out to his family was not his fault.

Twenty years later, in the nineties, time and life experience have given me a less simplistic political analysis of social problems. I still maintain, however "old fashioned" it may sound, that the capitalist patriarchal social and economic system has a stranglehold on the everyday people. I believe it needs to be changed. I believe we're affected as a group and individually . . . in our working and want-to-be-working lives, in our relationships with each other at work and in our homes. The political IS personal.

In the initial revision period of "The Father Poem," I found myself examining something I had ignored, denied, and wouldn't even have allowed myself to consider when I first wrote the poem. It was the fact that my father had choices. Why didn't I think about this earlier? My father hadn't changed since the poem was written. He was still dead. Our family history was the same. Apparently I was the one who had changed.

In the years between 1972 and 1992, I had been employed in factories just like the one my father worked in. As a blue-collar woman (the only female machinist in the three shops where I worked during that time), I was able to develop friendships with my coworkers. Many of the men were victims of industrial injuries and illnesses. Most of them were Democrats. Most of them belonged to a union.

We had a common struggle. It was "us against the bosses." We had a yearning for more control over our labor. We wished for more time off to do whatever we wanted. We could band together to make decisions that affected our work lives, whether it was fighting against a vicious foreman or putting our heads together to figure out a machining problem. Our tool boxes were not necessarily individual property, although they were respected. The real physical danger of our jobs forged team-work bonds for survival.

Even though these working-class men contended with some of the same unsafe working conditions and health problems as my father, they were not cruel to each other or to their families. I was introduced to the people close to them. Friendships developed that I still hold close to my heart. I spent time in their homes. They visited my home. They met my family. I saw the love these men demonstrated for their families. There was love in my own family.

By this time, the children and I were living with the man who would become my second husband. He worked 7:00 A.M. to 3:30 P.M. as a machinist at another factory. I grappled with the night shift at Allis Chalmers Tractor shop. We had differences, but we struggled through them together. We were partners in every sense of the word. There was a persistence that we had in common. A way of sticking out hard situations to the end . . . of resolving what you can and letting go when you can't see what else to do. And probably, most importantly, we tried not to take our work problems out on each other. It was difficult, especially being on opposite shifts. He would be sleeping at 1:00 A.M. when I'd get home from work. I'd call each week night on my eight o'clock break, and we taped messages to each other on an old tape recorder we kept on the kitchen table. He took care of the house and kids when I worked "nights." It stretched our relationship almost to breaking. Some of the kids tried to see how much they could get away with, since either one or the other of their "set" of parents was missing most of the time. We got along, but it wasn't a TV family situation comedy with a neatly wrapped up conclusion at the end of each half hour. It was damn hard. Some of the endings were happy. Some weren't.

In the factories where I worked for almost thirteen years, I also saw one or two men who were dangerous, self-destructive, and unpredictable. They were not the norm. They'd perform their jobs in a suicidal manner, burning up machine motors and breaking gear teeth in their frantic rush to work faster. Their accident rate was ten times the average, especially the afternoons when they'd come back to work after lunch break smelling like the taverns at the top of the hill. If they stayed at work to eat, they'd curse wives and girlfriends for packing some kind of food they didn't apparently like that day. They laughed about how they'd "knock 'em around to teach 'em a lesson." They were generally individualist and politically backward in their gut responses to oppressive work situations.

When a layoff was in the wind, and management ordered speed-ups in production, they would work even faster. They became hostile, suspicious, and even more dangerous to be near. In the factory's communal atmosphere where coworkers helped each other on a regular basis, they forced us to stay away from them through their antisocial actions. The closer it came to the layoff date, the more irrational was their choice of solutions. If working faster wouldn't stop the layoff clock from ticking, it must be something else. It must be *somebody* else. They blamed everyone who wasn't a white male, and said they shouldn't be working there. We were taking their jobs away.

I learned to avoid these people like everyone did. They could not be "reasoned" with. I saw that they chose to act the way they did. They were not robots whose arms, mouths, and legs were attached to strings. We all worked in the same factory. We were not all reacting to the worsening work situation in the manner that they were. Even some of the guys who went up the hill to drink at lunch time didn't act like they did. Though they were frightened, sad individuals, we held them accountable for their actions. They had no right to pass on their own personal feelings of oppression by persecuting others.

Neither did my father.

I began to understand that my own personal political beliefs did not contradict my right to hold him accountable. My father chose to isolate himself from the rest of his family. He wouldn't listen to people who tried to help them. I remember one doctor who made a house visit when he was off sick, telling him he wouldn't give him any more prescriptions because he wasn't following the dosage. My father chased him out of our house yelling obscenities. My mother told him more than once to quit his job and go on disability. He said she was crazy. I remember one of the very few times I was alone with him and not afraid. We were walking to the hardware store together. I must have been four or five years old, because I wore a red cape that I loved, and a navy blue felt hat with a brown and red feather, and the outfit didn't fit me by the time I started school. I remember looking up at him while we walked, and asking him why he was so mean all the time. He kept on walking, and answered, "Because I want to."

Understanding my father lies somewhere between examining his personal choices and his decaying health made worse by the horrible and dangerous conditions he worked under. His own childhood suffering must have also played a part. I remember him telling stories of how his father beat him with a horse-buggy whip on a regular basis.

I have yet to face the issue of my mother's responsibility in the arguments and chaos in our household. As an adult, I can't separate her misery and sadness from her own personal choices. Her torment was too much a part of mine. She was also physically abused by my father. But why did she appear to relish prolonging the arguments? Why didn't she take the kids and go back to her hometown to live with relatives or friends until she could get on her feet financially?

I can't answer my own questions. It's too easy to judge her by current social standards. It was a different era. She was a battered woman in a time before the term was invented. Did the situation she found herself in allow her to consider other options? Would she have listened if she did have help? Apparently, she just couldn't do it, for whatever reasons.

At the same time as my own blue-collar experience was helping me rethink my father's choices, something else was happened in my life. I was beginning to remember details from my childhood that I had formerly pushed deep inside. I was fourteen when I watched helplessly as my mother died on the dining room floor. Graphic scenes from her death haunted me on a daily basis. Sometimes these thoughts would grab hold of me in waves of real physical as well as mental pain. Memories of my father coming towards me screaming that he'd kill me if I tried to get help for my mother would cause my neck and shoulders to freeze into tightly wound muscle spasms. My stomach would ache. My nerves were constantly on edge. Sometimes my mind had real problems just being where I was at a given moment. I drifted off, disorganized, lost in the past. It was disconcerting and sometimes actually dangerous, especially if I was driving a car or running the machines at work.

There came a time when I finally ceased to deny the effects of my past. My partner and I had been together for seventeen years by this time. We had moved to California. Our kids were grown and on their own. Every time we agreed on an issue, be it about relating to the kids, "back home," or handling money or work questions, it seemed I would end up doing the opposite of what we had originally decided together without discussing that I had actually changed my mind. Our relationship was at stake. I loved him and he loved me, but we argued constantly. My actions and his reactions were pulling us apart.

I did not understand myself. Why did *I* make certain choices? Why did I stubbornly latch on to an opinion when I knew that I was wrong. Why couldn't I utter a simple "thank you" without thinking that a piece of myself was being torn away. Why couldn't I accept praise without wanting to hide? Why was I a writer unable to describe how I *felt*.

I began to work on myself as if I were machining a piece of steel that had been scratched and marred by outside forces. In the beginning I went to the library and got books about children of alcoholics. A half year later I tried therapy for the first time, but the therapist and I didn't "click." My husband continued to encourage me. He was also working on things in himself that he wanted to change. We decided to stick it out together.

Then I found Sandra. I was referred to her by a friend who also was seeing her for professional help. Sandra became my engine lathe of understanding. I was, at the same time, the machinist and the cutting tool. Hot metal chips flew into the air as the damaged metal was removed. Some of the pieces landed back on my bare skin, burning into my flesh, but I didn't stop. Some of the hot chips of my past ricocheted off me and landed on my husband. The work is still not finished.

And so it was that when I revisited "The Father Poem," my eyes, heart, and new political awareness, viewed my father and his actions in a more realistic light. I accepted the fact that he had choices. And even though his choices were colored by the effects that capitalism had on him, personally, as a working-class, blue-collar man, I realized that he still must be held accountable. I felt that to say to the world that my father "couldn't help it" would be unfair to the other working-class men I knew and admired, as well as personally dishonest.

A short time ago, I read the new version of "The Father Poem" for the first time. Again, people came to me expressing their gratitude for giving their feelings a voice. This time, however, many more *women* verbalized their *relief*. They said that the poem gave them permission to feel that they didn't have to forgive in order to understand.

"Focus" is the first new poem I've written about my father since 1972. The dream happened. Its sequences combined the reality of memory with dream fantasies. My father *did* have his picture taken for an advertisement. The repaired snapshot *is* included in the old family album I took when I ran away from home as a teenager. My father *did* mentally, physically, and sexually abuse me as a child. I really did awake from the dream, laughing, and feeling flushed, vibrant, and determined to record it. The words flowed fast and easily. Writing it was my personal victory.

The original title of the poem was "Entries and Exits," but it didn't seem to fit after I began to write this accompanying essay. When I thought about how my working-class background had affected "Focus," I decided that the topic of my family and its history could not have an "exit." The family events I'm aware of, and those that continue to open to me, will be with me as long as I have memories.

My family was like a team of injured players, needing each other to finish a game we never wanted to be in. Some team members died trying.

My sister and I are all that's left of our family. My brother died two years after my mother. My sister's seventy now, I'm fifty-five. We're just beginning to share our own personal stories of what it was like growing up in our family. I tend to talk about it more than she wants to, but sometimes she writes me long letters filled with her childhood ghosts and memories. I save the letters.

There is such a wide disparity in our ages and life histories that sometimes it feels that we came from separate families. Our father and mother were children of farmers. My sister spent most of her childhood in a tiny rural town close to relatives. I grew up in a large city. The parents of my sister's childhood had a small amount of money and an entrepreneurial view of the world. I was born at the end of the "Great Depression" as an unwanted surprise. My mother was a frustrated housewife dragged from the only place she ever wanted to live in by my father, a newly employed factory worker. My father's small chicken and egg business was history. The empowerment of self-employment was never to return. He had bosses telling him to work harder, faster, and longer, for the rest of his working life.

My sister said that our father's drinking wasn't a problem when she was a young child. He did it in taverns back then, and she doesn't remember him coming home drunk. By the time I came around he didn't have these kinds of personally selected booze boundaries.

These inner-family class and social differences are difficult for me to analyze right now. In any event, my sister and I don't discuss the topic very often and we *never* use class terminology. When we do speak our memories it's as if they were painfully sad scenes from someone else's photo album. And yet the telling of each story is accompanied by its own special sigh of relief.

My sister told me that she tore "The Father Poem" pages out of a copy of a book of my poems that I gave her six years ago. She wanted to keep the book, but she said she couldn't stand reading the poem about our father because it wasn't true. He wasn't mean just because of his job.

It took me twenty years to agree with her.

My sister and I live on opposite ends of the country. I flew out to visit her in the summer of 1992, shortly before this essay was completed. We hadn't seen each other for five years. We communicated by long-distance phone calls and letters. I was apprehensive about the trip. Therapy had helped me dig deep into my past. I wanted so badly to tell her more about these painful excavations. But wouldn't that be like asking her to shovel alongside of me? I felt confused, but I knew that I needed to show her the "Focus" poem before I would submit it to a publisher. I felt that the poem was way too personal to have her stumble across it by accident, if indeed it would be published. I needed to tell her about my recent childhood discoveries, before there was a chance they would be publicly shared. The incest issue was something I had unearthed slowly and painfully in the last four years, along with an enormous amount of self-guilt and shame. Now I wanted to tell this truth to the only person living who knew both my mother and father intimately.

A week before I left on the trip, I phoned my sister and said I had another poem about our father that I wished she would read. First she said she didn't want to. Then, later in the conversation, she changed her mind. I don't think it was anything I said. In fact we were talking about the mechanics of the trip itself . . . the flight number, how I was to travel from the airport, etc., and she suddenly said that I should bring the poem with me. I hadn't prepared myself for her to either want to see it or not want to see it. I just went into some kind of numbing state when I put the idea out into the air. Now that she actually agreed to read it, I instantly felt very frightened that I had asked her, and ashamed that I had even written it at all. I wanted to go back in time and erase what I wrote. For a fleeting second it felt that if the poem never existed, I could change the past and the incest wouldn't have happened.

Of course I didn't say any of these things to her. Talking feelings didn't happen in our family, and it's just now beginning between my sister and me. So I just said that I'd bring the poem with me and if she wanted to see it she should ask. I wouldn't bring the subject up. We agreed and finished discussing the flight numbers and shuttle logistics of Baltimore International Airport.

The second day into our visit, my sister asked if I had the poem. She had been telling me a story about when she was nine years old and our brother was born. Our father was working out of town somewhere. She and our mother were out for a walk with the infant in a baby buggy, when suddenly, our mother blurted out that she didn't want him anymore. She said my sister could "have him if she wanted him," and then she simply turned and ran up the street. My sister tried to hurry after her, but the carriage was heavy and awkward and she couldn't go fast enough to catch up. She said that she remembers pushing her baby brother home, changing his diaper, feeding him a bottle of milk, and placing him in his crib. When he woke from his nap she again diapered, fed, and eventually put him to bed for the evening. It grew dark, but still no mother. My sister waited on the porch steps and then went to bed herself. Much later in the night, our mother came home. Where she was all that time, no one knows.

My sister shares this pain with an air of anger, resignation, and strength. She is stubbornly determined that her past will not affect her present. I am sad, yet adrenalized. I feel sorry for that little nine-year-old girl. But I'm also so proud of this woman, my sister, standing before me in her kitchen. She never "went to therapy" but somehow in her seventy years, she has figured out how to live with these terrible memories and keep on going.

I tell her that I'm putting the poem under her jewelry box on her bedroom dresser. She can read it when she wants to in her own time. Then we go grocery shopping together. Her grandchildren are visiting. They want some kind of cereal they just saw on TV.

The poem stays there for another day. The next morning, as I am eating breakfast, she comes out to the back porch with a horrified look on her face.

"I read the poem. That son of a bitch. If he was still living, I'd kill him."

I feel suspended in mid air, like the fork full of scrambled eggs I'm holding above my plate. I am air. I am light . . . clouds of light fill my stomach and chest. If we were in a Hollywood movie scene, we'd hug or cry and some kind of fade-out music would fill the room. We don't hug. We don't cry. We're not in Hollywood. She's still talking. I'm still holding my fork full of eggs. I put it back down on the plate. I look at her face. It's vibrating. Her brows are knit. Her voice continues. She says the catalogue photo wasn't from Sears. It was a leather coat factory advertisement. He was a foreman at the factory and they asked him to pose with one of their sample coats. Our mother tore the photo up but she didn't paste it back together.

My sister is talking a stream . . . nonstop. . . . She said that she gathered the pieces and repaired the photo. My sister emphasizes each word, each fact, with the force of ancient righteous truths. I don't doubt for a moment what she tells me. So she, too, believes the poem she had just read. I love her. I feel loved. I feel cared for and verified. I am touched, and suddenly shaken by the fact that if she hadn't taped the picture back together and pasted it in the album I would never have seen it, years later. An integral piece of my own personal painful trip back in time wouldn't have existed. I am floating above the hot summer morning and I am shivering.

Weeks afterward, back home, I'm still flying in my mind, excruciatingly happy. I walk down streets smiling in a town that doesn't do that in normal practice. The lightness I felt at my sister's breakfast table has not left me. It is a wonder and delight.

My sister and I still have trouble *saying* that we love each other. I have no idea when and if that will change. Yet, her "swear words" after reading "Focus" were the biggest statement of love that I ever felt from her. I took a risk when I shared "Focus" with her. My sister took another risk and read it. We are both stronger because of our actions. We may live on opposite sides of the country but we are closer than ever before in our lives. I can't even imagine what I would have felt if she hadn't supported me.

The journeys of this past year have taught me that each family member owns their own yesterdays. Portions of those yesterdays are collective memories. I found my own frightening and separate, like blurred photos. I discovered that I could use the courage of my class survival instincts, the endurance, the team resourcefulness, to focus on revealing and facing the worst of these fearful memories. I'm slowly learning that I can follow the advice of a man, my husband, without worrying about being hurt. I'm examining my defense mechanisms. I am allowing myself to look at my own image and celebrate the things I love about myself, as well as viewing old habits I am determined to change. Just as with any kind of work, it's not easy. I get tired. When I do, I try to look back to see how far I've come.

I am a working-class woman. I have my own camera. I take my own pictures.

Lennard Davis

I was born in the Bronx in 1949. My mother, Eva Weintrobe, was born in Liverpool, England, in 1911, the daughter of a Lithuanian Jewish cabinet maker and his Polish Jewish wife. My father, Morris J. Davis, was born in London in 1898, the son of a Russian Jewish father who was a fishmonger and a Russian Jewish mother who was the daughter

of a rabbi. My mother and father both became deaf in early childhood through illness—my father around the age of one, and my mother at seven. They received a minimal education at residential schools in England and were trained for low-level jobs in industry. My father became a sewing-machine operator in the garment district, and my mother was a seamstress. We lived in a working-class section of the Bronx where I attended public school.

Lennard Davis is a professor of English at SUNY Binghamton. He is the author of *Factual Fictions: The Origins of the English Novel* (New York: Columbia University Press, 1983), *Resisting Novels: Fiction and Ideology* (New York: Methuen, 1987), and coeditor of *Left Politics and the Literary Profession* (New York: Columbia University Press, 1991). He is Book Review Editor of *Radical Teacher,* on the advisory boards of *The Arkansas Review* and *The Eighteenth Century: Theory and Interpretation,* and is cofounder of the Group for Early Modern Cultural Studies. He is at work on a book, *Theorizing Disability* (Verso), and stays involved with political causes on campus and the concerns of the deaf community. He is married to M. Bella Mirabella, and is the father of Carlo, fifteen, and Francesca, twelve—who teach him about injustice and freedom every day.

Lennard Davis

A Voyage Out (Or Is It Back?): Class and Disability in My Life

I

"Only connect" says E. M. Forster, and we all try. But the "only" is misleading. Is it as simple as "only"? Are these connections arbitrary? Made after the fact? Are they easily made? Too easily? For these purposes, I would like to think that there were connections, continuities between my upbringing, my politics, my work, my life. Only connect. But there may not be, other than as a fantasy of orderliness. Noam Chomsky has always struck me as an interesting case in point because he has steadfastly claimed that there is no connection between his linguistic work and his political work. Perhaps he is right. Perhaps he just could not see.

If I want to web my life with connective strands, I would draw them out beginning from my family's deafness. To me, my parents' deafness will always be inseparable from our social class. There are now greater opportunities for the deaf, but when I was growing up in the 1950s, the deaf were usually factory workers. My mother was an "alteration hand" in a department store and my father was an "sewing-machine operator" who sewed in the garment district of New York. The grind and rhythm of their work was to me part of their deafness, and their deafness was part of their work. I can say that I am who I am because of that conjunction.

I cannot say that everything about that conjunction was enabling. Life for me as a child was spare, depleted, gray. My parents, exhausted by their work, had little time to enrich my life. Their deafness added a greater barrier between me and any world outside. My mother took me to a museum just once in my entire childhood; we never dined out; occasionally we went to the park. My only enriched life was lived at school. Home meant boredom, television, and family squabbles. But school meant excitement, knowledge, harmony. Small wonder I became a teacher.

From my father and mother, I learned to survive. They had survival skills that most ordinary people can only imagine. My mother survived an early childhood attack of meningitis in which she lost her hearing, and my father survived an impoverished childhood and his own infant deafness. Survival is a double-edged form of salvation—you learn to tolerate high degrees of frustration and disappointment, but you forget how to regret and mourn the loss of what you might have had. You make do; you get by. My childhood felt like that of Dickens's orphan; I was old before my time, but I was wise.

My father tried to win at a life that others would have considered a failure. He came back each day from his menial job and told about his work in such a way that he made it seem to us that he was a gifted artisan—a Daedalus forging his inventions in a dingy sweatshop. And then on the weekends, my father would don his athletic shorts and shoes and train for his walking races. He had been a race-walker since his twenties, and he raced his last race when he was eighty. He even held the American record for twenty-five miles. His goal in life was to beat the odds, beat his lot in life, beat his deafness. His motto was: "Never say die." So he gave me a feisty raised fist that I still hold on to to this day. I think of it as a fist raised against the forces of injustice.

It was really at school, though, that my life opened. My father inspired me, but like many children from dysfunctional homes, I found my real mentors outside my family life. The principal of my public school, Sidney N. Levy, adopted me, gave me books to read, and once a telescope to study the stars. Kindly teachers took me under their wings. In my settlement-house summer camp, counselors talked to me of philosophy, life, ideas, and radical politics. In junior high school, an English teacher, Peter Poulakis, introduced me to George Orwell and Aldous Huxley. In high school, another English teacher, Ronald Greenhouse, nudged me into the world of bebop and the beatnik culture of the early sixties. School was always a place of wonder for me. I learned, I throve, and through the genuine interest of others, I managed to get myself into Columbia University.

I was a kid from the slums for whom the system worked. The public schools and the private charities like the Jewish Federation of Philanthropies, who ran my summer camp, seemed to produce people who took the time to teach me. And I was a willing learner. Moments of learning were organic, like the time that Sidney, the high school math teacher who lived in my building, sat me down on the curb by the abandoned lot and explained to me that the whole was greater than the sum of its parts. He was reaching for a metaphor, perhaps about our lives. He also told me to question authority; he said just because a teacher tells you something doesn't mean it's right.

So, I was, as Antonio Gramsci called the likes of me, an organic intellectual, being taught not necessarily in the schools, but on the streets, articulating the issues of my class. There were many sages amongst us in the Bronx. Mr. Zuckerman, the podiatrist who lived across the hallway, had a run-down office a few blocks away. The back rooms of that office were filled with a visual cacophony of scientific equipment—oscilloscopes, Van de Graff generators, electrical receivers and transceivers. Mr. Zuckerman let me wander through these rooms, hooking up one thing to another. I built my science projects back there, under his guiding hand. The Bronx was and is filled with people like him, with their local wisdom tucked into back rooms, so that an outsider who walked down the derelict streets would have no idea that behind these drab buildings were scientists as smart as Niels Bohr or Albert Einstein who just happened to be podiatrists by day. And there were poets, and painters, and geniuses of all sorts.

It is a contradiction of our culture that organic intellectuals who speak and articulate positions for their class frequently get tracked out of their milieu as quickly as society can arrange it. Of course, not all do, but I, for one, went to Columbia University, got my Ph.D., and taught for many years in elite institutions. In essence, I abandoned my class, and I fled from deafness. This was my voyage out. Most of my students would have little idea of the kind of world in which I grew up. But from time to time, I see someone like myself. Often they have rough edges and can come across as obnoxious or aggressive (I was) as they work out their awkward and contentious relation to the establishment; but other times they are shy and quiet. I always know their secret and their route, and share my story with them. Teaching, for me, has much to do with these moments of connection and revelation.

One student comes to mind. William Michaels (let us call him) was an African-American young man who lived in Harlem and each day climbed the fortresslike steps of Morningside Park, the geographical boundary that separates the ghetto from the university, to come to my humanities class in the early 1970s. He was a really smart student, and I was drawn to him. I probably was only five years older than he was. William's financial aid was inadequate, so he sold drugs to keep himself in college. One day he told me that he was quitting because his seventeen-year-old girlfriend was pregnant. Obviously the contradictions in his life were too great to stay in this elite institution. I called his mother and we both lamented his decision. I tried to get him to remain, but he had made up his mind. We stayed in touch for a while, but I always felt his loss, I felt the guilt of a survivor for having made it through college.

Now I am teaching at a state university, and I am surrounded by students who are the organic intellectuals of their age; some even come from my old neighborhood. Forty percent of the incoming students are the first people in their families to go to college. When I see a student with a bright eye and a quick tongue, I feel the deep connection of those moments when life and work make sense on the most profound level.

When I think of my work, I see myself as the doer of many things. What did they call Ulysses—the man of many ways? Perhaps I am trying to avoid the limiting trajectory of my parents' work, or perhaps I am acting out my father's attempt to break from that trajectory through his semi-career of race-walking. I think of myself as a teacher, as a writer—but I write many things, and each of them makes sense to me in terms of my upbringing. As an academic, I have written two books on the novel that attempt to place the "high" culture of literature in a political and social context that shows how such artifacts come from and affect the lives of less elite peoples. This was my mandate to show the effect of lower-class culture on consciousness. *Left Politics and the Literary Profession*, the anthology I coedited with M. Bella Mirabella, attempts to place the achievements of progressive politics in the analysis of literature over the past twenty years. I know that my class position motivated my point of view.

More recently, in addition to connecting with class-issues, I have reconnected with the issue of deafness. This was my voyage back. For me deafness had been something I associated with my parents, and despite all my interest in race, class, and gender, it never occurred to me to write about deafness in an academic setting. About three years ago I joined an organization called Children of Deaf Adults (CODA) and met many professionals in the field of deafness. From them, I learned that there was an academic discourse about deafness, and, after reading extensively, I have written a few articles on deafness, and am working on a book attempting to theorize deafness and by extension disability. Recently, I have been at work on a memoir, *The Sense of Silence*, part of which is included here.

I also do a fair amount of popular journalism—a kind of writing I always appreciate because it is popular. I would not want to write exclusively for the academic elite, and so *Redbook* or *McCalls* is as much a part of my sphere as is *In These Times, The Nation,* or *The Eighteenth Century:*

Theory and Interpretation. I recently wrote an article about how the deaf are abused by the legal and mental systems. This kind of reportorial journalism feels right—as I attempt to point out to society what wrongs it has done on the deaf, who are for the most part poor and in these cases African-American or Latino.

So, in essence, my working-class experience has been a guide to my life. It probably is no accident that my wife is also from the same background—both academics, we found each other and reconnected with our past while forging a present. But like my various working-class students, I know that, having left physically, I will never be part of the working class. Of course I am not part of the ruling class. I am one of those who belong to that tricky, in-between grouping known as intellectuals.

I wanted very much by the time I was in high school to be an intellectual. I remember that a fellow student wrote in my high school yearbook "One day we will run into each other in Central Park. I will be a music critic and you will review books for the *New York Times.*" This was a wish to be part of the intellectual world that seemed fantastically out of our reach. When I finally came to write some reviews for *New York Times Book Review,* I remember the feelings of cognitive and affective dissonance. But what would have surprised my high school self was the fact that the books I reviewed were on leftist art forms in the 1920s and the autobiography of a deaf actor. The pleasure of being myself at mid-life is the pleasure of realizing that I no longer have to flee from my working-class self and my deaf self; that the very issues of my upbringing—the Bronx, deafness, class position—are capacious enough for me to make my work.

I have not forgotten what it means to be working class. I would say that not a day passes by but that something reminds me of my origins. Being a professor connects me with issues, and even people, but it does not reintegrate me to my class in the way that my parents and my childhood self experienced the resentment of class humiliations, the lived experience of class injustice and class pride. I can remember and I can tap these memories, but I think it would be disingenuous to claim that I am still working class. There is a dialectic between the past and the present. The past is never effaced by the present. And like the unconscious, my class experience is perhaps the background radiation that informs daily action. But I do feel that I can never fully return to those origins. In the same way, I connect with deafness, but I am not deaf. Part of my consciousness is and always will be deaf; I am structured by deafness as I am by class. But I am not fully that which I write about. Perhaps it is true that the outsider is fully the only one who can write. And perhaps writers are never fully part of that which they write about. Writers are more often than not the silent observers of their culture; the spies in their families who take notes for future novels and poems.

For me such disjunctions get worked out in writing, in narrative, in articulation and teaching, and in struggling for a more just political process. I even live in a blue-collar neighborhood in the Bronx, but I am still an outsider—the professor. The voyage out may contain a return, but it is never entirely a voyage back. And the desire to connect is often more about desire than connection, despite the will for desire and the will to connect.

II

I have two balanced memories having to do with a dawning vision of my family's social class. The first is a dim recollection of a boat ride up the Hudson River. My father worked in the garment district for a manufacturer of ladies' coats and suits. I had only a faint idea of what his work was. I was just happy that he was working. His workshop organized a boat ride on a weekend for the families of the workers. I suppose that the International Ladies' Garment Workers Union must have set up the trip, since I do not think that his employer was that generous. The boat was rather large, like one of the sightseeing ships that take people around Manhattan island. There were lots of people—men, women, and children. All the men were dark and hairy, and had taken off their shirts so they could bask in their undershirts, the kind that have no sleeves so that their wiry arms, toughened at the sewing machine, extended in urban, athletic ways. The women were wearing cotton sun dresses, and children ran amok. People drank beer, smoked cigarettes, and engaged in a kind of loud jocularity that is reserved for holidays.

I immediately separated myself from my parents and ran around the deck of the boat, dizzy with the feeling of being on the water. I was amazed to see all these people. It gave me a sense that my father actually knew people other than the deaf, that his workplace was real and not just a door he walked through each day into a blankness that was my absence from him. There was a festivity and a beauty to that ride, as we sailed past the skyscrapers, past the Bronx, and up the river to Bear Mountain. The city dropped away, and in its place was the silent, gliding greenness of the banks of the Hudson. I suddenly felt part of something larger than myself and my family. There was a comfort in the feeling of being among workers sailing up the river with their families for a day out in the sun and nature.

Laughter, good-natured kidding, open space—the open, lung-filling space that I did not know, narrow as my confines were. These were the moments when I felt that life among the urban poor could be more than mere survival in dark, silent, shadowy byways of the city.

This positive memory is pierced by another more sobering one. One day I happened to go to my father's workplace. I am not sure how I got there. Perhaps he took me, or perhaps my mother stopped in to see him. Nothing prepared me for what I saw. I had lacked a vision of his working conditions. Certainly, the boat ride up the Hudson made me associate life and light with the idea of work. But there before me was a dark, cavernous loft filled with men and women hunched over sewing machines. The floor was drab and the varnish, if there ever was any, had long ago been erased by dragging feet. The walls may have been painted some color in the past, but they had achieved that final entropic state of soot-blackened gray brought on by fifty years of inattention. Workers with piles of disassembled clothes on their left would reach down, pick up a sleeve, attach it to a jacket body, and throw it down on their right side. My father was one of these people. I see him sitting by a window that fronted onto a brick wall. He is working in his tee shirt on a hot, humid summer day, wearing his reading glasses. He was probably in his early sixties. Around him was the unheard mechanical din coming from the rows of sewing machines, the large pressing machines that emitted bursts of steam. The ceiling seemed to be dark and full of hanging cables punctuated with an occasional bare, low-watt light bulb. Other people wheeled bins around and picked up the clothing body parts.

As my father saw me, he got up and greeted me with a big smile. He hugged me, and because he was delighted to show me off, introduced me to everyone he could get his hands on.

"My son, Lenny. Say hello to Joe."

"Oh, you're Morris's son. He's something! Does all his work and deaf and all."

"What he say?" my father would sign.

"You deaf and work," I would translate.

He seemed pleased with the condescending comments, so who was I to tell him not to be. He showed me around, and the more he showed me the more depressed I got. This was where my father worked. It was a dark, glum, humiliating place where nothing was beautiful, nothing uplifting. In the books I had read in school and the television programs I watched, fathers wore suits and sat in their dens. They went off to be professionals.

But my father, who could draw English cathedrals with delicate cross-hatchings, who held an American track and field record, who could mime Charlie Chaplin to a tee, was nothing but an indentured servant in a Dantesque form of industrial hell.

My father took me through the doors that separated the workers from the owners. Things were not exactly elegant, but the tone changed. There was carpeting, recessed lighting, and secretaries. My father wanted to show me off to the boss. He was a bald man with a cigar—weren't they all?

"Oh, is this your son!" the man said.

"My son. Say hello to Mr. Carmel."

"So, you're the son. You can hear?"

"Sure."

"Well, your dad is a really good worker. I can count on him."

"What say?" my father signed.

"You good worker." Again he was pleased.

"Tell him," my father signed, "you smart boy. Good student. You grow up and become electrical engineer."

This was only one of thousands of moments when my father asked me to tell hearing people things I knew I could not say. His idea of conversation was always out of kilter with the hearing world. I was reluctant to say it.

"Tell him," he insisted with that all-too-familiar exasperation beginning to burn through his facial features.

"I can't." I responded. The boss was watching, but losing interest.

"You ashamed of me?" My father signed again.

"No, it's just that. . . ."

"Tell him," he said, pushing me forward like a mother dog pushes her pup with a shove of the muzzle.

"My father says that I am smart. I'm a good student and I'll be an electrical engineer." I spit it out like a bitter pill.

"Good luck," said the boss without caring a bit.

My father smiled in delight at my transmission of his prediction of great expectations. Only I was humiliated beyond all bounds. Here in this place of desecration, my father came to work, was bossed around by bald men with cigars, performed routine repetitive tasks without even producing a coat, and came back each week with his envelope of cash.

A few years ago, I had a dream that there was another Depression and that I had lost my job. I had to wait on line to find work as a sewing machine operator. I was glad to get any job at all. Luckily, I was picked out from among the crowd of jostling men, and found myself going upstairs to a factory where I was seated at a sewing machine. I picked up some fabric and began to sew. I said to myself, "This isn't so bad." Then I realized that I had the whole rest of the day to sew. And the next day. I woke up and cried for myself, for my father, for all the people who work in factories and who have no say.

Of course, my father never seemed to mind. He would come home each day and was proud of his ability to work. He never said he disliked his bosses, except if they fired him. As he never complained about his deafness, he never complained about his lot in life. That was not his way. His way was to glorify what he did. He was the best worker, skilled in his craft, which I have no doubt he was.

Janet Zandy

I was born October 30, 1945, in Hoboken, New Jersey. Until I was ten years old, I lived with my mother, father, and sister in a four-room apartment in Union City, New Jersey. Then we moved into a duplex house in Lyndhurst, New Jersey, which my parents purchased with my aunt and uncle who lived upstairs. Lyndhurst was and is a working-class town about ten miles from Manhattan with a good high school sports program and a lot of racism.

My parents and their parents were workers. My maternal grandfather was a trolley car ticket collector. My paternal grandfather was a carpenter, and his father was a stone carver in Italy. My mother took home piecework, was a riveter for a short time during World War II when my father was "overseas," and worked

as a short order cook in a luncheonette after he died. Relatives and friends came to my mother's house not only because she was a good cook, but because they could trust her to keep their secrets. After World War II, my father found a production job at Trubeck Laboratories in East Rutherford, New Jersey. In addition to his paid blue-collar work, he offered his white-collar know-how to the family—interpreting official-looking forms and applications, mediating problems, and completing and checking tax returns so that the aunts and uncles would not have to turn to strangers.

In my high school yearbook, I announced as my life's goal: "Making my parents proud." In this photo my parents and I are beaming because I am accepting the $2,000 scholarship check from my father's company that would pay for my entire four-year college tuition at a state college. If my father had not worked for that company, I might not have gotten a college education, and he might not have died so young.

Janet Zandy is an assistant professor of Language and Literature at Rochester Institute of Technology. She publishes on women's and class issues, and is the editor of an anthology of working-class women's writings, *Calling Home* (Rutgers University Press, 1990). A political and labor activist, she is a member of ROCOSH (Rochester Council on Occupational Safety and Health). She lives in Rochester with her husband, William Zandy, and their children, Anna, a high school student, and Victor, a college student.

Janet Zandy

Liberating Memory

It is Parents' Weekend, a minor ritual in academic institutions. This particular Sunday in early October 1963, my father has to work the weekend shift at his chemical plant and cannot attend. I am disappointed because he is not there, but say nothing. I am a freshman scholarship student and a commuter. I live at home with my parents and sister. My mother and I drive together to Parents' Weekend activities scheduled for parents who have weekends.

We arrive overdressed and feel a discomfort we do not voice. We follow the crowd and sit on the damp steps of an amphitheater carved out of old Watchung Mountain stone. Within a decade much of the mountain will be leveled for parking lots, but today it is a shaded and beautiful outdoor theater. We listen to the welcoming remarks of some college administrator. Neither of us feels welcomed. I see in my mother's face a hidden sadness; I feel a shame I try to deny.

This is not a memory of continuation or development. It is a memory of rupture. The discrepancy between what my mother and I felt and the scene that was played out could not be acknowledged. We had intense feelings but we didn't have the language to identify and affirm them. We could only push the feelings down and go home.

Today, I cope with middle-aged memory blocks. I forget familiar names, repeat stories, blank out whole days. Old, acute shards of memory crowd out the short-term data and demand attention. I remember that Sunday thirty years ago because I cannot forget the consciousness of discontinuity between the two great loves of my childhood: my family and school. I loved school *almost* as much as I loved my parents. But, the more schooling I got, the more separate I felt from them. It is an old working-class story.

We didn't have a telephone until I was eleven years old. Even after the phone was a black fixture, there wasn't a lot of planning or scheduling. Calendars were there to keep track of birthdays, anniversaries, and deaths. Everything else just happened. My childhood was noisy. Company, usually relatives and rarely friends (who needed friends when there were so many relatives?) would stop by, never quite unexpectedly, on the way to other places. Out would come the coffee and cake, and the joking, teasing, and visiting continued until everyone was too tired or too full. When I was in high school and college and needed quiet to study, I would retreat to the basement, working at my old black desk, wrapped in a blanket during the damp, winter months. I was always excused to study.

My parents were conscious of the value of education to their daughters' future. They both had had to quit school after the ninth grade to get a job and give their pay to the family. My mother was the oldest daughter of ten children; my father was one of seven children. This is not counting the siblings who did not reach adulthood. There was a great sense of obligation on my father's side of the family; a great sense of responsibility and pleasure on my mother's side.

My father's Italian family lived in Hoboken, an enclave of first- and second-generation Italians who antagonistically shared the same crowded streets with third-generation Irish. They stubbornly kept Italian traditions of food and religion, but spoke English at home in order to help their children make it in America. I remember one uncle much touted within the family for having a white-collar job and working on Wall Street. He said little and kept his eyes down. The other five brothers were blue collars. My aunt, the only daughter, married late for an Italian girl and died giving birth to her tenth child. My grandmother outlived several children and died at ninety. She was always carefully dressed, manipulative with her children and their spouses, and insistent that her many grandchildren kiss her on the lips. For most of her long adult life she was a widow. Her husband, the grandfather I never met, left one morning for work and never returned home alive. He was a passenger in a car that was struck head on and he was killed instantly. The accident happened on Route 3 near what is now the Meadowlands, a stadium and racetrack, but what was then a thick marshland where crabs with low toxicity were netted by urban fishermen. By the 1950s and 1960s these marshes became one long garbage dump. As kids, my sister and I would roll up the car windows as fast as we could to beat the stench on Route 3. Heading east, it is the road that has the best view of the beautiful New York City skyline—on clear days.

My father hung out with my mother's oldest brother and that's how he got to meet my mother, avoid Hoboken, and spend a lot of time in Jersey City. My father was very smart, and always acutely felt the absence of what he called "the sheepskin." I remember the story of his stolen education.

When my father was living at home in Hoboken, something happened one day that brought everyone to the street side windows—perhaps it was a parade, a peddler, or a fight. While everyone's heads were poked out the window and their backs were turned, someone came into the apartment and stole the money that was supposed to be for Carlos's education. I say *story*, because even as a child I had a hard time believing that one.

So much of the goodness and generosity that is as much a part of my childhood as uncertainty and loss stems from my mother's family. My mother's mother died shortly after I was born. Anna was the daughter of a rabbi whose family lived along the German/Austrian border. She was sent to New York City as a child to stay with distant relatives. Whether the decision to send her to America was an act of rescue or oppression is hard to say. She told stories of having to hide in the skin of a cow when soldiers came into her village. No one explained why. She was apparently sent to America to be a servant in the home of wealthier relatives. One day, she was distracted while she was hanging clothes on the roof of the building where she lived. She fell. She recovered from that fall, but while she was recuperating she met Albert, an immigrant from Italy. Perhaps he gave her the first attention she had had in a long time. In one sudden shift, before she was sixteen, she was a mother, a wife, and an orphan. Her Orthodox parents in Europe lit candles, tore their clothes, and sat shivah. She was dead, but not dead. She never learned to read and write, but her children always praised her ability to travel all over New York City and the boroughs by reading the subway lights. Mostly, though, she stayed at home and worked—the daily battle against dirt in crowded spaces, cooking on a wood stove, scrubbing clothes on a washboard, giving birth to fourteen children, feeding the neighborhood "poor souls"—she worked. Many Sunday afternoons of my childhood were spent at the Jewish cemetery where we would place stones on her grave and visit.

Anna's inheritance to her children and grandchildren was a bone-deep knowledge of what it meant to be shut out. The aunts and uncles, brothers and sisters, trusted each other a lot more than they trusted institutions or any promises of the American Dream. They practiced an unpoliticized and unnamed socialism. Whoever had extra that particular week, month, or year shared it with the others. It came in the form of continuous, spirited, gift giving. My mother never shopped for my sister and me without "taking care" of some of the cousins. My uncle just happened to stop at the house after a trip to the butcher. When the aunts baked, the trays of cookies and cakes were for the Family, never just their own smaller household. No one asked . . . it was expected that each would recognize the other's need. And it was expected that any stranger who was on the arm of a member of the family would be heartily welcomed. I used to think that the same five-dollar bill was in constant circulation, only enclosed in different happy birthday, anniversary, and get well cards. Until the time came for braces, a car that worked, and a college education, it never occurred to me that my own family did not have much money.

Since they never had to be concerned with monetary accumulation or investment, there was space for play. They were gamblers. The aunts played the numbers. They would call each other and discuss numbers that figured in their dreams. Every once in a while, a number hit—for a few dollars. The uncles played the horses. In the days when there was no such thing as off-track betting, they would take the bus to the Big A, or Belmont, or contact their bookies. I remember one uncle giving me tightly folded pieces of paper to take to a local candy store. The guy behind the counter of this tiny, dirty shop was fat, cigar-chewing, and not particularly delighted to see children. I handed the paper to him. Sometimes I got a Three Musketeers bar for my efforts, most times not. Such was my short career as a runner. On Saturday afternoons my grandfather would demand absolute silence; uncles, aunts, and children would come to a complete stop so that the radio could be turned on and the race results heard. Every now and then a particular set of horses would win, place, and show, but usually there was just a flash of anger, something thrown at the radio, and then everyone would continue where they left off. On those occasions when I accompanied my uncles to the track, I noticed they were less interested in the physical animals and more interested in their scratch sheets. Sometimes they didn't even watch the race. What they loved was the luck . . . the thrill of risk . . . the possibility of momentary freedom from care . . . a chance to take care of the family . . . not the money, but the luck . . . the great promise . . . the charm . . . the dare and the desire . . . the Luck.

My protected, loving childhood and adolescence halted with my father's unexpected death in 1965 at the age of forty-nine. I cannot recover what is not completely lost. He would fit no stereotype of white maleness. Without an education or many models, he figured out a way to defy the worst in his own culture without abandoning it. He used his meager allowance from the paycheck he handed my mother to buy books for his daughters. Even in our tiny dwelling, our privacy was always respected. He shared all the domestic chores, and enjoyed his woodwork and garden. I never heard him

Janet Zandy's sister (Annie), father (Charles), and Janet.

utter a racist or sexist epithet. His life should have been longer. If he had had a physically safe work life, it might have been.

I was very slow to make that particular connection. It is too late now to piece together a causal relationship between his work at the chemical plant and the sudden cancer, embolism, and death. Despite the deep tiredness he carried from his shift work, my father seemed strong and healthy. He was hurt, occasionally, but never sick. Now and then, there was an accident at the chemical plant, some spillage, a minor explosion, and he would be sent home, the red burn marks tattooed on his chest. Long defunct, Trubeck Laboratories was once located on Route 17 near where it crosses Route 3. It manufactured expensive perfumes. Instead of Christmas turkeys, the men who worked there got little bottles of Shalimar and White Shoulders. There must have been "family days" since I remember walking inside the plant, holding my hand to my nose to block the acrid smell, noticing the open drums, the pipes, the noise of dripping chemicals. That smell touched everything my father owned or wore. I can smell it still. I often wonder how many of the men who worked at Trubeck Labs—before even the minimal restrictions of OSHA on the chemicals, the toxicity, the penetrating smell—survived.

My father was my intellectual companion and he was gone. I have no memory of my junior year in college but the transcript says I got straight A's. My college studies and my time at home were completely severed. I was so slow. I thought knowledge worth learning was inside the library, the classroom, and my professors' minds, not at home. There was no intellectual space to make sense of my private pain. Women, labor, black, and ethnic studies did not exist; there were no occasions to glimpse shared struggle. We learned the Anglo-American story and were implicitly told that was *the* story.

I graduated from college, found a job teaching high school English, and for two years lived at home with my mother and gave her my pay. I read Martin Buber, Nietzsche, Tillich, Gurdjieff, and Jung—but not Marx—looking for answers. I left for graduate school, protested the Vietnam War—a source of great tension in the family since all my uncles "served" in other wars at other times—married because my mother would disapprove of "living together," and became a mother and a feminist. Before I read the great feminist texts of the 1970s, it was the lived experience of delivering and caring for a child day after day, alone, that made me question knowledge in a profound way. I had bouts of anger, depression, and debilitating migraine headaches. Days and days were locked inside a punishing migraine. I had trouble speaking and could barely answer the telephone.

As an act of self-rescue, I joined community women's study groups and the editorial collective of *New Women's Times,* one of the early U.S. radical women's newspapers. Learning about women within the circle of other women enabled me to find a public voice. I was still angry, but now I understood why—at least partially. As we read *Sisterhood Is Powerful, Of Woman Born,* Mary Daly, Kate Millet, and Redstockings, we, collectively, began to construct the categorical differences of gender. We signed our letters "In Sisterhood" with good faith, as we began to test what "woman" meant in relation to race and class. Perhaps it was 1978 or 1979; we might have been reading a historical novel by a Black woman writer. I blurted out, "Well, slavery is gone; it's much better now." The only African-American woman in our study group, whose love for me I have never questioned, replied, "Easy for you to say, Miss Janet." Wilma Campbell reminded me that even though neither one of us may have a lot of money to spend in a downtown department store, it is not likely that the store detective will follow me.

The dream of a common language and the power to connect seemed to dissolve during my infrequent visits home to my mother. My female relatives tell me now that my mother was always "proud" of me. But too many conversations ended in constricted silence. My head was so much in theoretical radical feminism that I could not even see the conditions of my mother's life. And all she could see was the daughter she used to know. My mother worked in a greasy-spoon luncheonette serving heavy lunches to working people. Everyone in town knew Millie and wanted to have their sandwiches made by her. For all the years she worked there, I never once went in, sat down, and had a cup of coffee with her. Connections are easier to make in books. I could not replicate my mother's life—nor would she want me to—but I could find a way to affirm it without sacrificing my intellectual work. And that's when I began to collect and edit working-class women's writings.

For fifteen years I worked as an adjunct teacher of composition and literature in a local community college. At first, the part-time work seemed satisfactory because it enabled me to care for my children during the day and work evenings and weekends. As a child, I had never had a babysitter who was not a relative, and so day care for young children was not part of my inherited family epistemology. I was able to sustain this because my husband is an engineer who earns a middle-class paycheck. My students at the community college were familiar to me in their language, their attitudes about work, their values and relationships. Many of my full-time colleagues mocked these students for their malapropisms, their lack of class. Of course, these students did not lack *class*. Class was obviously inscribed on their fatigued bodies and in their desire for associate degrees that might earn them a little more take-home pay. What they lacked was the power of class definition. They also lacked the wanna-be-patrician, bourgeois sensibilities cultivated and nurtured in the greenhouses of graduate English departments.

At the community college I learned two profound lessons: how it was possible to connect lived working-class experience to the study of literature and how to organize and struggle for change. I developed and taught a course called Working-Class Literature and I organized adjunct faculty.

My usual zigzag movement between experience and theory became more focused. It was 1981–82 and I was publishing in feminist journals and newspapers, and claiming a public voice. The intellectual ground that was once my formal education was broken up. In the fissures and recesses I began to develop an alternate ground of being that promised location inside the dislocation. Without naming it, I was acting on Foucault's assertion that "knowledge is not just made for understanding; it is made for cutting." In the past, the cutting had been in the power of the owning class to cut down, literally, the lives of working people—but also, I came to realize, in the power of language and the academic elite to cut out working-class studies and sever workers from their own history and culture. It was time to cut in another direction.

I taught working-class literature to working-class students. I realize now that without overt autobiographical references, I was uncovering/recovering the integrity of my own working-class family life to produce curricula, texts, and cultural criticism. Here was a legitimate, powerful alternative to acculturation, nostalgia, or assimilation. I quickly found that the most difficult problem in developing a curriculum of working-class studies is the enormity of the subject. (This is not a problem, of course, for those who do not concede that working-class culture exists.) I organized my course around the interplay of three powerful pronouns: I, they, and we. Who tells the story? Who mediates it? And what is missing? I began with personal narratives, often oral histories, and ask students to do their own work autobiographies and interviews along the Studs Terkel *Working* model. We looked at writing of *witness*—the work of the next generation or the informed insider to tell the stories that were not voiced. We read Harriette Arnow's *The Dollmaker* and Maxine Hong Kingston's *China Men,* tracing the long journeys of "DP's"—displaced persons—in the land of broken promises. We looked at Lewis Hine photographs, listened to the music of coal miners, read contemporary poetry by working-class women, and studied episodes of resistance in the film *Salt of the Earth* and recovery in Leslie Marmon Silko's *Ceremony.* I grouped texts, photographs, music, and films in a montage that included differences of gender, race, and ethnicity around questions central to suppressed histories: What kind of work is going on here? Who controls it? Who profits from it? I wanted students to discover not only neglected texts, but also those conditions which thwart and suppress the production of culture. I was allowed to do this because I was a harmless adjunct.

If working-class culture becomes exclusively an object of study, and not a means of study, the larger struggle is lost. My intellectual work gave me political courage. I also knew that I had nothing to lose. When a full-time position finally opened after nine years as an adjunct, I applied, but was not given an interview. I tasted my own invisibility. I did not like the taste. I took Joe Hill's advice and started to organize.

I shared the labor of meetings, phone calls, letters, petitions, questionnaires, research, and talking, talking, talking with another longtime part-timer, Chris Munson, and a sympathetic female union president, Judy Toler, who was never reelected after supporting us. We won our first raise in ten years and representation at the union bargaining table. We made small gains, securing mail boxes, the right to assign our own textbooks, and inclusion in the college directory. I published a front page article in a Rochester newspaper and pushed for voting and meeting privileges in my own department. I became an outspoken critic of academic work exploitation at conferences and meetings. I had not lost my pungent working-class tongue. When I began adjunct teaching in 1972 I earned $875 a course; when I left fifteen years later as an adjunct associate professor, I was earning $400 more a course. I still had no benefits, no retirement, and no guarantee that I would actually teach the course I prepared. When the next full-time opening came up, I was not surprised when I was again not invited to interview for the job.

Opportunities for praxis in class struggle are available behind the academic gate; one does not have to travel to Wigan Pier. But it does mean confronting uncomfortable questions: how does my work rest on the labor of others? how can I use my power to practice democracy in the workplace? The increasing use of adjunct faculty is a piece of a larger labor story; white and blue collars blur in a common history of being overworked and underpaid. To be an adjunct is to be an academic "other," a category for academic managers, a flexible object, a thing. In the dynamic of this work relationship, I caught a tiny glimpse of the reality of my parents' work and that of so many others. I also learned there are alternatives to liberal humanism with its emphasis on individuality and its naive faith in progress. I was cutting my way back home.

Part Two

A Language of One's Own

Masani Alexis De Veaux

I was born one of eight children on September 24, 1948, and raised in Harlem, New York City. My mother was on welfare at the time and my father was in prison in upstate New York for the better part of my early childhood. I attended elementary and junior high schools in Harlem. Later, when we moved to the South Bronx, I attended and graduated from Walton High School which was located in a White working-class community in the North Bronx. Although my paternal grandmother was licensed as a teacher in North Carolina, when she migrated north in the 1930s, the only job she could secure was one as a maid. My maternal grandfather worked for the New York City Transit Authority laying tiles. This photograph was taken of me in an apartment in the East Village, New York City, circa 1969. I was twenty-one years old then and just beginning to imagine myself as a writer (at the time of this photograph, I was only writing poetry). Shortly after this photo was taken, I started work on my first book, *Spirits in the Street* (Doubleday, 1973).

Masani Alexis De Veaux is a poet, essayist, playwright, and political activist whose work is nationally and internationally known. In addition to the experimental novel *Spirits in the Street,* her works include two award winning children's books, *Na-Ni* (Harper and Row, 1973), *An Enchanted Hair Tale* (Harper and Row, 1987), and *Don't Explain,* a biography of jazz great Billie Holiday. Her plays have been produced on television, Off Broadway, Off-Off Broadway, in regional theaters and include: *Circles* (1972); *The Tapestry* (1976); *A Season to Unravel* (1979); the highly acclaimed *No* (1981); and *Elbow Rooms* (1987).

She worked as a writer, contributing editor, and editor-at-large with *Essence* magazine for twelve years. In this capacity, she examined a global spectrum of social and political issues important to African-American Women, Third-World Women, and Women of Color. As an activist, she has traveled extensively in Africa, Latin America, the Caribbean, Europe, Japan, and throughout the United States, working with various Third World Women's and Women of Color organizations, and is an active sponsor of MADRE, an international organization based in New York City, and a Board member of the St. Croix–based SISA: Sisterhood in Support of Sisters in South Africa. Presently, she is an assistant professor of Women's Studies and a faculty member of the American Studies Department in the State University of New York at Buffalo.

Indigenous Voice

Even *The American Heritage Dictionary of the English Language* will tell you that language be more than spoken words which can only be symbols that form, express, and communicate thoughts and feelings. In the dictionary's definition language be "any method of communicating ideas, as by a system of signs, symbols, gestures or the like." Question: how come all the dictionary "examples" of language refer to White/western cultural concepts? As in: "the English language," "the language of algebra," "Shakespeare," "Miltonic language," and "bad language." Answer: the dictionary was written by White people talking Standard White English. So language is really who's talking. And who's talking to who. Where they come from. What color they be. What education they got. Whether they be female or male. What they think about the world inside and outside of them. What they history is. Language be the gravel on the forked road that divides how I speak from how my fourth grade school teacher speaks: *The Teacher assigns a list of vocabulary words to use in sentences, for homework. The next day, she calls on me to use the word "galore" in a sentence. She re-explains to the class that the definition of the word means "too much or in abundance." I proudly stand and read from my homework a sentence I have heard my mother often say: "Yall got garbage de lore all round this house." My White, female Teacher informs me that there is no such word as "de lore." I am embarrassed and confused. It is a word I have heard my mother use so many times so many ways. I sit down at my desk feeling like a fool. I am an excellent student who prides herself on using words. On knowing how to spell and read and write. And I have a bunch of commendations and gold stars to prove it. When I go home, I tell my mother what The Teacher say. My mother is visibly angry. She bangs the food she is cooking into the pots on the stove. She is tired of hearing what The Teacher say to me. And she is tired of me repeating that shit. "Your teacha don't know nothin' bout what I know so she can't tell me how to talk you hear what I say?" she says.* I am nine years old when I realize that the language I speak at home is different from the language I am taught in school. And that the disdain on my teacher's face for the way my mother speaks, the

Black Female Language she teaches me, tells me that this language is considered "ignorant," "slang," and "inferior." As such, it is to be outbred-cauterized from my consciousness—if I expect to "make it" in White (meaning educated and cultured) society. If I expect to be successful by White middle-class standards of speaking. Whether the person I am speaking to—and being judged by—is White or Black, female or male.

The denigration of my mother's English—and by extension, Black language—as ignorant and inferior, is at the core of the cultural racism, and generations of language oppression abusively heaped upon us as speakers.

The language my mother taught me traces the cartography of our mutual, though differently experienced, racial, sexual, and class realities as African American women. It charts our speech *and* silence, through a landscape hostile to our self-defined survival. The class and culturally-specific ways we speak to and about each other record the lessons and strategies of our shared knowledge of what we know we know. When my mother told me "you was born with three strikes against you," she was telling me what life had taught her: Black women in our class were struck out of the game at the moment our lives began.

When I speak the language my mother spoke to me, I speak the history upon which I walk verbally, and write by hand. I remember: *As children, whenever we back talked to my mother or expressed any independent thinking, as in "I thought it was okay to do what I wanted, stead of what you told me to do," my mother always responded, "You thought like Nellie thought." Which, more often than not, was followed by the punishment of a beating designed to beat that trait out of you. I never knew who this Nellie was. And for years, for years, I wondered what was Nellie's relationship to my mother? How come she was always calling on this Nellie I never saw, to put us in our place? And then one day, while reading Angela Davis's book,* Women, Race, and Class, *I discovered Nellie. An enslaved young woman who was viciously whipped by an overseer. Her crime? Talking back and thinking for herself.*

Thinking like Nellie, meaning thinking for yourself and speaking up to "authority," was a punishable offense. And speaking your own words, defining who you are or will be, is unacceptable behavior for Black women. So learn to live by that rule, daughter, my mother tried to instill in me. Learn it from her, for my own sake, or from "them" later. Learn what you need to survive.

But to survive, Black and female and a writer, in this class-privileged society, I needed to resist. Loudly. Ground my words as a poet and writer in a tongue rooted in my mother's, but defined by own growing up in Harlem, in the fifties and sixties. One of eight children. Raised by a woman who once did "piecework" in a dress factory downtown. My grandmother, a licensed teacher but confined to earning her living as a maid. My grandfather, aunt, and uncles, working at non-professional jobs. Working all the time, just to survive.

I turned to the voices of other Black women writers. Finding community in their works, I was affirmed in my belief that I needed a language defined by my own standards. My own history. One which I must be prepared, once I spoke it or wrote it, to take the consequences of: Early in 1980, I was approached by Glenda Dickerson, a Black woman well known as a director in New York City's Black theater community. Glenda wanted to direct and stage a play based on my poems and stories. After several meetings hashing over which poems and which stories and editing the script, we still lacked a title for the piece. In the middle of one meeting, Glenda asked me to meditate on my childhood with my mother. "Try to remember," she said, "anything that stands out in your mind." I told Glenda the story of me and the broom. *One day when I was a little girl, maybe six or seven years old, my mother instructed me to get the broom and sweep the floor. Since I didn't want to because I was busy playing, imagining myself somewhere else other than the one room six of us lived in at the time, I told my mother, "No." Of course I got a beating for that, but now that I look back on it, it was the first time I publicly resisted the circumvention of my imagination and creativity, by what was expected of me as a girl.*

So *NO* became the title of the play that became a word-of-mouth success. Largely attended by a mixture of lesbian and heterosexual women of color from varying class backgrounds, it was originally scheduled for a two-weekend run the following year. It played for eleven straight weeks to sell-out audiences at the Henry Street Settlement House's New Federal Theater, on the Lower East Side. The New Federal Theater had a history of showcasing plays about the lives of working-class Black people.

Ironically, the words that created the play's uniqueness—the autobiographical words of the young girl sexually abused by her mother's boyfriend; the mother-daughter dialogue that pits a mother's middle-class aspirations against her daughter's working-class rooted analysis; the poems and stories of Black women balancing life in a heterosexist Black community, and a racist and sexist White world—were the very words some of the play's critics wanted to silence, their reviews a sad reminder of my mother's warnings.

But speaking up for myself, speaking my own language as I do, defining my sentences in the grammars of being Black and female, is rooted in the language I grew up listening to; and in the working-class environment I come from. So living in Harlem shaped my tongue. It shaped the sounds of language re-created daily. In conversations at home. On the street. Out of the mouths of leaders. Shaped the language I speak as a woman. Shaped my days as a writer-turned-graduate student at the State University of New York at Buffalo.

Harlem shaped me for the stance I took while earning my master's degree; and when researching and writing my dissertation. For I wanted it written in my own voice. Not in the "scholar-ese" of a White, male-dominated, academic, abstract language. Devoid of my class, racial, sexual realities. I wanted it written in the multiple languages I have learned to speak. Reflective of, and incorporating, my mother's tongue. Wanted it written within the frames of my own intelligence, creativity, and aesthetic. My own history. Wanted to celebrate and validate language spoken by women in my family—in an arena where the existence of our language has been systematically denigrated and denied.

I wanted to; and I did. When my proposal to meet a departmental language requirement by writing a critical essay exploring Black women's language forms was questioned, I argued that the study of Black language was as legitimate as the study of any other language; and worthy of serious academic pursuit. When members of my dissertation committee suggested good ideas housed in language that imposed their syntax over my indigenous own, I took in the best of their ideas. Threw away their dry husks of class-privileged language. Held fast to my right to speak as a scholar, in the syntax of my own tongue. Refused to deny the language of, and connections to, my community.

I have my Ph.D. now. And I am proud of that accomplishment. Proud that I have been honored with time to think critically; to reflect upon my history and the history of Black women. Upon the indigenous voice I speak, teach, and create with. And although I can speak "scholar-ese" when it suits me, I speak like a Black woman all the time.

Adventures of the Dread Sisters

We crossing The Brooklyn Bridge. Traffic is slow going. Bumper to bumper. And cars everywhere. Taxis blowing horns. It's Saturday morning. Everybody making it to Manhattan. Us too. We got to get there soon. Before the snow. Threatening to cover the city. Any minute now. We going to the RALLY AGAINST GOVERNMENT TRUCKS HAULING NUCLEAR WASTE THROUGH HARLEM. Every day for a week they been saying on the radio

> don't worry folks
> don't worry
> don't worry   it's safe

I might be only 15 but even I know ain't nothing safe. Not on no city street. Anything could happen. So I don't believe nothing the government says. Personally, I'm through with the government. Too many people ain't got jobs. And whole families be living in the streets. I'm for get rid of the government, give life back to the people.

We stuck on this bridge. We got 25 minutes to get uptown.

> Is that soot or snow I see
> falling up ahead
>
> Hope it ain't snow
> The windshield wipers don't work
> too tough
> Nigeria says

Nigeria and me we call ourselves The Dread Sisters. We're not real sisters. She's not my real mother neither. But she raised me. So we are definite family. We even look alike. Both of us short and got big eyes. Both of us got dreadlocks. Just like the Africans in the pictures in Nigeria's books.

We got twenty minutes before the rally start. We slow dragging our wheels over the bridge's skin. Our blue Pinto crammed between two screaming-yellow taxis. The East River below us. The gray sky above. Manhattan coming slowly nearer. I stare at Nigeria out the corner of my eye. She sucking her teeth. Mashing on the brakes. She hate to be late. She catch me staring. Winks. Locks her eyes back on the road.

My sister Toni and me been living with Nigeria ever since we was little. She adopted us. Then moved us to a house on Adelphi Street. Got a backyard and a attic. Got my own room and so do Toni. Got a home. Nigeria be like our mother and father. And for my money, I wouldn't have it no other way. But Toni ain't like me and Nigeria. Toni be liking boys. She don't like books. She like to straighten her hair cause she in high school. Toni be the last person to get up before noon on a Saturday. Don't care whether it's a life and death thing like a rally or not. The whole planet could blow up it wouldn't wake Toni up.

> Nigeria
> What
> I don't want to die in no nuclear war
> Ain't gonna be no nuclear war pumpkin

she says in her Colored and Progressive Peoples' Campaign office-voice

> God won't allow it
> People who make bombs
> don't believe in God

I fires back at her. And she don't say nothing but roll down her window. December hit us slap in the face.

Nigeria got a profile like a African sculpture. She be looking carved outta black wood. Her lips be chiseled. And she got a mole above her right cheek. Like somebody dotted her eyebrow. Ain't nothing moving on this bridge.

> It's what *you*   believe that counts

she finally says

> never play the game by the enemy's
> rules   fight back
> Whether it's bullets or bombs
> do the unexpected

A Language of One's Own

then she pokes her head out the window. The red leather Nefertiti-shaped crown holding her dreads falls to one side. Three lanes of cars plug up the bridge. From one end to the other. We move a little bit. Stop go stop. I open up my sketchbook. Flip through the drawings. Till I get to the ones I'm doing on Afa Tu Twelve. Which is this made-up planet. Where all the females become Ebabas hooded blueblack women who fly.

Nigeria gave me my first sketchbook. And taught me how to draw. She's a painter. Used to work summers on the boardwalk in Atlantic City. Doing charcoal portraits. One for 3 dollars or two for 5. Me and Toni used to go with her. I remember one day a old Black lady came by Nigeria's stall. She was old but she was beautiful. All dressed in black. With a black hat and veil. Black summer gloves. Some medals pinned to the lapel of her dress. She walked with a military step. She had watched Nigeria draw all summer. And now she wanted her picture done. So Nigeria sat the old lady down and started drawing. It took nearly 3 hours. To do a job that usually takes 20 minutes. By the time she finished there was a crowd of people standing around oooing and aaahing. Everybody was saying how the old woman had jumped into Nigeria's eyes. Poured herself through Nigeria's fingers. Liquified on the paper. The picture shimmered when it was finished. It made the old lady happy.

Daughter

she said to Nigeria

these is God's hands you got

and she kissed Nigeria's fingers and pressed a brand new 20 dollar bill in Nigeria's hand. And walked away. Humming *Life Every Voice and Sing*. Nigeria still got that 20 dollar bill. Which she keep in a black silk handkerchief. Tied with a red string and a little piece of paper. "1967" written on it.

The year Langston Hughes
died

she's in the habit of reminding me because he was her favorite poet.

Anyway we caught in this no-moving traffic. Nigeria not mashing so hard on the brakes now. We stop and go some more. It is cold inside the car. She leans forward. Rolls up her window. Sits back. I ask before I think not to.

> How come you never had no kids
> of your own Nigeria
> I didn't want any of my own
> I wanted some that belonged to the world

Then she don't say no more. Look like she thinking. I'm thinking too. I wonder if there's gonna be a world.

Over our heads the sky is thick with the threat of snow. We stuck on the bridge. Nothing's moving. And it's 5-to-the-rally. Nigeria reaches into the back seat. Grabs a bunch of flyers. Gives me some.

> If you can't get to the rally
> when it starts
> start the rally wherever you are

she says. And jumps out the car. Her yellow wool coat whipped by the wind. And I'm right behind her. Snuggled up in my big jacket. My neck wrapped twice with cloth from Kenya. We leave Miss Pinto in a herd of cars. Nigeria take one lane. I take the other. We passing out flyers when sure enough here we are in another adventure cause here comes the snow.

I was born in Detroit on June 6, 1956, the third of my parents' five children. When I was a baby, we moved to Warren, a working-class suburb of identical boxlike houses, small machine shops, and large, sprawling auto factories. My father's grandfather worked in the stove-works (Detroit was a center for stove-building before the auto industry took over). My father's father worked as a mechanic for Packard Motor Car Company for close to forty years, from World War I until Packard went bankrupt. His wife, my grandmother, was a homemaker. On my mother's side, my grandfather died before I was born. He held a variety of jobs, working for Detroit Edison, the power company, and operating a small corner store, which my grandmother helped him run. My father worked for Ford Motor Company until his retirement a few years ago. For most of that time, he worked in the office at the Sterling Axle Plant, the same plant I worked in to help pay my way through college. My mother was trained as a nurse, and managed to work one day a week after all the kids were in school. My grandmother, who lived with us, watched the children every Thursday while my mother worked. I attended the local public high school, passing by rows of machine shops on my way to school every day, a constant reminder of what awaited. One teacher, when we did something well, used to say, "Not bad for a bunch of hillbillies and Polacks." That's what we were, and we took it as a compliment.

Jim Daniels teaches creative writing at Carnegie Mellon University. His poetry collections include: *Factory Poems* (Jack-in-the-Box Press, 1978), *On the Line* (Signpost Press, 1981), *Places/Everyone* (University of Wisconsin Press, 1985), *Digger's Territory* (Adastra Press, 1989), *Punching Out* (Wayne State University Press, 1990), *Hacking It* (Ridgeway Press, 1992), *M-80* (University of Pittsburgh Press, 1993).

Jim Daniels

Troubleshooting: Poetry, the Factory, and the University

My high school was very proud of its auto shop, an addition built in the sixties with tax dollars from the nearby Chrysler plant. Every year, a tool company sponsored a big trouble-shooting contest at the school in which the competitors had to find a number of things wrong with a car in a limited amount of time. The champs were always written up in the school paper. Though I never entered the troubleshooting contest, I did end up writing about it for the school newspaper.

I never took auto mechanics, though my brothers did. In Warren, you were expected to be able to fix your own car. It was a matter of pride. A typical disparaging remark was, "That guy probably can't even change his own oil." Even my grandmother took an adult education auto mechanics course. I could change my own oil, and do other basic repairs, though I often relied on my brothers, and my father, for their advice and help. That was something they could give advice and help on. When it came to writing, I was on my own.

I often wonder what it was that put me on the path to becoming a writer—the path that took me to college, while so many others stuck around and took jobs in the plants. I think the early knowledge that it was okay to simply read for pleasure, and that the written word was something to be valued, contributed to my interest in writing. My mother has always been a voracious reader—I can still picture her curled up with a book and a beer waiting out the long nights for my father to come home from work.

My love of sports also contributed to my love of reading. My mother tells me the first words I recognized in the newspapers were the names of baseball players like Mickey Mantle, and Al Kaline, the Detroit Tigers star. My mother wrote me a note allowing me to take out adult books from the library so that I could have access to the sports biographies: *The Roy Campanella Story, The Harmon Killebrew Story,* and other literary classics. While I was in the adult section, I began to roam and by the time I was in junior high, I was bringing home books by Hemingway and Fitzgerald.

Through eighth grade, I had attended remedial speech class. The other kids, when they wanted to get to me, simply had to make fun of the way I talked. That too contributed to my taking refuge in books, and in writing. I could write my thoughts down without worrying about anyone making fun of them. In high school, I showed some of this writing to a couple of my teachers, and with their encouragement, I began to write what turned out to be poems. They told me I was writing poems, but I was resistant to that notion. My friends would scoff at the very idea—poetry was for wimps. At the time, I didn't like poetry—just about everything I'd read seemed difficult, boring, remote. It didn't seem to make any connection to my life. But the release, the pleasure I took from writing, became addictive. By the time I left high school, I knew I wanted to be a writer.

We didn't have a typewriter in our house, and none of us could type anyway, so when one of my teachers suggested I enter the *Detroit News* Scholastic Writing Awards competition, I was faced with the problem of getting my work typed. For Christmas that year, I received a note in my stocking saying that my parents would pay to have my entries typed. I ended up winning two honorable mentions, which, though not having the prestige of the troubleshooting award, did help legitimize my writing in my father's eyes.

Having the entries typed was my mother's idea. Because of all the overtime my father worked—seven-day weeks, twelve-hour days—he just wasn't around to think of such things. It was my mother's job to maintain the emotional relationships in the house. The home was her territory, and work was my father's. Then, I simply knew my father was not home and resented his absence without clearly comprehending that he had no choice. He had five kids, and he had to work when they told him to in order to support us. Our family life clearly suffered from his absence. A major preoccupation in my writing has been how our jobs, whatever they might be, influence and control our lives away from work.

To become a writer, I knew I had to go to college. I also knew I wanted to go away to school if at all possible, and when enough scholarship money came through, I headed for Alma College, a small liberal arts school a couple of hours north of Detroit. I had met two of their writing teachers at a workshop for high school writers, and I was excited about the prospect of working with real writers, but I chose Alma for another reason too. I had quit drinking and doing drugs near the end of my senior year in high school after nearly four years of progressively heavier and more frequent binges. Even after I had developed an interest in writing and decided to go to college, I continued to party with my pals, many of whom were simply waiting for graduation to take their place on the assembly lines. I had to get away and clear my head before I got sucked into the factories along with them. My oldest brother had attended community college one semester before quitting to take a job driving trucks for Chrysler, so I had seen how quickly it could happen.

Alma had two four-month semesters followed by a one-month intensive term during which you only took one course. I was in the middle of a course on Faulkner one spring term when my father called. My father never called me, so I knew it was something serious. He'd gotten me in at the plant for the summer, and I was to come home immediately for my physical. I had to drop the class, pack up, and leave. The summer jobs were starting to disappear, a harbinger of the layoffs to come, so I had to take the job while it was available. I carried Faulkner in my lunch bucket till I finished the books I'd already bought for the class. I smudged the pages with grease, squinting through my scratched safety glasses.

I still remember the dread I felt after my father called. I would be joining my friends after all. The money was good in the factory—I've heard it called the "Golden Handcuffs." The work was very difficult and monotonous, but for any teenage boy getting out of high school around Detroit, the chance to make the good money and buy a hot car (which you'd then be making payments on for years so you couldn't quit if you wanted to keep the car) was one that was often hard to pass up. Besides, our fathers worked there.

When I began work in the factory, I realized just how hard that work could be, especially during the heat of the summer. I had a variety of jobs there, including operating a cover-welder which welded steel "hats" on axle housing, and operating a press which stamped out axle housing halves. I mostly worked afternoons from three to eleven, which meant that the only thing to do when I got off work was to hit the bars. I quickly fell into my old drinking habits. I could sleep off the hangovers in the morning. What else was there to do anyway? I'd sit on the porch drinking coffee and waiting till it was time to go to work. I usually worked seven days a week, so those summers became one long blur of hard work and hard drinking.

Because of the hard, physical work, the darkness, the dirt, the noise, the language of the factory tended to be very colorful, often obscene, as if we needed to kick our language up a notch for it to have any effect. It was a bit of a jolt when I returned to school in the fall. *Fuck* and *shit* were probably the two most commonly used words in the plant, so common, I stopped thinking about them. Back at school, I could see people wince when I talked. Not that college students and professors never use those words, but the classroom demanded more decorum. I had to quickly tone down the obscenity and remember where I was.

I had gone to college thinking I wanted to be a writer, and once there, I wrote poems about growing up around Detroit. When I started working in the factory, I had no thought of writing about it. It was simply a way to earn the money I needed for the next school year. However, I soon found myself jotting things down on my breaks. Sometimes, it was some piece of advice one of the other workers gave me, sometimes it was an image. I'd often jot them down on old "ok" or "rejected" tags that hung on baskets of axle parts, using a paint crayon as my clumsy pen. I found one of those old tags—it simply reads "ropes of light." That image, of thin streams of light shining in the high factory windows about seven o'clock each evening, was the beginning of a poem called "Factory Jungle" in which those ropes of light became the vines that a factory Tarzan might swing on.

When I returned to college and began turning these notes into poems and showing them to my teachers, I began to realize what preconceived notions some people had of factory life, and the working class. For example, one teacher criticized my poem, "Factory Love," a tongue-in-cheek love poem for my machine, because he said factory workers hated their machines, their jobs, so it was an unrealistic poem. He totally missed the irony and humor that anyone in the factory would've picked up immediately. Who was he to tell me what factory workers thought?

Another time, Robert Bly, the well-known poet, visited the college, and one of my professors showed him some of my writing, including a poem about working as a short-order cook which details the frenzy of trying to fill an order for thirty cheeseburgers and thirty fries. Bly took me to task for not having enough metaphors in my poems. The whole idea of deep images seemed absurd to me in the context of the hectic, grueling factory. That kind of contemplation seemed like an incredible luxury.

One of the safety posters in the factory read "Daydreams Can Cause Nightmares."

I began to realize it was partially a class issue. For a long time, the only ones who wrote poetry were the people who had the education and the free time to write—the upper classes. Those who worked in factories and steel mills of this country in the early part of this century were often immigrants with minimal formal education, so their voices were rarely heard in our literature. As these voices have become more prevalent, the loud, raucous poems perhaps seem like cursing in class to those who associate poetry with gentility. An interviewer once asked me, "What beauty do you find to write about in the factory?" As if poetry necessarily had to be about beautiful things.

I continued to write poems about other subjects, but I found I struck a nerve when I started writing about the auto plant. For years, the factories were these big looming scary structures—one of which was eating up my father's life. I drove by them all the time, but they were mysteries. No one in our neighborhood talked about their jobs. Pretty much everyone worked for Ford, GM, or Chrysler, or one of the many machine shops—we never compared notes on what they actually did. It didn't matter. My entrance into that world behind the factory gates was an important part of my education. It enabled me to begin making connections between factory life and home life.

As I continued my education and read more poetry, I discovered that the people I knew the best and cared about the most were not showing up in what I was reading, which really bothered me. I was beginning to wonder if poetry *was* this high-brow thing after all. Then, in graduate school, one of my fellow students loaned me an anthology of poems about work edited by the Canadian poet Tom Wayman, called *A Government Job at Last*. It was the most exciting literary discovery of my life—even better than finding *The Al Kaline Story*. Here was an entire book of poems by poets who were writing about work, writing about *my* people. I immediately wrote Wayman care of his publisher, and he wrote back saying he was putting together a new anthology, and to send him poems right away. He published a number of them in that book, *Going for Coffee*—it was one of my earliest and most important publications because it made me feel there was a place for my poetry in the literary world. It gave me the confidence to continue with my work.

In 1981, after finishing my master's degree, I was hired to teach at

Carnegie Mellon University. I think my working-class background, and the tradition of hard work, may have been a help to me in landing this first teaching job. All through graduate school, I had been actively trying to publish my poems, and I'd published quite a bit in literary magazines, which clearly helped me on the job market. Many of the other graduate students were not sending their work out. There's a literary and artistic tradition of not appearing to pursue success too aggressively. It's considered crass. In my family, it's considered laziness. The work ethic my father instilled in me drove me to keep my work in circulation in the face of frequent rejection.

In 1985, when my first full-length book of poems, *Places/Everyone,* was published, I was nervous about how my family would react. They had read very little of my poetry over the years—they didn't ask to read it, and I didn't volunteer to show it to them. While much of it was published in literary magazines, I could be sure my family would never be exposed to it. The only magazines we had at home were *Reader's Digest* and *Newsweek.* A book was another story. They would find out about it, I was sure. I *wanted* them to. I wanted them to be proud of me, of our lives.

I dedicated the book to my family as a sign to them of the spirit in which the book was written—as tribute, not exposé. My father, who has always been reticent about his children's accomplishments, said little directly to me, but that Christmas there was an open house at the plant at which people set up tables and sold various crafts and things. My father set up a table with a pile of my books and sold them to the other workers. One of my brothers took a picture of my father selling the books. I treasure that picture as evidence of my father's love and support.

At home, my father has said things like, "Why don't you try to write a best-seller?" He's never quite understood the concept of poetry, nor the choice I made to concentrate on poetry when it pays so poorly and so few people read it. My mother has said things like, "You have a poem for two of your brothers, why don't you write a poem for your other one?" She is uncomfortable, just as my father is, with talking about specific content; nevertheless she is clearly paying attention. My family has been supportive without quite understanding what it is I do, and that's the case with many occupations, so I feel fine that they simply accept it.

When *Places/Everyone* was published, I had been teaching in the university for four years. While I had many favorable responses, both in the university and in reviews, at times the work was met with suspicion. One colleague wondered if I would be able to write about anything else,

Jim Daniels's father.

since I wasn't in the factory anymore. One reviewer wrote, "Now that he is a successful poet and university teacher, he can no longer write 'shammy' when he means 'chamois'; and he had to learn to say 'Mademoiselle' and 'Please pass the quiche.'" The assumptions of those comments seemed to be that I had got the working class out of my system now that I was a university professor.

I guess I took that as a challenge, for my second book, *Punching Out,* takes place *entirely* inside an auto factory. For me, it's clearly not a matter of "getting it out of my system."

It seems ironic that publishing poems about my background has given me the credentials for an academic job which has taken me further from it. While, after many years in academia, my everyday world is very different from the world I grew up in, and my poetry in some ways reflects the changes in my life, I want to always keep that other world inside me—it's part of my background and heritage, and I'm proud of it.

I still feel a strong connection to that world, a connection that the "drive" in the poem, "Driving Factory Row, 1989," tries to bring out. Driving past the workers on lunch break hanging around outside the factories, I felt both my connection to them and my distance from them. It brought back memories of my summers working on the line—particularly the iced tea carton, which was the same brand that was sold in the plant I worked in. I remembered guzzling those cartons, and squishing them, like the man in the poem, on those incredibly hot days when the foreman would be passing out pink salt tablets as if they were some kind of miracle drug.

But I was clearly not that man anymore, and I tried to temper my nostalgia for that past, to squash any temptation to idealize it by qualifying the joy I was imagining he felt. I knew it would be a joy limited by his knowledge that in a few minutes he'd have to go back in to deal with the heat and noise once again.

Writing not only saved me from the grim work, it saved me from a grim economic future. I also had to temper that nostalgia with the knowledge that many of the people I'd worked with back in the late seventies had permanently lost their jobs during the recession of the early eighties. No one I knew found a job that paid nearly as much as the plant did. College didn't necessarily mean more money either. My cousin, who worked full-time in the factory while going to night school in criminal justice at Wayne State University, eventually got his degree at about the time he was laid off. He did get a job working as a prison guard in the federal system—but he had to take a substantial pay cut.

One of the things I did miss about the factory was that workers' relationships and feelings about each other were much more clearly defined than they are in my academic job. If somebody thought you were an asshole in the plant, they didn't have any qualms about telling you so. On the other hand, I have seen quite a bit of subterfuge in academia over the years. At the end of "Driving Factory Row," I'm trying to contrast the kind of psychic cuts one might experience in an academic environment with the flesh-and-blood cuts one gets in a factory.

When I first started teaching in a university, I had a hard time decoding the way people talked to each other. Everything was subtle. I often wouldn't figure out what happened in a meeting until days later. A seemingly innocent remark about someone's new publication could actually be a veiled threat about someone's tenure case. In the factory, the union protected you from being fired. The lines were clearly drawn—the boss was an adversary. In the university, a colleague of similar age and experience, someone I might see as a friend, could turn out to be a rival, or an enemy, if it's clear that only one of us can get tenure. There are many more opportunities for back-stabbing, and, unfortunately, there are those who will take advantage of those opportunities. In the factory, I felt like I knew where I stood, even if I didn't like where that was.

On the other hand, little human interaction took place in the plant except on breaks. The machines were so noisy, I often felt isolated. Communication often took place in sign language. The drudgery and isolation wore me down. I needed a few drinks after work to feel human again. Many workers needed a few drinks, or drugs, *during* work hours just to get through the day.

In "Driving Factory Row," I needed and wanted to step back and look at the work from the perspective of an outsider, the outsider that I've inevitably become. I do hope, however, that it's the perspective of an outsider who was once there, who understands and appreciates—an outsider who will never forget. Maybe, finally, this poem *is* a little nostalgic for the simple clarity of that life. And if it is, well, then so be it. I offer no apologies.

Writing poetry is what took me away from the factory life and into the university, first as a student, and then, as a teacher. But writing poetry is also what has taken me back to that life, taken me back home.

Jim Daniels

Driving Factory Row, 1989

On this long sweat of an afternoon
driving Detroit's long straight roads
lined with the pale boxes
of small machine shops and huge factories
I pass workers wearing paper towel bandanas
eating their lunches outside the open shop doors,
men and women sitting on cardboard boxes
counting their change
counting the times anyone's told them
I love you.

Perhaps some things do give more satisfaction
than squishing an empty iced tea carton
in your fist, but the guy doing that
right now in front of Edwards Tool and Die
looks pretty damn happy.

It's been a few years since I did any
real work, wore any real shoes
did any real dancing
but I've been saving one band aid
from the plant hospital
for when I'm really hurt.

Reprinted by permission of the author. Originally published in *Labor Pains: Poetry from South East Michigan Workers,* Leon Chamberlain, Editor, Ridgeway Press, 1991.

Linda McCarriston

I was born in Chelsea, Massachusetts, in 1943 and grew up in Lynn, where I lived until 1968. I attended public schools through fourth grade, and then Catholic schools. My mother worked as a waitress, factory worker, domestic, bakery hostess, and, for most of her life, as a meat-wrapper in a supermarket. My father was a stationary engineer (working boilers, engine rooms) for American Oil Company in Chelsea. He earned his First Class Engineer's license at night, after serving in combat in World War II. My maternal grandmother, Marie Gosselin, emigrated from Paris, France, as a girl to work in the mills of Salem. She raised sixteen children to adulthood. My maternal grandfather, John Telesphore Parent, was born in Canada of Native American and French parents. He worked in maintenance at the General Electric in Lynn. My father's parents emigrated from rural Northern Ireland in 1911. Patrick McCarriston became a laborer, eventually working at the General Electric in Lynn. Margaret Reavey McCarriston worked in shoe factories. When they first arrived in Lynn, they lived in a garage and were on "relief" because of Patrick's poor health.

Linda McCarriston has published two books of poetry: *Talking Soft Dutch* (Texas Tech Press, 1984) which was an Associated Writing Programs Selection, and *Eva-Mary* (TriQuarterly Books, 1991), winner of the Terrence Des Pres Prize and finalist for the 1991 National Book Award in Poetry. She is the recipient of two NEA grants, Vermont Council on the Arts grants, and a Bunting fellowship. She is active in adult literacy programs in Northern New En-gland, was an adjunct faculty member from 1979 to 1991 in the Adult Degree Program of Vermont College, and Jenny McKean More Visiting Writer at The George Washington University. Currently, she is an associate professor in the Creative Writing Program at the University of Alaska, Anchorage. She has two grown sons, three stepchildren, and two nieces who are "part of the family."

Linda McCarriston

"The Grace of Form": Class Unconsciousness and an American Writer

Consciousness of class has its own history in this country, just as feminism does, and the two usually "present" as symptoms of health or societal de-cay—depending on which side of the Great Divide you stand on—at the same times. My experience as a poet has everything to do with that history, both the current vogue of a certain working-class mythology, and past periods of strenuous denial of class as a usable American term at all.

What I wish to explore here is secondarily the fact of class as a shaping element of my sense of self and my opportunity or lack of it "to become a writer," and primarily the difficulty of coming to that consciousness in the face of its denial. Although the same sense of walking, alone, a long hall of mirrors has characterized my coming to consciousness as a woman and as the product of a certain class, I believe that—in my history at least—the forces of class and gender have had separate, discrete applications. In both cases, however, my struggle to "tell it like it is" has been against the sure knowledge that if I did, the one to whom it was addressed would find it dismissable.

Increasingly certain that my experience is not unique, nor even exceptional, but common, I hope here to illuminate the role of my writing in the development of my own class consciousness, to reconstruct the complex class "dis-instruction" of my upbringing, and to explore my evolving sense of the relationship between my work and my world.

Fifteen years ago, when I had "gone back to school" and back to my writing after the years of absolute wife-hood (by which I mean a complete Other-identification and permanent underclass status), I wrote my thesis on Yeats, asking where he had acquired the authority that allowed him to speak as he did, as though he knew he were speaking for others. I knew I did not have that authority, and I did not know how to go about getting it. Moreover, I sensed that until I located a source of that stature, that voice, I would be stuck writing the tiniest of lyric poems, apropos only of myself, perhaps daring a little timeless and universal feminine allusion here and there.

The answer I came up with for my paper did not include a most significant set of factors, which today it must: that Yeats was an Anglo-Irish Ascendancy male, educated, of the class that brings forth artists and statesmen. Yeats himself, today, might well answer the question this way. His work drove into and beyond these limitations, though his right to do it rested on them.

I was a working-class Irish-American Catholic girlchild, grown into a working-class (by definition) wife, product of a complex education in ignorance meant to mold me to many uses, none of which would be served by a self-knowledge that encouraged my identification with the underclass, as a group, or women, as a group. I could hope to speak *like* Yeats, but not *as* he spoke. For he spoke out of his true social condition, his whole self, and I spoke only insofar as I could mime him, that is, fake the power that gave him speech.

Nor were my mentors, in 1977, about to encourage, about Yeats, a discovery so "radical," so "political." The ground of Yeats's personal authority was, for them, as it was for me, to be located purely in aesthetics. Yeats's political poems—dutiful lapses into civic consciousness—were simply overlooked. Politics had no place in the world of the timeless and universal.

Occasionally I wondered, during that time, where the *teach* of

Horace's *teach and delight,* as art's functions, had gone. What were we learning, I secretly asked, that we didn't already know? Why were we trying to "make it new," when it seemed there was *news,* and we were not able to tell it. To tell it, I understood, was to make something different from poetry. I wondered as well why we touted *no ideas but in things,* when in fact most of the ideas I was aware of were hidden, buried—confoundingly or consolingly—deep in people.

These questions gestated over a period of two years, during which I was eager for the instruction and approval of writers I admired and whose censure I dreaded, even as I felt my own work trying to veer in a different direction.

■ ■ ■

Much of my life which ought to have been the subject of my work was utterly off limits, except for those fleeting shadows of it that overlapped or echoed "the life of the poet" that seemed to me *de rigeur*: economic security, first (*need* was never the subject of poems, *desire* was), and second a fairly uniform set of values growing from a certain economic vantage point—hip, cosmopolitan, urban, psychological rather than historical in perspective, thus individualistic and marked by a "spirituality" utterly divorced from ethical, social concerns.

What I had heard called "a formalism of content" arose from this *Verstellung,* circumscribing both experience and artifact, and finally producing a formalism of emotional posture and range that, to my eye, accepted as adequate the received social order and quibbled only with the private soul or the significant other.

Though I could not have begun to articulate this back then, I felt the constraints acutely, particularly, discretely, like points of stress in ill-fitting clothes. Most of what excluded me from this point of speech as a poet was class. What did not exclude me on that count did so on gender, or the particular combination of class and gender that drew the circle in which I stood. It was OK to be a woman poet; it was beginning to be OK to be a mother poet. It was not OK to be a Tillie Olsen kind of mother—no nannies, no housekeepers, no dependable income except for what you earned and saying so. None of this discrepancy, this content—emotional and dramatic—was considered fit subject for the poems.

Thus I could find no way to explore in my work what drove me crazy for the first ten years of my return to writing. Off limits were not only the narratives of my life as a mother—married, divorced, remarried, without means, "adjuncting," raising children between two men of means, a "migrant worker in the Groves" of both Academe and Matrimony—but also the emotional response I had to it: indignation, outrage, grief, bitterness. In fact, looking back, I believe it was the emotional response to it that was really on the Index of Forbidden Attitudes. If I had been able to be glad-hearted in this torment, if I had been able to cast my experience as though I were on a permanent drip of Thorazine, if I could cast it—as I tried to do—in mythic terms, with their implication that my lot and my sons' was inevitable, the "human situation," "timeless and universal," lamentable but not changeable, I might well have gotten support for the poems that were discouraged.

Even as I entered the M.F.A. program, I was attempting to write poems about my family of origin, my childhood, poems of trauma and violation that stood beyond the pale and waved their dirty linen. These too were discouraged. In fact, at that time, beginning my apprenticeship in the psy-chological, individualistic tradition, I lacked a paradigm adequate for me to understand my experience. I did not know yet that when the impact of social forces as such on the individual is denied, the resultant stresses are seen as "intrapsychic," and "idiopathic," of unknown (ignored) origin, and the individual is "blamed." When social forces are recognized as causative of such "illness," the diagnosis must face the opposite way.

My entire education and American Experience had been in the tra-dition that denies these forces and construes going to the root of the prob-lem, radicalism, to be a subversion of the status quo. I had learned deeply—literature had assented to this vision and was still assenting in 1976—that radicalism, "subversion" of the established order, was un-American, in spite of America's origins and history. I had learned that we were "all in this together," and that those who spoke, the White Fathers, spoke for us all.

I hold myself responsible for not having ventured further in those years to find the required, other paradigm for my work, but it was turning out that, as I'd "gone back to school" to find out, I *could* write a decent poem, and my mentors were lavish in their encouragement, clear in their admonitions about what was good for my work, my "career." I began to run out of what was good—for my career—pretty quickly, and it was not until after I'd earned my degree that I wrote a poem in which it was clear that the speaker grew up in a tenement, not in the suburbs, that the speaker's father got dirty at work and the speaker's mother ironed his workclothes.

Moreover, I suggested in this poem that the worst thing that could happen in the family might not be simply the absence or distance of a proper bread-winning father, or the neurotic self-absorption of his wealth-bound wife, but violence, in the "normal order of things"—a massive cultural powerlessness.

Since then, of course, the pages of literary magazines have been filling with work that would not have been taken seriously by even the least of "mainstream" journals the year I earned my M.F.A., 1978. Now, it seems, working-class experience and characters, accessibility and an appropriate Whitmanesque diction have a much broader audience. In part, what Carolyn Forché recently called the "democratization of poetry," especially through the establishment of the National Endowment for the Arts, has permitted poets who are not of privilege to write, to have a crack at it. A renaissance of non-elite voices is evident, with an audience for poetry that seems as a result larger and broader than it was twenty years ago. And in part, the children of privilege are enjoying dressing down, as proles.

I can't hold it against them, of course, as I spent the best part of my teens and twenties, and my apprenticeship as a poet, studying the least nuance of label and inflection to try to pass as middle class. If I do resent the efforts of the *hip-geoisie* to pass as working class, in the arts or on the street, it is because, whereas proles attempt to assimilate up by denying their disadvantage, privilege denies its advantage in passing as prole. Chief among the advantages that the would-be proles possess is the wealth that allows them the fundamental necessity to create: leisure. When real proles want to write or be artists, they often make hard choices: between sleep and their work, for instance; between "vacations" and work; between dental and medical care and work; between economic security and work. The time to write must be purchased. And it is at that point that tooth decay proles and braces proles part company.

The romanticization of the underclass, people of color, women, all laboring folk, is of course nothing new; but the risks in inviting elites to adopt the "folkways" of their lessers—and further to speak for them, to depict them—are what they have always been. When the emotional content—grief, despair, rancor, alienation, hatred—is present in art that depicts underclass life, we are taught to consider that work propaganda. When the soundtrack is dubbed out, we are taught to consider it art. E. P. Thompson, the English historian, refers to such art as "the propaganda of the victors."

■ ■ ■

Where I come from, *class* means *money*. Whether or not you find it "tacky" for me to say it is a matter of "taste"—that is, your address on this or that side of the tracks. Where I come from, moreover, class is what we all aspired to, the look of it if not the substance. It was our American Horatio Alger duty to do so, to seem to be as safe, as healthy, as free to create, as our betters—not to show the strain of our lives.

I did a fairly good job of it, too, on a tight budget, both economic and cultural, and might well have continued on that track, as many of my hometown fellows have and as my father did, all the way to his death. All that he had become, except for his private victories, resided in his possessions: a closet full of clothes with the right labels, a domestic oriental rug and piece of Jordan Marsh art that he agonized over purchasing, and a car, new every two years, that might have been driven by a bank president or a polo player. And inked in his own hand, on all the shirts and linens that he sent out for laundering, his assimilated name, Bill Carr. There was no one but us at his funeral.

I find my father's failures, even his crimes, far less understandable in psychological terms than in historical, political ones. And I find my own ability to have escaped many of his sins and limitations, as well, in history, not psychology. If I were of his time, of his class and ethnic origin, of his family history and gender, I can imagine myself the same person.

The fact that I have done my life differently in some ways from his derives from my inclination to write when I was permitted to do so by opportunities that my family could not or would not provide. (This inclination to write, I must add, was the only one of several that I experienced as a child that required no money, no training, no gear—unlike my aspirations to be a priest, an archaeologist, a veterinarian, an oceanographer, all of which were off limits to me because of gender, and most of them because of class as well.)

And so were many others afforded that opportunity. Thus "class" is becoming classy again. It's "in." The myth of classlessness is in remission, and multicultural literacy ascends. But for how long? And to what end?

■   ■   ■

Grace Paley said at the summer 1993 session of The Meeting House Writers Conference in Enfield, New Hampshire, that you shouldn't write unless you have to, unless you are all but "driven nuts" to reveal what has been hidden. What that implies, of course, is the position of the writer herself as poised between the hidden and that from which it is hidden, a hard spot, I think, to be in. For that from which the hidden is hidden is really not a *that*, but a *whom*. The job of the writer is then to present one world to another world, to present one life to another life, a hidden life to one who would, by and large, prefer not to know it. That which is hidden is hidden for a reason. To reveal it is to make someone uncomfortable—or responsible, let's say.

To reveal what has been hidden entails, on the part of the writer, a *de facto* awareness of the gap between these two worlds, as well as an awareness of the resistance of "the reader" to know, truly, the life heretofore hidden. Not knowing, ignoring, is bliss, insofar as bliss is an equilibrium in which one finds oneself safe and comfortable. Horace's injunction that art must both teach and delight then becomes the task of the writer and the key to revealing what has been hidden, seducing the reluctant knower, with the pleasure, the intellectual thrill, "the terrible beauty" of the unwanted lesson: into knowing.

Paley went on to say, quite bluntly, "What we are doing is trying to create justice in this world." Omigod. In America? Why do we need to do that? Everything I learned told me we already had it. It's done, right? We already have justice. Democracy has come out of the oven, in America, and all "we" need to do is sit down and eat. And all poetry has to do, all literature has to do, all art has to do, at least here in America, is delight. Right?

Not according to Paley, but she was not there when I needed her fifteen years ago, and had she been, I would not have listened to her, as I was still identified with "where I was going," I was a *Moon River Poet,* and I would keep my eye on the prize.

But I got to the point where I could not write. All that I had in me, boiling in me, as Paley said, driving me nuts to be out, could find no way out. The grace of form, as she described it, could not descend. I decided, in 1984, to quit writing and get a Ph.D. Looking back, that was a decision to become daughter-of-Bill-Carr: Dr. Linda Carr.

It was in the astonishingly conservative, intellectually repressive halls of Boston University that I discovered class (with the help of a few daring intellectuals, all since gone) and its relevance to my own inner struggle. I discovered all that had been hidden from me, my own history. I already knew, in the maelstrom of my mind, *why* it had been. And the grace of form began to descend.

I read, in Alan Dawley's *Class and Community,* the history of my hometown, Lynn, Massachusetts. Though I had grown up within earshot of the big General Electric strikes, had witnessed fights at the gates between strikers and scabs, though I'd been proud myself to join the union when I was old enough to go to work officially at the Elm Farm where my mother wrapped meat ("flying up" from the out-of-the-till dollar an hour at the lunch counter to a $1.37½ an hour, with breaks, on the cash registers), I knew utterly nothing of labor's history. I knew nothing about the origin of the eight-hour work day, the bloody battles of unions in America, child-labor laws, "Labor Day," not even my own grandmother's role in organizing women shoe factory workers in the city years before.

I knew nothing of the great marches and strikes of this shoe-making town, nothing of the proud radical identity that reached back to before the Revolutionary War. And I knew nothing of its decline after World War II, the identification of American workers with the middle class, the flight to the suburbs, the decay of the social and organizational centers of labor in Lynn. I knew nothing but what I saw unnamed and saw internalized as "individual failure."

And I knew nothing about the strategies, documented in sermons and in public education policy, that had neutralized the power of that con-scious working class, as it had neutralized women's power. I saw my own "education in ignorance," for the first time, in its historical context—my upbringing as a working-class Catholic Irish-American girlchild cut off from every authentic shred of identity.

Get Out of Lynn, meaning "get out of the working class," was the loud and clear message I grew up with, and in Dawley I saw the evaporation of my father's whole life as I saw the evaporation of Lynn. The dematerializ-ing of labor history left us all, my father, my family, my town, with a sense of ourselves as *tacky,* as simply poor, the only town, the only man, the only girl who couldn't "make it," blameworthy by virtue of stupidity, laziness, unattractiveness. With the disappearance of class consciousness, each of us was isolated, to measure ourselves against the myth of classlessness and to fail.

One of the most remarkable aspects of this strenuous erasure of per-sonal history was my family's deliberate lying about its own origins and past. I know now how common this phenomenon is, parents' efforts to free their children to "better lives" by keeping the secret of their origin. I was astonished to learn that my father, the fifth of six children, was the first born on American soil, and of Northern Irish Scots-Irish ancestry. He had insisted the family came from the South, and came generations ago, scrap-ing, before he thought up *Bill Carr* and had the money to send his sheets out, to locate a relatively elevated status even in his tradition.

I read Boyer and Morais's *Labor's Untold Story,* its pages still uncut when I found it on the shelves of the Mugar Library. I read everything Robert St. George suggested, and all that Sam Bass Warner offered, and wrote my papers straight into the ossified core, right at the warnings that "I couldn't win."

At the age of forty-one.

On my side of the Great Divide it was *Eureka*. And on the other, *Paranoia*. Just as, in the few years previous, as I had come to consciousness as a woman, it had been *Eureka* vs. *Hysteria*. I remember learning that miners were recruited from all over Europe to dig for silver in the West—with promises, of course, of wealth and freedom—and when they arrived they were sent down in crews where no two men spoke the same language. Unable to identify, speak, and organize, each was left, to question himself alone in his confusion, disillusionment, anger, and despair. To find himself the only malcontent.

That tale remains a parable for me.

■ ■ ■

What class is, what classes are, to what degree and how individuals may move across class lines—these are matters for someone else to argue. Class *is*. And the denial of class, both in my personal family history and in the successive layers of culture that instructed me in ignorance, meant simply that I internalized my lot and was ashamed: of my bad teeth, my bad taste, my woody-looking reprocessed wool, my cardboardy shoes, my congenital poor girl's split ends and unbraced grin. And of everything that came out of my mouth, both what it said and how it sounded. An abusive homelife no doubt contributed to this self-image, but that abuse was completely consistent with, perhaps inevitable inside, the successive layers of social denial that shaped and sustained my culture. Ashamed.

So the shame realized itself most pointedly in silence. I was like a parrot that had learned to say a few human words and was praised for them, but could no more articulate for humanity the reality of my experience than the bird could. This shamed silence, alternating with an impulse to do what the Old Man sometimes did—just "tell them off" in such a way that he would not be taken seriously—was the alternating current of my confrontation with "my betters." The parrot or the pit bull.

■ ■ ■

To be poised where Paley says we must be, knowing the inner life, layered in shame, and articulating it in terms human enough to be heard and passionate enough to be moving, is the job.

The invitation, of course, is to be poised there but to continue forgetting where we have been on behalf of admittance to where we are meant to be. *Up.* Seemingly out of the underclass. The invitation is to repent of our tacky pasts and become acolytes in the true church of the middle class, memorizing the new prayers, the chief of which is the credo of classlessness. Kundera calls this process "organized forgetting," referring to his own history, and Adrienne Rich has written extensively warning women, in particular, to "resist amnesia."

Beyond the richness of a multicultural society, beyond the wisdom lost in the melting pot when the melting pot, as Lucy Lippard says, simply bleaches us all, why resist amnesia? Why keep the old wounds of labor history, class history, race history, women's history, open? And what relevance does any of this have for someone like me, a poet, not a historian, not a politician?

In *Praises and Dispraises: Poetry and Politics in the Twentieth Century,* Terrence Des Pres cites the work of many poets whose vision was indeed social. In fact, he points to Yeats as an example of the ancient bardic tradition, in which the function of the poet was to be "the voice of the tribe," the voice of warning, whose judgments, dispraises, were feared, and as honored as his (or her) praises were.

If there is a separate class to which writers may belong in America, it must be this one, one in which the writer allows herself her estrangement from her own origins, by becoming painfully conscious of their impact on her life, yet refuses the promised safety of "crossing over" to another class identity: by standing on that point that Paley knows so well, rendering one life to another.

The tradition of American arts and letters has been for some time a world of stasis, "mainstream," an arts from and of the center, where change does not take place. The angry young men of letters have traditionally been angry at their fathers—not as Antigone was at Creon, in response to the social order in which they find themselves, but at the delay they must experience before they accede to their place of privilege in it. They object to being sons for a time.

But the world is full of those who are its perpetual "children," those who will never accede to privilege though they identify with it, dress as though they had it, live, often, for its approval. This is how I experienced myself as a working-class girlchild, and how I experience myself today. In fact, the invitation for me to join "up" is fraudulent, hollow. I may still only "dress up."

One of the present obstacles to real identification as working class in America is the change of the economy from one of production to one of service. In much "working-class" literature, the situations are in fact of the past, when large numbers of workers labored together in mills and factories. Today, the "industrious poor" in cities are often in token "white-collar" positions, seduced in part by the dignity of genteel poverty into denying the real worth of their work. In rural areas—as in Vermont, where I have lived for years—it is the fortunate ones among the indigenous population who even get to remain, living increasingly in pockets of poverty outside the walls of the centers of leisure which they serve.

I have in mind here, too, especially in the present economy, those masses of unemployed "professionals" who are driven to take "consultant" positions, at all but minimum wage, and without benefits. Adjuncts in academic institutions, for instance, all over the country—in my own experience, virtually two-thirds of working faculty—produce the lion's share of a program's income and take home perhaps one fifth of the total salary and benefits package that their "colleagues," doing identical work, are paid. If class continues to have an impact on my life as a writer, it is surely in this fact, that like many women of my generation who deferred their own professional development while raising families and supporting husbands' careers, I have continued to live in an economic underclass, and, as before, the politics of the situation are obscured and denied.

To raise these issues directly is to risk retaliation. I allowed myself to be quoted publicly last year in an interview, saying that, because I have been an adjunct, my work has never been encouraged or supported by my academic institution as "real faculty" expects its work to be. I was fired as a result. Frankly citing the economic inequities between the minority and the majority of faculty was seen as "uncollegial," and I was dismissed.

This, in an autobiographical essay on class and the American writer, seems to me to be an important example of how our received myth of classlessness continues to exploit, in this case, two-thirds of a faculty population while guaranteeing that this vivid underclass will "keep the secret" for the sake of their jobs. A strongly class-conscious group, a group well versed in labor history and tactics, would know exactly where they stood and what they must do. Instead, my fellows—my colleagues, the adjuncts—dress like their betters, teach like their betters, allow the students to believe they are in fact "colleagues," and go without all that makes the professional lives of their betters possible.

Several years ago, one of these teaching "colleagues" and I mailed off applications for NEA fellowships together. He was a full-timer, a man whose education had been but a small part of his patrimony as the son of a Texas oil millionaire, and whose women had raised his children.

I commented as we left the post office that it cost a lot to get such an application together and into the mail. It did. He responded, "Yes, but be glad for it. There must be plenty of good competition out there who just can't afford it, and that gives us a better chance."

This was the first time in my life that someone from "the other half," that "other" tiny percentage, had actually uttered what my entire education had denied: that "the haves," as the Irish say, "keep all they have, take what they can." The man had betrayed, to me, if only briefly and only that once, what I had long felt I was up against though my whole world denied it.

To grow up without this consciousness—poor, laboring class, with one's eyes on the prize of middle classness, is to experience an education created by one's betters for their own ends. In the fifties, of course, we learned nothing about labor history, even my hometown's, nothing about slavery, nothing about the genocide of native peoples, nothing at all about women. The myth of classlessness included them as willing participants in the great dream, pulling together—so of course there was no working-class literature or art, as there was none for people of color or women. And still the impulse is to create an art that denies not only the existence of an underclass, but the human experience of living a life entrapped in it.

As Paley says, "what has been hidden."

Eric Frohnmeyer, in response to censorship of the NEA and its grants to "pornographic" work, pointed out the obvious when he said that art is intellectual research. Art, I agree, cannot take place at the center. "Mainstream art," or poetry, literature, is an oxymoron, a contradiction in terms. Mainstream art is but decoration, embroidery on the fabric of what is. Mainstream art, by definition, takes place at the static center, making the outworn new.

My experience of writing poems has been, I think, "the creative process," shared by all who allow themselves to be "inspired," breathed into, overtaken by something greater, outside themselves. I think poems are, as I've heard them described, "shortcuts to wisdom." In the poems I have read that are memorable, that at once teach and delight me, the movement is a plummet. (This is also true of those poems of mine that are keepers, the ones in which discovery is most profound, where I come to know something I didn't know I knew.) The poems explore some scene, some image, some habit, and plunge to its depths, penetrate the usual surface on which stands the ground of the institutionally known.

Because I am a poet, I find poems to be the most lucid route to the root. They jag down like lightning to their epiphanies, and their epiphanies are roots, and *root* is the root word of *radical.* To forbid the subject of the largest social functioning of the tribe to poetry is to confine the poet to a sandbox with a plastic shovel. Six inches, dear, and no more.

As I heard Howard Zinn reiterate a couple of years ago, the promise of American democracy rests upon the first freedom, freedom of speech. All social change that enacts the freedoms that democracy proposes comes from the bottom up. From "grass roots." Always has. Never has justice been extended, gratuitously, downward (except by Portia). Justice is always wrested away from those who are better off the less justice there is.

Zinn mentioned the night I heard him speak that he was turning away from the writing of history and toward the writing of plays, as he felt that art was a more accessible and effective way of speaking freely, to and about the tribe. I agree with him. In poetry, at least, the renaissance in both readership and writership is undeniable. What brings Paley and Zinn, Thompson and Forché, Dawley and Rich, Des Pres and Boyer together here in this essay is McCarriston. For me to forget what has brought me here would be, I think, a great sadness. For me to sequester myself in the sandbox for the sake of a shiny shovel and a new pail would be to fall victim to the great threat to democracy as Tocqueville foresaw it two hundred years ago: conformity, majority opinion.

■　■　■

I've smoked a few cigarettes with Bob, the literary night watchman, since I got here for my year at the Bunting Institute. We sit on the steps and drink coffee. He can't understand why I moved in three days before I was invited, and stay here night after night, right through the weekends, till he has to turn the alarms on. We have traded books. He works nights at Harvard, and he loves to talk books and ideas with the kids. They give him their used books. He's read everybody.

I tell him about this essay I am writing, having a hard time writing, not knowing "who I am," especially in prose. I ask him if he thinks there are classes in America.

"Oh yes," he says.

"Can you cross?" I ask.

"My dear," he answers, pointing to the entry to the institute from the sidewalk, "every time you walk down those steps into here you leave the real world. You cross. You have crossed."

I press on, "What's the real world, Bob? Why is this not the real world? What's the difference?"

"Well, it's like these kids at Harvard. They know where they're going to sleep. They know where their next meal is coming from, no matter what. They know if they've got a paper due and there's a party, that if they miss the party, they miss the party, but if they don't pass in the paper, they get an extension. They get in, they ask, they get an extension."

I say, "Well, yeah, but what about when they leave here. Aren't they scared? I'm scared. Aren't they going to have to worry about a roof over their heads and where their next meal is coming from then?"

"Nah."

"Why not?"

"Well, it's just what Harvard *means,* you know?"

"What does it mean, Bob?"

And here his language would have had to go from anecdote to theory, I think, would have called upon a vocabulary he does not know: the vocabulary it took me forty years to unearth, and without which, the grace of form could not descend.

Linda McCarriston

To Judge Faolain, Dead Long Enough: A Summons

> Your Honor, when my mother stood
> before you, with her routine
> domestic plea, after weeks
> of waiting for speech to return
> to her body, with her homemade
> forties hairdo, her face purple still
> under pancake, her jaw off just a little,
> her *holy of holies* healing,
> her breasts wrung, her heart

From *Eva-Mary,* TriQuarterly Books, Northwestern University, 1991.

the bursting heart of someone
snagged among rocks deep
in a sharkpool—no, not "someone,"

but a woman there, snagged
with her babies, *by* them,
in one of hope's pedestrian
brutal turns—when, in the tones
of parlors overlooking the harbor,
you admonished that, for the sake
of the family, the wife
must take the husband back to her bed,
what you willed not to see before you
was a woman risen clean to the surface,
a woman who, with one arm flailing,
held up with the other her actual

burdens of flesh. When you clamped
to her leg the chain of *justice,*
you ferried us back down to *the law,*
the black ice eye, the maw, the mako
that circles the kitchen table nightly.
What did you make of the words
she told you, not to have heard her,
not to have seen her there? Almost-
forgiveable ignorance, you were not
the fist, the boot, or the blade,
but the jaded, corrective ear and eye
at the limits of her world. Now

I will you to see her as she was, to ride
your own words back into light: I call
your spirit home again, divesting you
of robe and bench, the fine white hand
and half-lit Irish eye. Tonight, put on
a body in the trailer down the road
where your father, when he can't
get it up, makes love to your mother
with a rifle. Let your name be
Eva-Mary. Let your hour of birth
be dawn. Let your life be long
and common, and your flesh endure.

The Apple Tree

for my mother

More beautiful now than ever you were
in pale May blossom, or in August,
gravid again—your chained boughs
bearing, your skirts, stiff camouflage
arustle—you stand, past use, past
prettiness in the winter of your winter,
at the brink of encroaching woods, in the yard
of the old farm, where now, out windows,
curtains shake themselves like rags
from a lost cleaning morning. Here,
in the light that by noon takes
your shadow and carries it from the garden
to the barn, now, from your deep
seeking source under snow, drink long,
breathe slow, be still, as did the child,
she of the single body. The many that
found you and took you are fallen away.

From *Eva-Mary,* TriQuarterly Books, Northwestern University, 1991.

Joann Maria Vasconcellos

I was born on August 5, 1959, in Cambridgeport, Massachusetts, the youngest of six children. My brothers and sisters never forgave me for being six days late. I was due July 31 and had I complied, our birthdays would have run one sibling each month consecutively from June to November. The following summer my family moved to North Quincy, where my parents ran a neighborhood store at Five Corners. My father continued to hold down other jobs to make ends meet, including truck driver and postal worker. All four of my grandparents immigrated to the United States from the Azores. Their work included factory work, seamstressing, and public works. My maternal grandmother, Vavõa Trinidad, lived with us and was a second mother to me.

I became a physical therapist largely because my friend Wanda thought it would be a good job for us (she's now a toxicologist). Not having strong career guidance in high school, I thought Wanda's suggestion was as good as any; after all I liked helping others and I was a "people person." In my late twenties, having moved away from my working-class neighborhood and being under the influence of middle-class friends dreaming their dreams, I began to search for what I thought would be a good job for me. Eventually, the search brought me to graduate studies in sociology. Currently, I am a doctoral candidate in the Sociology Department at Boston College. I also have a M.A. degree in Feminist Liberation Theology from the Episcopal Divinity School and

B.S. in Physical Therapy from Quinnipac College. My research areas are popular culture and feminist theory.

Although there is much about academics that I enjoy, the incongruence that exists between working-class me and academic me leads me to wonder at times if I made the right choice. In order to maintain a semblance of sanity, I try to keep connected to my working-class culture. Amongst other rituals, I watch *All My Children,* pray to Vavõa, and have a daily laugh on the phone with my mother.

This is Joann Maria Vasconcellos's first published essay.

Joann Maria Vasconcellos

Laughter as Liberating Memory

There is something about the remembering. So sweet. Yet also so painful. For it can never be relived outside of my heart. I can't honestly say that it is one clear memory. No. It is a blur of times. A remembering of time after time. The ritual of women—and men—of family—at the Vasco house. The kitchen-table ritual. Of stories. Some words in English. Some in Portuguese. The smell of coffee. Stories. And. Laughter.

This laughter. Amongst the Portuguese and English words. In order to hear secrets, we pretended not to understand some of the Portuguese words. This laughter. Amongst the smell of coffee and malacardas. Um. The taste of malacardas. Still one of my biggest pleasures. Not quite donuts. Not quite fried dough. This laughter. Amongst the shouting and yelling. Back then, loud competitive talking made me feel alive. Yes. This laughter is what fills my mind. What I cannot re-create outside of my heart.

The place is gone. My family has moved on. Others now live in that place that holds my memories. They cook and eat and sit in that kitchen. Do these others hear the laughter? What happened to the leftover vibrations? Does that kitchen still hold a part of me? Does memory of me live in it, like memory of it lives in me? Have those walls forgotten me and mine? Sometimes I want to visit. It's not too far. Seven miles. But the thought of not getting what I want. The knowing I'll never be able to get what I want. Keeps me away.

Some of the family and friends are gone. There are times when I want to conjure them up. I insist that they come back to me. Especially Vavõa Trinidad, my maternal grandmother, who was like a second mother to me. Vavõa, how could you have gone before I knew just how important you were to me? Then I stop. For fear that she will visit me. Yes. I want her. But the thought that she may come sit with me leaves me in fear. I'm not my mother's daughter. My mother can commune with those who passed on. I am too frightened. I must live with only memories. The memories that at times are liberating. At other times are immobilizing. The memories which can never be re-created outside of my heart.

That kitchen on Newbury Avenue was the center of my world. That kitchen table was the center of the kitchen that was the center of my world. I spent hours circling around and around that kitchen table. Vavõa would be sewing in the corner of the room. Circling and running, with Vavõa nearby, I was content. The table is gone. Formica. I remember. Gray formica. I spent hours underneath the table. It was my haven. Coloring and sitting with Vavõa nearby. I spent hours on top of the table. Playing with buttons on the table. What a noise they made when I emptied that Quaker Oats box. Spread all over the table. Vavõa's buttons. They were jewels to me. My favorite toys. Gone. Special times. Those Vavõa-all-to-myself times. My brothers and sisters were off at school, my parents at work and I had her all to myself. Vavõa and I in the kitchen with the formica table.

Other times. Others at the table. We played cards. Canasta. Poker. Bid whist. Vavõa would tell us. Stand up. Walk around the table. Now change seats. That was the secret to changing our luck. I loved to play cards at that table. But this is a different kitchen-table memory. I'm more grown up being able to play cards with the others. No longer do I just get the conciliatory joy of merely watching others play. It's somewhat of an initiation. To be able to actually hold my own hand. No longer having to settle for sharing Ma's hand. I was a big girl now. Yet still this gray formica table was my favorite place. Along with the cards would come the laughter. And the stories. I wanted to hear them over and over. Mostly about the times before me. The cards gave us a reason to sit. Together. It was home. The kitchen. The gray formica table. The stories. The laughter.

Home. Gray formica table. There's definitely noise. Lots of people. Talking. Or more likely shouting and yelling. And laughing. Back then there was no TV at the table. Only sounds which originated in that room were allowed. That was plenty. Commotion. There's movement. Ma makes us lift everything off the table so that she can clean it with the sponge.

People up and down from the table. In and out the door. Without keys. People in and out the door without keys. There were smells. Coffee. Always coffee brewing. Sometimes malacardas. But that was usually early Sunday-morning-get-out-of-bed-and-to-the-table smell. I can vaguely remember Ricky's-camel-cigarette-burning-in-the-ashtray smell. There were touches. The feel of the plastic sticking to the back of my thigh on a hot summer day. Home. Sometimes I try and will myself back there in my dreams.

There are new kitchens where I try to relive the memory. But. It is never as sweet as the memory of Five Corners for me. The house that is filled with memories of grief. But also filled with memories of laughter. I try to recapture those times in my life. But. The resemblance is faint. The memory is sacred. It cannot live outside of my heart. This memory of kitchen-table laughter. That fills me. Has in recent times become my saving Grace.

How many times in these past years of not knowing who I am has this laughter saved me? What is this working-class girl who's supposed to be married but still is single doing in front of this computer? Why is she typing her own words and not the words of a middle-class boss onto these keys? Why is this working-class girl saying words like paradigm and hegemony and epistemology? Who is she/am I? I feel like a showoff. Like a pretend-to-be. During these times of uncertainty. The echo of kitchen-table laughter pulls me in. To myself. Remembering who I am.

The ever-present ambivalence brings me to the edge of sanity at times. I have not assimilated completely into the middle-class world of academics. I am a resistor of assimilation. What does that mean? I have privilege. Yes that is true. But I also have memories. Of used-to-be times. Of a kitchen table. And laughter. How can I stay true to myself and stay in this world? This world that objectifies the working class. How can I benefit the working class in this middle-class world? Or can I? Am I merely fooling myself? These questions haunt me. They leave me in a perpetual state of ambivalence. The ambivalence comes from the fact that I refuse to forget. Refuse to assimilate. I have learned to befriend the ambivalence and listen to her wisdom.

When I feel close to the edge. Not knowing who I am. Beginning to believe that I've made all the wrong choices. That's when the memory saves me. This memory of kitchen-table laughter. The sacred healing laughter. That always made it bearable if not better. The sacred healing laughter. That lightened the heavy load of life or maybe just made it easier to carry.

The sacred healing laughter. That helped me to realize that life is full of confusion as well as certainty.

We used this laughter to remember those who had passed on. My brother Ricky, who had stepped on a land mine at nineteen in Vietnam, was kept alive with laughter. "Do you remember the time Ricky . . . ?" Followed by laughter. My favorite story is the time that he taught me how to climb stairs the "right" way when we were visiting Washington, D.C. It was at the Lincoln Memorial. I learned quick. He couldn't catch me. How many times was that story told in that kitchen. Not enough for me. Not enough to bring Ricky back.

Vavo Trinidad, my maternal grandfather who passed on as Ma carried me in her belly, the grief sent to me along with her blood through the umbilical cord, was kept alive with laughter. "Do you remember the time Pa . . . ?" Followed by laughter. My favorite story is the one that they tell of him going for his citizenship. When he was asked who Columbus was, he answered, "Colombo von fa frio." Or translated. Once Columbus Day comes it gets cold. How many times that story. Often enough to make me feel like I'd maybe known him. Not enough to rid me of the emptiness of not knowing him.

Vavõa Vasconcellos, my paternal grandmother, who managed to maintain her sense of humor through a difficult life of tending to a family and putting button after button after button on mattresses in a Providence factory, was kept alive with laughter. "Do you remember the time Ma . . . ?" My favorite . . . I can't remember . . . the grief in the not remembering is too much. The remembering really can make the grief easier. You see. Vavõa Vasconcellos was my cousins' Vavõa. Their kitchen table holds her memories. Her laughter. Her stories. I am jealous. For this strong woman, whom I'm said to resemble, is a stranger to me. I long to hear stories of her.

The unbearable grief became more tolerable in the echoes of our laughing up our memories. Spirits were kept alive for me in the laughter. How I wish we had that formica table to sit around and remember Alan. My brother whose heart gave out at thirty-three. But. My family had moved. There would never again be a kitchen without a TV to sit in and laugh and remember. Alan whose laugh would rival anyone's I knew. It was more like a roar. When he laughed he meant it. His belly would move with it. His whole body laughed. And my whole body aches for missing that laugh.

We used laughter to laugh at authority. The college educated. The politicians. The church officials. The they-think-they're-better-than-us relatives. My favorite. How my Dad outsmarted his bosses. How he left the milk cracker factory with the conveyor belt going. He just couldn't take it anymore. My favorite. How Vavo Trinidad outsmarted his bosses. His presumed ignorance of English helped him to empower himself in the workplace. While others thought him stupid. He outwitted his superiors. We learned self-respect for who we were in the gasping for breath between fits of laughter. In the side pains that accompanied our laughing out loud so strongly and passionately, we learned to be proud of who we were.

In the laughter we resisted you're-not-as-good-as-us messages. In the laughter we healed from the grief and misfortune of our lives. In the laughter we could be the best of who we were. In the laughter we learned to forget. In the laughter we forgot our heartaches momentarily. In the laughter we forgot humiliation. In the laughter we forgot. In the laughter we learned to remember. In the laughter we remembered who we were. In the laughter we remembered who we loved. In the laughter we remembered.

There is something in the memory of kitchen-table laughter that reaches out through the years, grabs me, and wraps itself around me. It fills me up. Healing that split part of me. The feminist-academic-working-class me who wants to dance to Led Zeppelin after I finish that feminist theory book. When the confusion surrounds me. I call out for the laughter to heal me. I remember. But then I think. Oh shit! Am I becoming one of the college-educated-with-no-common-sense that we use to laugh at? Can I really be a working-class woman with a Ph.D.?

When did I enter this life that I'm not sure is mine? Was there one moment? Or a collection of moments? A cumulative effect that brought about the transformation? I'm not sure of the exact time or place. But. It happened sometime, somewhere in between leaving my home at Five Corners for physical therapy school and entering graduate school. A period of over ten years.

In the earlier years the laughter was still with me. It echoed inside me. It was strong and steady. I went with it. Loud. Boisterous. In-your-face laughter. I was the working-class life-of-the-party type. Then I became conspicuous. I learned. To pretend. That I too was middle class. I learned to be ashamed of the working-class me. I let the laughter die. I cut off my source. I learned a new language and a new laughter. I put up boundaries. Took space. Had issues. I even started to say my "r's." I enunciated. I forgot to remember.

Then I declared that I was a feminist. I began to study about sexism. Then racism. And. Class elitism. I began the journey back to the laughter.

The beginning of this journey is clear in my mind. It began one Tuesday afternoon in November. I was at my kitchen table. I heard a whisper. It was Vavõa Trinidad calling out to me. She had been trying to contact me for days. But I didn't know it was her. Until this wonderful Tuesday afternoon. For several weeks I had been mesmerized by the beautiful blue, late-afternoon autumn sky. Finally. This day. While staring at the sky from the kitchen table. I fell to the floor. I remembered. Vavõa had always said that she wanted to be buried in blue. So that she could blend in with the sky and make her way to heaven. She was calling out to me. Through the blue-ness of the sky. I finally heard her.

This was a turning point. I began to piece myself together. With the help of Vavõa and a growing community of wonderful women. I began to embrace the working-class me. I began to remember the laughter. At this point, I was studying Feminist Ethics and planning to find a paid activist position upon graduation. I decided ahead of time that I wasn't going to enjoy writing my thesis. Was I surprised when I came to look forward to the writing and research. This is when I began to consider staying in aca-demics. In the midst of the considering I had a dream. I was at school with my mother in a class where we were sitting in a circle, feminist style. All of a sudden my mother got up. She started to give a speech and wouldn't stop. I tried to get her to sit down, but she wouldn't. I was embarrassed. She was proud. I woke up and wept. My mother was the working-class strength in me that would give me a voice in the midst of feminist academic circles. I went trembling to see my advisor and asked her if she thought I was cut out for academics. Then I told her to be honest, that I would not be of-fended if she said "No." I was shocked when she said, "Yes."

The next year I spent applying for graduate school and depressed. I have yet to totally understand what the depression was about. It had some-thing to do with delayed dreams. Almost never had dreams. About how the working class is not given the space and ability to dream. About the stifling of almost had dreams. It also had to do with terror. I was terrified that I would never shake these pretend-to-be, impostor feelings. Till this day, al-most three years later, I still have times when I can't believe that this is me living this life. Ambivalence will always be part of my life as a working-class academic; the laughter helps pull me through. It helps me to stay connected to the working-class me. It helps me confront the times when I become filled with the self-importance of an academic. It helps me keep a perspective. A working-class feminist perspective.

This is the laughter that came to me when I began to visualize the performance piece *For Laughing Out Loud.* The echoes of the laughing-out-loud women of my childhood brought me through the process of creating this piece. Their laughter is heard in the character of Working-Class Joann, who helps to give Academic Joann perspective. This piece of work was the most empowering aspect of my first year of graduate school in sociology. I had been feeling beaten down. Confused. As if I would never make it through. Split. This piece helped me to remember the laughter. It helped me to join together the working-class me and the academic me. It helped me begin to see the wisdom that is present in the ambivalence. For the laughter I thank all the women who warmed the chairs around our kitchen table at Five Corners. I also thank all the men who yelled in from the other room, "What's so funny?" To which we answered, "Nothing."

Joann Maria Vasconcellos

For Laughing Out Loud

For Laughing Out Loud is a working-class feminist performance piece which uses performance, dialogue, visual image, social theory, and narrative to discuss laughter and the feminine mask. In discussing femininity as a mask, I question why women wear makeup, what is hidden behind the feminine mask, and can a woman be a feminist and still wear makeup? Potential answers to these questions are found in feminist theory and working-class sarcasm. Laughter is then introduced to the performance as ritual, empowerment, sacred, resistance and mask remover. The film *A Question of Silence* is used to explore the power of "knowing" laughter among working-class women, which leads to courageous mask removal in the film. Throughout the piece issues of class confront issues of gender. The introduction and conclusion, in particular, illustrate the struggles of a working-class feminist academic attempting to integrate her class background with her feminist scholarship. What follows are excerpts from the larger piece.

The story begins with Academic Joann standing in front of the television screen. Her back is toward the audience. Academic Joann is dressed professionally in a femme sort of way, with her black power-skirt, black pumps, and professional blouse and blazer. She is about to get ready for the masquerade. All of a sudden Academic Joann is startled by Joann's voice coming from a tape recorder placed behind her on an academic-give-a-lecture table.

Joann's Voice: Pst . . . Pst . . . Joann. . . . Come on Joann this isn't the masquerade. This is the real thing. They're all staring at you waiting for you to do something. Something intellectual or something academic or something theoretically profound . . . come on.

Academic Joann turns to the tape recorder looking nervous, puzzled, confused. But soon her attention is switched back to the television screen where Working-Class Joann dressed in a purple chenille bathrobe and reading the Star *tabloid demands her attention.*

Working-Class Joann *(whips the* Star *aside and declares angrily):* STOP IT! STOP IT WITH THE INTELLECTUAL–ACADEMIC–THEORETICALLY PROFOUND STUFF . . . OKAY? . . . IT MAKES ME NERVOUS! *(Cringes and returns to the* Star *)*

Working-Class Joann.
Photo by Stephanie Tilton.

Academic Joann *(to Working-Class Joann):* shh! *(Turns to Joann's Voice on the tape recorder and asks nervously):* are you sure this isn't the masquerade?

Joann's Voice *(whispers with a hint of sarcasm):* Listen girl, just between you and I, it's all a masquerade . . . but don't let them know that . . . you'll lose your power . . . control of the situation . . . that sort of stuff. Now just sit down, put on your mask and let's get on with the show.

Academic Joann obeys Joann's Voice and starts to sit down, when she is abruptly stopped by Working-Class Joann.

Working-Class Joann *(looking away from her* Star *tabloid, quite sarcastically):* YOU MEAN TO TELL ME YOU HAVEN'T PUT YOUR MASK ON YET . . . DAMN IT JOANN YOU'RE GONNA RUIN EVERYTHING. *(Sighs deeply.)* I KNEW THIS WASN'T GONNA WORK. *(Whispers):* YOU'RE NOT THE INTELLECTUAL TYPE. *(Goes back to reading the* Star.*)*

Academic Joann *(perturbed and nervous, says to Working-Class Joann):* cool it, will you. *(She then turns to Joann's Voice on the tape recorder and pleads):* listen get rid of her, she's gonna give the real me away.

Joann's Voice *(Obliging Academic Joann, she speaks authoritatively to Working-Class Joann):* Okay listen, you, you with the *Star*, you're going to have to leave. Do you hear me? Heeeey!

Working-Class Joann *(puts the* Star *aside snickering, sarcastic and really enjoying herself):* OHHH NO! I'M NOT MISSING THIS. I'VE BEEN WAITING FOR WEEKS TO WATCH YOU PRETEND YOU'RE NOT ME. NOPE. I'M NOT LEAVING NOW. *(Back to the ever-present* Star.*)*

Joann's Voice *(attempting to be diplomatic, compromising, turns to feminist process):* Listen. We can't go on with you taking up space on the screen. We need that screen for the multi-media effect, remember. Now, listen, we won't forget to put your concerns in the content. We talked about that. Okay?

Working-Class Joann *(looks up from the* Star; *far from satisfied, she continues with a thick sarcastic tone):* OH YEAH, MISS BIG SHOT MULTI-MEDIA ACADEMIC INTELLECTUAL THEO . . . THEORE—THE—O—RE—TI—CLY . . . PROFOUND SHOWOFF. *(Gives both Joanns a raspberry.)* THAT'S ALL I AM TO YOU NOW—NOWTHATYOU'REIN GRADSCHOOLJUSTPARTOFYOURCONTENT? FORGET IT! I'M NOT LEAVING. *(Back to the* Star.*)*

Academic Joann: damn it *(lets some slight anger show, while struggling to keep a professional front)* don't you remember? i only have fifteen to twenty minutes to pull this off. *(Now she's ready to give in to Working-Class Joann, anything to get her off the television screen.)* alright you can be in on it all . . . the content . . . the style . . . the questions . . . only if you promise not to be so sarcastic . . . you're going to get me in trouble. remember this is graduate school . . . this is serious.

Working-Class Joann *(peeks over the top of the* Star, *listening, puts* Star *aside slowly, sarcasm is gone, smiling, and feeling quite smug):* HUH THAT SOUNDS MORE LIKE IT! I JUST DON'T WANT TO GET LOST IN YOUR ACADEMIC SHOWOFF IMPOSTOR PRETEND-TO-BE ROUTINE. I DON'T WANT TO BE JUST PART OF THE CONTENT, ALRIGHT? I PROMISE TO HELP YOU OUT. YOU'RE GOING FOR THIS WORKING-CLASS FEMINIST ANALYSIS STUFF? WELL, YOU'RE NOT GONNA BE ABLE TO PULL IT OFF WITHOUT ME. I'LL COME RIGHT ON OVER AND HELP YOU OUT. OKAY? YEPYEPYEP. I'LL BE RIGHT THERE. JUST LET ME FINISH THIS ARTICLE ON NICK NOLTE'S MISTRESS FOR EIGHT YEARS. SHE HAS THE GREATEST RESPECT FOR THE MAN NOW THAT HE'S GONE BACK TO HIS WIFE. HOW DO YOU LIKE THAT?

Working-Class Joann finally leaves the screen and Academic Joann turns down the volume on the television and sits down to put her makeup/mask on. She dumps the contents of her makeup case on the table, sets out her mirror and begins to put on eyeliner.

Joann's Voice *(with a slight hint of exasperation):* Okay . . . Okay . . . finally here we go.

TELEVISION SCREEN: Scene from *Nine to Five* where Lily Tomlin, Dolly Parton, and Jane Fonda are laughing out of control, followed by scene from *A Question of Silence* where the women burst into laughter in the courtroom.

Joann's Voice: This project is about laughing-out-loud women. It's about laughter as ritual. Laughter as empowerment. Laughter as sacred. Laughter as resistance. Laughter as masks removed. That is the laughter which provides women the space to remove our masks. Laughter that heals us from the wounds that are hidden behind our masks. Laughter as solidarity for women who laugh in the face of absurdity. But before I get to laughter, I'll be talking about the masks which laughter is hidden behind. "Womanliness therefore could be assumed and worn as a mask, both to hide the possession of masculinity and to avert the reprisals expected if she was found to possess it—much as a thief will turn out his pockets and ask to be searched to prove that he has not the stolen goods."[1]

TELEVISION SCREEN: Images of professional femme women on the screen . . . Grace Van Owen from *L.A. Law* and Erica Kane from *All My Children*.

Academic Joann *(stops the eyeliner for a moment):* what the hell does that mean? er, excuse me, could you elaborate more on the significance of that excerpt? please? *(Continues on with eye shadow.)*

Joann's Voice: Well, it was written by this woman Joan Riviere. She's a psychoanalyst, so she's into Freud and stuff. She seems to think that woman, now don't take offense, but women like you, need to wear this mask of femininity in order to hide the fact that you may be displaying masculine traits. For example, if you're giving an academic lecture, you'll dress feminine to detract from the fact that you can sling the intellectual bull just like one of the guys.

At this point, Academic Joann checks her femme self out and gives it a humph.

Joann's Voice: She talks about one of her analysands who tends to flirt with her male colleagues after one of her lectures. She explains this behavior as "an unconscious attempt to ward off the anxiety which would ensue on account of the reprisals she anticipated from the father-figures after her intellectual performance." [2]

Academic Joann *(finished with the eye shadow, on to blusher):* interesting? interesting, so not only do I dress feminine, but I also act feminine after

Academic Joann.
Photo by Stephanie Tilton.

to detract from the fact that I'm just as smart as they are. where does the father-figure stuff fit in?

Joann's Voice: Well you know the psychoanalysis stuff always goes back to the early years. In this case it's something about her wanting her father's penis. Oedipus. The oral-biting sadistic stage. Something like that. Also, this woman's intellect is connected with her father, who was an intellect himself. So she is associating her male colleagues with her own father.

Academic Joann *(with extreme sarcasm):* CERTAINLY SOUNDS INTER-ESTING, BUT I DON'T THINK I WEAR MAKEUP BECAUSE I WANT A PENIS. ALSO, HOW DOES IT WORK IF YOUR FATHER'S A TRUCK DRIVER OR WORKS IN A FACTORY OR A SECURITY GUARD LIKE MY DAD? CERTAINLY MALE ACADEMICS DON'T RESEMBLE HIM.

TELEVISION SCREEN: Images of Madonna's video *Vogue.*

Joann's Voice: Maybe not. I admit her logic is hard to buy with our skepticism towards the psychoanalytic approach. Yet, her uncovering of this phenomenon of female academics being super femme is intriguing. Why do you wear makeup, doll face?

Academic Joann *(chuckling):* Well, I'll tell you this much . . . I was into the feminist butch look, my hair was real short and I didn't wear makeup for years. I started wearing makeup again as kind of a revolt against that. I was becoming too dogmatic. Also, it had something to do with class, girlie girl things as a way of bonding with my old working-class buddies. Yet, I'll be honest with you, sometimes I hesitate before putting on my mask. Wondering what it's all about. If I can *really* be a feminist and wear lipstick. But, for today I'm the masked feminist.

■　■　■

TELEVISION SCREEN: Yet another Joann. This time she's wearing a mask ready to pantomime the following dialogue:

Academic Joann: Now I can understand this smiling thing. How we have to be polite, good listeners, forever attentive. As women we are masked. Hidden behind the image of who we should be.

TELEVISION SCREEN: Masked Joann hand on chin leaning forward with that attentive active listening look.

Academic Joann: Smiling that oh-that's so funny look

TELEVISION SCREEN: Still with the lean forward pose, but smiling broadly.

Academic Joann: when we WANT TO SCOWL.

TELEVISION SCREEN: Leans back and scowls.

Academic Joann: Nodding that so-fascinated look

TELEVISION SCREEN: Nodding and pointing with finger, as if to say, good point.

Academic Joann: when we WANT TO YAWN.

TELEVISION SCREEN: Leans back slightly and puts hand to her mouth and yawns.

Academic Joann: Bobbing that oh-yes-you're-so brilliant look

TELEVISION SCREEN: Bobbing and smiling and bobbing and smiling some more.

Academic Joann: when we WANT TO LAUGH OUT LOUD.

TELEVISION SCREEN: Hands up in the air and bursting out in laughter.

Academic Joann: That part of the mask I know well.

TELEVISION SCREEN: Before disappearing, masked Joann nods one last time. This time she means it.

Academic Joann: Yes, we may wear our masks for many reasons. Gloria Anzaldúa writes in her introduction to *Making Face, Making Soul/ Hacienda Caras,* a collection of writings of women of color struggling to remove their masks and make their own faces. "The masks, las máscaras, we are compelled to wear, drive a wedge between our inter subjective personhood and the persona we present to the world . . . These masking roles exact a toll. . . . After years of wearing masks we may become just a series of roles, the constellated self limping along with its broken limbs."[3] Despite the toll. We smile. In denial. For survival. Not knowing what else to do. We smile and nod and bob.

TELEVISION SCREEN: More makeup commercials.

Academic Joann: We smile on the outside but inside we want to scowl to yawn to laugh right out loud at the absurdity of it all. *And there are times. When we feel safe. That we laugh. We laugh right out loud. We remove our masks.*

TELEVISION SCREEN: Wilma Flintstone and Betty Rubble share a laugh.

Academic Joann: This is what I want to turn to now. That sacred space of laughing-out-loud women, where we can remove our masks.

TELEVISION SCREEN: Lucy Ricardo and Ethel Mertz share a secret pact as well as a ritualistic laugh.

Academic Joann: Laughter. Ritual. Sacred. Healing. The energy in the laughter moves us forward. We peel off our masks. We dare to speak the truth. We dare to laugh right out loud. Mary Daly defines "The Virtue of Laughing Out Loud" in her book *Wickedary* as the "lusty habit of boisterous Be-laughing women: habit of cracking the hypocritical hierarchs' houses of mirrors, defusing their power of deluding Others; cackling that cracks the man-made universe, creating a crack through which Cacklers can slip into the Realms of the Wild; Virtue of Crackpot Crones whose peals of laughter peel away the plastic passions and unpot the potted ones."[4]

TELEVISION SCREEN: The opening scene from *Roseanne* where the family is playing cards around the kitchen table. It ends with Roseanne winning the pot and laughing heartily with her mouth wide open.

Academic Joann: This image of laughing-out-loud women is a strong image that I take from my working-class background. A *source of strength* for me is the *image of women laughing around the kitchen table.* The sound of *MA'S hearty laughter* remains a powerful force for me. *SHEILA MA-HONEY'S giggling. AUNT LIL'S boisterous laughter* which literally shook us up. *MARINA'S cackling* with her nose going up and down. *JUDE'S loud and compelling howling.* And *VAVÕA* with her more *refined and sophisticated laughter.* These are all images that are dear to me.

When I began to think about this project I wanted to think of an image that confronts power. I visited my imagination. Once there I wondered. Or is that wandered. About. Wonder about. An image that resists power. It was waiting for me there. It tickled my imagination. My imagination started to giggle. LAUghing. LAUGHING OUT loud. FOR LAUGHING OUT LOUD. **FOR LAUGHING-OUT-LOUD WOMEN.** That was it.

Notes

1. Joan Riviere, "Womanliness as a Masquerade," *International Journal of Psychoanalysis* 10 (1929): 306.
2. "Womanliness as a Masquerade," 305.
3. Gloria Anzaldúa, *Making Face Making Soul/Hacienda Caras* (San Francisco: Aunt Lute Foundation, 1990), xv.
4. Mary Daly, *Wickedary* (Boston: Beacon Press, 1987), 142.

David Joseph

I was born June 30, 1954, in Arlington, California. Most of my early schooling was in the public schools in Mt. Vernon, Washington, on the Skagit River north of Seattle. After eighth grade I was selected to participate in Project Catch-Up, an intensive summer program for culturally disadvantaged underachievers at Western Washington State College in Bellingham. I became the poet laureate of Project Catch-Up and returned subsequently to become a staff member. I also audited the music classes of Mlle. Nadia Boulanger in Paris in 1979 but managed to garner no other degrees worth mentioning. My father was a retail clerk and my mother a grocery clerk. Both were union members. They met in Bremerton, Washington, where my mother grew up, when my father was in the Navy. My grandfather was a shipbuilder in the U.S. Naval Shipyard in Bremerton. My grandmother was in charge of eight children and the family farm in the watershed near the Bremerton shipyard. Generally, males on my mother's side went into the Navy and returned to work in the shipyard. Females generally met Navy boys and married. My grandfather on my father's side died in a mysterious accident when my father was young. My step-grandfather was a member of the Carpenters Union. I lived with him and my other grandmother in Riverside, California, and Reedsport, Oregon, for one year after the death of my mother. I have vivid memories of riding on their boat with them on the mouth of the big Umpqua River in Oregon. The snapshot of me, prob-

ably taken by my father, was taken on the blacktop in front of the basketball hoop in the backyard of our house in Stanwood, Washington, on the way to Camano Island on Puget Sound where we moved following my mother's death. I think I was about seventeen, and the year would have been 1971. In the photo I appeared as I wanted to be seen by the world with a measure of dignity previously not allowed while my mother had been alive. My confidence and self-esteem have always been so low that I've felt I didn't take good pictures on those rare occasions when someone would actually think of taking one of me. So this photo seems triply rare and precious. Many things were lost when our house burned down a few months before my mother's death. However, my father took a lot of slides and snapshots which he'd had at one time. But several moves and two divorces later for my father, I don't know how much he may still have in his possession or where they may be if still in existence.

Until recently David Joseph was an unemployed clerical worker with no prospects for ever working again in his occupational field, having been laid off by the University of California, San Francisco, after twelve years' service. Although contractually he was supposed to have had rehire rights, the UCSF Personnel Department had been discouraging about his prospects, until the intervention of the AFSCME and Walter Johnson, secretary-treasurer of the San Francisco Labor Council. Mr. Joseph is active in the labor movement and a member of AFSCME Local 3218 and a delegate to the Labor Council. He participated in a union-sponsored panel in which he detailed some of the practices which caused employees of companies such as the University of California, San Francisco to develop carpal tunnel syndrome. Mr. Joseph has been a contributor to *Synapse,* the news weekly at the University of California, San Francisco. Other publications have appeared in *The Rockefeller Quarterly, The Huron Review, Rolling Stone, Central Park, The San Francisco Review of Books, Iron* (in England), and the anthology *Homeless Not Helpless.* He appeared in the film *Navy Town.* He is the editor of *Working Classics,* the magazine of the creative work of working people. He speaks and appears on panels at various conferences discussing workers' writing and literary theory. For now he lives on his sailboat in Richardson Bay near San Francisco with his wife, Carol Tarlen.

David Joseph

Breaking Through
the Sounds
of Silence

Because of my working-class background, it is very difficult for me to speak, write, or concentrate. There are walls around everything, and when I try to communicate, I must bludgeon my way through, unfortunately usually unsuccessfully. To speak or write or do anything at all is a tremendous struggle. This idea of struggle has kept me going, so far, battling against seemingly impossible odds to express my own viewpoint on my working-class life and experiences. Struggle has kept me alive.

No one in my family told stories. Communication does not seem to have been one of their high priorities. Consequently, I have had little means of developing a narrative framework by which I could begin to grasp what happened to them. Whenever I would ask questions, which would be often, I'd be met by a silence of incomprehension. In this total absence of an orally transmitted identity, one of my brothers just made up a background for himself. This inability to get answers about the most basic matters of genealogy or a family story, which has been one of the frustrating experiences of my life, seems to represent a collective impotence. Marx's axiom in *Capital* that the working class does not exist apart from its own conscious knowledge of itself would mean that we were working class in objective fact only, since we had no received body of information by which to define ourselves.

Even when the connections were miraculously offered, I missed the moment of opportunity. For example, at one point a few years back before my grandma lapsed into her oncoming senility, she offered me a leather-covered booklet containing family charts. For some reason I did not understand this was my once-in-a-lifetime chance and did not snap them into my clutches at that instant, and so the window closed forever.

Perhaps it was because of my inability to interpret words and gestures that I was unable to respond appropriately in the situation; since language was not one of the great shared arts of my family, I was not then and am not now able to follow what people are trying to say unless they do so in a straightforward matter-of-fact manner. My grandma, though quite lively and interested in things, had no sense of humor. She said that the comics in the Sunday paper weren't funny. My grandma was shaped like no other human being I've ever seen before or since, kind of like a five-foot-diameter human ball with a big, round Okie face, no breasts that I could make out, wide hips ideally suited for a birthing machine. Her short, stocky, strong arms and legs were perfect for the arduous chores of farm work.

My grandma's biscuits were the size of small loaves of bread. Potatoes were called spuds, and mashed potatoes were always referred to as smashed spuds. She had strong hands for milking cows. She slopped the hogs, gathered eggs from the hen house and started churning butter, all before breakfast. Every morning would find her chopping wood and lighting the stove to cook and heat water.

Grandma admired all her grandchildren. She was fond of giving us affectionate hugs, and we were fond of receiving them. The only words from Grandma were ones of admiration. Grandma meant food and hugs.

The one "fact" my grandma managed to impart to me about her upbringing was that her father or her grandfather, I'm not sure which, had been a healer. Whatever that was I didn't and don't know, except that they were politically suppressed by medical doctors, but this identity seemed to be significant to her, at least enough so to tell me.

My grandpa on my mama's side was terse, gruff, and grumpy, given to scowling alternated with frequent outbursts of anger. I was terrified of him. When he wasn't working in the U.S. Naval Shipyard, he busied himself with the endless chores involved with keeping up the woodland farm they had built. When he rested, mostly watching television, sleeping, or taking snuff, he wanted no one to disturb him. He wore several layers of clothes in the hottest weather. I admired him for the farm buildings he had constructed with the help of his sons, but most of all for the concrete dam he built on the creek on their land which connected to the pipeline to the house and formed the gravitational system for their drinking water, running downhill a distance of several acres—the whole thing I thought quite ingenious.

Grandma and Grandpa had eight children, four girls and four boys, my mama being the second oldest. Grandma had been born in Oklahoma. She and Grandpa were married in Idaho, I think. Mama spent her childhood near Boise before they moved to the woods outside of Belfair, near Bremerton, Washington, across the Puget Sound from Seattle, so that Grandpa could work in the U.S. Naval Shipyard in Bremerton. Kitsap, the county they lived in, had been a hotbed of radicalism with a contingent of the Industrial Workers of the World (IWW, also known as the Wobblies) organizing in the back woods there earlier in the century, but there was never any consciousness of that history either. The family were, however, staunch, New Deal Democrats, nonreligious and nondenominational as far as I could tell.

My uncles often spoke in mumbles, slurring their words so I couldn't understand what they were saying. When asked what they said or to repeat themselves, they got flustered, frustrated, or mad. I, and one of my brothers, have had the same problems. Even today people sometimes don't respond when I speak, possibly because they do not hear me.

Perhaps the silence that surrounded them led my mother and aunts to become obsessed with religion. They became Jehovah's Witnesses. Mama was the first to convert. Dad refused. The rest of the family ridiculed our beliefs. For example, Jehovah's Witnesses were not supposed to take blood transfusions. A rumor had spread among Witnesses that Wonder Bread had blood added to it when it was made. My uncles were fond of cracking jokes at us as they chomped down their sandwiches of Wonder Bread. But we were really afraid to eat the stuff for fear of ingesting the blood.

Growing up as a Jehovah's Witness was tough all round. It set us apart immediately from our peers in the classroom. From the flag salute first thing in the morning through the celebration of every holiday from Halloween to Christmas, which we were prohibited from celebrating, we were marked as different, and by no means could we explain the reasoning since it all had to do with dogma which made no sense. The religion seemed to be centered on the idea of denial of joy.

One thing connected with the religion as far as my family was concerned was an obsession with truth, that is, with telling the truth. We were so impressed with the idea of always telling the truth that I was left without the conception of how to stretch it for purposes of survival. I still have a difficult time trying to elaborate the truth, which puts me at a considerable disadvantage when it comes to the job search.

Grandma and Grandpa had been serious disciplinarians. There was a big, black leather strap hanging off the wall in their house. My mama was also a true believer in corporal punishment. Another thing that I noticed was that some of my aunts seemed to have an extreme dislike for their dad and never wanted to be left alone with him.

My parents were unable to spend a great deal of time with my two brothers and me. We had each been born eighteen months apart, so we were all infants and toddlers at the same time. Our mama had to deal with the formative development of all three at once, and she couldn't handle it. She constantly complained of migraines. I bore the brunt of her anger. She beat me a minimum of once a day, my middle brother a little less than me, my youngest brother a little less than him. The beatings increased in frequency, duration, and severity. She said she did it to me because she loved me, which was bewildering. Though I thought that she probably really did love me, being belted and bruised all over my body, raising welts and drawing blood, did not seem like affection to me. This so-called discipline was supposed to correct my bad behavior, but I was always at a complete loss to know what, if anything, I had done wrong.

The fourteen years I lived with my mama, she physically and emotionally abused me every day of my life. Her abuse included assaults with anything at hand including the furniture. One of my earliest memories is of Mama chaining me to a clothesline behind our house. As I became a teenager and her abuse continued unabated, I warned her first that if she didn't stop I would fight back, and then, whenever she started striking me, I defended myself.

Shortly after I began to strike back, she was killed in a car-train collision when trying to get to work on time at the supermarket where she clerked. She had attempted to cross the railroad tracks that crossed the one-lane dead-end dirt road we lived on ahead of an oncoming train. She needed the job. She needed to be on time. She needed to cross the tracks. Such was the dialectic that ended my mama's life.

Her passing caused me great grief and, simultaneously, great relief. It ended years of misery for both of us, yet left me with no shared resolution of our relationship. It has been years now since I could recall the sound of her voice, such as when I would hear my name called and spring bolt upright in bed. Unfortunately the pain of the blows is still very much with me.

During all that time Mama spent beating me, my dad was mostly silent, watching television. The nightly ritual from the moment my dad arrived home was an endless barrage of rage and sarcasm from Mama about her situation, some of it rational, much of it not, met mostly by Dad's silence. Mama was literally screaming for help, and not just to Dad, but to everyone within earshot, especially all the relatives. She would scream, "I'm crazy, I'm going to kill myself, I want a divorce." She was telegraphing her distress signal, and there was no way anyone could have missed it.

What has always amazed me was how everyone could choose to ignore her. Rather than intervening to save her, they were muddling through their own lives, apparently thinking she was just that way and that everything would always be the same, never seeing the train coming.

Mama continued her monologue interminably. My dad used the TV to tune her out. The sound of my mama's voice, my dad's silence, and the television's imbecility went on late into the night, long after I went to bed. With no bedroom door to shut out the roar coming from the living room I heard every word from my mama's mouth and every sound from every program. I didn't get much sleep. I was tired in the mornings, never ready to wake up. I was tired all day. The routine was always the same. It never changed.

Dad also had a retail clerk job—as a shoe salesman in a department store—to tune out. Both my parents were rank-and-file members of the Retail Clerks union, but I don't remember them ever discussing union business. If they attended any membership meetings, it must have been a rare occasion such as a contract renewal. At that time the Retail Clerks were pretty dispirited, being under the thumb of the state Teamsters boss who controlled them, even though they were an AFL–CIO union. The Retail Clerks did not have a reputation for being democratic. Fundamentally, though, my dad wasn't suited to his job. He complained that he got tired of spending his days looking at everything from the point of view of women's feet. He later took a variety of low-paying jobs, doing everything from farm work to clerking in a convenience store. He was always proud of the work he did and enjoyed showing me around his places of employment.

The third thing my dad used the television to tune out may have been a troubled childhood. I was able to divine that his mother and father had divorced, and that sometime afterward his dad had been killed in some kind of mysterious accident. Even in school my dad had apparently been pretty mute. In probably the only story I ever did hear him utter, his teacher asked, "How do we brush our teeth?" My dad said he thought he knew the answer to that question. He was proud, excited to be able to know an answer and get himself called upon. "Up and down," he said. The schoolmarm replied, "Wrong. Up and down on the uppers and up and down on the lowers." My dad never spoke again in school.

Dad's inability to construct a personal history that I can carry with me is a constant in my life. I once gave him a tape recorder and asked him to record any memories or descriptions of anything he wanted to on it, thinking it might be a way he could express himself. The method had worked excellently when my girlfriend's dad, a truck driver, had tried it, and we even ended up publishing one of his stories in my magazine, *Working Classics*. But with my dad nothing ever came of it.

In school I was a butt of jokes, because I lived on the wrong side of the tracks, had the wrong religion picked out for me, had parents who made their living by the wrong occupations, and was socially maladjusted because of my home life. Though considered bright scholastically, I was thought of as a troublemaker. I went on to become the class clown and an outcast. I got progressively into more trouble.

In 1968 I was sent to a summer program at Western Washington State College in Bellingham. It was called Project Catch-Up and was designed for adolescents who were underachievers. The kids who attended Project Catch-Up were white working class, Chicano, and Native American. I loved it. I thrived on it. For the first time in my life I got the attention I craved. I loved the other kids. They were my people, my peers. They all came from culturally disadvantaged backgrounds just like myself. They were diverse, excited, and physically appealing. Unlike the kids who sneered at me in my school, the Project Catch-Up kids didn't deny one another's essential human dignity.

1968 was a defining year for everyone everywhere. Workers and students around the world were rising up. May Day in Paris. The Summer Olympics in Mexico City. The Democratic Convention in Chicago. Black Power. La Raza. Indian Power. Women's Liberation. Gay Rights. The Anti-War Movement. Millions marched against the war. Soldiers in the states were organizing themselves into unions opposing the military hierarchy. It was scary, but wonderful, a giddy and naive time, when it seemed that the whole world was about to rise up into revolution, or if not the whole world, at least the United States. People seemed determined. They were very hopeful.

The idea of struggle, the very word "struggle," had a profound effect on me. It was like a mantra. All I had to do was say it and apply it to whatever was at hand. It meant I could fight back. It meant I could solve problems a little at a time. It was a word, the possibility for personal power in my own life. It meant that everything was not always the same. Things changed, and I could have something to do with it. I did not have to just take everything lying down. I could actively have some say. Even within my own thoughts and feelings, I could struggle with an idea. I could replace a bad thought-pattern with a better one. Struggle saved me.

My only survival tool has been struggle. How have I used it? I would struggle to get up in the morning, struggle to wake up, deal with my depression, with the pain of having been abused the first fourteen years of my life, with thoughts of suicide; struggle to go to college, complete my courses, go to my job, do my tasks; struggle to write, to connect one word to another; struggle to love another person. I would struggle to remove myself from a bench where I would sit for hours at a time, so that I could go to class. Every day was struggle, every moment. Every day I would say to myself, "What can I do today?" If I can accomplish only one thing all day, at least that may make a difference. I have to consciously think of it all the time, to try, to do, because it doesn't come naturally. It isn't natural, not to me, not even now. I am still struggling with struggle. Now as I write I am again painfully aware of the silences that have controlled my life. History and the economy have run out, and I know how it is to be discarded as so much human excrement. In 1980 I got a clerical job at a university. It was unionized, modestly salaried, secure and steady—in fact, everyone considered it a job for life with a good pension plan for retirement. But concomitant with it was the Reagan counterrevolution, which would represent the redistribution of wealth to the rich accompanied by the withering away of the middle class. After twelve years, I was laid off.

This job meant a lot to me, since I had no hope of ever getting "professional" employment. Although I attended college, I never finished. I felt alienated from my middle-class peers. Writing papers was agony, because the linear, rational thinking required of them was impossible for someone with my background. Therefore, the working class for me is something there is no escape from. It's an eternal present as well as a memory.

The university's Personnel Department had evidently decided to weed out all former employees it deemed undesireables. I had been chosen to go on the compost heap for not fitting the new professional business image. My speech was too stumbling, too halting. Too working-class. Although I have tried to improve upon my communication skills in order to fit in to the new environment, there is a certain level of development which it would be impossible for me to ever attain. I am not going to be able to transcend my working-class background completely. I wouldn't want to even if I could.

One woman in the Personnel Department read to me from my Personnel file, all about how badly I interviewed. Some of the comments management had written into my file had been quite vicious. I was already feeling bad enough from being arbitrarily laid off; this wasn't the encouragement I needed to send me off on a job search. Her "help" succeeded in making me feel miserable.

My family used a system of coding which I use to write poetry and fiction. Where this system leads from here I don't know. My family spoke in the language of violence, of physical and emotional abuse. They spoke too in the language of silence, not just of suppression, but also of being overwhelmed by their lives. My mama screamed in an inchoate agony for help. My dad spoke in a pantomime guiding people through the sites and substance of his worklife. Between the poverty of spoken communication and the onslaught of desperate verbiage, I found the impetus to connect words into a descriptive lyric and an attempt to create a story based in context out of the coding and pantomime.

In his book *Silence,* John Cage, the composer, explains how in music silence is the part which occurs apart from the composition and performance, that is, it is extra-musical, not really silence at all, but actually everyday sounds. These everyday sounds occur all the time, before, after, and simultaneously with the music. They may be heard during a pause or a quiet passage. They are essentially purposeless as far as the composing and performing of music is concerned, inasmuch as the purpose of music is music. As Cage was interested in composing a music of sounds, he felt an affinity with their "purposelessness" and so created a music of athematic purposelessness.

The literature of the working class consists of the purposelessness of silence. But sounds are not necessarily purposeless; their own purposes may just be irrelevant to or in contradiction with music. There is the literature of the cultural elite, and then there is the working class. We are outside its scope or purpose. Part of its purpose is to deny the working class's existence. We are murdered while the old-moneyed family goes on to inherit Howard's End. John Cage could be famous for his purposeless music, whether it had any significance or not, because of his education in the academies of music and his connection to eastern establishment art circles. A working-class artist has none of these options available.

Recently I saw *The Long Day Closes,* an autobiographical film written and directed by Terrence Davies. Just as in his previous film, *Distant Voices, Still Lives,* his working-class English family sang a lot socially— a remarkable phenomenon, possible only prior to the advent of television, I thought. Then I remembered how one of my brothers and I used to sing together in the back of our station wagon on our way to our grandma's, how my dad enjoyed playing phonograph records of musicals. One, *Carousel,* was a powerful and tragic tale of a carny worker in a sailing town. My dad loved it, but my mama hated to hear it. The story and its music are overwhelmingly sad. To this day that record still has the same effect on me. Despite the sadness, the music provided a catharsis my dad apparently needed. Like my mama I sometimes cannot take listening to it, but sometimes I feel a need to. Somehow through the music the words take on more significance, the lyrics become poetry, the poetry of the tragedy of ordinary people's lives.

Georges Sorel in *Meditations on Violence* said that the working class would have to organize itself in obscurity. Like my mama hiding in plain sight, the working class is resigned in obscurity. This principle certainly is true when we consider the art and literature of the working class. Jude remains obscure.

Any art of the working class is not going to be encouraged and brought to light by the power elite who own, operate, and control our society. If they select any such work for commendation, they do not necessarily have our best interests in mind. Therefore, working-class art and literature are do-it-yourself projects. That silence equals death is not only true for AIDS survivors. The working class must break through the walls of silence.

In Haiti workers are paid fourteen cents an hour. But is that low enough? The owning class will not be satisfied with a wage of one cent a century. The corpses' bones can surely be ground down to a fine powder. In these dark times it is imperative that we seize the means of creation.

Part Three

Places and Displacements

Maggie Anderson

My father's family was from Preston County, West Virginia, and nearly all of the men and some of the women worked on the railroad. The men were machinists or engineers; the women worked as dispatchers. In the second generation, some of them worked for the West Virginia Pulp and Paper Mill. My mother's people were small farmers in southwestern Pennsylvania, on the West Virginia border, and some of her family in the second generation worked in the coal mines. Since my connection was strongest to the women in both families, I also remember their domestic labor. My father's sister Nita hauled water, stoked their coal furnace, and washed clothes on a wringer washer into the late 1960s. My mother's sister Grace, who lived alone in a tiny apartment in Grafton, West Virginia,

was a case worker for the West Virginia Department of Welfare. My parents had college educations, became teachers, and left the West Virginia mountains. They were singular exceptions in their families. In the second and third generations, only two of us had education beyond high school. My cousins work as service workers, and there are only three of us still alive.

My education and my writing remain exceptions in my family in my generation, as in my parents'. I become more and more convinced of the difficult truth Thomas Hardy has his character, Jude, come to in *Jude the Obscure:* "It takes two or three generations to do what I tried to do in one." My parents tried to move from one class to another in the space of one generation. My mother's early death sent us right back home. My cousins did not attempt that path, and while the distance I have come as a teacher and a writer has been far, geographically I have come only two hours away from the West Virginia border. No one else in my family ever left the state.

This photograph of me and my father was taken when I was about seven years old. I have no photographs of myself from the time of my mother's death when I was nine until after I graduated from high school. My mother was the family historian and the record disappeared with her death. I had one aunt who had a photograph album and there were some adolescent photos of me in it. The album, along with all my aunt's belongings, was destroyed in the 1985 flood which put her house in the Pulp Mill Bottom in Parsons, West

Virginia, under water for five days. I don't know the exact date of this photograph, but it would have been shortly after we learned of my mother's illness. We were in West Virginia for the summer. My mother took the picture.

Maggie Anderson is the author of three books of poems, *A Space Filled with Moving* (University of Pittsburgh Press, 1992), *Cold Comfort* (Pittsburgh, 1986), and *Years That Answer* (Harper and Row, 1980). She is the editor of *Hill Daughter,* new and selected poems by West Virginia poet Louise McNeill (University of Pittsburgh Press, 1991) and coeditor of

A Gathering of Poets (Kent State University Press, 1992). Recent poems by Maggie Anderson have appeared in *The American Poetry Review, The American Voice, Ploughshares,* and *The Women's Review of Books.*

Among Maggie Anderson's grants and awards for her poetry are two fellowships from the National Endowment for the Arts and grants from the Pennsylvania Council on the Arts and the West Virginia Arts and Humanities Commission. She has been a resident fellow at the MacDowell Colony and was the Isabella Gardner Fellow there in fall 1990. Maggie Anderson teaches creative writing at Kent State University and she is a member of the Board of Directors of the Associated Writing Programs.

Maggie Anderson

> "A place that ever was lived in is like a fire that never goes out. It flares up, it smolders for a time, it is fanned or smothered by circumstance, but its being is intact, forever fluttering within it, the result of some original ignition."
> —Eudora Welty, "Some Notes on River Country"

Two Rivers

I was born in 1948 in New York City to parents who were the first generation to have education and to leave their working-class families in the West Virginia mountains. My father taught Latin at a private boys' school and my mother taught political science at Hunter College, yet they had worked out some ways of carrying the mountain culture with them. My father sang West Virginia songs and union songs, and he taught them to me. My mother made small vegetable gardens on the fire escapes of every apartment building we lived in. Every summer we went back to West Virginia to visit the family. It was important to my parents that I know the world they had come from, but they clearly had other ambitions for my life. They wanted me to achieve what they had, only more easily. To me, shifting back and forth between these two worlds was dizzying. I lived something like what W.E.B. Du Bois, speaking of race, calls a life of "two-ness."[1] For most of my childhood, I inhabited two worlds, not wholly at home in either one.

From my parents, I learned to speak two languages, and in the car on the hot drive back to New York at the end of summer they retrained my speech. In my summer world were the tiny railroad town in the mountains where my aunts and uncles lived, the fast river that cut between the steep hills, and the winding drives up dark hollows to visit one after another of our kin. In my school year world were tall buildings and buses, museums and concerts, and the large houses of my wealthy friends who had house-keepers and gardeners and who gave birthday parties with hired clowns. My life was divided in this way, culturally and regionally, until I was nine years old and my mother died.

My father tried for a time after my mother's death to maintain his as-similated life in New York, but when I was thirteen years old he gave it up. He did what all good mountain people do when there is trouble: he came back home. West Virginia was only partly "home" to me, and I spent the first few years there bored and impatient with my teachers and my class-mates, homesick for subways and exhaust fumes. I was mocked for my ac-cent, my clothes, and my noticeably better education, and I learned to make my own assimilations, gradually shedding my city speech and my knowledge of what is referred to in the mountains as "the outside world." Through the convincing social pressures of adolescence and the shared parenting of my father's brothers and sisters, I became a West Virginian. This was not what my mother and father had dreamed for me, but it was the home my father was able to offer. I lost immediate access to the urban middle-class privileges my parents had hoped I might come to take for granted. What I acquired was a more one-dimensional, and a more solid, sense of home.

I loved my father's people fiercely, with all the complicated angers and sorrows of kin. I learned to accept their teasing, and their admiration, of the unique position my father and I had in the family, our "book learn-ing," and our worldliness in comparison to their lives. From the privileges I had as a young child, I knew there were more possibilities than their cir-cumscribed lives allowed, yet I had also seen how difficult it was to attain these, and to maintain them once attained.

There is a telling passage in West Virginia writer Mary Lee Settle's novel, *The Clam Shell,* that defines something of what I remember of my father's complex assimilations to the New York City world of my early years. When my father sang the old mountain songs for his middle-class New York friends, it was a kind of cultural curiosity, quaint and fraught with self-parody. Even as a child, I was made uneasy by it. But his singing was always clear and whole with his sisters in the summers, after supper on the porch. My father had to learn to joke his past into his present, and he probably often hated himself for that implicit denial of his people.

The heroine of Settle's novel leaves her hometown of Canona, West Virginia, to go to a women's college in Virginia, "the school picked . . . by generations of hope."[2] She learns almost immediately how her home is perceived by the wealthy Virginians who are her classmates, and she learns equally quickly the value of self-parody to the assimilation process:

> "West Virginia!" she says, and that way of saying it, that edge of amusement, will diminish me over and over again at moments of triumph or exhilaration. The coal trains, the sad-faced quiet men, my father, the Jenny Lind shacks, the sumac, the manners tight as muscles, the flowers that grow near trestles, the iron wheels shunting, the waterfalls, the tall trees, the wild sharp cliffs, oh I am them all, coal and green leaves, slag and shale, dirty river and blank-faced mountain silence. I turn into the light, casting for a self presentable enough, cunning with stupidity. I walk into the mirror of her dull eyes. I hate what I see there: I see, for the first time, parody. I play for safety, placate, become my own jester.[3]

When she parodies a banjo player and sings a mountain song, the other young women ease into laughter and clapping, and she learns how the social currency of shame is also internalized rage:

> So, in our ways, we betray our pasts. It is a part of the remaking of the East Coast in its always hoped-for image. It is for this so much blood and money has been paid. Now that I have done it, for the first time, a raw, red vessel fills in me, and I know what it is to hold angry blood that cannot burst into words.[4]

While the temptation to deny my own connections to West Virginia has sometimes been strong, my clearest memory of denying the whole of myself through parody is of parodying "city people" for the benefit of my West Virginia friends. Eventually, I came to hate myself for that betrayal, as I hated my father for what I perceived as his, and my father and I resented, misunderstood, and grieved for each other out of the complexities of trying to move in the space of just one generation from one class to another, and then of being forced by circumstances to move back.

I remember less about my mother. She became ill with leukemia when I was seven years old and spent most of the last two years of her life in and out of hospitals. My mother had been raised on a small farm, and I remember that she wanted me to know the names of trees and flowers and plants. She took me to the Bronx Botanical Gardens and to parks in New Jersey where she taught me how to tell a maple from an oak by the shape of the leaves. I can recall only one or two conversations with my mother. When I was about to turn six, she asked me if there was anything special I wanted for my birthday. Since I had been learning the wonders of elaborate birthday parties from my wealthy friends at school, I told her I would like to have a party. She turned suddenly somber, or maybe angry. Her question was no longer casual, and she frightened me with her intensity. I remember that my mother took me by the shoulders and her voice echoes still with the resonance of instructions from the dead: "I don't care what you do with your life, but I *don't* want you to want a party." Although I am sure I have exaggerated the ferocity of her injunction through the years, I am also sure that I have not invented what she said. A class-based lesson for the second generation: "This is not a good, or even a possible, thing to want. This is going to cost you. It is not going to be fun." As an adult, I have read into her words what she did not say, the unspoken "for people like us," by which I am sure she intended both our sex and the roots of our lives in another class, in another place. My school friends in New York could afford parties, both economically and in the sense of the leisure to wish for them. This was a luxury, my mother's words implied, that people like us could *not* afford.

This is the personal, the anecdotal, the stories of one individual life: a mother who died before I knew her, before I knew to ask the questions I am now burning to know and cannot ask. How did she make that enormous leap? What did she give up? What did it cost her? How did she even conceive the idea of it? And what did it cost her mother and sister to support her ambitions, the *one* among them who might break the pattern of generations of limited possibilities for women, especially for women of the working class? I remember a deep sorrow always on my mother's face, and the few photographs I have of her reflect that. She is almost never smiling. It is impossible for me now to know how much of her sadness might have been due to her illness and pain and how much the result of some other grief, or exhaustion, connected to the struggle of her own necessary assimilations. My own grief is that I cannot ask her.

My mother's lessons and my father's songs were designed to teach me working-class mountain culture. From their examples and their lives, I learned that the community is more important than the individual, and that the achievements of any one individual are the achievements of the group. Because my parents had managed to move some distance away from the working class themselves, the tone of their messages to me was that of an urgent witnessing. Despite my father's sometimes self-parodying assimilation, he did not fail to teach me the Florence Reece song "Which Side Are You On?" and there was never any doubt in my mind about which side was the "right" one. Both of my parents had been chosen from their families of origin to get "*the* education," and everyone else worked so that they might achieve. The strongest lesson they passed on to me was that the individual from the working class achieves *for* the group, on behalf of, and because of, the sacrifices of a community of others.

When we returned to West Virginia, my father wanted the help of his family in raising me. The additional reason for the move back only recently occurred to me: that the life we had in New York City required my mother's (larger) salary as well as my father's. My father was able to return the emotional support his family gave us by helping to pay their doctor and hospital bills and by providing extra money during long strikes and layoffs. My father and I were odd in the family, but we were also a valued part of a network of kin.

When I was in high school, it seemed to me as if I would have to make some kind of final choice between West Virginia and "the outside world." I imagined only two options since it was that bifurcated culture I had been raised to. The friends I had who did well in school had the same burning to get out that my parents once had. Because of their intelligence, their gumption, and the economic support of their families, my parents had educated themselves out of the working class and out of the hills. They had taken what the self-deprecating regional joke calls "Reading, writing, and the road to Ohio." The lesson was not, however, lost on me that my mother's death had sent my father right back home, and that his family had taken us in. I think I came, for a time, to love West Virginia even more intensely, or perhaps simple-mindedly, because it seemed to me that my parents had abandoned it. I sentimentalized working-class West Virginia and yearned, in a way, for what my grandparents had raised their children to fight up out of: hard labor and the exotic geography; the comfort of the old country's foreign tongue. Much later, when I began to try to write seriously about the lives of my West Virginia people, I wanted to tell the story clearly and without sentimentality. It has taken me many years to realize that to tell our story clearly from my point of view, I must acknowledge fully *both* my worlds.

This is, of course, a privileged struggle. I have never worked in a factory or a mill, but I have seen the marks of that labor, and the domestic labor of my aunts, on bodies and faces and imaginations. Yet, as a writer who is two generations away from the working class, I find it impossible not to write of those lives, even though my own relationship to them is painful, ambiguous, and complex. I had to learn that the assimilated middle-class existence my parents had made was a temporary one, and my own life choices have been compromised, as my parents' were, by the love and pull of kin. I did not leave West Virginia until I was forty years old, after all my people had died. I live now, not in New York City, but in Ohio, where I teach at a state university and where I like to believe I have something of particular value to offer the first- or second-generation working-class men and women who are my students.

In some ways, my perspective has been that of an outsider, and much of my work has been occupied with insider/outsider concerns. I have lived among people whose lives are very different from my own, and I sometimes feel an awkward intimacy. I am always wary about what I assert that I understand. I know the lives of the working poor and the unemployed in West Virginia because they are the lives my people lived. But I have known something of the lives of privilege also because, for a brief time in my early childhood, I was a marginal insider in those worlds. I have felt largely protected from the harsh labor of my family and the economic tenuousness they lived with. Yet, I never felt "marginal" to them. For me, marginality exists only in that other world where, as my mother told me when I asked, "Politics means money, who has it and who doesn't." No matter how much middle-class credibility I may have achieved for myself as a tenured academic and as a writer, I always feel only limited, temporary, conditional inclusion. And there are still many days when I cannot believe that I am actually paid for reading and talking about books.

From the world my parents wanted me to inherit, I learned books, art, curiosity, language, the right fork to use at the dinner party, and a small degree of the confidence of privilege. From the world my parents were born to and the one my father took me back to, I learned determination, humor, the harsh lessons of class in our country, and a sense of community. In my poems, I want to write in the cadences and idiosyncratic phrasings of West Virginia mountain speech, as well as with the diction of my educated and formally trained intelligence. I want to write about the lives of miners and steelworkers because I know those lives, but I also would never want to pretend that I have worked in that way or that I have not had the opportunity to read a lot of books. It would be pointless, self-deprecating, and insulting to my people who made it possible for me, to deny the indispensable privilege my education has been. Yet, it pains me to realize that nothing in my education prepared me to witness as eloquently as I would like to their lives, or even to my own in relation to class. Much of my writing has been a struggle to unite my "two-nesses," to speak with the full breadth of my experience and understanding.

In the poem "Long Story," I have included some "rules" for mountain storytelling: "a good story takes awhile," and "if it has people in it, you have to swear / that it is true." There are several stories in the poem, and several interlocking communities of people: the kids I am walking with, the "toothless Field sisters" and "my Uncle Craig," the "miners with amputated limbs" and those sealed up inside the mountain at the end of the poem. The poem incorporates both literal accounts and metaphorical ones. The final image of the poem is based on several historical mine disasters in West Virginia. My own position in the poem is tenuously at home. This is only "one of the places I think of as home," and my insider-ness is emphasized through the creation of an outsider "you" who does *not* know "this place, or how tight and dark the hills / pull in around the river and the railroad." I have a solid, accepted place in the community. I am not a stranger here; the kids know me and they know my dog. But I also, by implication, think of some other places as "home." The kids and I both "know mines like (we) know hound dogs," and my outsider-ness is somewhat like that of the children: I know the mines but do not work in them. The suggestion, of course, is that my people do. In "Long Story," the central focus is not an individual but a community of people, and the carriers of that community's stories are the children.

The difficult struggle for those of us who are first- or second-generation daughters and sons of working-class people is never to forget where we came from and never to deny what we have been privileged to learn. My working-class roots are also intricately tied to a particular region of the country, the place my parents came from and the place they left when they tried to move beyond the class they were born to. As a child, I saw these two places in terms of the two rivers that wound through them, the Hudson River in New York City, and the Cheat River in Preston County, West Virginia, where we went every summer. Now, these rivers seem to me metaphorically evocative for what they suggest also about the complexities of class in my life.

The Hudson River is both straightforward and complex. Its passage is paradoxical since it contains both salt and fresh water and flows in two directions. I remember it as scattered with ocean-going ships, ferries, and tugboats passing the Little Red Lighthouse under the George Washington Bridge. It is a river of transport and possibility, efficient and busy with boats. Along its banks, I was born and my mother died. The Hudson is my river of origin, yet its bridges were the path my mother took away from me, to the other side.

The Cheat River is fast and, largely, unnavigable, full of sharp turns and unpredictable depths. Every summer three or four children drown trying to swim in it. It seems to get lost sometimes below coal tipples and canyons of trees where the road goes up. Just south of Morgantown, the channel narrows and it becomes a deep lake at the end of the Cheat River Gorge. I know the way this river turns and threatens, floods and cheats us, the way it draws us in and can destroy. I also know how wild and extravagant it is, churned up in spring by whitewater and sunlight.

In my writing, I want both of my rivers and both of my languages: the books and the questions my parents educated themselves, and me, to value; and the beautiful speech of my people who lived all their lives along the Cheat River, who worked on the railroad and in the pulp mills and in dark kitchens, and who spoke a language necessarily welded to tools and labor. My people knew what they could afford to know, and they knew I was learning something in "the outside world" that was different and large. Not all of them thought this was a good idea, but none of them was ever afraid to say what they thought. Although all of them are dead now, their talk goes deep in me, and tricky, like the slippery truths of the rivers.

Notes

1. W.E.B. Du Bois, *The Souls of Black Folk* (New York: New American Library, Signet, 1969), 45.
2. Mary Lee Settle, *The Clam Shell* (New York: Charles Scribner's Sons, 1971), 27.
3. Ibid., 95.
4. Ibid., 96.

Maggie Anderson

Long Story

> To speak in a flat voice
> Is all that I can do.
> —James Wright

I need to tell you that I live in a small town
in West Virginia you would not know about.
It is one of the places I think of as home.

When I go for a walk, I take my basset hound
whose sad eyes and ungainliness always draw
a crowd of children. She tolerates anything
that seems to be affection, so she lets the kids
put scarves and ski caps on her head
until she starts to resemble the women who have to dress
from rummage sales in poverty's mismatched polyester.

The dog and I trail the creek bank with the kids,
past clapboard row houses with Christmas seals
pasted to the windows as a decoration.
Inside, television glows around the vinyl chairs
and curled linoleum, and we watch someone old
perambulating to the kitchen on a shiny walker.
Up the hill in town, two stores have been
boarded up beside the youth center, and miners
with amputated limbs are loitering outside
the Heart and Hand. They wear Cat diesel caps
and spit into the street. The wind
carries on, whining through the alleys,
rustling down the sidewalks, agitating
leaves, and circling the courthouse steps
past the toothless Field sisters who lean
against the flagpole holding paper bags
of chestnuts they bring to town to sell.

History is one long story of what happened to us,
and its rhythms are local dialect and anecdote.
In West Virginia a good story takes awhile,
and if it has people in it, you have to swear
that it is true. I tell the kids the one about
my Uncle Craig who saw the mountain move
so quickly and so certainly it made the sun
stand in a different aspect to his little town
until it rearranged itself and settled down again.
This was his favorite story. When he got old,
he mixed it up with baseball games, his shift boss
pushing scabs through a picket line, the Masons
in white aprons at a funeral, but he remembered
everything that ever happened, and he knew how far
he lived from anywhere you would have heard of.

Anything that happens here has a lot of versions,
how to get from here to Logan twenty different ways.
The kids tell me convoluted country stories
full of snuff and bracken, about how long
they sat quiet in the deer blind with their fathers

waiting for the ten-point buck that got away.
They like to talk about the weather,
how the wind we're walking in means rain,
how the flood pushed cattle fifteen miles downriver.

These kids know mines like they know hound dogs
and how the sirens blow when something's wrong.
They know the blast, and the stories, how
the grown-ups drop whatever they are doing
to get out there. Story is shaped
by sound, and it structures what we know.
They told me this, and three of them
swore it was true, so I'll tell you
even though I know you do not know
this place, or how tight and dark the hills
pull in around the river and the railroad.

I'll say it as the children spoke it,
in the flat voice of my people:
down in Boone County, they sealed up
forty miners in a fire. The men who had come
to help tried and tried to get down to them,
but it was a big fire and there was danger,
so they had to turn around
and shovel them back in. All night long
they stood outside with useless picks and axes
in their hands, just staring at the drift mouth.
Here's the thing: what the sound must have been,
all those fire trucks and ambulances, the sirens,
and the women crying and screaming out
the names of their buried ones, who must have
called back up to them from deep inside
the burning mountain, right up to the end.

I was born September 9, 1944, in New Rochelle, New York. My father, Peter Mirabella, worked in his father's hardware store for a while and then became an office manager for a small business. His parents, Michele Mirabelli and Giuseppina Sperano, were both born in Altamonte, Calabria. My grandfather came to the United States from Italy and after finding work sent for my grandmother. Michele Mirabelli had two small businesses, a hardware and grocery store. My mother, Ida Capasso, was a housewife her entire life. Hermother, Rosa Volpe, came from the city of Amalfi, and her father, Dominick Capasso, came from the city of Caserta. He had owned a small grocery store for a while, but when he died he was driving a garbage truck.

M. Bella Mirabella is an associate professor of humanities in the Gallatin Division of New York University and codirector of the Gallatin Abroad Program in Florence, Italy. She is co-editor of *Left Politics and the Literary Profession* with Lennard Davis (Columbia University Press, 1991).

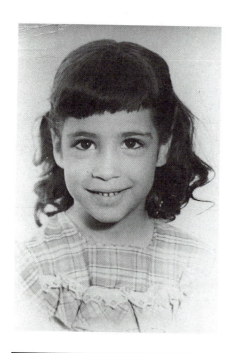

These two essays, "Connections" and "The Education of an Italian-American Girl Child," are companion pieces; they are part of a tapestry, some larger picture that I am putting together leading to a reclamation of memory, history, self, and place. The first piece concentrates on a trip to Italy fourteen years ago and the experience of affirming my place in that country's history. The second, while echoing themes from the first, centers on how I managed to become the "educated woman" I so dreamed about. Both record a life journey I am making and in that sense are like chapters in a book yet to be completed.

M. Bella Mirabella

Dedicated to
my father
Peter Mirabella
(1913–1986)

Connections

Ten years ago while still in graduate school studying for my Ph.D. I wrote the following:

I am the granddaughter of Italian immigrants who fled the poverty of Italy for a chance at what they hoped would be a better life in America. I imagine they left impoverished farms in the arid, cream-colored region of Southern Italy—at least my father's family did. Mother's family came from the town of Amalfi, perched high above the turquoise-blue Mediterranean. I wonder what they did—were they poor fishermen, shopkeepers, or laborers who could not find work?

So they piled into boats and came to New York City. Both sides of the family settled in the small ghettolike Italian section of New Rochelle, never really knowing each other though their children met and flirted with each other at school.

Grandpa Mirabella was a large-nosed, gruff man who had two businesses, owned some land, and fathered seven sons and one daughter. I do not know too much about Grandpa Capasso except that he had seven daughters and one son and was killed, still a young man, while getting out of a truck. He found a job in America and his death too. But Grandma Capasso made sure all her girls married, and would have forced Uncle Tony to do the same if he had not died of cancer at twenty-six. My father tells

First published in *The Gallatin Review,* Winter 1986–1987, pp. 16–22.

me he asked his father if he could go to school, but Grandpa Mirabella said "no" because he wanted his son to work in the hardware store. None of his sons or his daughter finished high school. Mother says none of her sisters considered doing anything other than what her mother had done—marrying and having children.

But somewhere on that journey from small villages to the American melting pot my family forgot that Italians were craftspeople even if only in a domestic sense. Grandma Capasso made pasta by rolling the dough out on a large enamel table with a long thin broomstick; and I hear that Grandpa Mirabella made his own wine and had a huge garden. But soon these shadows of the old country faded, and the family—grandparents, parents, uncles, aunts, nieces, cousins, nephews—all, every last one—turned from Italy, embraced and were absorbed by the enormous, indifferent, bland American culture.

So I sit at my typewriter putting my ancestors on paper, surrounded by a vast family of people I rarely see and who know little about me except that I live in New York City and am still in school. I feel a cord running through my center which ties me to those people, and the cord stretches to those small villages I have never seen though I have dreamed of living in them. But I am confused and bewildered about where I stand in all of this long history. Am I the one who is connected with this past because I see and feel the roots of it all? Or am I the fool, and has a joke been played on me? Has the entire strain, the long stretching generations of breeding Italians who lived and died so that I could sit and write this, lived and died for the questionable destiny of composing America's middle class? And am I the one who has fallen away and gotten lost in my endless amassing of useless knowledge? Have I cut myself off from them, or am I returning to the family of craftspeople?

I wrote this when I first began to think about my place in American culture and what it means to be an Italian-American. Since then I have thought a good deal more about this issue, and since then I have returned to Italy and to the villages that were the birthplaces of my grandparents.

It was seven years ago that my husband and I drove along the treacherously winding curves of the Amalfi Drive to the village of the same name. I knew there would be no relatives left for me to meet. I had always heard how Grandma Capasso and her brothers and sister had left Amalfi—some to go to the United States and some to southern parts of Italy where they settled in Calabria and Sicily. Grandma, only a girl of fifteen, had come to the United States.

So I had not expected to meet any relatives, but I also did not expect the beauty of Amalfi. The village—white and sparkling above the Mediterranean—climbs up the mountainside. It seems to cling to the mountain, perhaps protecting itself from the sea which had at one time been the livelihood of Amalfi. Now the village seems to thrive on tourists. Perhaps some of the tourists are like myself who come to see if there is any connection between themselves and that exquisite place.

Faced with the serene beauty of Amalfi I could not but wonder how my family must have felt to have such a magnificent haven, to have left a place of such loveliness and peace for the eastern United States. But more importantly I wondered how they felt leaving their history, their culture, their community.

Grandma Capasso had often talked of Amalfi. She spoke of the Chiesa di San'Andrea—St. Andrew's Church—and its huge stretch of stairs that leads up to the church doors and a view of the village and the sea below. The church plays a very important role in my family's legends, legends about Great-Grandma and her assignations with the spirits. The story goes that Great-Grandma went to very early mass each morning. One morning—so early it was still dark—the peasant woman made her way through the narrow, twisting streets of Amalfi to San'Andrea's. The morning was quiet and though quite dark, she noticed that a black dog—*il cane nero*—was walking behind her. The *cane nero* even followed her to the church and up the many stairs. As Great-Grandma made her way up, she turned to look at the dog and the stairs below; she and the dog were completely alone. She went up the last few steps and waited there for the church to open. But when she turned again the *cane nero* was no longer there. In the animal's place was a lovely woman, a woman of radiance and peace, a woman who—according to Grandma Capasso and any other relative who knows the story—was the Virgin Mary. This is how I recall hearing the story from Grandma Capasso, but my Italian relatives added that Great-Grandma entered the church with the *cane nero*. In the church were all the people she had known who had died. When she turned from this scene, she saw the Virgin in place of the dog.

I went to the Church of San'Andrea. On my way I walked past walls laden with bougainvillaea, past an open kitchen door with a chicken calmly resting next to a washing machine; I walked under laundry hanging from windows above and through the narrow streets wondering if I was passing some ancestral home. I did not see the *cane nero*, but I felt that I had somehow touched my past by being in that beautiful village above the sea and in that church that has always held such an important place in our family mythology.

After Amalfi we journeyed south to Calabria. We were not even certain of the name of the town from where my father's family had come—it was either Montalta or Altamonte. Besides this confused name, we had three other facts my father gave us that he had heard from his father: the town was the highest spot in the region; the town was so high that, although you were in the mountains, you could see the ocean; and finally, as he put it in a peasant's lively tone, the town was so high one could piss on everyone else. Keeping these family facts in mind and after seeing the village of Altamonte on a modern and ancient map in the Vatican we decided Altamonte was the right place.

My thoughts during the trip to Altamonte were different than the thoughts I had as I drove along the Amalfi Drive—in Altamonte there was a very good chance that we would find relatives. This idea was unsettling. After all, what would I say? What would they say when we showed up? My Grandfather Mirabella had left his home at the end of the last century; he never returned and the family no longer communicated with us.

We drove east straight from the sea, into the mountains. We drove for miles with no village in sight. It got later and later, and after what seemed like hours we saw a walled mountain village in the distance; that was Altamonte. We came to two roads and an old gentleman walking along. "Which is the best road to Altamonte?" we asked. He paused, stamped his feet to test the surface of the road, and then said matter-of-factly, "*É equale*"—"They are the same." We continued on.

But it was another man we met along the way who turned out to be very important. His car had broken down and he hailed us as we rode by. "Where are you going?" he asked. "Altamonte," we replied. "Good, I'll go with you; my car is not working." We tried to avoid taking him; hadn't everyone in the North warned us of wily robbers behind every tree and down every street in the South? But before we could say a word he was in the car. Chattering away in a mixture of Italian and French (although we spoke to him in Italian) he asked "Why are you going to Altamonte?" "To see if my relatives still live there," I replied.

In the town, which was ancient—its church is from the twelfth century—and a bit run down, we parked our car. Our passenger insisted we go to a local bar and have a coffee. The cafe was tiny—it had just enough room for a small bar and a square table in the corner where a few old men were playing cards. As we stood at the bar and sipped our espresso the bartender asked our hitchhiker who we were. "They are looking for their *parenti*"—relatives—he replied. That was really how the whole thing happened. Once I said the name Mirabella—which is really Mirabelli in Altamonte—the bar came alive. The owner knew Mirabelli; they lived on via Balbia. "I remember Michele," one man said. "He married Josephine Sperano and moved to the United States," another said. They were talking about my grandparents; my grandmother had also come from Altamonte. Then an amazing thing occurred. One of the old men shuffled over, took my hand and said "*Conosce* New Rochelle?"—"Do you know New Rochelle?" Now this is the place where I was born and where most of my relatives still live. The coincidence of this moment shocked me. But as the old gentlemen explained, he had in his earlier years gone to New Rochelle to find work, but unlike my grandfather, he had returned to Altamonte. We learned that villagers often chose the same place in the United States to seek work; in this way they would have friends and family awaiting them.

Our hitchhiker decided to return our kindness by taking us to via Balbia and the home of Vincenzo Mirabelli. I had actually traveled thousands of miles for this moment but now that I was about to meet these people I had thought about for so long, I was terrified. Would these relatives be awful? Would my Italian fail me? I had not learned Italian at home, but had to study it at school. My family had lost the language. Here was I not only about to meet people I had never seen, but speak to them in a language I had taught myself.

When the hitchhiker knocked on the door and no one answered, I suggested we leave. "*Dorme*," he replied. "He's sleeping." It was four o'clock in the afternoon and most of the village *was* sleeping except for the few people—including the old man and woman still wearing the traditional wide-legged black velvet pants and dress of long ago—who came out to see what the knocking was. The green shutters above opened out. A man in his late sixties with gray hair stuck his head out of the window and looked down at the three strangers below. "It's your relatives from the United States!" yelled our hitchhiker. In a few moments Vincenzo Mirabelli—who had put on a tie before coming down—opened the door. He shook our hands and kissed us. He embraced us as if he had always known us. It was only later sitting at the kitchen table and drinking grappa that we learned that Vincenzo was my father's first cousin; we were actually related. Although I had mumbled in those first moments that I was the grand-daughter of Michele Mirabelli, Vincenzo had had no idea who we were. He had just welcomed us in because he thought we were relatives. This was all he needed to know.

In our visit with him, his wife, daughter, sons, their children, and cousins chatting over huge bowls of pasta and drinking wine, we learned more about each other and tried to fill in what had happened over so many years. In all our time together—we have been there twice—we were always made to feel as if we were family. I particularly recall one meal with cousins who lived in the countryside outside of Altamonte. The meal took hours to prepare and we sat and talked while Rozina and Catarina rolled individual pastas out on a board they held between them on their laps. We were sitting in a summer kitchen away from the house and everywhere around us were the flowering broom, the fields and the hills of Calabria.

This kindness, hospitality, and instant recognition of the family bond—as if the families had never lost touch—was repeated on our trip to Acireale in Sicily. Here we met the relatives of my mother's mother who had left Amalfi for the south. They settled in Sicily on the sea south of Taormina very close to the spot where Odysseus fought the Cyclops. They expected us. A cousin in California had always kept in touch with this part of the family. So we had written and they had said "Come."

When we arrived, they—two families—were waiting to greet us. Clotilda had baked miniature cream puffs and we ate and sipped espresso while they showed us photographs. Some of the pictures were very old; one was of my great-grandparents, another of my grandmother Rosa dressed as a young girl of the Edwardian era surrounded by her parents, brothers, and sister. Soon after this photograph was made Rosa left Italy and never returned.

We spent days with our family in Acireale—they showed us Catania, Aetna, the markets; they fed us foods we had never eaten; but mostly they welcomed us as members of the family.

These ties, these connections, this bond—these are the things that we have lost here in the United States. It did not happen right away. I remember when Grandma Capasso was alive we had enormous Christmas dinners with thirty relatives and food—especially desserts—for a hundred. I recall that in my childhood I was always surrounded by relatives. Now almost all my aunts and uncles are dead, but even when they were alive the individual families began to spend holidays alone; today the extended family only gets together at weddings and funerals.

Many of my relatives have little interest in Italy—some do not even know from which province their family originally came. Although we all grew up in the Italian section of New Rochelle, only one uncle lives there now. Sociologists will say this is assimilation, that we have all learned to become part of the American culture. But I am not convinced that this is a good conclusion. If immigrants cut themselves off from the land and culture they have left, they cut themselves off from their history. My history in the United States begins at the close of the last century. But what of all the centuries before, what of all the other people, what of their accomplishments, struggles, fears, their hatreds and loves? What happens to all this, this life, this heritage?

With the denial of this heritage often comes self-loathing. I grew up embarrassed to be Italian. When I saw those new Italian immigrants, those young men in my neighborhood, I wanted nothing to do with them. They looked sad, miserable, and afraid standing there in short woolen jackets buttoned up tight and their hair cut short. I hated them for looking sad and miserable. I was better than they were; *I* was an American; they were not. What did they know? Nothing. They could not speak the language; they did not know how to behave; they did not belong. But what I did not realize then, was that in rejecting them I was rejecting myself. After all, they were just like my grandparents fifty years earlier. These new immigrants were experiencing what my families had experienced. And would the newcomers abandon the land of their birth too?

My grandparents tried to hold on to their culture, but my parents' generation could not. They realized that the predominant culture here did not think too highly of Italians or for that matter of any group which stood out and was different. So my parents assimilated. They did not speak Italian, dressed as American as they could, and left the old neighborhood. Perhaps my parents wanted to be recognized as people and not stereotypes.

I recall one incident of stereotyping that shocked me in my early years. One of my sister's high school friends thought that because we were Italian our home should resemble the set for an Italian comedy. Our mother, short and fat with a bun at the back of her neck, could always be found in the kitchen perpetually preparing tomato sauce; above her head hung the required sausages, garlic, and tomatoes. My father, of course, had a shape similar to my mother's, only with a large mustache, and made his own wine. But when my sister's friend visited, she was shocked to find my all-American mom in her all-American kitchen.

I have always laughed at the foolishness of this story and I still recognize and reject the blindness of the stereotype. But I also mourn the loss of those sausages and tomatoes hanging in the kitchen. I mourn the loss of those touches that said this place was a bit different from the rest of the world outside. They said that this place had a special tradition, something to be proud of. These touches, as mundane and domestic as they are, nonetheless, reminded me that being Italian meant that a rich culture was behind me, that I could embrace my historical past, not shun it.

Obviously these are only symbols of a previous way of life, but the loss of these symbols signals the loss of a more complex and precious thing—that is the loss of the family tie. Before my trip to Calabria I do not think I would have acted like Vincenzo Mirabelli. I would not have opened my door, my arms, and my heart if a stranger had knocked at my door one afternoon and said, "Hello, I am your cousin from Italy."

I realize that people must accept and become a part of the new country to which they have moved. But it seems that some kind of balance is needed, a balance which will allow people to keep some of their old culture and history while embracing the new.

In looking back at what I wrote ten years ago, I think I have found some of that balance.

M. Bella Mirabella

The Education of an Italian-American Girl Child

There were never any books in my home when I was growing up above my uncle's Italian grocery store, unless you want to count my sister's and my school books and, yes, I almost forgot—the Junior Encyclopedia. But there was no library, no collection, no "real books" except for three books from my father's youth. One was a red, tattered, much-used Webster's Dictionary. The other two had almost an aura about them and were regarded as rare treasures by my father. I see them now, bound in faded purple cloth with gold lettering: *The Scarlet Pimpernel* and *The Count of Monte Cristo.* I remember my father showing me these books; he held them with great reverence, his voice calm but filled with joy as he recalled how much he had enjoyed them. He still remembered the many adventures contained between the covers of those books. Even at that distant moment long ago, I wondered to myself why the house was not filled with more of these magical wonders and delights Dad seemed to treasure, but I never really formed that question to myself for many years, and I never asked him.

My father in many ways had the soul of a poet. He was a gentle man with a violent temper. He was frustrated and angry because he loved ideas, art, music, literature, but he could never really indulge in these wondrous things. I use this word wondrous because this is the feeling he conveyed to me. Those two adventure novels were marvels to him; he could never get over how the authors managed to sweep him up into their worlds each time he had read them. My father thought these books were great literature. He respected them; he honored them; he approached them with great humility and he conveyed these feelings to me.

He felt this way about music too. Some of my fondest memories of him are when the two of us sat together and listened to classical and swing music for hours. He would buy *Reader's Digest* collections of swing and classical music. We would sit together and listen, album covers and records scattered about. We would swoon over Mel Torme, Tony Bennett, and others and with each tune, Dad would lovingly point out musical details. He loved this music, the music of his youth, but he loved classical music too. We had wonderful days together when we listened to Tchaikovsky. He loved Tchaikovsky's symphonies, the great power and sway of the music, the tempestuous passions. And I loved it too. We spent hours listening to the *Romeo and Juliet Overture,* he carefully explaining to me how the music revealed the Shakespeare story. I loved these precious moments: my father and I together, alone and at peace. And always he conveyed to me love, respect, and awe for these exquisite results of the human will to create.

But except for this modest music library and the three precious books there was nothing else. There were no trips to museums nor theaters; there were no concerts, except at home with Dad and the phonograph. When I look back and wonder why my father did not indulge himself in these precious delights I must see that he was a man who felt he did not really deserve these pleasures. Since my grandfather had not allowed my father to go to college, he, disappointed but resigned, accompanied his more fortunate friends to Columbia and sat in on classes. He never tired of telling us about these moments at Columbia. He was so close and yet so very, very far, a man who loved ideas, and who desired an education, but who had never even finished high school. He had hoped when he married my mother that he and she would spend quiet evenings together listening to Brahms and Tchaikovsky and reading books to each other. But my mother hated classical music and was never a reader.

So there was my father wanting knowledge but thwarted at every turn. Although the books as well as the music were revered almost as symbols of the divine in earthly manifestations, the books in particular were there as symbols of the unattainable. They were not really his or ours; we were really not allowed to partake of them. Dad never read *The Count of Monte Cristo* or *The Scarlet Pimpernel* to me and I find it significant that I have yet to read them myself. Nonetheless, those two books were signs to us that something splendid was out there, just beyond our reach; we could look, but we could not partake. When Grandpa Mirabella said "No" to his son Pete, he said no to a great deal more. Dad translated that to mean, in good Catholic phrasing, "I am not worthy. Others can read great books, and drink from the golden chalice of knowledge, but not I." Getting a real education was frivolous and aggressive at the same time; it meant defying his father's wishes; it meant running the risk of cutting himself off from his family, his heritage, his class. This was too high a price to pay—best to take what small pleasures there were from music and incidental reading.

My father communicated the same message to my sister, Joyce, and myself, not out of malice but from what he perceived as his own profound sense of failure. In his thoughts, we too, through some kind of awful, primeval inheritance reminiscent of Greek tragedy, were doomed to be failures with him. This feeling which grew out of his own personal history was further complicated by the dilemmas that result from the working-class, immigrant experience. Troubled by money and never feeling accepted in this country as persons of Italian heritage, my father and we his children faced a paradox of sorts. On one hand, we revered being Italian and fervently held on to our culture while feeling embattled by the huge, overwhelming American culture which relentlessly encroached on our family. On the other hand, paradoxically, we were also mortified by our heritage, convinced that we had to give up everything Italian in order to be accepted and become American. From the adults, we children received a two-sided message: "Stay here and remain Italian"/"Leave and become American." Caught between these two worlds, we could find no place of comfort. Education confounded this dilemma by further threatening to lure us permanently away from our culture and our class.

The constant worries about money fueled this antieducation feeling.

My mother was very ill all through my childhood, and my parents could never free themselves from what seemed to be unspeakably terrible debts. It is not surprising then that my parents would have been unwilling to spend money on education such as college. However, in our early years, through an unfortunate geographical accident, we lived across the street from a Catholic school and my parents decided they could pay $50.00 a year to send my sister and me to St. Gabriel's grammar school and then later the all-girls high school. St. Gabriel's was a terrible school in every way. Although we suffered and complained, my parents, with deluded earnestness, felt they were "sacrificing" to give their children a special education. During those school years my fellow students and I were tormented by poorly educated nuns and lay teachers who hated children and felt that daily humiliation and ridicule—their central pedagogical principle— would make us good soldiers of God even if our minds and spirits atrophied in the process.

When I look back on these years I am always newly astonished by the memories I carry. I am still particularly horrified by one experience I had. One morning in the sixth grade, we nervously sat at our desks awaiting our mid-semester grades. Our teacher, Miss Dunn, always relished these moments of high anxiety for the children. Miss Dunn—with teeth so buck she spat on us when she spoke, forever fiddling with fallen bra straps—terrified us; she always seemed to be in a bad mood and could be prompted to attack at any moment if we made even the slightest wrong move.

On that fateful day before the ritual of distributing the report cards began, Miss Dunn said, "I would like the following students to please stand up." She then began to call the names, in alphabetical order, of course. I was consumed by terror when I heard my own named pronounced. We all stood up, poor, miserable eleven-year-olds that we were, trembling in our maroon and gray uniforms waiting for the horrific verdict. And down it came like a condemnation from on high. "Students," she said, "look at these people. They are examples of failures." Suitably diminished, we sat down, unable to look at our classmates. No one ever mentioned this crushing moment to us; they knew that at any time it could happen to them.

This experience was one of many over my ten years in Catholic school. Certainly, my early education at the hands of these nuns and Miss Dunn types furthered my feelings of exclusion from the world of learning; the daily brow-beating did not make me feel that I was worthy of such pursuits. However, sometimes those teachers made us read selected great books; one of these was a withered old nun, my senior-year English teacher. We were to read books and write reports. She would not be engaged in any way; rather she dozed at her desk while we worked. While this is not an experience likely to help students develop critical thinking skills, it did give me the opportunity to read such books as *Murder in the Cathedral, The Idylls of the King, Jane Eyre, Great Expectations,* and *David Copperfield.* In these books I found the pleasures my father had hinted at when he showed me his own precious volumes. Although the happenings in the stories were certainly remote from my little daily existence, they nonetheless touched me very deeply. After all, I knew how terrified and guilty Pip felt, how all alone and abandoned by the adult world David felt. I was spellbound by love turned to hate with Thomas à Becket. I was swept up in the magic of romance and King Arthur. In my own life had I not also longed for some mystical occurrence to rescue me? These books suggested to me that there was another way to live; there was life beyond the mean, narrow, unimaginative existence I lived; there was knowledge beyond the paltry offering of St. Gabriel's.

I graduated from St. Gabriel's with dreams of more education, but I was not really prepared. Although I had secretly yearned to be in the college prep group, I chose the commercial group because I knew what was expected of me. My parents reminded me that our lives were more practical and difficult. The acquisition of knowledge could never possibly be one's life, and it could never possibly make anyone enough money to survive on. I could content myself with reading in my spare time. When my sister had wanted to go to Parsons School of Design—she was a talented artist and designer—my parents said she could not go. My sister's obligations were at home where she could work and help support the family.

When I told my parents I wanted to go to college, they gave me the same answer they gave to Joyce, the same answer Grandpa Mirabella gave to my father. But when my mother said "Women don't need to go to college because they get married," she put a new twist on the matter. I needed to work in order to get money, but whatever efforts I made would be worthless because eventually I would defer to some unknown future husband who would take care of me. Because my mother was always struggling with money, there was nothing malicious or particularly odd in this sentiment, which she shared with my aunts and other female family members. What else could a woman do other than marry after a brief stint at some menial, degrading job? Uneducated, unskilled, afraid, the women of my mother's generation looked upon their daughters with anxiety and concluded that we would be safe if we married. A youthful marriage to some suitable Italian young man also meant that the heritage was secure.

Although some first- or second-generation immigrant families might encourage their children to be educated, this was not my experience. I am reluctant to make generalizations about Italian-Americans, but much of the resistance to education I encountered was the same that had confronted my father—education would take me away from the Italian clan. Making money was a valued pursuit, but not if it would take one away from the family. My particular dilemma was complicated by gender. Education was unthinkable; like other women of my generation, I was expected to tend the house. One of my female, Italian-American students once quipped that we were expected to be home stirring the tomato sauce, and although this may sound amusing, it's true.

None of this was ever said to me directly, but I understood it, and it made me uneasy. Even if I was to go along with the Prince Charming idea for a while, I still had no idea what to do with myself while I was waiting. My parents expected me to work in an office, and this looked like my fate, until a solution came to me in the form of the community college. Here was a compromise, I thought. It was very cheap and I could woo my parents with the idea that I would study secretarial science. But even this victory was hard won; I had to promise to work during the summer to pay the tuition. So off I went to Westchester Community College. It is difficult for me to say how much I loved—and treasure the memory of—this institution. Although I actually majored in marketing (a subject I loathed), I was still in college. It was higher education and an escape from the mind-and-spirit-withering school experiences I had in St Gabriel's. It was exposure to ideas, even if some of them had to do with debits and credits in the columns of my accounting balance sheets. Although I did have to take marketing and accounting, I also studied history, writing, and the most beloved, literature. I was actually reading *The Odyssey, Oedipus Rex,* Dante, Goethe (which I pronounced Go-eth for a while), and Shakespeare. I had read *Macbeth* in high school and although I knew it was a momentous moment when I picked up that book, the truth is I had no idea what it meant. But there I was in college reading *Hamlet,* another try at Shakespeare. Ah, Shakespeare! My father practically swooned at the sound of the word. I, too, practically swooned, tantalized by Shakespeare's language but equally confounded; I knew I was in the presence of greatness, but there was a wall between me and the sweet beauty locked within. One afternoon, however, sitting in my girlfriend Celeste's backyard, the veil dropped and suddenly it began to make sense. I had found the key and I, the kid who lived above the grocery store, was reading Shakespeare. For the first time in my life, I had books on my bookshelves sitting beside *The Scarlet Pimpernel* and *The Count of Monte Cristo*.

It would be wonderful to say that from that great moment in Celeste's backyard, I soared to unknown heights, getting A's all the way, winning scholarships to Harvard, and easily sailing into the "celestial kingdom" of the Academy, but, alas, the battle was not so easily won. After my glorious two years at WCC, reality stood before me once again in the form of my parents; they had allowed me to indulge myself in a bit of education; I had been able to read those precious books, but now there would be no more dabbling. But what was a woman in the 1960s going to do with an Associate's Degree in Marketing? No, it was the life of the secretary for me. I brushed up my stenography and found a job at the General Foods Corporation in White Plains. However, within the first week, trudging from the enormous parking lot to the enormous building complex with its warren of corridors, escalators, stairways, I vowed to go back to school and become a teacher, no matter what it took. And while I made myriad typing errors, flubbed dictation, forgot to make the coffee, sent people the wrong things, made spelling errors, and generally despised the petty world of business (I was, after all, working in the roasted nut division), I plotted my escape. It took a couple of years, during which I took courses in history and literature at night, read Thoreau and Emerson, and posted above my desk Emersonian aphorisms such as "Whosoever wishes to be a man must be a nonconformist" to the dismay of the white-collared men under whom I toiled.

Of course, my parents did not know what to make of this. My mother was particularly dumbfounded. But with my father, it was different. One evening I announced that I was going back to school to become a teacher. He answered me with a pained expression on his face. "How are you going to pay for it?" When I think back on that night I see that he realized at that moment that this was something I really wanted. He would not try to stop me because I was in some sense doing what he had always wanted to do himself. But coming from the working classes, always struggling with money, he was afraid I would fail. He could not support me through college, so what was I to do? He was horrified at the thought of student loans. How could I knowingly put myself into debt after what he had been through? But that is what I did; with the help of those loans, a cheap apartment, part-time jobs during the school year and work at General Foods in the summer, and groceries from my parents every once in a while, I survived. My mother thought me crazy; my father watched silently in secret delight and joy.

College was everything I had hoped it would be. For a young woman from the Italian section of New Rochelle, Hunter College in the Bronx in the 1960s was as awe inspiring as the hallowed halls of Princeton. This was a four-year college, with real professors, ethnically diverse students, foreign films made by persons with unknown names but who I knew were important, and so many literature courses. With joy and trepidation, I entered my first philosophy class. I could barely understand anything in philosophy; I had no vocabulary, no possible way to make sense of such a discourse. My literature courses were also a challenge. One English professor had been a rock 'n' roll disk jockey; at least that is what he said. I could never quite believe that a man with slicked-back hair, a waistband up to his chin, an excruciatingly boring manner, and a specialization in Restoration drama could ever have flipped those Elvis disks around.

The real cruncher was Professor W. Although he modeled himself after an English don, even saying "murther" for murder, he was really one of those nuns from St. Gabriel's in disguise. He had studied his teaching techniques at the same school of education—the school of ridicule and humiliation. Unfortunately, he taught Shakespeare. He had the self-serving notion that we could learn about the theme of love in four Shakespearean dramas by his reading every line of the plays to us. There was, of course, no discussion from us and barely any interpretation from him; there was only Professor W., gray-suited, condescending, self-congratulating, forever reading. He was bringing culture to the Bronx barbarians, many of them like myself, Jewish, Italian, African-American, Irish kids from working-class families in a free institution. Some of the students were more educated, more familiar with great literature and he rewarded them with praise for their "sensitivity to the text." But for those, who, like myself, had never read these books and were weak in punctuation, he had nothing but scorn and the red pencil. My particular sin was the semicolon; he barely acknowledged my ideas, but with deadly red pencil in hand he decorated my papers with corrections and nasty insults which floated above my modest efforts. But despite Professor W.'s cruelty, including postcards home listing my spelling errors, I survived, made friends with the semicolon, and most amazing of all, I now teach Shakespeare.

I love to share these stories with my students, particularly the horrors of Professor W. I want them to know that I, too, suffered with Shakespeare, that I also suffered with teachers, that I have not forgotten, and that I will never do that to them. They gasp when I tell them about Miss Dunn too. I tell them this story when I am giving them my take on failure. There is no failure in my classroom I tell them; there is only struggle, process, learning. Often I encounter students who remind me of myself toiling in college, feeling overwhelmed. I was often befuddled, but slowly I began to acquire a vocabulary, a sense of history; I began to feel more comfortable. I began to become the educated woman I had always dreamed of being. I began to claim those books for myself; I was no longer the proverbial small child outside the shop window, who could only look and not touch. I see this happening to my students too. Recently, during an oral exam, a student related how he had entered college feeling all those books belonged to others, but now as he was ready to graduate, he felt he had made them his own. He found the pleasures within them and they were his.

Although I always rejoice with these students, I recall that as I embraced knowledge, I also knew I was slowly leaving the clan. I had disregarded the wisdom of my mother and the aunts who firmly believed that education threatened whatever Italian heritage we had left. But their fears about loss of culture were bound up with class as well. They knew they were very low on the class ladder; they had been low on that ladder in Italy too. It was always understood, though never really spoken aloud, that one from the clan who acquired too much education might gain entry into that other world and anyone who did and looked back could only have disdain for those who remained behind. Perhaps this was another reason why Grandpa Mirabella had said "no" to my father.

When I graduated from college, I wanted to go to graduate school but once again I felt stalled, afraid. Initiating each stage of my education had been exhausting; it would have been so much easier if I could have made that journey without the burden of Grandpa's ancient disapproval and others' weighing me down. But this was not my lot, and literally trembling with fear I applied and actually went to graduate school.

From the moment I started out on this course and throughout all of graduate school part of me felt like a fraud. I felt like one of those Italian immigrants I had seen on the street in my neighborhood when I was a child. If those professors only knew who I really was, that I was like those immigrants, they would not have allowed me to stay. If they knew that there were only three books in my house while I was growing up, they would have asked me to leave. There I was in a classroom with students who had studied at Vassar, Amherst, and Smith. They dashed papers off with incredible ease while for me writing papers was unspeakable torment. They spoke about Hardy and Austen as if they had been reading them for years; I sat in class terrified of making a "stupid" remark. I constantly wondered how I would ever keep up. When I had announced to my mother that I was going to graduate school, she had returned with, "Haven't you had enough?" There were many days in graduate school when I wondered if perhaps she had been right.

Feeling completely out of my element in every way—in terms of class, education, background, ethnic group—I cannot say I was actually "happy" at graduate school. Once again, however, I loved the learning. One of my professors, Julian Moynahan, was the perfect antidote to that old curmudgeon, Professor W. Talented, intelligent, witty, and kind, Julian is a great teacher and has always been a source of encouragement to me. It was Julian who told me I would make a fine teacher and it was with teaching that I began to feel confidence in the academic world.

When I received my first teaching assignment while still in graduate school I was thrilled. The day before my first class I walked into the empty classroom to try it out, see what it would feel like. I said a few words aloud; they echoed in the hollow emptiness. I felt a bit embarrassed to be talking to myself, but I realized I was in a special moment and I continue to feel that about the classroom. It is almost a sacred space where I come together with my students to question, discuss, argue, agree, disagree, laugh, and generally have a thrilling time fooling around with ideas. When I walk into the classroom I bring with me the memories I have related here. When I walk into the classroom I dispel the powers of the Professor W.'s, the nuns, the Miss Dunns. When I enter that space I try to bring with me some of the excitement I feel about books, about learning and whatever joy and pleasure I carry with me into the classroom is because I fought a long hard battle to get there.

Over the years I have thought about this odyssey of mine a great deal; certainly the writing of this piece has forced me to rummage around in the storage boxes of my past and try to make sense of it. I used to feel that educating myself meant a break with my Italian past, but my journey to Italy years ago showed me that I could embrace my Italian heritage. In a similar way, my success in the classroom comes in part from my working-class consciousness. I feel this particularly in my conversations with young female students with families who are against their education and who refuse to come to their graduations. Like myself, they are torn between family obligations and desire for a life of achievement. My family feared that an education would take me away and in some ways it did. They were wrong, however, about the disdain I would feel. In my pocket, as it were, I carry a rich treasure; it is rich with the memories of my struggle to be educated, memories of growing up and being Italian, and the memories of being part of a tradition of honest work and toil.

The writing of this essay has been a reclaiming of the past for me, an opportunity for me to affirm it. I think of my father and those two faded, purple volumes, and I think it is time that I read them. It will be a lovely connection, a connection to my past hopes and dreams and a connection to my dear dad who loved those books and all books so much.

Barbara Fox

I was born in 1940 in Brooklyn, New York. I am the child of working-class parents, the daughter and granddaughter of union organizers, dockworkers, paper handlers, mill-wrights, New York City transit mechanics, bookkeepers, housewives. The grandchild and great-grandchild of Irish, English, Russian-Jewish immigrants. People who panned for gold in Australia (and found some), who married sailors (and were disinherited), who dug the Liverpool–Mersey tunnel, wrapped soap for Lever Brothers in England, and who were rabbis in Russia. They all converged on America in the early part of this century. My own parents continued these patterns by moving us to California when I was eleven.

There seem to be very few photos of my father and me together. That may be because he was the one who generally took the photos, and by the time I was a teenager we did not spend a lot of time together. This picture was taken the night of my senior prom. My grandparents were at our apartment as well. My father's arm is around behind me, touching my mother's arm—they touched a lot. I was their oldest child, their only daughter—all dressed up, about to graduate from high school and go on to college. We were all very excited. Much to his annoyance, my father had given my date (who would become the father of my children) money to pay for our limousine.

Barbara Fox is a painter who teaches art appreciation and art history at the National Technical Institute for the Deaf at Rochester Institute of Technology. She has had solo exhibits at Wells College, the University of Rochester, and Pyramid Arts Center in Rochester, and her work has been part of several national group shows. Her artist book *today* is in the collection of the Museum of Modern Art, the Albright Knox Gallery in Buffalo, and Printed Matter in New York City. She is a member of the Board of Governors of the New York Foundation for the Arts. Her involvement in political activism began with the Civil Rights and antiwar movements. For several years she was a member of Rochester Women's Action for Peace, and she continues to be involved in feminist activities. In her work she uses the events—both personal and political—that were, and are, part of her life.

The Black Work

What could all that movement and disruption and dislocation have meant to all the members of those generations? What has it meant to succeeding generations? The experiences and the consequences of moving in just this one family are enormous. Generations of us continue the process. But each time it occurs, it causes disruption. And each time it occurs it requires the development of new understandings of how-to-be in the new place. Each new generation of movers has had to find the cultural signals which provide road maps and entryways into the new place. People need to know how to behave, how to fit in; they want to know how to be like others already arrived, already comfortable. At the time my grandparents arrived, this country's media was filled with virulent racism, fear of immigrant groups, and antisuffragist propaganda. These campaigns of hatred were in many ways successful. We all still live with the consequences. For my parents' generation the focus of this organized hatred would be on Blacks and Communists.

My family accepted many of these ideas as their own, never seeing this as part of a larger picture in which they too were part; in which they too were oppressed. For them it was part of the process of becoming, and being, American. They believed the propaganda, and they developed the appropriate feelings and attitudes to match the ideas. What had been sociological and external to them, became psychological and internalized. My family, and many other families in similar circumstances, arrived in this country to be confronted with powerful macroscopic cultural forces telling them who and what was acceptable in this culture. These belief structures of larger historical forces became reflected in the microscopic values and cultures of many families. What was external and new to them as aliens and immigrants was then passed on and internalized as American Truth. As I write our story I have begun to see the layers of these developments. For me, their prejudice became like pentimenti found in paintings, many layers that have gone before, that in fact add to the totality of how we be-

"Black work" refers to an alchemic process of combining, as in a compost, disparate elements which eventually transform into the real value and goals of alchemy—the true awakening of human potential. It seems ironically appropriate to use it here.

come who we are. These exist like ghosts in my life, in conflict with the warm and loving people I also knew them to be. The hatreds are also like threads through our family, creating both cohesion and disruption as we pass from generation to generation.

I have asked myself, what was it like to be an immigrant? Yet I know what it means to become disconnected, because I too moved. I moved, not to another geographical place, but to a different social, cultural place. It was expected of the children of my generation; we were to do better than our parents, to go beyond. We were supposed to become part of the American middle class. This expectation was in the air after World War II, just as the hate campaigns had earlier existed. But did anyone understand the implications of that? Did anyone understand what would happen in families? While the connections to the past, those pentimenti, are there, what is also there is loss. When I think about my own history, I realize I have had my family's migrations as an example.

I have often grieved the loss of my family's stories, cultural stories from the "old countries," but to most of my family those things were frivolous, unimportant. I wanted the fabric of those kinds of stories. Sometimes my grandmother, my mother's mother, would tell me stories of her childhood, of her family, of her romance with my grandfather. She was the only one who shared those secrets, and I seemed to have been the only one interested in them. Her stories of Liverpool at the turn of the century were like stories out of Dickens: scrubbing the porch steps and the brass door knob, being offered a doll by a strange man, being chased by her furious father through back alleys. One of her stories was, in fact, prophetic. It concerned my grandfather and his mother. Some years after they settled in the United States, there had been an argument between mother and son and the connection broken. Nana wouldn't tell me what the argument had been about, but the silence between mother and son continued until someone informed my grandfather that his mother had died. She was gone; there was nothing more to be done. This breaking of connections is not uncommon with us. This is part of the dynamic that has enabled us to leave a home country.

Holidays brought all my mother's family together. We generally celebrated at my grandparents' apartment in Brooklyn. These gatherings were always exciting and nourishing to me, even though the potential for my father's drunkenness and anger grew as I got older. Thanksgiving was a turkey dinner, but Christmas was roast beef, and best of all, my Nana's Yorkshire pudding and roast potatoes covered with rich, dark gravy. Dinner was served in the living room and at least three people had to sit at the table while perched on the edge of the couch—with its prickly upholstery. After dinner my grandfather would play the piano. He could pick out any tune and play it by ear. He had never studied music, but it was his great love, and it is something two of his children have continued. We would sing popular songs, and inevitably, someone would join him in playing "Heart and Soul" and English children's songs.

Being at my grandparents' was like a cradle to me. This was THE place of warmth and acceptance for me. I was their only granddaughter—the first child of their only daughter—and they lavished their affections on me. I was never happier than when I was with them.Their funny English sayings and nursery rhymes, their tea and scones, their gentleness and pride in me, were irresistible and delicious. Their apartment was on the ground floor of a four-story walkup. Everyone knew everyone. Most of the other families were Jewish and Italian, though my grandparents had managed to find other English immigrants in the neighborhood. On summer nights people sat outside talking about the Brooklyn Dodgers and playing the ball game "Hit the Penny" with their children. I can still feel those days and nights.

Eventually all my family left the city and my grandparents moved to Florida. They have been dead many years now and few of us see much of each other. Recently, though, I was told about a family dinner to which I was not invited. It was a Thanksgiving dinner involving three generations—the oldest to the some of the youngest. The conversation was enlivened with the introduction of a racist joke and continued on with virtually everyone participating in this almost family ritual. When I first heard about this family gathering, I was hurt to have not been included, but then I thought about what would have, or could have, happened if I were there. Would such a conversation have occurred? Would there have been a confrontation? Would I have wanted to be there? The answer is yes, I would have wanted that. Yes.

While the racism is real, I have come to understand that it also serves a purpose in our family of being a kind of social glue. Or as a kind of diversion. It provides conversation when there is none, when people have no real intimacy between them. This is particularly true of the men in my family. It is all too common for the topic of race to come up, and to be used as the connection between them all. We are not people who discuss things out in the open. While each member is part of the family, real discussion of problems, or controversial new ideas, took place in smaller groups, within immediate families, or between particular people. Acceptable topics which affected or connected everyone were limited, are limited.

For years the topic of race caused the most heated and hurtful arguments between my father and me. The issue of race became the metaphor for things we should have resolved as parent and child, but did not, could not. Just as the racist jokes served as a diversion for my family as a whole, issues of racism and prejudice served the same purpose between my father and me. When we should have been working through personal problems, we learned to disrespect each other's views.

As a laborer, a skilled tradesperson, and as a union officer, my father taught me very early about the abuses suffered by working people. He would readily criticize governments, officials at all levels, including union officers. He understood how structural arrangements made the working classes powerless, and in the next breath he would dismiss entire groups of those same powerless people. His intolerance of Blacks, Italians, Jews, was not something that could be rationally discussed. When I suggested, at age eleven, that it might be better for the world if everyone were to make the same amount of money, my father—with great disdain—called me a communist. In 1951, that was not a sought-after label.

In contrast to his anger was his love of singing and playing. How many times had my father sung "Daddy's Little Girl" to me, at me? How many times did I want to sink through the floor when he began? It was mostly sung in bars and at family gatherings where adults would become drunk, especially and predictably, my father. When I was a very small child, I remember and I have been told, we got along very well. We spent hours and hours together. We took long walks in the country, I played and watched him make wonderful things in his shop. I went with him when he did carpentry jobs at other people's houses. As I grew, his talents as a parent decreased while his drinking increased. Ultimately it took its toll with physical and psychological consequences. He was caught between a generation which thought its children should be seen and not heard, and one which encouraged its children to talk and discuss things. His solution was to talk as long as there was no dissent. What later seemed to me as closed-mindedness may have been his way of being protective; if we didn't talk about things, there would not be problems, and we would not fight. Discussions for the sake of discussion were unheard of. Discussion was for giving instructions, describing the truth; not for expanding awareness, understanding concepts. Given my father's view of the world, it must have seemed frightening to have his daughter not accepting his boundaries. He must have feared for me, he wanted to protect me, but his response was to try to silence me by rejecting my questioning and my pushing. He was a wonderful iconoclast yet it frightened him when he saw that reflected in my behavior. One Sunday when I was nine or ten or eleven he walked me to church. I had been fasting and planning to receive communion. As we neared the church we stopped in a candy store and he offered me a chocolate milkshake. I accepted immediately. That was a wonderful lesson for me: it took the wind out of the sails of the church in a way that remains with me still. When I later participated in civil rights demonstrations, my father was not able to apply that same distance to other entrenched belief systems. He was horrified that I would go to Washington, D.C., and leave my daughters with only their father to care for them. But more accurately he was just horrified that I was participating in civil rights demonstrations.

The story of my grandfather and his mother was repeated between my father and me—we became angry with each other. The inevitable topic which caused our anger was race, but the issue was something else—he was unable to control my world. His response was to refuse to speak to me again, and then he died. He died without any talk between us, without forgiveness on either side, without softness, without reconnecting. He was simply gone. To describe exactly what happened between us is very difficult. It creates a sense of tattling, of betrayal for revealing family secrets. It creates shame for exposing the most awful things. But to continue the hiding prevents changing, prevents the healing and repairing so necessary. As I struggled with this dilemma, someone suggested I ask my children and my grandchildren what they thought. I read most of this already written chapter to my nine-year-old grandson, Spencer. Then I told him that the overt reason my father stopped talking to me was because Spencer's mother, my daughter, had given birth to a child whose father is black. My daughter had given birth to my beloved grandchild, Spencer Michael Walker. I went on to say that that wasn't the only reason. My father, despite his bravado, was fearful and felt a need to control his world. That my daughter had a mixed-race child out of wedlock demonstrated that everything was out of control; it meant moreover that all my political activities had resulted in exactly the kind of thing he had feared, and he would have no more of it. When I asked Spencer what he thought about all that, if he felt angry, he said, "No, I don't feel angry, I feel disappointed." As I sat there with this child, this new beginning, this potential, I felt deeply proud, deeply connected.

It was my father who taught me about art, about music, about beauty.

Barbara Fox, *Requiem for a Dead Father #2*, 1986.
Oil and collage on canvas. 3' × 4'.

I learned about them during the countless hours spent in his basement shop as he made toys for my brother and me, or repaired cabinets for others, puttered, made things, or just cleaned up his area. This was the foundation of my love for art, for life. It was he who would clean out the refrigerator to create exciting strange breakfasts, or would come home with huge amounts of bread and cake and cookies from the kosher bakery hours before a Jewish holiday. It was he who would create a picnic on the living-room rug, because it was raining. And it was he who moved us cross country to California, stopping as we drove to explore the snake farms along Route 66, and the Grand Canyon, and the desert, and other wonderful things. He urged us to open the windows so we could smell the heat in the air.

We drove out west in our brand new station wagon in 1951, my parents, my brother, my father's mother, and me. I would lie on top of all our belongings in the back of the car, looking out the back window and watching the road go past, watching the miles add up between where we had come from and where we were going. Before we began our migration to California, my father took us to Manhattan from Queens, where we lived. We went to art galleries and museums, and to the Empire State Building—for one last look at this place we were leaving. We went to a Greenwich Village art gallery and the work there looked Giacometti-like, may even have been Giacometti. None of us understood this work, but it was important to him that we see these things.

In the Renaissance, young boys were sent to work as apprentices to artists. Girls were never sent or allowed such opportunities. If a girl happened to learn to make art, invariably, she learned those skills from her father who was an artist, and her training was informally sandwiched in between her domestic training. Some of us have never stopped doing that—sandwiching in art. It is still also true that women who become artists are often the daughters of men who are artists.

My father was offered a sculpture apprenticeship rather late in life—he was in his late twenties. He was married and my mother was pregnant with me. Feeling it was not feasible, he refused this opportunity to become a sculptor. But he never stopped making art of one kind or another. Sometimes he carved wood, sometimes he made toys, or cabinetry, marquetry, or metal sculpture. His lack of formal training and critical skills frustrated him. It was also obvious in his figures, but it never stopped him from making his art. Sometime before he died, he exhibited his work with a group of regional artists in Florida. It gave him great pride and satisfaction to have people look at his work. Also around that time, he gave me his wood carving tools. I had begun to make woodblock prints and he sent me the tools along with handwritten instructions and illustrations on how to sharpen them in just the right way. Knowing I am using the same tools my father used, indeed the same ones he used when I would watch him work, makes a very special connection. He looked at some drawings of mine at just about the time I was beginning to take my work seriously and he admired their realism. "That's what's important. Forget that abstract stuff. This is what's really good. Do it this way. Don't forget." His criticisms were devastating. "What a stupid drawing! That's not what a woman looks like. How could you draw like that? Here, this is the formula for drawing the human figure. This is the way to do it." The frustration he would pour out may have been a reflection of his own disappointments, but they were hard to hear, and rarely helpful. His best teaching came when he wasn't doing it, when he was just loving being in his shop, or figuring out how to do a project.

When I first began making pictures, I wanted to draw what I saw. These images were alone, never in a context, never placed on anything, in anything. They floated on my paper and on my canvas—beautiful in their solitude. It was easy for me to become lost in the complexities of the objects. I took pains to choose things with folds (I still do—clouds and curtains are common objects in my paintings). It gave me great pleasure to create a sense of the movement of the folds in my leather bags, or boots, faces even. The desire to get it right through my drawings, and later my paintings, was painful—I had not yet developed my artistic language. How many hundreds of drawings did I do, dissatisfied with every one, before I arrived at the place I knew as skill! Then that alone was no longer enough for me. It was art without consciousness, as I was without consciousness. I had stopped working and thinking politically for several years. I had concentrated on finishing my degrees and raising my daughters. As I worked towards making substantive art, I felt strangled, locked up, inarticulate. Now I wanted literally to speak through my work. I wanted to tell stories with my pictures, I wanted to show things that were true for me, to me. And I wanted now to paint as well as draw: to make art, to love the experience of painting, composing, creating.

What developed finally, and in some form continues still, was a long series called the Black Paintings. At the beginning they were completely abstract, though over time I have come back to recognizable images. I would use old paintings, covering them with thick blackness and collaged and painted objects, but always leaving parts from the original painting, or the canvas itself, showing through. I have a need to acknowledge what has gone before, like the acknowledgment of generations. There is a deep satisfaction knowing that under the surface of my paintings are other paintings, other ideas: the connections of the pentimenti. The blackness was a response to my feelings of silence. But it was, and it is, more. It is thick and richly tactile. Or it is thin as a stocking. It can be matte or shiny. There is the possibility of its representing emotions, as well as its importance as a formal element. I was overwhelmed by color and its implications, and blackness gave me an avenue by which to experiment. I was overwhelmed also by my returning sense of involvement in political issues, and the blackness provided a way of clarifying my voice. The development and the struggle with the black paint has gone in many directions and has added strength to the works, and to me. It, too, like the issue of race, is a kind of metaphor for the political and the artistic issues I now incorporate in my work. What began as first timid steps into the act of painting, which is al-

Barbara Fox, *Overt Consequences,* 1988.
Oil, charcoal, ink on canvas. 4' × 6'.

ways on a completely abstract level, have developed into strong, clear directions. My father was wrong about many things; one of them is that art is not about copying what one sees.

As I struggled with my painting, the Women's Encampment for Peace and Justice, near the Seneca Army Depot in upstate New York, was just developing. It was an exciting and energizing historical moment. I joined a group of women from Rochester who had begun meeting to support the women at the Encampment. As our group worked and studied, the issues ranged from militarism to other issues of peace and social justice, to the universal problems of women. The focus of our work has been on understanding the force of patriarchal domination and on how we can empower ourselves and other women in the face of this vast power. It is not merely to rid the world of injustice, but to examine the structure of it and to make that structure clear. With that knowledge it is easier now to understand why my working-class family was, and still is, so intolerant. It is no more acceptable to me, but I see where it fits into the scheme of things. My way of responding is to incorporate these issues into my art—to image the chaos caused by alcoholism, to paint pictures of children killed by the Contras in Nicaragua, to express artistically the injustice that women experience.

Traditional art criticism has not looked generously upon the joining of art and politics. Nor has it thought highly of the combination of autobiography and art (as is especially true regarding women's art). Combining all three has become my goal. I have turned my back on the cautions about such things. Looking carefully, and reading carefully, it has become clear to me that art, in fact, has rarely been about much else. Perhaps life itself is mostly about these same things.

Finally, a word about my mother. Growing up I did not feel close to my mother—essentially I was my father's daughter. I have always felt that I had been identified as being more his child, and that my brother had been identified as my mother's. While we all lived in the same house, there was a separateness. My growing up struggles were almost exclusively with my father, my mother going along with his position on virtually every issue. She shared my father's attitudes about most things, including his refusal to speak with me. Since his death she has continued to live in their mobile home in Florida by herself. But since that time, and truly for the first time, she and I have spent long hours together or on the phone talking about the state of our family, past and present. She comes to our home, visits with her grandchildren and her great-grandchildren. I believe she loves us all. We have together, very slowly and very quietly built a connection which had never existed before. I have come to accept not being able to change her prejudices, but I have also come to understand that I love her in spite of them. We have truly nurtured a peace between us.

Maxine Scates

I was born in Los Angeles, California, in 1949 and attended California public schools from elementary through high school. I received my undergraduate degree after flunking out of one California state school and earning reentry to another by attending a community college. In my five and a half years as an undergraduate, I worked first as a usherette at the Fabulous Forum, a Los Angeles sports arena, and later as a cashier at the *Queen Mary*. My mother worked in factories before and during the Second World War. After the war, she worked as a clerical worker for the L.A. Police Department, and then for twenty-five years as a clerk, and finally an assistant librarian with the L.A. Public Library. At seventy-five, she still works as a volunteer at her local elementary school library. My father was a truck driver, mostly for the Department of Water and Power, until the age of forty-seven when alcoholism and war-related injuries forced him out of his job. He now lives at the California Veterans Home. My brother, Allen, a teacher and author of several books on the game of volleyball, holds undergraduate and graduate degrees in physical education from U.C.L.A., where he has coached the U.C.L.A. volleyball team to fourteen N.C.A.A. Championships.

Maxine Scates holds degrees from California State University, Northridge, the University of Oregon, and Oregon State University. Her poetry and essays have appeared in *Agni, The American Poetry Review, The American Voice, Ironwood, Prairie Schooner, Poetry East,* and many other journals. Her first book of poems, *Toluca Street,* won the 1988 Agnes Lynch Starrett Poetry Prize from the University of Pittsburgh Press, and subsequently the 1990 Oregon Book Award for poetry. She has been the recipient of fellowships from the MacDowell Colony and the Oregon Arts Commission. She has taught poetry and writing throughout the state of Oregon in the Artists-in-the-Schools Program, at Northwest Writing Institute, at Lane Community College, and as poet-in-residence at Lewis and Clark and Reed Colleges.

Leaving It All Behind?

I grew up in the fifties and sixties in Los Angeles in a white working-class neighborhood, a featureless postwar housing tract a mile east and north of L.A. International Airport. There, difference seemed to register in terms of religion: Protestant, Catholic, and Jew. The only sense of ethnicity was present in Marietta Diveckia's family, which had fled Hungary in 1956, or Joey Mandel's parents, who both bore the tattoos of the concentration camps on their arms. Of my playmates and schoolmates, I seemed to be the only one with grandparents living in Los Angeles. Joey and Marietta's families had come from other countries, but other children's parents had all come from the Midwest or the East and usually in that vague time before or during the Second World War. By contrast my mother's mother, my grandmother, had been born in Los Angeles, her mother an immigrant from Mexico—a fact that seemed to have nothing to do with our own Irishness, an Irishness that had less to do with ethnicity than erasing anything Mexican—and her father the son of a carpenter from Missouri, who had come West by covered wagon in 1886 and, as I would later find, was also a member of the Knights of Labor. I knew nothing of my father's family, but I did know that I was unique in that both of my parents, and my brother, born before the war, had come from no farther than downtown Los Angeles.

Nonetheless, in my neighborhood the similarities so far outweighed the differences that on 97th Street everyone seemed very much like us. The fathers were veterans of the war; the houses had been purchased with GI loans. The men, many of them alcoholic, were bonded by the common experience of the war and the women were isolated from each other. Or do I remember only my own mother's isolation? For the unpredictability of my father's alcoholism dominated and isolated our family, and almost all of our social interaction was confined to other members of my mother's family on occasional visits to my grandparents' house downtown on Toluca Street. As a result, my family did not seem part of anything as much as apart from everything. Ours was a tiny, oppressive household in a large sprawling, segregated city that I knew no more of than the car and later the bus route between those two houses.

And as to those houses? In my own house the environment was unpredictable and chaotic—filled with physical and psychic violence. The environment on Toluca Street, however, was more predictable. There, my grandmother, Nana, was a drugged and shuffling presence intermittently institutionalized (as her mother had also been) after a series of mental breakdowns that had begun in 1930 at the age of thirty-two with the birth of her sixth child. There, I learned much of both the internalized and externalized hatreds of racism as my family, led by my grandfather, a retired L.A.P.D. sergeant, both denigrated and denied Nana's mother's and thus Nana's Mexican heritage, and there my grandfather both brutalized Nana and mocked her silence, a silence I grew complicitous with and a silence that feeds me now.

In my family everything we were was to be denied out of a sense of shame that we were not like everyone else, and that, of course, became the goal, to be exactly like who we thought everyone else was. Within the realm of that denial and its attendant secrets falls the denial of my great-grandmother's racial identity and her own institutionalization, which I only learned of as an adult; the ignorance of and thus the denial of my grandfather's role in Nana's mental illness; and the denial of my father's alcoholism.

My mother was the source of much of this story of denial, particularly with regard to the circumstances of the institutionalization of her mother and grandmother and with regard to my father's alcoholism—and with reasons I now find understandable. My mother was twelve years old, the second eldest, when her mother disappeared into Norwalk State Hospital for the first time. She was eighteen when Nana returned. To this day she has willed herself not to remember much of what happened in those years. Married at nineteen, she had to get on with her own life. In order to do this she pieced together a version of how things should be out of the picture of life the dominant culture presented her with—a version refining and eclipsing her own childhood where her father became a good Irish cop and her mother's breakdowns and ensuing silences a frightening aberration. As the circumstances of her own marriage worsened, she could not bear to acknowledge its violent unpredictability because as a Catholic she saw no way to leave it. Busy surviving day to day, busy forgetting, she neither had the time—as I do now—nor the words for presenting her own invisible story, for exploring the obvious contradictions between who we were and who we were supposed to be.

In that exploration I have come to recognize a sense not only of a cultural but of a moral void associated with growing up in a white working-class environment because of the feelings of secrecy and shame connected to that overall denial. Moreover, in my grandfather's denial of my great-grandmother's racial identity, a prohibition passed on by his children to their children, there was also the explicit articulation of racism, which rather than being held in secret was very much a spoken part of what I remember and what I learned and which was not only directed toward my grandmother—within the family—but, in both houses, was also very much directed by the male members of my family toward society at large. So, too, do I feel hatred as a part of that void, a void because, based as it was on secrecy, shame, and the hatred of others as well as ourselves, no consciousness could exist which could join with that of others to permit an understanding of the social and economic circumstances that had created that oppressive atmosphere.

Given these circumstances, perhaps it follows naturally that one more thing we were not was "working class"—a phrase I doubt that I ever heard as a child. We were "lower middle class," a phrase I clearly remember as a response to a question I must have asked as a teenager and spoken by my mother with such insistence that it was *what we were not and what we might be* that I registered and still retain. It is that contradiction that both becomes the locus for my own experience of white working-class identity and the place I often find myself writing from, a place which because of the insistence that it be left behind confirms for me that growing up in a white working-class environment did not mean having an identity—it meant looking for one.

As a result, when I think of where I locate my working-class identity, I think not of an experience solidly grounded in a sense of class consciousness or community, but rather, based as it was on negation, an absence of it suggesting that identity was, aside from our exultant Irishness and the vacuum of our own fears, available in everything we were not. In college, where I first encountered the concept of class and class consciousness, my naive understanding of those terms did suggest the specific representation of a whole identity. Consequently, my first and, no doubt, romanticized consciousness of the working class suggested values which embodied struggle and solidarity. Yet if that definition was true, who was I? Where did I come from? It would be years before I could begin, or, in fact, even want to begin to answer those questions.

Though, as I've said, I doubt that I'd ever heard the phrase in childhood, my family *was* solidly part of the working class. My father, an eighth grade dropout who had come home from war shattered both physically and mentally, was a CCC-trained truck driver. However, by the time I had reached fourteen, his alcoholism had caught up with him and forced him out of a job, as my mother, with the blessing she had waited years for from the Catholic church, had finally forced him out of the marriage. For my father, I don't think there was ever any question of who he was: what he didn't have and knew he would never attain left him defeated. I see him tired, his clothes grease-stained, coming home from work each day and settling in to drink. He knew that change would never occur. Recently, he told me that there was not a day of his working life that he did not hurt. It is only now, in old age, that he recalls with pride the work he did in the forties and fifties driving truck, as did all of my uncles, for the L.A. Department of Water and Power. Then, he knew that his body would be used for labor as it had been used for war, and what he was left with was passivity and a helpless rage which, inevitably, was expressed toward us.

For my mother, things were slightly different. She had a high school education. Although she had worked years in factories before and during the war, after the war she had graduated to clerical work in the L.A.P.D. and later in the L.A. Public Library, where she worked for twenty-five years, first as a clerk typist and later as a librarian assistant. My mother wanted more, and I think that is perhaps because within the workforce she did make the move from factory to clerical work, although for a woman without a college education that work offered little advancement. Nonetheless, working in a library made her respect words, if not love them herself, because in them she understood what she could not do as she understood what I, perhaps, could do. But even that understanding was undercut by her abiding sense of what she called her "inferiority complex," a complex which, due to my shyness, she was sure I had inherited, and which, in turn, left the means by which I might "be" anything vague. Of course my mother was a contradiction herself because there was so much that she believed she could not do yet did without knowing it, exactly because there was no public and certainly no private validation of what she had accomplished in surviving. Thus, even as she pushed me away from one identity and toward another, she could not quite name the latter except by denying the former.

As I entered adolescence, I had come to accept Nana's silence along with the denial of her racial identity as unquestioned fact; it was the immediate presence of my father's defeated alcoholism which had become too obvious for anyone to ignore, and which had come to embody all I did not want to be. All I knew of working-class identity was the compelling drive to leave it behind, like my brother, who had left home when I was eight, and who, with at least the minimal encouragement and expectation accorded a male, was already a U.C.L.A. graduate. And I did. And therein lies not my mother's story, but my own, a story painful, I think, in its clarity, though I doubt that it is atypical. It begins at that point in time when my mother was no longer the source—when I entered into complicity with the story I was joining and as a result became separated from my mother by the very thing she had urged me toward.

I recognize complicity most certainly in the years when I attended a mostly middle-class high school. I remember my first creative writing class, in which the teacher asked for responses to a sketch I had written of the living room on Toluca, the piano top covered with endless dusty photographs chronicling birth after birth—and the response of one of my classmates, "Well, obviously they're Catholic." I think that was the first moment when I clearly saw myself defined as other. Moreover, I think those were the years when I recognized that "leaving behind" was no longer an abstract notion but could actually and actively be accomplished—and perhaps that was because I could concretely begin to see what I could become.

During those years, my best friend was the daughter of a wholly middle-class family. My friend's mother did not work. She spent her afternoons playing bridge, and my friend's father was an aerospace engineer. I spent many afternoons after school at my friend's house. I liked the way my friend's mother treated me. Though I was an indifferent student, I was a reader and so was she. She, after all, had a subscription to *The New Yorker.* I was the recipient of many kindnesses from that family, yet something else was also taking place in my association with them. It came in my friend's mother's perhaps spoken, perhaps implied suggestion of my own mother's dependence on me—the sense that my mother was holding me back—and most explicitly it came in my failure to defend my mother against such accusations.

It came also as I learned the subtleties of class etiquette. For instance, one weekend I was invited along on their sailboat for a trip to Catalina Island. Before I left, my mother gave me five dollars to pay for my food which, out of a sense of obligation to her, I did offer somewhat embarrassedly, though I knew both before and after its refusal that it was not appropriate even as I assumed we could not return their hospitality. At the moment of that refusal I think I began to dissociate myself from what I felt to be my mother's inadequate social understanding.

However, what I was learning is perhaps best exemplified by another incident which occurred toward the end of my senior year. Through a friend of my mother's, my friend and I had landed jobs waiting tables and cleaning cabins at a dude ranch in Wyoming for the summer between high school and college. I had never been out of Los Angeles for more than a week and was thrilled at the prospect of such an adventure. When we returned home in the fall, my friend would go out of state to school, and I would go to one of the California state schools. I had applied because I had friends who were going to college, rather than at the behest or encouragement of the school counselor, who, all along, had suggested secretarial school as the most promising route. When I returned home in the fall, I would also find that my mother had often walked the five miles to work that summer because she didn't have busfare, but rather than have me stay home and work—rather, in fact, than hold me back, she had kept silent. I would hate her silence, though of course I could not have been entirely ignorant of our finances since my father had long since stopped paying child support.

But all of this was preceded by this incident. As our departure for Wyoming had approached, my mother had decided to invite my friend's parents to dinner to discuss and celebrate both our graduation and departure. It was quite an occasion because even though my father was long gone my mother still rarely invited people to dinner. But the occasion was marred because somehow the invitation, carried by me, was misdelivered so that my friend's parents did not arrive at the appointed hour. As we waited, my mother's nervousness became more and more apparent. And when they did arrive they had already eaten and my mother, who never cried, was clearly near tears. The evening dissolves after that—my mother's awkwardness, my friend's parents picking at the food. Was I responsible for the miscommunication? Possibly. Or did my friend's mother intentionally misunderstand? I don't know. But I suspect that I sabotaged that dinner out of a sense that it would not meet the standards of that other world I was growing aware of—though, too, perhaps my memory of this incident is influenced by the more general sense of regret I have now for the separation from my mother that was taking place in those years.

In the years that followed I did go to college, and I did finally graduate because in the sixties education in California was almost free, and a student who hadn't begun with much interest or belief in her possibilities could wander in with a vague desire to write precisely because the door was open. Through that open door, I found my way to a wonderful teacher, the poet Ann Stanford, and finally to an M.F.A. program in a graduate school out of state. There, I began my apprenticeship as a writer. Eventually privileged by marriage to a middle-class academic, for some years I was supported and given time to write, an apprenticeship that included years of writing about paintings and travel, years of forgetting who I was and where I came from, of believing I should write in the present because I didn't see how to write about the past. Yet, finally, because writing is an action which can lead us toward truth, I found that the "voice" I was looking for was inevitably located in the place I had come from. My first book, *Toluca Street,* in part, attempts to portray the lives of my family. But the work I include here, from my second book, *Forgiveness,* while continuing the attempt to portray their lives, also attempts to address contradictions of my own identity, an identity formed by what I now recognize as the working class and existing in the middle class.

I have only just begun to realize the complexity of that identity, formed by denial of what one is or was, colonized and, through that colonization, then inevitably complicitous with what one is joining as that first identity is suppressed. Part of that complicity is that it took me some years to recognize that it even existed, and thus that intentional distancing is now part of my topic as well, as is my by now quite overwhelming desire that the circumstances and the forces at work in my parents' and my grandparents' lives be understood. I want their lives to be visible in all of their contradictoriness. I want my work to express not only the loss in the silences of three generations of women but also the waste of my father's addiction. I want the reader to understand what caused us to hate rather than value ourselves and others.

Finally, I hope my work offers a sense of why my family could not speak and what kept them from speaking. Words that had they had them might have lent their lives a visibility and validity they did not feel they had, words that I hope offer them and others that validity now. Words that had they had them might have offered them the opportunity for change as those words have offered me that same opportunity. For, of course, it is precisely because I am privileged, through education and through the ongoing action of my writing, that I am able to identify both the colonization and complicity. I hope the result is a shared experience that does form a version of the contradictory and complex nature of working-class memory and identity, an identity that despite my middle-class existence *is* the grounding of the identity I speak from. And it is, finally, the identity I must own, if I am to continue to believe, as I do, that art is an integral part of a conscience that both calls for and is capable of creating change.

Maxine Scates

Mockingbird

My mother sings it to me,
the song her grandmother Lila
played for a mockingbird fallen from its nest,
a human singing *Listen*
as a mockingbird replied,
and listening
the baby bird perched on Lila's finger
until it finally sang.

I remind her that when I was a child
she sang this song for me,
but now I want to know more of Lila.
I know she was sent north from Mexico City
to a convent in Los Angeles.
I know she painted, she stitched,
she raised birds and ran a restaurant,
and I know that like her daughter,
my grandmother Nana,
Lila was institutionalized.
One year both
were locked up at the same time.
I want to know what sent them
stunned, drugged, or strait-jacketed
to sit behind barred windows of different wards.
I want to know what mother knows,
the images fast on memory's glassy eye.

But here,
farther south than I was born,
in the gardens of the Self Realization Temple
overlooking the warm sea
and surfers riding endless waves,
my mother freezes at the answers.
Sometimes it's better to forget.
Still, I insist, what of life in Mexico,
did Lila ever tell her?
No, never Mexico, but Lila taught her
to make the lizard face that children loved,
took her to a flower show, the movies,
and when they went for a drive in the valley
Lila picked wild mustard for the birds.
But as she recites what I've heard before
I hear the notes
of something else, not Lila's life.

A bird is singing now,
I ask what bird? My mother tilts her head
and listens, a mockingbird, of course.
It goes on answering itself
caught in its trilling.
But does it have a real cry?
She hadn't thought of that,
and I am ten again
as she calls from the kitchen window
of our house
bent under a sky that presses down,
Look up! she shouts, *Look at the clouds.*
They can be anything.

My mother, source of my story,
tilts her head
and this seems a fluid place,
a warbling that holds its own.
Eucalyptus rattle, red calla lilies
filter light, carp swim in their dim pool,
as my mother sings her song,
a melody gone on so long that like the bird
I think she doesn't know her cry,
answers she can't give me
locked beyond these words
she taught herself to sing.

Legacy

Finally reconciled,
I am forty years old
when my father reaches out and swats my ass
from his hospital bed,
and then I remember touch was allowed there
near the couch that sat by the heater
under the crack in the ceiling made by an earthquake.
There, in the privacy of the home
where a woman's body, or even a child's,
was a casual thing
to be handled,
slurred like the carnal language
describing our bodies.
There, where his language defiled
as it touched on all of our secrets
as he spoke of those who might want
what we didn't have yet either;
there, in the little house
in the all-white neighborhood
of truck drivers, of car salesmen and deliverymen,
of wives who were clerks and factory workers
of wives who were housewives
of wives who were beaten and fearful.
There, with the roots of hatred
and of self-hatred,
with the words rising up in my mind now,
words I'd wish anywhere but in the depths
of my consciousness:
You lying sack of shit.

But why not those words?
Aren't we all mired in it?
And in the forgetting of it?
There, where his hands reached out
from their place on the couch
to swat, to fondle, to maul—
hands that hurled bowls and ashtrays,
hands that hurt and hurt even themselves

"Legacy" first appeared in *Agni* 33 (1991).

when they hit because they were wired together,
shattered and scarred by the burning.

And wasn't that were the sweetness
that returns in age as benignity left him?
When he was blown away from his shipmates
who died in that burning?
Or did sweetness leave
when the eighth grade dropout
rode the freights across country
through the depths of the thirties
with five dollars in his shoe
afraid to take the shoe off?
Or did sweetness leave somewhere before,
part of a more obscure legacy?
All of it swirling, askew,
coiling in him
so that in it with him
we were enveloped, sucked in.
Do you see what I mean? *In it*
we didn't know where to go or what to do
because though I can tell you now
I could not tell you
on the day I opened the front door
to my father and a woman
both staggering drunk and oblivious to me
as they headed for the bedroom, and then,
just as I'd begun to believe in my invisibility
his friend Bob washed up out of that craziness
saying *How about a kiss?*
pushing against me
and then *That's not so bad is it?*

My father would have beaten his old friend if he'd known,
would have seen what he did was wrong
because as he believed nothing else was
he believed I was his,
what he couldn't see
was what he was doing to me.
Distance tempers my anger,
or what I saw one day in his swollen hands,
one hand resting on the steering wheel of the Peterbilt,
the other gripping the gear shift.
Then in the roar of the engine
and the grinding of gears
as the desert stretched on

and he stared straight ahead
obligated to see nothing but that road
I came to understand something about labor.
Then I saw what he did not see,
maybe what he never had seen,
in a silver boulder that loomed suddenly
by the side of the road promising everything,
in the books beside me on the seat
that my mother had brought home
from the library where she worked,
and later, in the surge of the river
below the hydroelectric plant
where he had hauled the transformers that day.

There, in the motel where we stayed
sleeping in the same bed
I can remember nothing of that room
and I think some part of me
will always rest with him
because I haven't yet given it up,
or maybe because nothing did happen, maybe because
that day I'd seen something too of his loneliness
away from the house where we all lived
where a distance was beginning in me
where I saw that already he was drunk
but was nonetheless grateful
for some small tenderness drunkenness made in him
that wanted to show me the stream
behind the motel, the glittering stones
and the small fish that swam there.

Reconciled?
Yes, because he is mine,
because I am far from harm,
because his was the legacy left him
and, in turn, what he has left me
at the bottom of what I don't say
stifling the promise of change
in a country drunk with lies and forgetting.

Carol Faulkner

I was born August 13, 1958, the sixth of seven children. I grew up in Garrettsville, a small town in northeast Ohio. My mother worked in a rubber factory most of my childhood. My father was a welder in a machine shop. During the Depression, he worked for the Civilian Conservation Corps surveying the Everglades. His parents were truck farmers in Florida—though my grandmother was a schoolteacher until she married my grandfather. I think they were a bit proud, having once run a large farm in Georgia until the boll weevils ruined them. My mother's father immigrated from Poland as a teenager and worked for a steel mill in Cleveland. I never met him or my mother's mother or my father's father and, to tell the truth, I don't know very much about my mother's family history.

Carol Faulkner earned her Ph.D. from the University of Oregon in August 1992. She teaches at Lane Community College. She writes fiction, and her academic interests are class and narrative structure.

Carol Faulkner

My Beautiful Mother

My father says my mother was the most beautiful woman he had ever seen. When he walked down the beach with her jaws dropped and heads turned. There is a picture of her, her long bare legs draped over the side of a rocking chair, blouse tied under her bust, and she is postcard beautiful with her curling dark hair. It seems strange to me now as I look at her sturdy square body, her Polish nose and peasant ankles. Seven children and thirty years in a rubber factory have thickened her. They don't make bracelets for women like her. My mother's hands are so big she buys large men's gloves. She says they were once like mine. She had wrists like mine.

I used to sit in the car and watch the workers come out when my mother picked up her paycheck. They came out of those doors like miners, black-faced, dangling white cigarettes, like some freak birth, and my beautiful mother too. She always wore homemade dresses—A-line, sleeveless cotton print dresses. The ones for work had a grayish black stain across the belly where my mother leaned over the table sorting innertubes. My father didn't like pants. Besides, dresses were cooler. In the humid midwest summer, temperatures in Polson Rubber reached 117 degrees and that was at night. My mother had a small rotating fan to cool the sweat that trickled down the small of her back.

She slept from 7:00 to 9:00 every evening in the bed that my younger sister and I shared at night. Sometimes we let her sleep till five after because we forgot and sometimes just to give her five more minutes. "Did you iron my dress?" was the first thing she'd ask. And if I had been able to tear myself away from the television during commercials, it would be hanging over the railing still warm. Then I'd make her lunch—when she was on a diet, hardboiled eggs and a package of soda crackers and, always, Rolaids for her stomach. From the bathroom, she'd call down the stairs and ask me to bring her a pair of socks. "And don't bring me any holey ones." I would stare into her drawer trying to imagine which ones were holy. I guessed she didn't want to wear anything holy to work. Half the time I would hand her the socks and she would unfold them and say, "I told you not to bring me holey ones." I must have been twelve before it clicked and I understood what she was asking for. She dusted the floor silvery smooth with the baby powder she sprinkled in the heavy-soled black shoes she wore so she could stand for eight hours over a table inspecting the dull, black tubes. Just before she left, she stood on the back porch and sprayed her hair, big choking clouds of "White Rain." She put on her bright coral lipstick in the mirror that hung by the door in the kitchen next to the ceramic sacred heart of Jesus. She left at twenty of ten in a flurry of where's-my-scarf-did-you-remember-my-Rolaids, a welcome distraction from the horror I felt each night.

Even through my painful adolescence I kissed my mother good-bye each night for fear that she might not make it home, that the factory might not spit her out the next morning. Sometimes my mother would be throwing-up sick, and it sickened me to watch her go to work anyway. Sometimes she didn't make it through her whole shift and she would come home quietly in the middle of the night. Hot August nights people fainted and slipped down to the concrete sometimes hurting their heads. I don't know if my mother ever did. She never said. I remember the whispered stories of men who had their fingers or arms pulled off in giant rollers and lay on the floor passed out from the pain until someone found them. And now, my mother keeps the cancer count. Fifteen years after Polson Rubber moved to Tennessee, over half of those ex-workers have survived cancer, or died of it.

My mother distrusted the union leader with the Italian name who represented something dangerous—a man who was never satisfied, who threatened to shut down the factory every two years, to interrupt her desperately needed paycheck. She voted always to accept the contract, always to unseat the corrupt union leaders who asked for more, more, more, and during contract negotiations she parked under the lights and hoped that her tires would not get slashed. The shop moved to Tennessee anyway. She never said so directly, but I know she blames the union because the faceless owners were too big, too invisible to blame and, I think, if she started down that road the blame would never end.

Before graduate school, I too worked in a factory—partly because I couldn't imagine myself in an office and partly because I needed to know more about my mother's life. Seven years later I could still run any one of those machines. My muscles memorized the movements. It was too loud to talk, too loud to hear a walkman even. The boredom was so numbing, that I taught myself to slice off the tiny plastic pieces in the presses and read at the same time. Second-long snatches of Thomas Carlyle, thirty pages in an eight-hour shift. But my mother didn't read *Sartor Resartus*. I wonder what she thought about all those years. I try to imagine the despair with which my mother must have driven to her factory unable to put her children to bed or read them a story. I understand now the thwarted maternalism behind the way she used to make the bed over on top of my sister and me when she got home in the morning, just before she went to sleep herself. For me, it was a magical moment that marked her return. I would pretend I was asleep while she let the sheet fall like a parachute over my face before she tucked it down again. It was as if I floated down into a peaceful relief. Another time she had returned whole.

My mother cleans houses now, and when I go home to visit I clean them with her. I am angry that she still does it, but I cannot stop her. I long ago gave up hoping to see some of my own anger reflected in my mother's face. She leads me around the houses pointing out all the beautiful things, and I feel her reclaiming me, bringing me back to the life I grew up in. It has always been this way, a parachute and a rock. My mother warns me to do a good job. She tells me how her employer once hid change under the elephant-foot stool to see if she moved it when she vacuumed. I would laugh if I could. With anger and despair I go about scrubbing floors. I take a petty pride in noting the grammar and spelling mistakes on the notes my mother's wealthy employers leave. I desperately wish my Ph.D. would lift me out of this, but I know it never will—never in the way I sometimes want it to help me leave behind the story of my childhood, of my mother. It isn't really a matter of whether or not I do or don't clean houses while I am on vacation. Memories of my mother will always haunt me.

My mother says she never thought she would get old and fat and ugly. Once when she visited me, I stopped at the University, and she stayed in the car. She said she was tired. But I knew better. She thinks I am ashamed of her and her eighth-grade education. And the truth is, I have been most of my life. But I am even more ashamed of my shame. In grade school sometimes the teacher would make us tell the class what our parents did for a living. It seemed that most mothers didn't work at all, and I masked the truth by saying my mother was an "inspector." I was always glad that no one asked what that ridiculous title meant. When I got to high school I tried to talk her into getting her GED. She answered the way she always did. Her "no" always sounded like "yes," always left the hope I'd get my way. My sister persuaded her to take a first-aid class to better herself. I quizzed her while she cooked dinner. She grew flustered and red-faced over and above the flush caused by the stove's heat. She failed the test. And I dropped the GED.

I understand the feelings that my mother suffered. When I first came to the study of English, like a foreigner I kept a notebook of words which were the currency of the field: "indeterminate," "discursive," "problematic," words I had never heard spoken. I kept my list covertly and cynically, as a hedge against failure, but I knew that I would have to become conversant in this "discourse." That secret cynicism covered a much greater confusion of emotions—insecurity, desire to fit in, desire to remain intactly different.

A college education was never my birthright, but something I always knew I had to struggle to get. I was sixteen when my mother came to my school, pulled me out of history class, and told me the shop was closing. My father was already disabled by then, and I went back to class dazed with a picture in my head of having to forget college and go to work to support my parents as my father had done before me. It's hard for me to explain what getting an education has meant to me, but more and more I ask myself what good is it to have arrived if I have to pretend to be someone else when I get there. What I really want is to be accepted and respected for who I am within the academic community.

There has been considerable pressure from both sides to abandon my working-class roots—as if class, unlike race or gender, could be stripped off with one's clothes. The graduate school I attended happened to have a union for graduate teaching fellows. I became president of the union, a move that was particularly unpopular with the head of my department. Later I was advised to leave this information off my vita if I wanted to find a job. And each time I called home my family would ask me if I was "done with all that" as if I had been experimenting with cocaine or dabbling in the occult. I think many in my family would like to see me embrace the American Dream even if it means culturally abandoning them. At the same time, many of my colleagues are uncomfortable with the anger that sometimes seeps through my rhetoric.

There is little precedent for accepting the experiential validity of my working-class perspective in academia. The tendency is to theorize class in order to prove that it has a place at the university. When I wrote my dissertation about class in Willa Cather's fiction, my adviser insisted that I put my readings in a Marxist context. I had nothing against Marxism, but I wanted to write about Cather because I couldn't reconcile her romantic portrayal of Antonía with my mother's life. I was offended that she made a villain out of Ivy Peters, the only working-class man who exhibited any anger toward the upper classes. I couldn't join in Cather's celebration of docile, selfless working-class characters because they reminded me of the way my mother identified with her employers. I wanted to make others realize that these were stories that could only be written by someone who didn't live the working life she portrayed. I wanted to bring unrealized dreams and aching backs into my discussion of the issues that matter to me. I did end up translating my readings into academese, but there were times when I felt like my own voice was being drowned out by the academic language, that I was being distanced and alienated from my own past.

On the one hand, theoretical paradigms have helped me realize that the working-class story is the flip side of every narrative of individualism. Now, each time I read a novel about (in Cather's words) an "exceptional individual," I wonder about the faceless many that make such a narrative possible. Can the story of an individual's rise even exist without the implicit backdrop of those who are denied individuality and denied opportunity? Where are their voices? Who will tell their story? I want to recover these buried stories, but I don't want to lose my ability to make others see them through the lens of my own experience. The truth is that academic language has helped me make important observations about the working-class narrative, but as often as academic language helps me express a complex concept, it takes away the concrete, personal language I need to say what I want to say about working-class experience. It is not that no one at the university identifies themselves with the working class; the danger is just that we become advocates for, and we cease to be voices of the working class.

More and more I realize that academic language is not just a new vocabulary. My working-class community operates by a different system of communication and values. The standards I grew up with aren't the standards I meet at the university. I know how to sew clothes, put in a garden, can my own vegetables, change the oil and spark plugs in my car, put up drywall. In my family, that's gender equality. By that yardstick, the feminists I work with would be considered pretty helpless. These fundamental differences in the ways we approach issues have to be recognized by the academic community no less than the working-class one. Understanding, as they say, is a two-way street.

Several years ago, after he could no longer work, my father wrote his autobiography. He wanted me to edit it, but I couldn't. It wasn't like any books I had read. It just wouldn't fit itself into the patterns of literature I knew. It wasn't until years later when I read Jack Conroy's *The Disinherited* that I understood that his story was part of another tradition with which I was entirely unfamiliar and which my academic training had not prepared me to appreciate, let alone enjoy. Now I know that his writing grew out of a different way of experiencing the world, a way that is devalued. My mother understood that better than my father or I. Even if she could have found her own time to write, she would never have believed her life was worth the telling.

I recently attended a conference in which a popular author talked about being bored by writing that doesn't have enough play in the language, that tries too hard to "mean" something. I was really struck by what a privilege it is to splash around on the surface of language—and what an insidious form of discrimination against groups who use language differently. Earlier, she had explicitly condemned academic elitism, but she was unwittingly endorsing a concept of language which was classist. When I am confronted by contradictory stances like that, I want to say to my academic colleagues: I've learned your language—now you try to learn mine.

With the exception of a single sociology course, I never heard anyone discuss class when I was an undergraduate—certainly never with regards to literature. I silently suffered in the belief that I was the only one who came from such a background and that my background was vaguely shameful. That's a feeling that is reinforced by assumptions made about the working class. I think most people assume that by getting an education I have left my working-class past behind—and that I would naturally want to. All sorts of assumptions and blindspots about working-class life are encoded in our literature and unconsciously reencoded by literary critics insensitive to what it means to be working class. A woman I taught with once complained to me about her students' lack of enthusiasm. "I'm sorry, Carol," she said, "but I think it's a working-class attitude." Most of her university students were not even working class. Her belief was based on ignorance of, rather than contact with, the working class. Now that I'm a teacher I know that students and future teachers *learn* that the working class and working-class issues either do or don't have a place in the classroom. I know how important it is for me to say, I am working class and I do belong here.

It is not easy for me to bring my working class-ness into the university. When I speak about class in the language I grew up with, there is always the danger that someone will follow me into my old kitchen without the sympathetic eyes I take there. I remember the care I took deciding who I could bring home when I was growing up. I once brought a friend home

and she laughed at something my father said—no doubt she was just being
a typical kid—but I was so sensitive, so aware of a sense of inferiority that
I never asked her over again. I feel just the same way now. I want to protect
my family from people like my colleague who would see in them all the
things that she hates. Yet by protecting the people I care about, I insulate
those academics. As long as I keep quiet, my colleague never has to confront the prejudices she grew up with. She remains complacently ignorant
of the people she condemns. It is not just the academic community that
pressures me into silence, but my own vulnerability. I can gauge how close
I come to saying what is genuine for me by the discomfort I feel as I write
it. Do I sound naive? Am I being maudlin? Am I revealing too much? When
I began to work on this piece, I was part of a writing group that read our
work aloud once a week, but I couldn't read this piece out loud. It's too
filled with myself. I feel like I'm violating professional decorum, but who
else will tell this story? I must be able to speak as a working-class woman
because, above all, subjectivity is what has been denied the working class
all along.

I am constantly negotiating my position between my past and my
present. Right now, I live with a foot in each of these worlds, and I'm not
entirely comfortable in either. Yet, for all my confusion, this is a story I

need to tell. I see the world through memories of my mother. I will always carry her with me, into my academic life which as yet seems to have scant room for the anger, shame, and grief I feel. I continue to struggle to tell my mother's story, my story, and to understand them both. Despite all her worry about my union activities and all my anger at her steadfast subservience, I like to think my mother would have been like me. And, perhaps, with seven children and without my education, I would have been like her. Telling our story is, for me, a matter of recovering the reality of the working-class existence, exposing the tendency to rewrite that story in order to transform oppression into a character-building experience, refusing the image imposed on us from the outside. It means speaking *as* a working-class woman, not just *for* working-class women.

Part Four

Cultural Work

Wilma Elizabeth McDaniel

Editor's Note: Wilma Elizabeth McDaniel did not want to be interviewed and did not want to write about herself. She says, "It kills me to say I wrote this . . . I did that. . . ." This biographical material is culled from her letters to me, bits of press release, articles, and an interview with Jennifer Lagier in *California English* (March/April 1987). I am indebted to the poet Julia Stein for bringing Wilma Elizabeth McDaniel's work to my attention.

The Poetry Which My Life Has Required Me to Write

Wilma Elizabeth McDaniel is a poet and living witness to the Dust Bowl "Okie" trek to California. Part Cherokee, she was born in 1918, the fourth of eight children, into a family of Oklahoma sharecroppers.

> My background was one of unremitting hardship and poverty. It was a patchwork of rundown houses with privies and hard water that one could not make a suds in without using lye to soften it. The daily struggle was for basic food, clothing, and shelter, the latter entailing the frequent use of pots and pans moved around to catch rain from roofs that always leaked.

In the thirties her family left the oppressive 100-degree day heat and barren land of Oklahoma and migrated with thousands of others to the promised green of California.

> Our survival in the San Joaquin Valley could only bring better conditions materially. I cannot always say the same thing of spiritual survival. We found, quite often, a terrible malaise of the spirit, people who did not realize what they had given up in emotional ties and comfort for a full stomach.

She has been both a farmworker and a poet most of her life.

> It is truly difficult to talk about the forces that shaped my poetry. I have always been a poet. This is literally true. I wanted to respond to life around me when I was no more than three or four. I wanted to take the world to myself to cry out to people around me of its magnificent beauty. I actually feared they would miss it if I did not tell them that it was there. By the age of eight, I had to be about my calling. At fourteen, I summoned every iota of courage I could muster and took a poem to a tiny newspaper. It was published.

In 1973 her first book of poetry was published. Her books include: *A Primer for Buford, Sister Vayda's Song* (both from Hanging Loose Press), *A Girl From Buttonwillow* (Worm Wood Press), and *Tollbridge* (Contact II). The poetry included here is from her unpublished collection, *Shawls*.

> I'm enclosing some poems from a collection which has been gnawing inside me for several years. Of course, it begins at the beginning (with working women). Indeed, doesn't it always

end with working women? Those my age are still working to help their children make house payments.

Anyway, I have envisioned a rather large manuscript of working women's poetry, about 106 pages under the title *Shawls*. I am sending you a quarter of it. Good angels, knowing my bad eye problems, translate and type my poems. I'll receive typed batches as time permits these working women to do this heroic service.

In response to my request for some autobiographical writing and a photograph, she says:

I'm going through old pictures, the only ones I have of myself have yellowed too much to copy. They obviously should have been better preserved. Someone said it was the chemicals some photographers used then. My most satisfactory representations of myself as a child are tiny pen and ink drawings my mother did from memory. In her early nineties and impaired with arthritis, she would draw these pictures with only a few strokes. Invariably, I am running along dusty roads, picking wildflowers, calling up doodlebugs, in absolute amazement with the wonder of life around me.

It is strange that quite a bit is written about my poetry, read in schools, but so *little* is being *published* outside of small presses such as Hanging Loose in Brooklyn, or the feminist Broomstick in San Francisco. I feel almost certain that you will receive few entries from cotton-picking poets, two-room school academics, but let 'er rip. I'm coughing up postage.

Sincerely,
Wilma Elizabeth McDaniel

Dessie Upshaw
Headed West

When a relative called
her to come work in the
Portland shipyards
Dessie had never traveled
outside rural Missouri
and wondered what she
would eat on a long trip

Among fourteen women
on a Greyhound bus, she was
the only one who wore a dress
and cotton stockings
and carried dried fruit in
her shopping bag

In Kearney, Nebraska
she ate a handful of raisins
which held her over to
Ogden, Utah
where she ate a dried peach

By the time they reached Portland
she was down to only
a few wrinkled prunes
and fretted about that

A fellow traveler told her
not to worry
Oregon abounds in fruit
they've got acres of prunes
and pears and miles of
apples to pick
they don't just grow ships

Italian Community Trying to Figure Out Dustbowl Girls 1936

From Amalfi Junction's
fertile vineyards oozing wine
or taking siestas on cool
shaded porches
their eyes of glass and silver
eyes of watery brown
All eyes searched the coming
road
and saw only dreaded gypsies
with bare feet

They could not see yellow dust
was beauty
when it colored the hair
of girls and held their footprints

The entrenched could only say
people worth their salt
working hard
already had a home

They forgot so easily, the same road
led everyone to this place
these hardvoiced people who
believed God still lived in Rome

Wilma Elizabeth McDaniel

First Spring in California 1936

The Okies wrapped their
cold dreams in army blankets
and patchwork quilts
and slept away the foggy winter.

From doors of tents
and hasty shacks
they watched for spring
as they would watch
for the Second Coming of Christ
saw valley colors change
from skim milk blue
still needing sweaters
to pale green that filled
their eager eyes with hope.

As they worked and waited
the Valley burst forth with
one great color, gold,
flaunted poppies over acres
of land.
Women hunted for fruit jars
and tried to can the flowers
in case next year did not
produce a bumper crop.

In a letter from Wilma Elizabeth McDaniel, December 1, 1991.

Wilma Elizabeth McDaniel

San Joaquin School

So young and new in California
there were still green blades
of grass in my long hair

when I knocked at the door
of Beginners School
I had everything to learn

that pomegranates could grow
outside pages of the Bible
and real men wear turbans

At fifteen I couldn't know
how vital it was to make
a list
of things I had never done before

And mark an X by things
I never would do twice
pan again for gold
and learn that it was fools'

It was terribly hard
but I learned to measure
distance
from my bedroom window
without a telescope

Until then I never cared
how far it was to the moon
or who lived there

At straightup midnight
in the May of all Mays
I saw there *was* a man in
the moon
with a Portuguese face
young and round like
Silva's milker

When I turned my head
his eyes followed me
like any boy on Planet Earth

and he was sad when
I closed the curtains

Wilma Elizabeth McDaniel

Shawls

In that period no one
understood how climate
can affect a woman
thin her blood to water
or freeze her soul to ice

Perhaps I lived too long in
the shadow of Santa Glacia
wearing my shawls to ever
thaw out

And adjust to light that blinds
and gives me vertigo of spinning
melons
and giant peaches without fuzz

I start for the orchard
and lose my way in a parking
lot of pickups
jostled by a six-pack crowd
of silver-buckled levis

And tanktop girls with fake
eyelashes who stare at me
in disbelief

A stereo is moaning out
They Call The Wind Maria
but no one seems to feel its
chill except me

I get my old glacial shiver again
and long for the heavy shawls

Pat Wynne

I was born at the beginning of World War II in the Bronx, to secular/radical Jewish parents. Irving and Rose met in a writing class at night school. Rose Parker, born in Rumania, was proud to be related to Anna Pauker, head of the Rumanian Commun-

ist Party from 1948 to 1952. Irving Wynne, born Isidore Weinman, was the son of Russian socialists. My grandfather Nathan distributed radical literature in the Ukraine before he fled persecution in the early 1900s. As a child, I spent my summers at Golden's Bridge Colony, where I was immersed in workers' culture and struggles. The photo depicts me and my son, Richard Lehrman, circa 1970.

Pat Wynne is a singer, composer, pianist, and voice teacher. She graduated from Music and Art High School and Hunter College in New York. In addition, she has an M.A. in Women's Health Counseling from San Francisco State University. Since 1980, she has been performing her original songs—about experiences in the real world of cutbacks and downsizing, dreaming and dating—in night clubs and concert halls. Based in San Francisco, she is a member of the Freedom Song Network, and has sung at more picket lines and rallies than she can call to mind. Her latest project is *Working Women's Stories and Songs,* an evening of interwoven oral histories and songs, which she performs with Carma Muir Berglund.

Days of a Red Diaper Daughter

June 1992: Little Joe's, North Beach, San Francisco

Over an Italian dinner, a dozen people sat at a long table after a Freedom Song Network concert at the San Francisco Art Institute. Four of us started singing:

> You can tell a Red
> From the bumps upon his head
> From the vitamins he's fed
> And even when he's dead
> You can tell a Red!
>
> You can tell a Red
> By the way he combs his hair
> By his winter underwear
> By the fact he's everywhere! *

That's one of the songs from the Henry Wallace campaign, his 1948 run for the presidency on the Progressive Party ticket. Who else remembers these songs? We Red Diaper babies grew up in the United States of America, but it felt as if we were on another planet: the Red Planet.

1950–1960: The Bronx

Shhhh! Shhhh! I remember being warned over and over again to be quiet whenever I spoke about anything political in my home. We lived in a two-room walk-in apartment in the Bronx. Our windows were at street level. People could look in.

Shhhhhh! A clop on the head if I didn't obey.

My parents believed that FBI agents were outside the window, listening to everything we said. I was nine years old in 1950. I thought my parents were crazy. Who were *we* that FBI agents would listen at our window? It shaped my attitudes toward my parents: I devoted myself to remaining sane in the midst of their insanity.

*Author unknown.
Copyright © 1994 by Pat Wynne.

I was always aware that my family and I were living on the fringes of American society.

There was a disjointed, disconnected quality to our lives. There were so many *contradictions*. I suppose being Jewish didn't help. My parents' immigrant mentality had fused with the ingrained caution learnt in threadbare Depression childhoods. And add to that the Holocaust.

Working class, Jewish, and "Progressive": that combination brought a lot of personal joy, but also a lot of pain. And female too: well, it's amazing I grew up with any self-esteem at all.

The message I got from my parents was: go to school, get all A's.

"You got 90% on your test? What happened to the other 10%?"

"Practice the piano! Remember you're a scholarship student. You have to excel."

But then, if I want to be a performer? "Get a teaching credential, then you'll always have something to fall back on."

My mother encouraged me to be financially independent. She felt trapped in her marriage because she didn't have a profession.

"Never be in a position where you have to depend on a man." That message was constantly repeated.

She had worked as a beautician for many years, but she'd be damned if she was going back to that. She hated to be financially dependent on my father, but she couldn't change her life. She wanted mine to be different.

We lived in a Jewish neighborhood in the West Bronx. During the early 1940s, my parents had given up their apartment in the city every year, to live upstate in Golden's Bridge from May to December. They bought an acre of land there, and slowly built a little summer house. When World War II ended and all the servicemen came home, finding an apartment was suddenly very hard. Finally, my parents tracked down a two-room apartment for $40 a month, on the corner of Walton Avenue between the Concourse and Jerome Avenue, near 170th Street. That was our home from 1945 to 1955.

Two rooms! Living in that tiny space with those two high-strung people wasn't easy. No one had enough privacy. At first, we all slept in the same room. Then, when I was nine, they bought a Castro convertible sofa, and Dad went to sleep in the living room/dining room/kitchen. I never thought about the implications of that change; I just moved into his bed. Without my little bed, there was more space in the bedroom for a big upright piano.

The only place you could really be alone was the bathroom. I escaped there regularly to read. Even that was problematic, because my father, an amateur botanist, often experimented with exotic plants. I was afraid that the carnivorous Venus flytrap and pitcher plants growing on the window-sill in back of the toilet would grab me and eat me.

A child of secular, Marxist Jews, I didn't go to Shul. My parents said the progressive middle Shul in the co-ops on Allerton Avenue in the East Bronx was too far away. The fact that I studied music every week down on West End Avenue and 83rd Street in Manhattan didn't seem like a contra-diction to them.

Said my father, who'd been given a Bar-Mitzvah, "Religion is the opi-ate of the people, and don't forget it." (As I matter of fact, I haven't.)

When Passover came around, my father refused to eat matzo. All year round, he ate matzo with great pleasure, but through the Passover holidays, he insisted on having a loaf of bread on the table.

A walk-in apartment has no stoop, no stairway, no lobby. The en-trance is right at street level. Anyone passing by, all our Jewish neighbors, could see right inside, and know that we were violating Jewish tradition. So, my mother kept the shades down for the whole week of Passover. At school I was the only child without a matzo sandwich; the other kids asked questions I couldn't answer.

My parents taught me about anti-Semitism. Although I was brought up to believe that all people are created equal and, unlike our neighbors in the Bronx, we never used racist language, my mother told me I was never, ever, to date anyone who wasn't Jewish, because, in the end, they would call me a "dirty Jew."

My father had changed the family name from Weinman to Wynne because he felt that would help his law practice (the law practice he never started). They named me Patricia, I'm sure, to protect me from anti-Semitism. Growing up, I was the only person I knew with that name; it felt special. Then, in high school, I found out every fourth person, male or female, was called Pat.

Disguised as Pat Wynne, I've often heard anti-Semitic slurs and com-ments, over the years. In those situations, I identity myself as a Jew, and confront the perpetrators. I sometimes think it would be easier to have a Jewish name.

In many ways, I led a normal Bronx life. I roller-skated on the side-walk, I played A-My-Name-Is-Alice with my pink spaldeen. I jumped rope. I went to PS 64 and Junior High School 117 with the other kids from the neighborhood.

We danced in the corner candy store to doo-wop records. We had an after-school girls' club. We knew which boys were in which gangs. In the fifties, I dressed with collar up, tight skirts with a slit, saddle shoes, a high pompadour and long curly hair. I dressed tough, and I talked tough.

But for three hours a week, I was trained to be one of the "little ladies and gentlemen" at the Pardee School of Music on West End Avenue, where I was a scholarship student between 1947 and 1953. Miss Pardee lived in a bubble of gentility, and held us to her quaint standards. She did teach me musical skills, though; building on that training, I was later accepted to Music and Art High School, without which I would not be who I am today.

Besides the streets of the Bronx and Miss Pardee's, I had a third life: my life in Golden's Bridge Colony.

1940–1959: Golden's Bridge, Westchester County, New York State

About 100 acres, Golden's Bridge was incorporated into a Colony in the 1930s. Only workers were allowed to buy land: no bosses, managers, or foremen. My parents built a tiny six-room house, eventually creating a three-room rental unit out of half of it.

We were weekend gypsies: schlepping and hauling, schlepping and hauling. Packing the car, unpacking the car. Dad's old sedan barely made the trip.

Golden's Bridge was a prefigurative community, the workers' utopia, but often there was trouble in paradise. The adults would throw chairs at each other and curse in angry Yiddish at the colony meetings. Sometimes they fought about tenants and beach passes; sometimes about Stalin and Hitler. We kids would listen outside the barn and giggle.

For a long time, my mother was secretary of the colony. My dad never talked to anyone, but grew gorgeous vegetable gardens.

Golden's Bridge was where I lived my *real* life. When I got to the country, I could breathe. I could move around without restriction. I could walk barefoot. I could hide out and never see my parents all day.

There was a day-camp program, and wonderful people came to be our counselors. Our favorite was Ernie Lieberman, who was a member of People's Songs and later a Limelighter. Pete Seeger came to visit. I still remember the day he taught us, "Way down south in Yakkety Yak, a bullfrog jumped from bank to bank, because he'd nothing better for to do."

Everything was for the children, for us: for the next generation who would change the world.

My friends, some of whom I'd known since birth, came from similar city apartments and progressive families. We understood each other in a way that was not possible with my nonpolitical friends from the Bronx.

As a girl, I felt equal to the boys, physically and intellectually. I played punch ball and softball with them—noncompetitively, of course. I swam across the lake when I was eight or nine, to pass the Big Raft test. At the day camp, we went on hikes, learned folk dances, and entered puberty with boys and girls we'd known all our lives.

We were encouraged to take our talents seriously, to explore culture: finger painting, sculpture, folk dancing, ballet ("Sit at the piano, Patsy, and practice," said my mother. "You're very clumsy"), woodworking, singing.

We ran wild. We broke into the barn, we raided gardens in the fall. We followed the camp counselors around, spied on them, and wrote accounts of their secret kisses in the camp newspaper. (I wrote the gossip column.) We stole their cigarettes, and buried them. By the time we were twelve, we were smoking the stolen cigarettes ourselves. We had a kissing club. One night, my friend David broke into the little grocery store, painted all the Kotex red, and strewed them all over the camp.

Our behavior was tolerated because we were, after all, the hope of the future. The revolution would be won for us and our progeny. In Golden's Bridge, we had permission to be completely ourselves. No wonder I felt fully alive there.

We developed strong ideas about right and wrong. We knew about causes. We collected money in slotted cans for Willie McGee and the Scottsboro Boys. We knew about racism, union busting, Mother Russia, and Red-baiting. I remember the cars and buses that came back from the Paul Robeson concert in Peekskill. All the windows were busted; people were bleeding. Local thugs had thrown rocks at the audience as they were leaving the concert. We heard about the police, how they'd looked the other way.

In Golden's Bridge, we had a sense of belonging to a community, and to something larger than ourselves. It was the one place that I felt at home.

1986: Panajachel, Guatemala

My father lived in Guatemala for twelve years after his retirement from the Post Office. He kept his home in upstate New York, and spent the warm months there, April to October. Every winter, he was in Guatemala. He made a gypsy life for himself, echoing the Golden's Bridge years.

In the winter of 1986, I visited him. On our daily walks, he told me stories about his life, things I hadn't known before, although he never did admit that he'd been a member of the Communist Party.

He told me how he was accused of being a Communist while working at the Post Office. The eight other men who were also accused got together and hired a lawyer to defend them. My mother, always worried about money, wouldn't let my father join the group.

For ten years, Dad said, he was put into a dark room where bright lights were shone in his eyes. There, he was questioned over and over again about his Party affiliation, his house in Golden's Bridge. They asked about other members of his family, those suspected of being in the Party.

Unaided, he denied everything over and over and over, and he never lost his job.

Golden's Bridge? "I live in Golden's Bridge because I like to garden," he'd say. "I never talk to anyone. I only tend my garden." Actually that was true.

"My brother? I never see my brother except at family gatherings, twice a year. I never talk to my family. I don't even have a telephone."

Endless denials. Endless interrogations.

The other eight workers who hired the lawyer had lost their jobs long ago. Steadfastly, my dad held on, held on, held on, waiting for his pension.

My father gritted his teeth and worked all his life at a job he hated, just so he could get his pension. I'm happy to report that he lived twenty-five years on that pension, and got to do a lot of things before he died.

My father was extremely shy and introverted, and the McCarthy purges made him more so.

He was the second of eight children. His parents came from Russia at the beginning of the century, driven out by pogroms. My grandparents were socialists. Grandpa was politically active in Russia prior to the Kerensky revolution.

They brought their politics with them, and raised their children to be socialists. My grandmother was one of the women who organized strikes against the kosher butchers in Brooklyn in the early part of the century.

They read the socialist Yiddish newspaper the *Forverts* until, at a certain point, my grandfather switched to the *Freiheit,* the Communist Yiddish paper. My grandfather was a tailor, in the garment workers' union. This is my legacy.

The family was poor, but my father managed to put himself through college and law school by working full time in the Post Office. He graduated and passed the bar in 1936, at the height of the Depression. Not aggressive or assertive, he was afraid to leave the security of his civil service Post Office job for low-paid law clerk's work. Alas, he never practiced law, and stayed in the Post Office till retirement.

He took every civil service exam offered, and passed them all. But he never took any promotion that would make him a supervisor of other workers. He couldn't be a boss: it was against his principles. Of course, it also didn't suit his character.

He was in the Post Office Players, and acted in Clifford Odets's *Awake and Sing* and other plays by progressive authors of the thirties and forties. He took the Great Books course at the public library for twenty years. He supervised my reading from elementary school on, and was still sending me books until he died, in 1990.

My parents were working class, but not uneducated. Their education and their politics gave me a global perspective. By the time I was twelve, I'd read a long list of English, French, and Russian classics: *War and Peace, The Brothers Karamazov,* Gogol's *The Overcoat,* De Maupassant short stories, Dickens. I read Steinbeck, Dos Passos, Howard Fast. My parents said comics, romance novels, and movie magazines were "crap"; I read them at my friends' houses.

My parents met in a short-story writing class in night school. Though my mother never graduated high school, she was well read and wrote poetry. She also loved music; she always had the radio turned to concerts and opera.

Ahead of her time, my mother believed in good nutrition. She bought only fresh food, and planned meals that were especially healthful. The summer vegetables from their gardens sent them both into paroxysms of delight. In classic European fashion, she then proceeded to boil everything to a pulp.

We ate fresh fish, too: bass and blue gills. My dad would take me on his expeditions. First, he dug for worms, writhing night crawlers; then, he led the way to some railroad trestle on the reservoir, where passing trains threw gravel at our heads, or to a weedy corner. Usually, my line got caught in the rushes, and Dad would yell, "You can never do anything right."

1960–1973: The Red Diaper Daughter Grows Up

When I took sociology in college, we were told that society could be analyzed into three classes: upper, middle, and lower. I discussed this theory with my father, who took a fiercely different position.

"There are only two classes," he'd say, in his Brooklyn accent, "the woikers and the capitalists!"

"But Dad," I'd protest, "the professor said—"

"I don't care what he says. There are only *two* classes: the woikers and the capitalists!"

It drove me nuts. After all the turmoil of the 1950s, I wanted to fit into the mainstream. I wanted to turn my back on politics. I wanted a "normal" life.

I got pregnant and got married before I finished college. After graduation, I gave birth to my son, Richard.

My marriage quickly went sour. My husband, Marvin, expected me to take over from his mother, who'd lovingly ironed his sheets and underwear.

We'd been married in her front room, in an orthodox Jewish ceremony that included me, the bride, only as a passive chattel to be given away. I probably started to hate him as soon as he broke the glass at the end of the wedding.

I felt trapped, unready to have a child. I expect Marvin felt trapped too. He never offered me money for clothes or other personal things, which made me determined to get out of the house and earn my own living. I started substitute teaching when Richard was nine months old. Six months later, I got a full-time job.

I taught music at PS 9 in Brooklyn. I joined the UFT, and became a strike captain in one of the first teachers' strikes in New York City in the early 1960s. Of course I joined the union: I was still Daddy's little girl.

When I separated from my husband, after four years, it felt like I'd been let out of jail. Being a single parent was a breeze compared to the oppression of marriage! (What would Mama have said?)

I got involved with a black man who lived in the Lower East Side (later to be called the East Village). We were together for several years, and I loved him deeply, though we didn't live together or marry.

In my life, I've had three important interracial relationships, two with African Americans and one with an African man. My father had always impressed upon me the equality of all people. Unlike my mother, he totally accepted my relationships with men who were neither Jewish nor white. I've always respected my father for his lack of hypocrisy.

Racial attitudes also changed the way I regarded my union.

In the 1960s, the Ford Foundation set up three community-controlled schools in New York: one in Oceanville–Brownsville, Brooklyn, IS 201 in

Harlem, and another school in the Manhattan Twin-Bridges area on the Lower East Side. Facing this new power of largely black communities, white teachers in the city began to feel threatened and challenged. Many were accused of racism and fired from the three schools.

The UFT called a strike. I advised my principal to keep the school open, which he did. For the first and last time in my life, I did the unforgivable, at least as far as my father was concerned: I crossed the picket line and went to work during the teachers' strike of 1968.

It was difficult to unravel the skeins of unionism and racism in that strike. I decided to support the black community I worked for at PS 9, rather than participating in my union's strike. Though in my own life I continued to teach in the black community, and socialize in the black community, it was a very difficult and confusing time for me.

I often think about that strike. Most of the white teachers in the UFT were Jewish, and that strike marks the beginning of the overt break between Jews and African Americans on the Left.

1993: The Mission District, San Francisco

When my father died, he left me enough money to make a down payment on a small house. The realtor called it a mini-mansion. It has high ceilings, bay windows, a few large rooms. As much as anything, the peacocks in the stained-glass panels on the front door caught my attention. Besides which, we could afford it.

I love this house. It represents security in unforgiving times, as long as we can keep up the monthly payments. But it doesn't define my identity.

My parents brought me up to define myself elsewhere, not in material things. That didn't always feel so good. In high school, when I asked my father for money to buy things, things close to a teenager's heart like clothes or shoes, he told me I wasn't a "factory owner's daughter," like the other girls. Those aspirations weren't appropriate for me. To my dad, all the other kids were the offspring of factory owners, no matter what their actual parentage might be.

Visiting my girlfriend Jeannie, I was amazed that she didn't know how much money was in her purse. She'd tip her bag upside down, pull out all the loose change, and count it. Depending on the total, we'd go to a movie, or go for a walk. I was on a stricter budget. When I was commuting to Miss Pardee's music school, my mother gave me my exact subway fare, not a penny more, not a penny less. One day, I got on a train going in the wrong direction by mistake, and had to ride halfway across the system until I found a station where I could transfer from train to train without paying again. I arrived home terrified; the next week, my mother counted out the exact fare again.

My dad's refusal to be promoted, principled as it was, meant we were always living on a limited income.

Many of my middle-class friends—the factory owners' daughters— received a clear message from their parents: "Whatever you want to do, you can. You're beautiful, talented, bright: go out and conquer the world. We'll help you." The message I got from my family was different. Growing up in the Depression, hounded by Red-hunters, my parents were cautious and paranoid. Although they wanted me to excel in a career, they doubted that success was possible. They couldn't encourage me to find my dreams; they encouraged me to secure a pension.

About one thing, my dad had no doubts at all: he knew what was right and what was wrong. As a child, I was never allowed any feelings of my own; I was held to another standard, a rational standard, a nonmaterial value system. That was hard.

I look back now, and I see that my parents' value system, their common purpose, was so strong as to be almost a kind of spirituality.

My parents' values gave them the sense of community that we struggle so hard to find here in the city. And they passed it on to me. It's the deepest core of my life; I can't live without it. When I left home, I tried to be "normal," to fit in, but the roots were too deep.

Since I moved to San Francisco in 1973, I've been repoliticized: active in the San Francisco community schools as a parent, then in the radical psychiatry community, and in the 1980s as a political musician and cultural worker.

I joined the Freedom Song Network soon after its founding. It's a loose network of political musicians, serving groups that work for social change. Many of us are Red Diaper sons and daughters. In ten years, we've sung at picket lines, marches, demonstrations, rallies, banquets, and benefits for unions and a rainbow of good causes in the Bay Area. I also compose political songs, and perform them in concert settings, in small-group arrangements.

Integrating my music and politics—the schools my parents sent me to and the principles they taught me every day—is the closest I've come, as an adult, to feeling as I did in Golden's Bridge Colony. I've come home: it's not exactly the Red Planet, of course.

I was brought up to believe in the truth. All the children in Golden's Bridge were seekers after the truth. Isn't that why we used to follow our camp counselors around and write up their transgressions in our newspaper? Over the years, the truth has become more complex, but it hasn't died. I know I'll be pursuing it, as activist and cultural worker, for the rest of my life.

Pat Wynne

Silences

Class background is a mystified concept in this "classless society." When I was a young girl living in the Bronx, my parents pushed me very hard to achieve in school and in my music studies. Yet at the same time I was re-

Pat Wynne at Golden's Bridge, circa 1965.

ceiving a mixed message from them. "Be a teacher, have practical goals—the entertainment business is too insecure. What if you don't make it? Don't aim too high." Was it their immigrant mentality, sexism, or their working-class insecurity?

Consequently, my song writing, rehearsing, performing were always activities done "after work." If work was too demanding, or I got sick, or my child got sick, or my husband needed something—those were the priorities in my life. I never thought I could be successful, because the message was that I couldn't succeed. I didn't receive "permission" to try, as I would have if I had come from a middle-class or upper-class family.

Permission is a concept I didn't understand until I was an adult. I would see mediocre performers who thought that they were wonderful. Where did these feelings, so elusive to me, come from? When I investigated further, it invariably turned out that they had come from affluent families. They were reared to believe that the world was waiting for them. I was not raised that way. My way was a cautious road leading to a position of security—preferably with a pension.

As a voice teacher I see so many of my most talented students come to their voice lesson exhausted after eight hours of work that means nothing to them. Their voices suffer, their progress is slow. My students deserve the luxury of time to work on their music, their voice, their art, their career. But alas, the most talented often suffer. Their priority is survival. The world sometimes loses the best art to economic constraints.

When I read Tillie Olsen's book *Silences*, I was moved to write this song, which is dedicated to Tillie Olsen.

CHORUS: I just want to sing about the song,
          It gets born but it takes so long,
          You know the world is full of silences and when silence lasts
              so long,
          There's a miracle in a newly written song.

1. Does the lady have a room of her own,
   Does she have to compose while she's ironing?
   Does she get up at dawn before it's time to feed the kids?
   Is she burning the midnight oil, midnight oil?

2. Does that old computer screen make her eyes burn,
   Does the office manager make her cry?
   Did the band rehearsal end just as her morning shift begins?
   Can the waitress memorize her lines, those darn lines?

CHORUS

3. Praise the artist who is struggling to survive
   She's got a voice that won't be silenced,
   Did Cole Porter scrub the floor, Richard Rogers mind the store
   How much work goes into every song, every song?

CHORUS

I was born on February 19, 1950, in Queens, New York. Most of my family (from my mother's and stepfather's side) were political refugees from the Greek community of Smyrna (now Turkish Izmir). My biological father's family was from the northern Greek city-town of Kastoria, known for providing some of the world's most skilled furriers. I was raised by my mother, Phyllis Linakis (her father's name) Mantsios (her first husband's name) Simitopoulos (her second husband's name). My mother was a single parent for the first ten years of my life and worked as a seamstress at home and in garment shops to earn a living. I attended Public School number 170, Junior High School 217, and Jamaica High School.

Both class and ethnicity played an important role in my upbringing. I grew up in a poor but fairly diverse neighborhood that bordered on a large Greek community. Life in the neighborhood revolved around street culture, which provided me with a bottom-up view of the world and equipped me with a sense of combativeness and determination. Life within the Greek community revolved around the Church, which my mother made sure I attended regularly. As a result, I grew up being both an altar boy and a street hood; I learned to play Greek tunes on the accordion (the instrument of preference at the time, for those who had neither the money nor the space for a piano) while also learning to pick locks. This essay is dedicated to my mother, who throughout it all kept me alive, taught me perseverance, and provided me with a sense of ethics.

This photo was taken in July 1954. It shows me with relatives welcoming my paternal grandmother on her first

visit from Greece. The ship she arrived on (in the background) was named *Nea Hellas*—"New Greece." I am fourth from the left; my mother is second from right.

Gregory Mantsios is the director of Worker Education at Queens College, CUNY. He oversees the college educational program for union members, its Extension Center, and its Labor Resource Center. He earned a bachelor's degree in sociology and a master's degree in urban studies from Queens College, and a Ph.D. in sociology from the Union Institute. He publishes articles on class, education, and the labor movement, and lives in Montclair, New Jersey, with Paula Rothenberg and their children, Alexi and Andrea.

Gregory Mantsios

Living and Learning: Some Reflections on Emergence from and Service to the Working Class

It is six-thirty in the evening. It's already been a long day: ten hours of meetings, telephone calls, and paperwork. The classroom I am now in is beginning to fill up with a new crop of students. They are here for their first college orientation. Unlike their more traditional counterparts across campus, these students are not recent high school graduates. They are older and, in fact, many of them have never been to high school, earning instead a high school equivalency diploma by taking a standardized exam.

As the director of Worker Education for Queens College, it's my job to tell these students about college requirements, tuition rates, and grading policies. It's also my job to tell them why a college education is important and what it will mean for their lives now and in the future.

No matter how many times I do this, it never comes easy. As I look around the room, it's not myself I see sitting in those classroom chairs but rather my parents and their contemporaries—not as they are now, but as they were when I was a teenager. It seems odd; I cannot imagine them in a college classroom either then or now.

Some of the students in the room are in their early thirties, many considerably older. Some speak perfect English, many speak broken English.

Some are white, most are black or Latino. Some are native New Yorkers, others recently migrated from the South. Many are recent immigrants from Eastern Europe, Asia, or Latin America. By day, these students work in garment shops, on construction sites, in warehouses, on assembly lines, and in high-rise office buildings. By night, they enter the world of the "non-traditional student" in a fairly traditional college setting. It's been a long day for them, too.

Why are these working adult students enrolling in college when so many others like them do not? It is because they are members of unions that have established educational funds to enable them to enroll in a college degree program either on a tuition-free basis or at minimal cost. Eight unions participate in the program, enrolling nearly six hundred students. Some unions provide reimbursement to students who successfully complete their course work, others provide full or partial scholarships. One union provides full tuition, fees, and book expenses for fifty of their members, all garment workers, to attend classes in this program. The Education Director of the garment workers is with me at the orientation to address his member-students.

As I look around the room, I am struck by two things. First, that all this is made possible by labor unions—those institutions that have somehow become a dirty word in the U.S. While big business and conservative politicians blame unions for all of society's economic ills, progressive politicians scramble to distance themselves from unions for fear of damaging their political careers. Yet it is these very organizations that are providing working people both with social services and with self-respect. As many in the room will tell you, it is the union that fights for their rights, protects them from hazardous working conditions, and brings them a modicum of dignity at the workplace. It is also the union that fights for the social services so many poor and working people depend on and provides these services when government fails to do so or do so adequately.

The union has brought these members to our college program. It not only provides the educational funds that make it possible for union members to attend college, it has actively recruited, counseled, and cajoled its members into taking advantage of this educational benefit. The union leader who is addressing his member-students at the orientation ends his talk with the words, "Knowledge is power: seize the power."

The second thing that strikes me is that I am facing a group of people who are commonly portrayed in our society as lazy, unproductive, and selfish. Our movies and television serials depict them as crude, our comics stereotype and mimic them as dumb, and our news media suggest that they are a greedy lot that have outpriced themselves in the global labor market. Workers always seem to get a bum rap in a class society.

The everyday life of the worker-student in front of me is a hard one. Most of them work at physically exhausting, mind-deadening jobs that require both physical strength and mental stamina. Many work a second job after hours or on weekends in order to get by. In some cases, they earn no more than the minimum wage. Even those who do earn considerably more cannot be sure that they will have employment throughout the year. For the construction workers in the room, there will be only twenty-six weeks of work this year.

They raise a family and keep house without the advantage of paid helpers. They cook, clean, shop, and take care of their children on their own in the little time that is left after a day at work. Time and economic class are inevitably intertwined: everything takes longer when you are pressed for money. Whether it is the time needed to shop comparatively or the time it takes to use public transportation, getting through everyday life is fraught with inconvenience or peril, or both. Finding the time and the energy to take college courses seems like a Herculean task. This is a life that is in sharp contrast to those who shape our cultural stereotypes and who are fond of making pronouncements about the problems with the U.S. labor force.

But the hardened faces that fill this room are filled with hope as well as with hardship. And hope, like hardship, has a class character. I often ask new students what motivated them to return to school. Some have very specific goals in mind, but most have limited and vague aspirations: to pick up some skills, to get a better job, to earn a little more money, and increasingly, to get out of a dying industry.

While their younger, middle-class counterparts are often filled with great ambitions for accomplished careers, successful business ventures, and recognized professional achievements, such aspirations are rare with working adult students. These students want a decent job and the ability to carry on an intelligent conversation and they hope we can help them with both. I remember reading an account of one working-class student who put it this way, "I just want to be average."[1] Class also has a way of reining in the spirit.

It sometimes astounds me that such a vague promise of a better life through education inspires considerable sacrifice among the poor and working class. One student told me, "I slaved all my life to send my kids to college, now it's my turn."

Another student said, "The union is terrific: it gave me an opportunity to go to school and better myself and I would be a fool not to take advantage of it."

But it's not all that simple: both unions and education have a spotted history. And what really troubles me is the ambivalence of those workers not in the room—the ones who don't attend union meetings, read the union newspaper, or take advantage of union services. Perhaps worse still, I think about the workers we spoke to and failed to recruit to the program. If unions are so great, why is it then that they so often fail to interest, let alone mobilize workers? And if education is so great, why do so many drop out of school in the first place and then fail to continue their studies, even when someone else is paying for it?

For every worker touched by the labor movement, there are countless others who think unions are irrelevant at best, corrupt and counterproductive at worst. For every student enthusiastic about his or her studies, there are countless others who have dropped out of or even been destroyed by the educational system. Not all have fared well by unions or by education. All this makes me reflect on my own past and I cannot help but feel that the ambivalence both towards unions and towards education is justified.

I was immersed in a class struggle, of sorts, almost from the day I was born. My father, a fur worker who immigrated from Greece, was by all accounts a good, decent, kind, hard-working man. He died of a bleeding ulcer before I was ten months old.

My mother is a sensitive but tough woman who had a particularly difficult life. Her mother died of pneumonia six years after arriving in the U.S. from Greece with my grandfather. My mother was two years old at the time. Her father returned to Greece to raise his two young children with the help of his sister. Within days of arriving in his homeland, he was taken prisoner by Turkish soldiers and was never seen again. My mother and her brother continued to live in Greece with their aunt. Eighteen years later, her brother returned to the U.S. and in four years' time had earned enough money to bring over my mother. For the next five years, they lived with relatives in a Harlem flat. My mother did factory work to contribute to the household. At age twenty-nine, five years after arriving in the United States, my mother married my father.

Married for barely two years and with an infant son, my mother had to face the unexpected death of my father and deal with the sudden loss of a loved one for the third time in her life. Rather than raise her son in a strange land without any money or employment, she gave me up for adoption to a wealthy uncle of hers who had made money in real estate speculation and who she believed could provide me with both comfort and security. His own son had recently died in the Second World War and I was the replacement. The terms of the agreement included a stipulation that my mother never divulge her true identity to me. After six months of heartache, my mother secretly returned to her uncle's house and kidnapped me back. Her aunt and uncle adopted another child a year later. I wasn't told any of this until I was in my twenties.

My mother raised me with the help of her brother, who moved in with us to share the rent and expenses. He was a warm, vivacious man who sold insurance to the Greek community in Jamaica, Queens. Eventually he was to become a leader in the community: a local activist who emerged as a compromise candidate between Jews and Blacks for District Leader in the local Democratic Party. His service to the community would influence me in more ways than I knew at the time.

Like most girl children in Greece, my mother had been taught to sew at an early age. Since this was the only marketable skill she possessed that would allow her to stay home and take care of me while earning a living, she sought work in the garment industry. One of my earliest memories is of riding the subway with my mother every Wednesday morning. She carried a large cardboard box tied with a cord and held with a wooden handle. We walked several blocks from the station and entered one of the hundreds of garment storefronts that lined the side streets of midtown Manhattan. The large plate glass windows in the front were covered with dingy yellow plastic sheets to protect the already-badly-faded dresses on display. I found it hard to believe, even at that age, that this was a place of business.

We walked to the back of the store, past dozens of women operating sewing machines, greeted the shop owner, and placed our cardboard box on a large table for the owner to open and examine. The boss was friendly enough, but examining my mother's work was a serious and stern matter. He spread dozens of fur collars out on a table, lifting and turning each one as he ran his hands through them, his eyes squinting as he examined every stitch. These were the fur collars, soon to be attached to women's coats, that were so popular in the fifties and it was my mother's job to take a piece of unfinished fur and make it into a clean, smooth, elegant collar. After the boss nodded his approval, a worker from the shop carried away the merchandise and presented us with a new cardboard box filled with another week's work.

Back in our apartment, my mother sat for hours working those collars. In the winter, she sat on a footstool by the window: in the summer she took her work out to the fire escape where, propped on some cushions, she worked until sunset. She was happier working outside because among other things, she knew intuitively that the fur hair and microscopic fur dust visible only at certain angles in the bright sunlight would settle and accumulate throughout our apartment, presenting a health hazard to us both. She wrapped everything in plastic and mopped constantly. To this day, more than thirty years after she gave up "homework," my mother wraps everything—everything—in plastic. For the "privilege" of doing her work at home and on her own time, my mother was paid less than the shop floor workers, had no job security or benefits.

Unions have always opposed "homework" because it undercuts wages and undermines the union. But without "homework" at the time, I don't know how we would have survived. Naturally, my mother didn't care much for unions.

After ten years as a widow, my mother broke the traditional Greek taboo and remarried. My stepfather, like my father, was kind, gentle, and hardworking. He worked as a merchant marine for twenty-four years before jumping ship in New York. Born in the same town as my mother's family, he settled in the states at the age of forty-five. Equipped with no knowledge of English, but with a penchant for hard work, he spent his life in the U.S. working in restaurant kitchens. For years he jumped out of windows and hopped over fences to avoid immigration inspectors. As an "illegal alien" he worked off the books at or below minimum wage. He was always paid in cash. Years later when he finally gained citizenship, he got his first real paycheck. It was at that time, too, that he first became a union member. Ironically, it was his boss who signed him up for the union, telling him he was required to do so. For my father, it just meant one more deduction from his pay.

One memory that stays with me from this period is the night my stepfather brought his boss and the boss's wife to our apartment. The wife had recently purchased a gown that needed alteration and, knowing that my mother did this sort of thing, came over for a fitting. When, for the first time, I saw my mother get on her knees to pin up the boss lady's gown, I was suddenly filled with rage. I hated them for being so rich that they could bring my otherwise very tough and proud mother to her knees.

The neighborhood we lived in was situated between a stable working-class community to the north and a dirt-poor black community to the south. It was a commercial and transient district of storefront businesses and residents who lived on the margins of society. We had more than our share of neighborhood drunks and "white trash." There were half a dozen transient hotels that doubled as houses of prostitution. It was a tough neighborhood even by today's standards. Guns and drugs were around, even if not as abundant as they are now; switchblades, brass knuckles, and burglar's tools were also quite popular at the time. Most of the kids I knew on our block wound up dead or in jail.

I started working at a relatively young age and took on a number of jobs. I worked as a stock boy, bellhop, messenger, and later as a janitor, cab driver, and gem runner (transporting diamonds and other precious material to and from the jewelry district). I also spent one summer making pizza and another one hawking beers at ball games. None of these jobs were unionized.

Here I was working in unskilled, low-wage jobs and part of a community most in need of a voice and an advocate and yet the labor movement failed to reach me—failed to touch me in any way. And these were the days of "big labor" with a public image that rivaled that of "big business." It all seemed irrelevant to me at the time. It's ironic that it wasn't until I started teaching in college and making a decent salary for the first time in my life that I went to my first union meeting and walked my first picket line.

The advantages of schooling, like the advantages of unionism, were late in coming to me. For the most part, I hated school. I thought it was a boring and hostile place. I also had trouble with the English language and that didn't help matters. My mother spoke in Greek at home and insisted that I do the same, even as she frantically tried to master English. She went to night school to improve her English and sent me to after-school classes to improve my Greek. In afternoon school and at home, I was learning the ways and customs as well as the language of the Greeks.

Based on appearances, my primary school experience should have been a positive one. Public School 170 was literally a little red school house at the top of a grassy hill. There were only two classes for each grade, making for a relatively small and intimate school community. The school was racially integrated and had a rich ethnic and linguistic mix: Russians,

Poles, Latinos, Asians, Jews, and Greeks. The kids also came from what appeared to me to be economically diverse backgrounds: workers and shop owners, apartment dwellers and homeowners. (In my mind, the sons and daughters of shop owners were rich kids. They were, after all, the children of businessmen and property owners, even if their business was a coffee shop and the home they lived in a row house.)

The school, however, was far from idyllic. The building was old, outmoded, and in constant need of repair. The playground was a barren parking lot with a gravel surface that ensured bloodied kneecaps whenever anyone fell. The third floor was reserved for a girls' vocational high school program. Within a decade, the school would be demolished completely and replaced by a much larger modern school building.

Semi-annual report cards at PS 170 listed six grading categories, in the following order: 1) social behavior, 2) work habits, 3) health habits, 4) language arts, 5) math, 6) other areas (social studies, science, music, art). There was little doubt in my mind that these reflected the school's priorities. Reading recent accounts of inner city schools, I am not sure, that priorities are very different today, despite the rhetoric.[2]

There was one message that predominated throughout my early school experience: it was my teachers telling me "this is the way we do things." Language arts meant grammar drills, spelling quizzes, penmanship evaluation. All this was counterposed in my head with the way I was used to doing things in Greek. There was absolutely nothing in those six years to inspire me about the written word. Primary schools in those days were called grammar schools, for good reason.

Math, too, was taught in a mechanistic and unimaginative way. Social studies, to the extent that it was taught at all, was a collection of dates, names, places, and facts, none of which either spoke to me or interested me. On the one hand, all this was foreign and disorienting to me; on the other hand, the listening, memorizing, and repeating over and over was the most tedious thing I had ever experienced. I alternated between feeling intimidated and being bored to death.

No matter what my mother said, school just didn't seem that important. Economic class does have a way of determining what a kid thinks is important. I remember the day in fifth grade when school officials were conducting their annual in-class eye exams. For two years I had been cheating my way through those exams to avoid having to wear glasses. My teacher had suspected for some time that I couldn't read the blackboard, so she asked me, once again, to identify the letters on the eye chart, this time reading backwards. I flunked. It is ironic because I never cheated on class tests: that just wasn't worth the bother. Cheating on eye exams was a matter of survival. I was going to be in for some pretty rough times in the neighborhood.

With glasses, my schoolwork improved. My strategy, however, remained the same and revolved around getting by. Like so many others, I just wanted to be average. Once in six years I said something brilliant about a math problem on the board, astonishing both my teacher and myself. Overall, I was content with being mediocre and this characterized what would remain a fairly lackluster academic career for many years to come.

Much more was going on, however, because in addition to the basic academics, I was learning how to be an American: I was learning how to fit in. It was not only a matter of learning how to dress, speak, and look, I was also learning what to like and what to dislike. And it was not simply a matter of accepting and conforming to a lifestyle and set of values, but of internalizing them. I remember, quite vividly, the day in sixth grade when I changed, forever, the way I pronounce my last name. I traded in the harsh sounding "Mann-choz" of northern Greece, for a much softer sounding "man-sios" because it sounded a lot like the way Jayne Mansfield pronounced the beginning of her last name. I also remember responding to the question "what are you?" by telling people I was Catholic, because that sounded less foreign and because someone told me that Greek Orthodoxy was closer to Catholicism than to Protestantism. This was, of course, years before Hollywood and Olympic Airlines were to create images of Greek Zorbas and dancing in the aisles that would endear Greeks to a significant portion of the U.S. population. As for me, I ended up feeling shame and guilt both for being foreignlike and for wanting not to be. I just wanted to be average.

For others, the black, Latino, and Eastern European kids, it was worse. While I was presented with models that held out the hope of assimilation, they were presented with models that challenged their very being. Everything we were being taught made who they were and what they were beyond redemption. These were the days of fierce battles to maintain racial segregation: they were also the days of the cold war, evil empires, and school shelter drills. Without a conscious attempt on the part of the school system to teach tolerance and respect for differences, everything we were taught reflected and reinforced the prejudice and intolerance we saw around us. Teachers were obsessed with eradicating Black English in the school, textbooks provided us not with black history but with glimpses of "exceptional" blacks, and administrators adopted a patronizing tone when addressing black kids: all of this confirmed the messages we were getting from outside. Ordered to duck under our desks to avoid annihilation by Russian missiles at the sound of special school bells, it was no wonder we were afraid even to talk to our Russian classmates. Much of the racist sentiments and most of the anti-immigrant sentiments we picked up had less to do with race and ethnicity than it did with class. No one had to tell me that Polish jokes were really jokes about class: they were about everything we did not want to be. I would chuckle nervously, knowing I was about an inch away from rock bottom.

School was dominated by the ideologies and personalities of the white middle class. We were fed values and lifestyle models which were simultaneously presented as universal and lacking in ourselves. What counted was white not black or brown, American not immigrant, middle class not poor or working class. So different was less, inferior, inconsequential, and inadequate and we all quickly learned to see the enemy within us. We were developing prejudices and self-hate that would take a lifetime to overcome.

Some of us could harbor fantasies of being "average" more easily than others. As white kids, we believed our second-class status was temporary: if we worked hard, perfected our social skills, and entered the middle class, we too would be average. But skin colors, like gender, are irreversible. And if you were unfortunate enough to be handicapped by class, race, and gender, like most of the girls on the third floor, then you were surely doomed. Boys could learn to make decent money working with their hands; the girls on the third floor were learning to type and cut hair.

Most of us eased the pain and got back our self-confidence on the street, not in the classroom. Tough kids who behaved in class earned the privilege of going outside to clean blackboard erasers. Some reward. Kids that didn't give up and withdraw, became defiant and confrontational. The classroom increasingly became a battleground.

The battle was lost in Mr. Zago's junior high school class. Mr. Zago taught by the force of sheer terror and his routine was a fairly simple one. He would slowly walk around the room, stop at a desk, call out your last name, and ask you a question. If you knew the answer, he would move on to another student. If you didn't have the right answer, he would slam a yardstick on your desk, an inch from your face and hands. He would then tell you to stand up, berate you, and ask you a series of additional questions, each one a little harder than the one before it. After humiliating you at your desk, he would have you go to the blackboard and ask you to write out answers to still tougher questions. You would find yourself sinking deeper and deeper into a nightmarish pit from which there was no escape. The ordeal usually lasted ten or fifteen minutes. At least one student was put through the ordeal each day. Mr. Zago's boot camp approach to teaching got me to do my homework, but I forgot everything he taught me the last day of class.

By high school most of us knew our fates were sealed. Sociologists could have told us all along that there is little class mobility in the U.S. They could have told us that despite the wonderful rhetoric to the contrary, the rags to riches stories and the "we are all middle class" image of America were largely myths—but we were finding out for ourselves.

The older kids on the block weren't making it. At best, they were stuck in the same type of dead-end jobs our parents had. As for my own generation of kids, we were now armed with cars, drugs, and a swelling sense of machismo and anger. Our childhood pranks were increasingly turning to criminal activities. One kid was arrested for car theft, another for selling drugs. Still another fell to his death jumping roof tops. Through it all, I survived. In the neighborhood, I avoided arrest: in school, I managed to stay average. When I decided to go to college, my friend Ray beamed, "The rest of us aren't going to make it, Greg, but you will." At that moment, I felt both that I had betrayed my friends and that I had an enormous responsibility to them. This was not a social responsibility: it was an individual responsibility to make it for myself.

I reached my lowest point in college. I was enrolled in a Western Civilization course, a degree requirement that could have been and should have been one of the most interesting courses of my academic career. Up to then, I had been taking remedial courses and struggling with the mechanics of math and the English language just to get C grades. The Western Civ course was a bust. I couldn't focus on the lectures and I couldn't concentrate on my readings. My mind would drift and I would daydream or struggle to keep my eyelids open. I couldn't connect either to the teacher or the readings. I forced myself, tortured myself, to study and after a lot of cramming, I managed to get a D. This pulled my grade average down to where I was within fractions of flunking out. All the self-doubts and all the ambivalence about going to college reached a crisis point. My friends were doing other things: I had abandoned them for this? I wasn't cut out for this sort of thing. It seemed that the only question left for me was whether to drop out or let the school throw me out.

My Western Civ professor is now a colleague of mine at Queens College. He doesn't remember me, of course, and I have never mentioned any of this to him. I have had few encounters with him, but when I was seated opposite him at a reception a couple of years ago, I had an urge to reach across the table and shake him.

What kept me going through all this? Certainly thinking about the alternatives—death, jail, dead-end jobs, and the army—helped. The urgings and the model of perseverance offered by my mother helped too. So did my ties to an ethnic community beyond my immediate neighborhood. These ties provided a sense of ethnic pride, broadened my circle of friends, and offered additional role models.

There were also some positive experiences in my earlier schooling, though not by curriculum design, that helped me keep things in perspective. In sixth grade I had a teacher who would send his son into school to substitute for him when he couldn't make it. The son, who had a bohemian quality to him, brought his guitar to class and sang folk songs. It was the first time I appreciated the beauty and power of language. The music and lyrics touched me in ways that no poetry book ever did.

Another teacher once played a Malvina Reynolds recording of "Little Boxes." I don't remember the teacher's name or anything about her class, other than that it was a writing class, but the song went like this:

> Little boxes on the hillside,
> Little boxes made of ticky tacky,
> Little boxes on the hillside,
> Little boxes all the same,
> There's a green one and a pink one,
> And a blue one and a yellow one,
> And they're all made of ticky tacky,
> And they all look the same.
>
> And all the people in the houses,
> All went to the uni-ver-sit-y,
> Where they were all put in boxes
> And they came out all the same,
> And there's doctors and lawyers,
> And business exec-u-tives,
> And they're all made of ticky tacky
> And they all look just the same.
>
> And they all play on the golf course
> And drink their martinis dry,
> And they all have pretty children

And the children go to school,
And the children go to summer camp
and then to the uni-ver-sit-y,
Where they all are put in boxes
And they all come out the same.

And the boys go into business
And marry and raise a fa-mi-ly
In boxes made out of ticky tacky
And they all look just the same.
There's a green one and a pink one,
And a blue one and a yellow one,
And they're all made out of ticky tacky
And they all look just the same.*

In the days of TV shows like *Leave it to Beaver, Father Knows Best,* and the *Life of Riley,* "Little Boxes" offered a radical re-visioning of success. Maybe being middle class wasn't all it was cracked up to be, after all.

In fact, "little boxes" were springing up all over. Levittown was, at the time, a newly developed, massive, planned community on Long Island that promised to make a private home, front lawn, and garage a reality for every American. Since I had already given up on the Levittown promise (my mother was to live in the same four-room apartment for forty years), folk music made me feel, "can't have it: don't want it." This was no small comfort.

Around this time, one of my teachers assigned *The Other America,* by Michael Harrington.[3] This was the first book I ever read from cover to cover. I read it out on the fire escape. For once, I felt someone was paying attention to those of us who were not part of the "affluent society." It was a revelation that not only were there others like us, but that there were others in situations much worse than ours. Why hadn't anyone said this before? Why were the only images of America presented in the classroom and in the media those of an affluent middle class? Much later, I was to become a colleague of Harrington at Queens College. He continued to inspire me and became a friend.

My eighth grade social studies teacher, Mr. Gatto, was the first teacher to have a real influence on me. He taught a wonderful class, assigned interesting readings, and demonstrated a caring manner, even when he was tough. One day he pulled several boys aside, including one of the toughest, meanest kids in the class. Mr. Gatto convinced us to join his theater club. I had never been to the theater and it seemed the strangest of all suggestions. I still don't know how he paid for it, but he took us to Saturday afternoon matinees. After a performance of *The Great White Hope,* he took us backstage to meet James Earl Jones. I never forgot that performance or that day and I have been going to the theater ever since.

Listening to folk songs in class and going to the theater with a teacher were not major happenings, and yet they had a profound effect on me. Folk songs of the beat generation provided me with an alternative perspective at a fairly young age and such a perspective, whether it comes from a counterculture or a political movement, is critical for those trying to survive poverty and deprivation in a society which prides itself on its abundance. Theater, on the other hand, exposed me to a middle-class art form that was appealing: its social commentary stimulated me to think about the world as well as about personal and social issues. I learned to appreciate cultural expressions, even if they were mainstream or what I considered "high culture." Theater was fun, moving, meaningful, even self-critical at times. Maybe middle-class life, values, and talents had something to offer after all. That such trivial events could have such a major impact, is indicative both of the paucity of the educational system and the resiliency of the human spirit.

Folk and theater, however, were only seeds: my real awakening came in college. After my Western Civilization course, I knew I had one more semester left. If I didn't pull my average up immediately, I would be out of college on my rear end. I registered for a sociology course with Mike Brown, a demanding but very popular teacher. (I always thought it tragic, that at most large, urban public colleges, the system of letting seniors and juniors register first meant that freshmen and sophomores got closed out of the best classes at the most critical juncture of their academic career.) Mike was very exciting and dynamic and exposed me to a completely different way of seeing the world. In his class, I read C. Wright Mills's classic *The Sociological Imagination* and learned what was probably the most important lesson of my life.[4] I learned that far from being individual and personal problems, most of the troubles that I and my friends and neighbors faced were broad social issues. They were systemic issues that demanded structural and public policy changes. I was beginning to learn that if I were to understand my own experiences, I would have to locate them in society and in history. By the end of the course, I was convinced that our compassions were skewed, our priorities reversed, and our institutions fundamentally flawed. I was also convinced that society need not be this way. Mike didn't offer any easy solutions, nor did he suggest models to emulate: he did offer ideas and experiences to draw on to make a better world. I was developing vision.

I never worked as hard as I did in that course. From that point on I got nothing but straight A's. Some teachers and courses were more interesting and more socially relevant than others, but it didn't matter. I was determined to learn as much as I could and to develop my own perspective.

Identifying with society's underdogs wasn't difficult for me. Although it had not been an easy lesson for me to learn, my uncle had been teaching me all along to identify with the "common people." He had become a Democratic Party stalwart because, as he was quick to tell me, the Democrats best represented the interests of poor people, immigrants, minorities, and working people. When he stayed up all night listening to the election returns, it conveyed the impression that the interests of the "common people," if not the Party, mattered. Now it was all coming together.

It wasn't, however, simply a matter of identifying with the underdog: I was developing an important set of principles to guide me. I remember visiting family in South Carolina: they were not much better off than we were and they were certainly just as nice. But when my sweet, vivacious older cousin sternly reprimanded me for unknowingly walking to the back of the bus with "What are you, a nigger lover?", I knew she was speaking not only for herself, but for the other white working-class people on the bus as well. Now I was learning to distinguish between good working-class instincts and bad. I was also learning that when my neighborhood friends spoke to and of women in insulting and degrading ways, that there was something fundamentally wrong both with them and with a society that encourages such attitudes and practices. I was developing a class loyalty that was informed and principled—a class loyalty that made sense.

My classmates and I were being influenced by the social movements around us. I was learning from the civil rights movement and the women's movement as well as the antiwar and anti-imperialist movements. I am convinced that these movements would have never reached me if I had not been exposed to their ideas in college.

It wasn't long before I became a social activist, myself. I became active in campus organizing, and later I joined the government's ACTION program, and became a full-time community organizer. I was learning important organizational and interpersonal skills. I was also learning from the Left, the Old Left as well as the New Left.

My understanding of and identification with labor unions were tied to academe as well. A former classmate of mine moved to California and became an organizer for the farmworkers' grape boycott. While visiting her, I worked briefly on the boycott myself and was deeply moved by the moral and political strengths of the farmworkers' cause. I spent many an afternoon in front of supermarkets convincing customers to shop elsewhere. I was part of a very effective team of picketers and we turned back hundreds of would-be shoppers. When the boycott as a whole proved to be effective, it gave me a tremendous sense of collective power.

A year later, having earned a master's degree in Urban Studies, I got my first full-time teaching job at William Paterson College in New Jersey. Within a few weeks of my appointment, I got caught up in a statewide faculty strike over salary and class size. This too, was an effective strike with considerable student and community support. Shortly afterwards, I was elected to union office and became increasingly involved in union activities. After two years on the faculty, I was fired for my union activities.

My interest in labor unions was growing and I sought out and found ways to connect my new interest with my academic work. I was asked to teach an "Introduction to Labor Studies" course to a group of electrical apprentices enrolled at Empire State College. This was a group of young working-class men and a few women, not unlike my neighborhood friends. Just about everyone of them hated being in class, or so they told me on the first day. In most cases, they had chosen to become class-A electricians (construction) precisely because they wanted to work with their hands rather than continue with school. After signing them up for their apprenticeship and at the union's request, the industry board overseeing the apprenticeship program imposed a two-year college requirement. While the industry board provided full tuition for these apprentices, this endeared them neither to the union nor to my class. They were a very rowdy bunch, but over time they began to give me the benefit of the doubt. Together we read quite a bit of labor history. It was only one of the topics I planned to cover, but it grabbed them the most and we stuck with it for the entire semester. They, too, had been taught that poor and working people were inconsequential in our society. Now, we were learning about the courageous working-class heroes and heroines who fought for the rights and benefits most working men and women take for granted today: the minimum wage, the forty-hour week, and the right to be treated with dignity and respect. From those apprentices, I was also learning how to bring my academic knowledge and skills to my community. The following semester,

I was appointed director of the program: a program that was to grow to nearly fifteen hundred students at its peak.

Compared to the apprentices, the Queens College students in the room with me now are older, perhaps wiser. Most have already been in the labor force for quite some time. What do I tell these worker-students about college and about the college career they are about to embark on? I tell them that, done right, higher education, like union struggle, can be an empowering and liberating experience. I tell them that education doesn't have to be boring, rote, or degrading: not ticky tacky, not little boxes, not all the same.

I tell them that education can be inspiring, enriching, and self affirming: that in college they will learn to think critically and creatively; that when they are exposed to middle-class, male, Eurocentric ideas and values they will be identified as such and that other values and ideas will be presented as equally legitimate; that they will struggle with ideas and learn to articulate well-thought-out arguments; that they will build their self-confidence: that they will be exposed to teachers who will infect them with their enthusiasm; that they will be challenged and that they will grow, individually and collectively.

I also tell them that I sincerely hope that we fulfill our promise to them: that we have created a special worker education program that provides them with pro-active counseling, special tutoring, small classes, and exciting and caring teachers: that we have designed a special worker education curriculum which, in addition to some of the more traditional course requirements in the liberal arts and sciences, includes such course requirements as Writing and the Literature of Work; Latin American Literature; African-American Literary Traditions; and Work, Class and Culture: that in addition to the college's fifty majors, they can choose special courses of study in Public Policy or Labor Studies: that we have created a new bachelor's degree in Applied Social Sciences with the explicit purpose of organizing a course of study around finding solutions to social problems and around developing strategies for social change; that our faculty and staff are committed to providing them with the knowledge and skills not only to make them better informed and more effective worker-citizens, but to become advocates in their communities and leaders in their workplace.

Yes, ambivalence toward education and toward unions may be justified. But we are doing our part and they must do their part to make these institutions more responsive and effective. Our Labor Resource Center at

Queens College was established to encourage discourse on the future of the labor movement. It organizes workshops and conferences with the active participation of rank and file members as well as union leaders. At the same time, the college's Academic Senate provides a forum for discussion and debate on policies and practices. It is a particularly interesting forum because administrators like myself can attend and speak on the floor of the Senate, but cannot vote. Decisions about college policy, including admissions criteria, degree requirements, and retention standards, are voted on by representatives elected by the students and faculty: one-third students, two-thirds faculty. I make a point of telling them that they have a right and a responsibility to help shape college policy. It is a responsibility to make higher education and unions into viable instruments for social change and for a better world.

And yes, knowledge is empowering. But there is another motto to ponder: "Discimus ut serviamus." It is the college's motto, and though it is buried in the college bulletin so that hardly anyone knows it, and rarely uttered so that those who know it forget it, and written in Latin so that those who see it may not understand it, it is particularly relevant: "We learn so that we may serve." It is a motto to be taken to heart by anyone emerging from the working class.

Notes

1. Mike Rose, *Lives on the Boundary* (New York: Penguin Books, 1989), p. 28.

2. See, Jonathan Kozol, *Savage Inequalities: Children in America's Schools* (New York: Crown Publishers, 1991).

3. Michael Harrington, *The Other America: Poverty in the United States* (New York: Penguin Books, 1962).

4. C. Wright Mills, *The Sociological Imagination* (Oxford: Oxford University Press, 1959).

I was born in Washington, D.C., in 1939 during the time when the hospital in Arlington, Virginia, did not admit "colored" people. After I was born, I was brought to live in the house of my grandparents in Halls Hill, a former slave enclave in Arlington. This was the neighborhood where I grew up. My grandmother was a midwife until it was outlawed through the efforts of organizations which I understood included the American Medical Association. My father worked as a receiving room clerk at the Bureau of Engraving in Washington, D.C., and my mother was employed as a domestic worker most of her adult life. My mother was my father's second wife. His first wife died in childbirth. I was my mother's first child, but the third of six children, one of three girls. I grew up between the boys. The first two were seven and eight years older than me, the third was three years younger, and my sisters are seven and eight years younger. While I was still quite young, we moved to a new, but small, wood frame white house. I was baptized in our neighborhood's Baptist church where I sang in the junior choir until I left home to go to college. I attended racially segregated schools. While in the eleventh grade, I became the lead plaintiff in a class action school desegregation suit which was filed against the school board of Arlington, Virginia. However, I never attended desegregated public schools because the suit was not won until after I finished high school. At Hoffman-Boston High School, I won many awards, which led me to a full undergraduate scholarship in mathematics. From Arlington I went to undergraduate school at Hampton Institute in Hampton, Virginia. This photograph was taken of

AERODYNAMIC SMOKE TUNNEL

HOFFMAN-BOSTON HIGH SCHOOL
HAMPTON, VIRGINIA

me when I was presenting my first science project in state competition for "Negro" students in Virginia. At the time, I was in the eleventh grade. I was very nervous and I was probably answering a question put to me by the panel of judges. I think I tied for third place. People always told me that I acted like an old person, but, as you can see, I looked young for my age. This was a problem when I became a young professional computer consultant because clients often thought I did not have the experience needed to handle their project.

Clarissa T. Sligh is an artist/photographer. Her work is based on telling personal and community stories in multi/mixed media form. She is the recipient of a NEA fellowship in 1988, a New York State Council on the Arts project grant in 1990, and an Artiste en France fellowship in 1992. Her work is widely exhibited and collected. She is the author of two artist's bookworks, *Reading Dick and Jane With Me* and *What's Happening With Mama.* She is national coordinator and cofounder of Coast to Coast: National Women Artists of Color. She has a B.S. in mathematics from Hampton Institute, a B.F.A. in painting from Howard University, and a M.B.A. in finance from the University of Pennsylvania. The broad range of her career and life experiences includes work as a computer programmer at NASA's Manned Space Flight Program, as a financial analyst on Wall Street, and as a teacher of art and photography.

Clarissa T. Sligh

Reliving My Mother's Struggle

I grew up in Halls Hill, a former slave enclave just outside of Washington, D.C. As a child, I would listen to the grownups talk about how everybody was kin to everybody else. They never exactly said if Mr. Hall had been the white man who had owned everybody. They had a way of leaving out parts of the story that they did not want to remember. I wanted to, but I never asked anybody more questions about Mr. Hall. I figured that it was probably one of those questions that the answer was "children should be seen and not heard." That's what grownups said to us if they didn't know the answer to something or when they didn't want to hear our mouths. But, I loved to hang around and listen to them talk and laugh about this one and that one. It was one of the few times they relaxed and enjoyed themselves.

The most valuable property and the store and restaurant on the highway were owned by people who had been closely related to the former white slaveowner. They were about as white as anybody could look, but my momma said that it didn't mean anything—that there were plenty of colored folks who looked like that all over the South. Since they owned so much, they didn't have to "work like a dog" like everybody else did. But, the men often got into fights over women. And the only time I saw the women was when they were sitting on their wide porches in their rocking chairs.

To this area my grandfather, Thomas Thompson, came looking for work. He had grown up the favorite child and only son of parents in Goldsboro, North Carolina. He had studied carpentry at Joseph K. Bricks, a small boarding school in Enfield, North Carolina. In what was considered the peanut farm belt, it was set up by a white organization, the American Missionary Association. Except for picking cotton and peanuts, there was little other work to be had where he came from.

By way of the grapevine, he had heard that a lot of building was going on in the Washington, D.C., area. He came with his clothes folded neatly in a cardboard suitcase and went from construction site to construction site, until he got a job carrying bricks. During that time, the most respectful thing that whites could think of to call us was "Negro." Most of the Negro men were employed to dig the ditches, carry the concrete and bricks, and do any other heavy or dirty work that needed to be done. After a few months, he went back to Goldsboro, got married, and brought my grandma, Lillian, back to live with him. They rented a room in one of the Halls Hill homes where people took in boarders.

Grandma Lillian began to let people know that she was a midwife and healer. No one else was doing it, so most of the people in the neighborhood began coming to her. She listened to their stories, bandaged them up, and delivered their babies. She and Thomas frugally saved every spare penny they got. Soon, he was able to buy a plot of land in the neighborhood. He got help to clear it and began to build their house. As he worked in the evenings and on weekends, people in the neighborhood came by and talked to him. They saw how good he was. Eventually, he sat up his own business and began to build houses for them. Over time, they had three babies, two girls, Naomi, Dorothy, and one boy, Clarence, who would later become my father.

Two generations later, when I was born, my parents brought me home to live in that house which my grandfather had built. I was the first granddaughter after three grandsons. My grandmother was delighted to have me around. I did not know it, but times were hard. No one knew where my grandpa was. He had disappeared. Most of his money and property had been lost in failed banks or to back taxes.

As I grew up, my grandmother would always say to me, "Spend your time getting an education. No one can take that away from you."

I did not realize what she meant for a long time. When I was little, no one ever mentioned Grandpa or spoke his name. I was not to meet him until after I was four years old.

When my grandpa came back, it looked like he and my grandma resumed living together like nothing had ever happened. By this time, my father was a grown man with four children. He and Grandpa didn't see eye to eye on a lot of things. Grandpa always reminded him that he had to follow his rules when he was in his house. That meant my father could not drink any alcohol or smoke his cigars or pipes. Although I was only four, it was clear to me that my father did not like it that his own father had returned. For us grandchildren, however, he always had a very soft touch and a twinkle in his eye.

He told us stories and recited poems. He sang us songs which he accompanied on simple musical instruments like a harmonica or string piano. He easily found work using his building skills as a handyman. He earned enough to take care of my grandmother and to help my father make ends meet. I did not understand why, but my father and Aunt Naomi continued to say behind his back that he was trifling. After I grew up, I asked my grandfather what had happened during the years when he had disappeared and no one knew where he was. He told me he was on the road following an itinerant evangelist gospel preacher.

He said, "I was sick and nobody knew what was wrong with me. The doctors gave me up for dead. That man was a faith healer. I swore to him that if I was healed that I would never go to a doctor again and that I would serve the Lord the rest of my life. He saved my life."

One day my Aunt Naomi was fussing bitterly about my grandpa being the cause of them losing everything they had had when she was a young woman. How she and my father had to save their homestead from being lost to back taxes and how they had had to take care of their mother. I could see how bad it made her feel. She talked about how her parents had helped to feed half of the neighborhood while she was growing up. She was an exceptionally smart and proud woman. I told her the story that Grandpa had told me. She became furious and said she didn't believe a word of it.

She said, "During the time Papa left Momma, he was on the road running after women. Women were his biggest weakness. He could never get enough of them."

When he died much later, at the age of eighty-six, she and my father threw all his poems in the trash.

I didn't care what she said, my grandpa always had a smile, a joke, a song, or a story for me and my brothers and sisters. He was a bright star in my life in our small blue-collar neighborhood. No Negro teachers or doctors lived there. Our preacher rented a room in an elderly widow's house. Many of the men and women had completed high school, but still held the low end of the pay scale federal government jobs. My father was a mailroom clerk. Others worked as day laborers and domestic workers, which is what my mother did. In terms of getting work, it didn't much matter if you had an education or not. You made more money and could be "your own man" if you had a skill. Except on weekends, life seemed grim. Like my father, most of the men wanted to wear a white shirt, suit, and tie to work. Unlike him, most of those men moonlighted to make ends meet.

With six children, we didn't have much money—but we were surrounded by clear blue skies, clean water and streams, clean grass and fruit trees. My grandmother had planted cherry, apple, peach, and pear trees while the house was being built. We had enough food most of the time. For fun we pitched horse shoes, climbed trees, shot marbles, and played other games. We grew most of our fruit and vegetables. In winter, we ate a lot of bean and potato stews. The vegetables and fruit my mother had canned during the summer brightened up those winter meals. Along with my brothers, I helped to chop wood in order to start the fires in our coal-burning furnace. The coal bin was empty many times. My father had to go and pay cash for the coal before it was delivered. The man who sold it lived up the street. During the summer he sold blocks of ice which my grandma used in her icebox and which we chipped up to make ice cream. Up until I went to junior high school, we drew well water for drinking and bathing and went to the toilet in our outhouse. Many people in our neighborhood did. This was a normal life for us.

My first memory of my family's lack of money, of having to do without because we could not afford it, probably came when I was around eight or nine. That was when my Mom had the fifth and sixth babies. The seventh baby died when she was one year old. The three were born only one year apart. I remember being told, "I know you will understand." Over time, they became the words which my mother used to gain my agreement to remain silent about wanting something which most of the other neighborhood children seemed to have—like shoes during the summer.

Not long after, I began to notice that people who had more than us felt that because we had to scrape to get by, that they were better than us. I began to believe it too. Momma said they worked harder, had more than one job, and handled their money better than us. She tried to push my father to get a second job. He refused to budge. After work, he went to his cousin's house and spent his time drinking and hanging out with his friends. It made my Momma furious, and, she would take it out on me and my younger brother.

Besides doing my home chores, I worked to make money any kind of way I could think of. I ran errands for people in the neighborhood. Most of the time, they would give me a nickle, but if they felt rich on paydays, I got a quarter. I collected soda bottles for deposit refunds. After I became thirteen, I began doing domestic work and any other low-paying odd job I could get. After all, we had learned how to work real hard.

I grew up between brothers. Despite being beaten up by them when I was young, I felt very close to them. As a younger sibling, I would do anything to be around them. During the same time, I saw clearly the man/woman dominant/subordinate struggle that went on between my parents. Although I never said the words, "I do not want to be like my mother or marry a man who is like my father," they went through my mind a lot. Despite the fact that my mom went to work every day, my dad would never lift a hand to help her with us kids or the housework. When she complained about it, he would say that it wasn't a man's job, that he did not want his boys doing housework, and that she did not make me help her enough.

He'd say, "How is she going to keep a husband if she does not know how to cook and clean house?"

My mother did not argue with him. But, she quietly resisted his opinion. She was the one who saw to it that things got done. She made sure that all the work was divided between all of us, and saw to it that my brothers learned to cook, clean house, and take care of the babies too.

I hated my mother's life. She had been very pretty. If we "got on her nerves," she broke switches off young trees, and yelled and screamed while beating me and my younger brother with them. She was afraid of the other women in the neighborhood. She would tell me about all the things my father should be doing, things she had stopped telling him about because he would not hear it anymore. She would not leave, even though she constantly complained about things being very hard.

So even though I did not know it, part of my goal was not to live my mother's life.

As the first girl and third child of six children, I had no competition being the keeper of our family photograph album. Snapshots were tucked in drawers all over the house. I collected and put them together. I found, in somebody's trash, a big heavy book that had been used for Christmas card samples. Before pasting the photographs down, I spent weeks arranging and rearranging the pictures to compose a story about my family life. I wanted others to know who we were, how we saw ourselves. I fantasized that it would become a permanent artifact testifying to our real history. I felt that it would counter the news media's accounts of who we were. Except for one or two so-called "exceptions"—our black spokesmen, who were usually selected and approved by "the establishment"—the Washington daily newspapers usually portrayed us as criminals or on welfare.

So, the words still scrawled on the pictures and pages are mostly mine. They had expressed my personal need and desire to display pride in my family and to create for myself a sense of identity and security.

As an adult, I still carry the image of my own mother's struggle to try to make ends meet, of her humiliation and self-sacrifice, of the dresses that she made becoming overly faded, of her underwear full of holes, of her one winter coat continuing to come apart despite her repairs, of her despair over my father hanging out at his cousin's house to drink, of her walking up the hill to catch the bus which took her to her domestic "days" work at a different white woman's house each day, of her endless agony to make sure that us six kids lived in in what she called "some kind of civilized manner."

Her dream was that I would go to school—go to college, since she had not been able to figure out how to get there herself—so I would not have to live like her. I don't remember when I knew it, but it was a concept I alternately rejected and embraced. Rejected, because even though things were hard, we kids were close, we had developed a self-reliance and way of thinking independently about things that I could see that "being better off" did not seem to perpetuate. Embraced, because I saw that my Negro schoolteachers and classmates favored those who dressed better, and with more money you could do that and not have to live what my mom called "from hand to mouth."

When I got my first full-time professional employment as a computer programmer after five years of college, I felt very proud of myself. I had earned the distinction of being the first in my family to get that far.

About two years later, I was one half of a young Black American couple. Our friends thought we had it made. We were both employed professionally. We had two cars and a new baby. We remodeled our house which had been in a formerly all-white neighborhood in northwest Washington, D.C. To be young and Black in America in the mid–1960s was to be in a world that promised to open up to endless possibilities and change. That did not turn out to be the case, but my generation, while still too young to vote, had been major participants and leaders during the Civil Rights Movement. We put our bodies on the line to bring down the walls of racial segregation. We wanted to change, to revolutionize America. And we did. Dense walls of Jim Crow laws designed to keep us second-class citizens began to crack. They had been kept in place by law-abiding Christian white Americans through legal and violent means. As more and more people made the decision to put their bodies on the line of fire, the walls of Jim Crow laws began crumbling down.

Within the first two months of our marriage, however, we discovered that our ideas about the roles each of us would play within the relationship were from jarringly different and opposing perspectives. The man who, before marriage, seemed so different from my father was in reality almost a replica of him. Why hadn't I seen that? I, on the other hand, had no intention of reliving my mother's life. After a few pitched battles, I escaped the marriage and left him in the house.

In less than three years after getting married, I was a divorced single mother, working long hours, living in a high-rent district, spending more than I earned, and partying with my new single friends. One morning I woke up with a terrible hangover. I drank in order to act like I was having a good time. I hated the "small talk," the pretense at friendliness, the waiting to be asked to dance, the constant jockeying to avoid being raped. I could not understand my very intelligent Black women friends. They wanted husbands. I did not. I knew I did not like this kind of life.

With my head feeling like a bruised watermelon and my stomach like an army had marched through it, I asked myself, "What do you really want that would just be for you?" Going within myself for answers had been a way I had learned to survive when I couldn't figure things out.

No one could have been more surprised than me when a clear image of me painting with watercolors flashed into my mind. I had enjoyed it only briefly as a preteen. Making art was something I had given up in junior high school. I felt I had to make an economic choice. Wasn't that the reason we had to go to school? I picked the college curriculum. That meant art classes were out. I consoled myself with, "Besides, you aren't good enough."

But now while I worked as a computer programmer, I attended painting classes at the Corcoran School every weekend I could. For about one year, I spent most of my spare time learning to see and how to mix paints. Like most working-class people, I liked art but I did not understand how anyone did it other than as a hobby if they were not rich.

During that time period, I saw a performance of the Guinea Ballet. I was twenty-eight. It was my first time to see a lot of Black people on stage who had feet, hips, and hair like mine. I saw that they were not Black people who looked or acted like they were white or seemed to know anything about the need to do it. The Black men saw the Black women as beautiful. They were proud and seemed to like and enjoy who they were. That night, I decided that I would go to Africa and see for myself what it was like to be in a predominantly Black culture.

In order to do it, I moved to a cheaper apartment, got a second job, paid off my bills, and began to save money. I said nothing to my family about it. I knew they saw Africa as the "savage dark" continent. That was what we were taught in school. My friends were puzzled. They could not understand why anyone would want to go there. I could not explain it myself.

Rather than talk about it to people, I simply focused on the task at hand. Getting the money together was a lot easier than I expected. I was ready to go in one year. I took my four-year-old daughter, Tammy. Much to the distress of my family and her father, we spent the next year traveling across the African continent.

While there, I began to understand what it meant to grow up in a culture where you learn to see who you are through the eyes of people who are not only different from you, but who consider you inferior to them and themselves superior to you. I saw that it had made me different from other Africans. Although their countries had been colonized, they did not carry my kind of anxiety and terror. They did not have to act cool in order to hide their fear. They did not always have to check out the scene to see if it was OK or safe to be where they were. Children were a natural part of community life and women kept them close. No one seemed to be embarrassed or ashamed of the way women's bodies looked and functioned. They could breast-feed their babies or enjoy braiding their hair in public or in friendly company.

I began to see that growing up an American Black, I learned to hate the blood of Africa that I carried in my veins. The psychological and physical control and abuse that was passed on to me through my family had stamped on my mind that I was inferior, that blackness was something bad, that whiteness was beauty and power, that to survive I had to merge my interests with the master, that I had to destroy who I was. I had learned to feel ashamed of our blackness, our kinky hair, our spirits, and our drums.

Africans, who did not have much, insisted that they shared their time, homes, and meals with us. It was the first time that I was among people where having a lot of material things was not a requirement for you to be worth your human life. Even though my hosts insisted that I share in their life, I often felt bad taking what was being offered. One old man told me, "You are a stranger in a strange land. One day I may be also." I knew my family would not relate to strangers in that way. I wondered if it would ever be possible to repay these kindnesses.

When I returned to the United States, I suddenly knew that my life of trying to "get ahead" was no life at all. I could not force myself to spend the rest of it poring over computer printouts from the time I woke up in the morning until the time I went to bed at night. For the next three years, I moonlighted as a consultant while working my way through an undergraduate art program at Howard University. I learned to draw. I studied African, the beginnings of European, and African-American art history. I changed my lifestyle in order to do it. I purchased an old Volkswagen and moved into a room in my parents' house. Except for one or two of the young professional partygoers that I knew, all of my friends completely avoided me. It was as if I had an exotic disease and they did not want to catch it.

I completed my art studies when I was thirty-three. Before finishing, I searched for work hoping to use my new skills, even though it would pay less than computer programming. I ran into an old friend, a civil engineer, who was in graduate business school. He convinced me that I should apply. He talked about how job opportunities were opening up for Blacks in big business. I thought about my nine-year-old daughter, Tammy. We were not destitute, but we were just getting by.

Some of our neighbors refused to let their children play with her because they saw my painting of a nude model that I had done for a classroom assignment. By this time, schools in Arlington had become integrated, which meant that Black children now went to the white schools. Whenever she tried to tell her teachers about her experiences in Africa, they would tell me that my daughter was highly imaginative. They let me know that Tammy's father had their sympathy because I was the weird artist.

I could have gotten a full-time job as a computer programmer—but I did not have the stomach for it. I applied to business school. Somewhere in the back of my mind, I knew I still carried my mother's dreams for me. Again, I found myself making an economic decision to use academic studies to get a job. Late that summer, I received a letter from the Wharton School notifying me that I had been admitted on one of those loan-scholarship packages. I was delighted but scared. The price of admission was very high, but I had no idea of how high until quite a few years later.

After business school, I moved to New York with my daughter and began working as a financial analyst. Almost immediately, I began to feel lost and disconnected in the regimentation of the corporate world. I could not wear blue pinstripe suits and imitate the men the way a lot of women could. The idea of making art gnawed at me. I tried my hand at it when I got home from work. I found that I had lost my skills, and at the end of the day, I had no creative energy left. I gave up trying. I kept telling myself, "In a year from now I will be living in another place."

After about six years, I finally put an ad in the personal column of the *Village Voice*. That was how I began to meet some artists. I worked on a few of their projects. Not long after that, I began to make super 8 films and slide narratives of my own. I was interested in the narrative, cartoons, and film—in time changing in space. I didn't know it then, but I felt I had totally lost contact with my own voice.

Working in the traditional white male bastion of Wall Street was exciting, but I saw how abusive classism was. The obvious dislike of women was worse than I had ever seen. Anybody who was different in any way was treated like a leper. Having come from the South, for the first time I could see prejudice in action against white people. Most complained bitterly and would turn around and pass the abuse to someone they felt would not give it back. Sometimes it was directed toward whoever was in the next lower position. Sometimes they got on the telephone and directed it toward their wives and children or whoever would answer. No matter how it was passed on, it made me feel pretty sick. No matter how hard I worked, I was expected to work even harder. I felt that my being a "token" was an excuse to keep out all other people who were "like me." After all, the firm's "Equal Employment Opportunities" requirements had been filled.

Two years later, I began a diary of self-portrait sketches.* My goal was to make one a night for one year and to allow the gestalt of each day's experience to emerge. I began to see that my life was little more than a continual rehashing of my worst fears and anxieties. After nine months, I tried to include my mother in the drawings. This act raised heavy walls of fog in my mind. I did not understand what was happening. In an effort to work through it, I pulled out the big book of my old family snapshots. Looking at them, I asked myself, "How did you get me to this place?"

My mind reeled through scene after scene of me trying to belong wherever I went—to work, to shop, to live. I could look a certain way, but I always felt like an outsider. Most of the Blacks I met were middle and upper-middle class. It was okay, but there seemed to be no place where my working-class experience fit in. In trying to express something about it, I began combining words with some of the photographs. My goal was to briefly work through these vague and uneasy feelings by writing down memories while constructing snapshot collages.

As I looked at the old family pictures, I remembered myself as a young person sitting on the floor, pasting them into the book. The images reminded me of how my bonds of affection with family members had been laced with barbs of conflict and violence. My stomach, my shoulders, and my face tightened up as I looked at our smiling faces. I remembered how I had cut out people I did not like. Now these cuts penetrated my adult memories like a sharp knife. Shadows of terror, anger, confusion, and guilt felt like a solid steel trap door.

As I reshot and reprinted the pictures, forgotten childhood experiences—many of which were taboo—began to re-emerge. I wrote the stories on yellow pads. I was transported back to another place, another time. Each evening after my job, I worked in the corner of my friend's studio. It made me feel wiped out, bent out of shape, or just real bad. I could not escape. I felt like I was wrestling with something that I couldn't see or touch. I knew it was a matter of life or death. I desperately wanted to live.

I exhibited the collages a year later. They were printed on a heavy etching paper coated with brown light-sensitive chemicals. I thought of

---

*Portions have appeared in "Taking the Private Public," in *She Was Lost Is Remembered,* edited by Louise Wisechild (Seattle, Washington: Seal Press, 1991): 147–149.

Clarissa T. Sligh, *Play with Jane,* 1988.
Silkscreen print.

them as newly framed memory pictures from my distant past. Although it was clear that they were reconstructions, I felt guarded about showing them. Embarrassment and guilt about "betraying family secrets" made me feel like I was being disloyal.

Could the viewers be nonjudgmental? Would they think my experiences had been tough only because I had been poor and Black? Would the work be dismissed as being too personal? I knew it moved beyond what was then acceptable to speak out about. It put me and the viewer facing each other over my chasm of shame.

Some people thought the work was naive because I used the voice of "the child." However, some people were able to talk about and let me know that they "got it." The work was different from anything I had seen. I struggled to create a visual language which had meaning for me. Even though I felt very vulnerable and tentative about it, I knew I had to continue. At that time, other artists were not yet openly personal in their work in that way. It was hard for me to consider it a valid statement. I moved around in circles while trying to bring myself back to it over and over again.

I did not know it then, but I was struggling with my terror. Each time I made an image which acknowledged my hurt and pain as a woman, I felt disloyal to my brothers and to all Black men. Perhaps it was the beginnings of my search for myself as a woman. I do know that I began to accept the fact that no matter what I said, I could not speak for all Black people. I felt that some would rather not hear my voice, but now I had to speak for me.

For the first time in my life, "us" meant "us women." At the same time, I met only one or two women artists that I felt connected to. I could tell by their assumptions that regardless of their "race" few understood about being working class. I wondered if there was a place for my voice. Yet, I began to learn from them how much I had not been able to acknowledge how hard sexism was on me. I could not tell one kind of prejudice

He was her husband when they played "HOUSE".

Clarissa T. Sligh, *He was her husband when they played "House,"* 1984.
Van Dyke print.

Clarissa T. Sligh, *Waiting for Daddy,* 1987.
Van Dyke Brown print.

from another. It just seemed everything got hard at a certain point. Through them, I began to learn to see the woman I had become. I began to appreciate my mother's struggles and her goals for me.

Finally, in 1984, I decided that I would leave Wall Street and try to work full time as an artist. I had no idea what that meant. I was really scared. I thought about my grandfather who had left everything behind in order to save his life. Somehow, in some way, I knew I was following him.

Today, making my art has become a way of learning what I know, a way of being conscious of how and why I learned it, a way to heal the scars and learn new truths. It has become a way to learn to trust my own gut feelings, my own thinking in a way I never could. With each new piece, I can see how I still work around my edges and walk around in circles. Sometimes I reach my center and the work flows well. The process is not predictable. I never know how long it will take or if it will happen at all. I now work harder and longer than I ever had to. Sometimes, the more clarity I get, the more I seem to get lost. Most of the time, I do not really understand the gesture, what I have made, until long after it has been done.

Steve Cagan

I was born on November 20, 1943, in New York City. When I entered the tenth grade, I was also entering my tenth public school—the schools were in Brooklyn, the Bronx, Queens, and Battle Creek, Michigan. My grandparents were all Jewish immigrants from the Pale of Occupation in czarist Russia. When I knew them, my paternal grandfather was a salesman for Metropolitan Life, my grandmother a housewife. They lived in Glens Falls, in upstate New York, and I rarely saw them. My maternal grandmother was a sewing machine operator in the garment trades in New York City. Her husband abandoned her while my mother was still a child. I never knew him. My father grew up a serious athlete, and was undoubtedly headed for a career in physical education when he was sidetracked by World War II. He finished his education after the war and became a social worker. My mother grew up in the Bronx; I knew her mostly as a homemaker until I reached high school when she began a career as a personnel worker in large social service agencies.

Steve Cagan is currently a freelance photographer and unpaid political activist in Cleveland, Ohio. Most of his activist photography is centered on El Salvador. The photo shows Steve, on the far right, meeting with Salvadoran community leaders. He has exhibited and published broadly. In 1991 he published *This Promised Land, El Salvador* (Rutgers University Press) written with his wife, Beth. It has been released in an updated Spanish-language edition by Editorial Arcoiris, San Salvador, in 1993. He will be spending 1994–95 on a Fulbright teaching and helping develop the Master's program in the Department of Journalism and Communications at the University of El Salvador.

Steve Cagan

Activist Photography

My earliest memories are of life in a "temporary" housing project for de-mobilized World War II military in the area called Canarsie, in the farthest reaches of Brooklyn, where we lived for four or five years. This was a colony of working-class people who had neither family resources nor pro-fessions to fall back on. The area was divided into two areas—in one, people lived in quonset huts, essentially halves of corrugated metal tubes laid on their sides—a military construction expedient left over from the war. The rest of us lived in rows of tiny attached prefabricated houses, with postage-stamp back yards and even smaller front yards.

But for the large numbers of young children, we who would later be called "baby boomers" (I was actually born during the war, and my two sisters were both born in Canarsie), our relative poverty was no hardship. What I remember, rather, was the sense of openness and freedom about the place. While our parents were trying to establish the directions of their lives after the war, we ran the empty streets and open fields in packs. There was little traffic in the area, which was isolated from the rest of Brooklyn, but there were some special visitors—like the Dugan's bakery truck, selling packaged baked goods door-to-door. I wonder how those muffins would taste today—in my memory, they are delicious.

Canarsie remains for me a period of unspoiled childhood joy. My fa-ther, who before the war had been active in the Communist Party in the small upstate town where he grew up and a serious athlete—he had started his college education on athletic scholarships—was working several part-time jobs and going to school, eventually getting a social work degree. I remember occasionally walking him to the bus stop and taking shelter from the wind under his long overcoat.

My mother, like most of the women in the project, was primarily a homemaker, and was busy making her contribution to the population ex-plosion in the community. She also had been politically active on the Left before the war. Her older brother and sister-in-law stayed in the CP throughout this period; as I write this, my aunt remains an active and in-volved member.

The simple demands of survival occupied all my parents' energy during those early years, and I have no recollections of anything that resembled the kind of political activity that would later become the center of family life for us. But even at this tender age my sisters and I were getting information and values from our parents that were the foundation of what was to come. Much of this was given to us in the form of stories—stories about union struggles and about racism, about Jews and about "Negroes," and, very importantly, about how our grandparents came over from Russia.

My mother's mother came to this country after the 1905 Revolution. Like many poor Jewish women and men, she ended up as an "operator," working in the garment trades in New York. I only saw her as my grandmother, a woman who always seemed old to me, who spoke a broken English, who would visit us for a week or so at a time from where she regularly lived with the "other" part of my mother's family, the people who weren't in the Left. But my image of her includes things I never actually saw, but heard so often from my mother that I think I can see them: my grandmother leaving the Bronx apartment early in the morning with her sewing machine strapped to her back—she brought it home every night to do some extra piecework; my grandmother refusing to teach her two daughters to sew—she told them she was afraid they would break her precious needles, but my mother always felt she didn't want them to hurt themselves, or perhaps to follow her into the shops; my grandmother as an active unionist. I didn't see those things, perhaps, but they were part of my environment.

In the early fifties, we moved *up* to a low-income city housing project in the East Bronx, where I spent an important formative four years, from third to sixth grades. The physical changes were dramatic, and they meant the loss of the palpable sense of freedom we had in Canarsie; I could no longer essentially roll out of bed into the street, but had to take an elevator eight floors down. The population was much denser, and the entire environment much more urban. In time, this began to feel so normal to me that I remember as a teenager thinking of unattached individual family houses as isolated and vulnerable.

The class environment was also different; we had left the temporary and artificial atmosphere of postwar reorientation and entered a solidly working-class project. Most people here had "regular jobs," and even the "professionals," like my own father, were essentially low-paid public servants. And, of course, it was a heterogeneous community, including large numbers of African-American and Caribbean families. Our housing project was a multi-racial and multi-cultural island surrounded by a sea of entirely white, primarily working-class, and decidedly hostile, neighborhoods.

This was the height of McCarthyism and the postwar witch-hunts and blacklists. One day my parents supervised an apartment full of kids; all of the other adults had gone to Washington, D.C., to demonstrate against the impending execution of the Rosenbergs. It was in an atmosphere of some fear, and a great deal of caution, that I began to awaken to some political realities. My parents and their friends would talk about unions, about political issues, but frequently in undertones or in circumlocutions. I have a vivid memory of being hushed by a friend when I said in school that "of course" I thought the Rosenbergs were innocent. That must have been in the fifth grade.

Most of our parents, including my own, were struggling to achieve economic stability—at this juncture, my father had regular work as a social worker, and my mother did occasional typing in the apartment to make a little more money. Despite their former ties to the Communist Party, like many of their friends in the project, they had little connection with any political organizations. This was a product both of the lack of time left by family and job responsibilities and of the repressive national atmosphere. However, the political, social, and family environment in which we lived provided them with abundant opportunities to discuss their values—their pro-peace, anti-racist, pro–working class, and pro-union attitudes—with my sisters and me.

They needed to help us understand why living in a mixed neighborhood made us not very welcome in the public schools (along with the other kids in my building, I attended three public schools in four years, without our address ever changing). They had to help us understand and deal with the regular expressions of racism we ran into—school friends whose parents wouldn't let them visit us in the project, racist comments around us, sometimes directed at close friends. Once I was playing in my room with some friends, and we started to construct an imaginary baseball team out of major league players we liked. I offered one who was rejected because he wasn't good enough, "and anyway, he's a nigger." My parents had to explain to me what the word meant, and more important, to help me confront the racism in kids who were otherwise very likeable. One very upsetting moment came when the Boy Scout group I had belonged to for a few weeks would not allow a black friend to join—I quit in horror, but also in bewilderment.

But this education could not remain at the level of stories and moral support. When the schools issued dog tags to students "so your bodies can be identified if the Russians drop an atom bomb," my mother not only objected, but refused to allow me to wear mine. I didn't quite get it—I was only in the third grade at the time, and remember thinking it was pretty cool; it reminded me of my father's army dog tags.

And our parents were drawn into a kind of open activism as they had to struggle for such amenities as traffic lights to get us safely to school. I remember my mother and other mothers forming a baby-carriage picket line across a major intersection, allowing only doctors and school buses through. Watching them, I felt there was something special about those women, though of course I couldn't put that feeling into words. But I was proud of my mother. The Left adults in the projects participated as parents in the schools, in the period in which in New York City the parents were breaking away from the PTA to form the United Parents' Association.

This environment, and my parents' reactions to it, provided me with three very important lessons; I think these are at the core of everything I have done deliberately since then. First, issues of class and race—and of racism, discrimination, and oppression—were very concrete and immediate, and what I learned at home was not some kind of Left catechism, but tools for responding to everyday realities. The notion of solidarity was something very real to me, and political perspectives were to be sought to help deal with problems that were imposed on us by the world outside.

Secondly, I saw that it was possible to struggle for change, and that those struggles involved making connections with other people. While my vocabulary didn't include words like "struggle" and "activism," the adults around me were explaining by their behavior what activism was. And I saw the possibility (although without any explicit expression of it, of course) of rooting one's identity in such struggles. Actually, this seems to me to be the source of a deep and lasting optimism.

Finally, and for me perhaps the most profound and important impact of all of this was that I came to measure the value of personal activities by the effects they had on other people. Satisfaction and sense of accomplishment were to be found somehow in being effective—and being effective meant succeeding in making the lives of the people around you better.

This almost inevitably led to political activism at a young age. While still in junior high school, I started participating in anti–nuclear weapons marches and some civil rights activities. By high school, I was a coordinator of the picket lines in the Bronx during the Woolworth boycott of the late fifties—every Saturday I would ride my bike to the various picket lines and check on attendance, morale, and effectiveness. The Woolworth boycott had a dramatic effect on me, as it did on many of us, because it forced us to confront the hypocrisy of our teachers, many of whom had been preaching about "tolerance" and against racism for as long as we could remember, and now performed incredibly contorted steps to avoid taking a stand on what seemed the outstanding moral issue of the day.

At the same time, I was also active in work against civil defense drills in the schools. This activity was the first that required me to confront authority directly. Although in retrospect our activities appear very modest and even timid, at the time they seemed tremendous enough to us. When our teachers would tell us to get under our desks, we would refuse to move. When they directed us to "safe" areas in the school, we would gather in front of the principal's office. Some students were harshly disciplined for these activities in other schools, or even merely for wearing the blue armbands that identified us.

There were two other important developments at this time. First, along with a small group of friends, frustrated with our inability to get access to the media that so distorted the world as we knew it, or even to have a way to reply to the unfair characterizations of our own positions and activities by teachers and school administrators, I began to see the importance of outreach and grass-roots media work, and began editing an early underground publication.

Our little paper was mimeographed, written mostly by ourselves, stapled together in my family kitchen, and distributed hand-to-hand. It was a very modest project, and it didn't last very long. But it gave me a sense of the rewards provided by doing that kind of work, and was a step towards a commitment to "media," broadly understood.

The second development began one day when I was about fourteen; my CP uncle came to our house and suggested to my parents that they go in together to buy a 35mm camera that was on sale for a younger cousin's bar mitzvah present. They accepted the suggestion, but decided for good measure to buy a camera for themselves—it really was a good sale. That turned out to be a momentous decision; using that camera was the beginning of a relationship with the medium that has deepened, and become more complex, over time.

Later, in college, I remained active in the civil rights movement, as well as becoming involved in the newly-resurgent student movement, in solidarity work with "Third-World" liberation struggles, and especially near the end of my college years and into graduate school and beyond, in the growing activities against the war in Indochina.

Again, there were a few developments that had important consequences for my later directions: all through high school and college, I never had any doubts about my participation in the civil rights movement. Indeed, my only regret was that I never made the commitment to go South, to devote my entire life (as it then seemed) to the struggle. A majority of the people I worked with were African-Americans, but any doubts about the appropriateness of a white, Jewish man's participation, even (on a very local level) in leadership, were easily dismissed. After all, this activity was ultimately rooted in the injustices and insults I had personally seen; it was an outcome of my commitments to childhood friends. And it seemed so eminently right and moral.

But in 1965 things began to change. With the development of the Black Power movement, many whites in civil rights work felt they were no longer welcome. Others of us felt that the new activity was a logical and reasonable outcome of the empowering quality of previous civil rights work. And it made sense to us that the key activists and leaders in the movement for Black liberation in this country had by and large to be Black people.

Of course, one felt a sense of loss; not only your own life, but an entire era, was changing. Indeed, I think that we have never recaptured the personal, social, and moral rewards of working at the height of the civil rights movement. But we also gained a great deal, an understanding of the need to be more self-aware, more critical of our own roles. After this, I was never able to lightly dismiss concerns about my "place" in support struggles. This is not to say that I was unable to participate; most of my political work has been in solidarity organizations and campaigns. But it has required me to approach that work with perhaps more sensitivity to the needs of the people we are trying to support.

During my college years, I started hanging out with people who were looking for a "scientific" basis for their socialist ideas and activities—a basis that Marx and Engels explicitly argued for. I was close to a number of people in the Communist Party when I was at City College, and in graduate school with other, more independent Marxists. But I was always dissatisfied with the notion that economic and political theorizing could provide the basis for long-term commitment, the kind of commitment that makes one examine every day's activities to see how they fit, that was provided by that special combination of living in "the projects" and being given a framework of political and class-based values by my parents. This was later seen by colleagues and coworkers on the Left as an "anti-intellectual" position, but I don't think it is—rather, it is an insistence that theory must be an integrated part of a whole life of the movement, of organizations, and of individual activists. I came to feel that living for theory is as sterile and ineffective as living without theory.

By this time, it was pretty clear to me that the only real options for work that could satisfy my need to have a political effect were in political organizing, in teaching, or perhaps in media work. In graduate school, I quickly tired of self-absorbed graduate students and the isolation from "real life" that university literary studies seemed inherently to generate. A moment perhaps more illustrative than critical in this process came during a Spenser seminar, when a fellow student explained that she was "seriously concerned" about Spenser's use of a particular word deep in *The Fairie Queene*. I was stunned by this; curiosity seemed justified, mild annoyance perhaps, but deep concern? Hoping to salvage the possibility of an academic career by entering a more relevant field of work, I switched from English to history. But despite doing quite well in graduate school, I found the attractiveness of organizing was too great, and the negative aspects of what I saw as a detached and uncommitted life were too overwhelming. I quit school to work full-time in grass-roots political organizations.

Within a few years, with a baby on the way, my wife and I both found ourselves working as academic "gypsies," teaching part-time—and being politically active—in several colleges at once. Then, in 1970, we made a decision that turned out to be quite momentous in our lives. An organization we belonged to, New University Conference, decided to expand, and we went to work, sharing a job as organizers. We left New York for Cleveland, Ohio, where we have been ever since. Times changed—NUC declined and folded within two years, Beth found work at a local university, and I entered a long period of unemployment, teaching a very occasional course, working as an unpaid organizer in various projects, and giving freer rein to my long-repressed desire to devote more time to photography.

Now I increasingly began to see myself as a photographer, but my attention was always divided between photo work and other, more directly "political," organizing activity. My first idea that it might be possible to integrate these areas of life came during my work with the Indochina Peace Campaign, when I began seriously to document our own activities, and

After climbing up the near side of the ravine that ran through the middle of the Salvadoran refugee camp in Colomoncagua, Honduras, a group of women and children look back at a group of dwellings on the other side, 1988.

finally was part of a small media delegation that toured all the countries of the region in 1974.

Since then, my major work has been in projects about factory closings and unemployment in Ohio, and later about the popular movements in Nicaragua and El Salvador. In both cases, I have been photographing in areas in which I was also politically active in other ways.

It's common for artists and other creative workers to describe the ways in which their early life experiences are reflected in their work. These are, of course, easier to understand in artistic work that is about the artist's life, or when—as suggested by the all too common and ultimately unconvincing platitude that all artistic work is really autobiographical—artistic production is seen primarily as an opening into the artist's consciousness, as if somehow the artist her- or himself were a very interesting subject. This very projection of the artist as the center of interest is one of the reasons I am loath to refer to myself as an artist.

Obviously the ideas, attitudes, and values shaped by early experience strongly affect one's choices of content and message and the way in which

Washing dried corn, the first step in the production of tortillas. In the camp at Colomoncagua, making tortillas was done in the collective kitchens, treating this very time-consuming task, traditionally the responsibility of women in their own homes, as a social responsibility, a workshop task, and freeing women to participate in other communal activities, 1989.

Liberating Memory

Demolition of an old powerhouse in the flats, 1977.

one works. Even though it is financially unrewarding, my commitment to political photography has been more important to me than the full-time commitment required for what is normally understood as a successful career in academia. My teaching position on the art faculty at Rutgers came to an end because I tried to integrate "art," scholarship, and activism rather than maintain the academic detachment—and academic ineffectiveness—considered acceptable by the university administration.

My background has also affected my relationship with my photographic "subjects." For the last five years (a period during which I was still also working in academia), I have been working with a community of Salvadorans, first when they were in a refugee camp in Honduras, and later when they returned to found a new community in El Salvador. Like many "documentary" photographers working in cultures or subcultures different from their own, I have had to think about the significance and consequences of my work. And in particular, I've once again had to confront the question of my "right" as a white, privileged North American photographer to work in an impoverished Central American community. Before that, I had been confronted by similar questions as I documented the struggles against factory closings and their devastating consequences for working-class communities in Ohio. In the end, I've been able to project a particular theoretical justification for my work that is based on seeing it as part of the struggles of the people I am photographing. Of course, "seeing it" this way would not be enough. I have come to understand myself not as a political or sympathetic documentary photographer, but as an "activist photographer" in an active relationship with my "subjects." This has meant abandoning the detachment and "neutrality" often expressed as goals by such workers, and to enter as an active participant in organizations and campaigns in solidarity with the communities whose lives and struggles are my photographic subjects.

My need to justify my work by holding it up to a set of ethical and political tests has grown directly out of my childhood environment, and the confrontation between the values I learned there and the professional, academic, and artistic worlds I came to occupy later. For me there is a direct link between my need to know that my photographs in a Salvadoran community are part of the effort that community is making to change its life, and seeing my mother standing in the street, with my little sister in a baby carriage, blocking traffic to force the city to install a traffic light.

Part Five

The "We" Inside the "I"

I was born in 1946 in New York City. My father was an immigrant pipefitter, a rebellious son of a hand-to-mouth rabbi, and his unsuccessful innkeeping wife, neither of whom made it beyond the Russian Pale. A Lower East Side Jude the Obscure, my father once published in the leftist press and shared his 1930s compatriots' literary radicalism. My mother's shtetl parents did make it over, labored mightily in the garment trades, and preferred the *Jewish Daily Forward* to the *Daily Worker*. Mother, who flirted with metropolitan leftism in the 1930s and very early 1940s, long taught history in New York schools.

This photo of my father and myself was taken in the early 1950s, at Fire Island, in the community of Ocean Bay Park—an interesting choice for my parents, since the same New York Communist Party members they so disliked in the immediate wake of the Moscow Trials summered there during the HUAC era.

What follows is a memoir of my father, at his finest as a worker-writer in a period of his life he preferred to forget.

Laura Hapke is a professor of English at Pace University. A graduate of The Garden School and Brandeis University, she holds advanced degrees from the University of Chicago and the City University of New York. She is a consulting editor of *Belles Lettres: A Review of Books by Women;* her scholarly writings include *Tales of the Working Girl: Wage-Earning Women in American Literature, 1890–1925* (Twayne/Macmillan, 1992), *Girls Who Went Wrong: Prostitutes in American Fiction, 1885–1917* (Bowling Green University Popular Press, 1989), and a score of articles on women's/American/labor studies in periodicals such as *Mid-America* and *The Journal of American Culture.* She sees her task as the rediscovery of those toilers of the past, particularly women, whose breadwinning stifled them, whose (mainstream) society scorned them, and whose literary imaginers, however sympathetic to their lot, often misrepresented them. Her forthcoming book is *Daughters of the Great Depression: Women, Work, and Fiction in the American 1930s.*

Laura Hapke

Homage to Daniel Horwitz

Last night I dreamed my father had just died and bequeathed me a half-used spool of thread. In my dream my mother scornfully waved a hand at so paltry a legacy. I woke, to disagree: he had left me what he had, and what he was. If by now I cannot stitch an homage to him with it, I am no daughter of Dan Horwitz, proletarian writer of the thirties.

My father died five years ago, during a sweltering New York City August that is still remembered as cruel, cruel. He had withstood a hungry boyhood in Jew-hating Russia, gathering grass to boil for soup. Always the outsider, naturalized citizen or no, he had been knocked in the face on a construction site (accidentally? he made so many enemies in the union one never knew) by a falling bit of metal. That was in the 1940s; a few years earlier, the Depression at its height, he had been hit even harder, in his psyche—more of that later—by his split with the CP over the Moscow Trials. But it was weather and old age that did for him in the end. That last week, as usual, we were quarreling bitterly, in person, then, for the last time, by telephone. His last words to me and, of course, the world, were "What's the use?"

When I go to the movies, I see grizzled but indomitable Clint Eastwood, chain-smoking toughie Humphrey Bogart, even mindless Arnold Schwarzenegger looking obdurate, and for a moment each assumes my father's likeness: as he was when confronted with a snooty putdown from my mother's educated pals; from a string of maitre d's who wanted to seat him in the back; from a doorman, when I lived in a building nice enough to have one, who took him for a mafioso.

I cannot recall the first time my father stopped being an embarrassment and started taking on a battle-scarred heroism that Hollywood stars can still make a buck on. Or rather when I first realized that I should not be ashamed that he was crude, coarse, blue collar, out of bourgeois place, only ashamed that I was ashamed. It may even have taken my decision to write the essay that follows to begin an exorcism of my genteel academic past, to cast off the snobbery about working-class people piped into me at my pseudo-real-thing private school. More of that later, too. In any event, it is a casting off that continues pretty haltingly, as I hardly trot out my proletarian parent in my courses on the literature of the 1930s—courses, I might add, sneered at by colleagues for the "thin" literary merit of Mike Gold's lyrical *Jews Without Money* or Agnes Smedley's brilliant *Daughter of Earth*.

What I do know is that the spool dream and the apparitions in the movie theaters are signals that my apologies to Dan Horwitz are long overdue. I did not create the consumption-worshipping and status-stalking that estranged us when I was a young girl, but God knows that even past graduate school I have held them as dear enough. Ironically, I came to realize the vitality and timeliness of working-class literature some years ago through sheer disgust at the kinds of literature that *were* extolled in the academy—and the kinds of scholarship that extolled them. Maybe I became a real person from a surfeit of literary criticism.

Prologue

Jackson Heights, Queens, 1950s

It is late afternoon, perhaps four, a time when schoolgirls and blue-collar workers are home. My mother, a teacher with a drawer full of medals from the Hunter High School for Gifted Girls (where, though a garment worker's daughter, she appeared in a play *speaking in French*) and Hunter College (she graduated at nineteen), is either not home or shut in her room, doing those mysterious "lesson plans" that occupied her afterschool hours during the 1950s. My father, who, to my ten-year-old's certain knowledge, never finished grade school, sits on a sofa, observing me. He wears work clothes, laundered but spotty, though, I am aware, not as soiled as the ones he wore to work. We look at each other, he from the corner sofa, I from across the room. We have nothing to say.

The pages of the *Daily Worker,* New York City, 1933

Cliff lay low on cold grass beneath an overcast sky waiting for a freight. He shivered. He had been lying on that same spot for a couple of hours and was getting restless. He let loose a shower of curses. Finally he heard the shrill moan of a locomotive. He jumped to his feet. The black belly rushed in with a maddening speed, throwing up a maze of ruddy sparks. Cliff threw himself forward. Cinders got into his eyes and blinded him. When he opened his eyes the train was disappearing around a bend.

"Where in hell is this limousine rushin' to? An' may be I'm gettin' to be too damn slow. But a fellow could kiss himself good-bye tryin' to make it," he muttered.

He looked up. It'll rain soon. Maybe snow. "What am I going to do now?" he asked himself, scratching his head.

Should he go back to town? Blackwell was no soft spot for hoboes. The handouts were poor and the cops were tough. He had to go far out of the station to hop a train. He hated like hell to go back. But he hadn't tasted any food since early morning and now dusk was snooping down [sic] on the wide fields. His stomach ached with a burning pain. He must go and pick up something.

— from *Going East: A Novel of Proletarian Life*

In 1933, my father, Daniel Horwitz, later Daniel Harris, a twenty-nine-year-old Lithuanian Jew who came to the United States illegally a decade before, made his entry in the ledger of thirties' literary radicalism. *Going East,* a novel of vagrants and strikers, appeared serially in the *Daily Worker,* whose circulation was then rising, though the paper had yet to hit its Popular Front stride. In *The New Masses,* Party devotee Mike Gold has christened the form my father and many others were practicing: the revolutionary novel. Horwitz, though he would never receive the critical notice greeting the "hobo jungle" fiction of those like Nelson Algren (*Somebody in Boots,* 1934), Edward Newhouse (*You Can't Sleep Here,* 1934), or the already world-weary Tom Kromer (*Waiting for Nothing,* 1935), had matriculated at birth (in Russian-occupied Eastern Europe) in what most workingmen called the college of hard knocks, and *Going East,* though apprentice work, at least broke into print. Native-born proletarian authors like Kromer knew the rough and tumble too, but, more formally educated, they enrolled in the school of life much later than my father. Perhaps, too, Dan's very authenticity—he was, after all, a skilled laborer by day and a writer by night—intrigued the editors of a paper whose over 30,000 readers understood the troubles of the foreign-born no less than those of the American working stiff.

In any case, I have it now, now that he is dead, his notebook of clippings, pasted carefully into a small, black, crumbling leather binder, the entire serial of his curiously American protagonist, "Cliff," who is described under the one-column headline "Novel of Workers' Life Begins in 'Daily' Tomorrow," as "a youth driven to hoboing by unemployment, . . . finally finding a job . . . and taking a leading part in the strike." Beside the blurb is a nice photo of Dan Horwitz, with all of his hair, and sporting the suit jacket, shirt, and tie that Depression Era workers wore even on the breadline and at sitdown strikes. Only two things had my father crossed out, sometime between 1933 and HUAC, quite methodically, in strong dark ink: the title *Daily Worker,* and the date.

In 1956, when, inhabiting a small Queens apartment with my parents, I began to sit up and take notice of life, I knew nothing of all this. Not for me the bittersweet life of the Red Diaper baby: I never felt *my* parents could have been the Rosenbergs. How could I? By then my father, and, in the only malleability I ever knew her to exhibit, my mother, had swung far, far right, and it was a dinnertime diet of "the Commies," "the Commies," "the lousy Commies." My mother was even writing a book, never finished, establishing the guilt of that unreconstructed CP twosome beyond a shadow of a doubt. (For whom? Were those mourning the now-dead Julius and Ethel likely to be swayed? And did the J. Edgar Hooverites need more polemic?) If I knew nothing of the black leather notebook then, I knew *that.*

But this is not what I want to write about. What concerns me here is that a few years later, when I was fourteen, I saw the clipping book for the first time. My father came over to me, shyly, and placed it in my hands. He did not tell me what it contained, only that it was something he had written. As I opened it, I saw his photograph, started to read the words "Novel of Workers' Life . . . ," and my mother entered. My father swept the notebook out of sight, where it spent another two and a half decades. I never saw it in his hands again.

Not long after, I began to gather literature on a then distaff-side, debutante-ridden Vassar (accepted for admission but too fearful to attend, thank God, I chose a more democratic place in the end), stalk the aisles of Saks Fifth Avenue after school, and go the hairdresser's weekly to straighten my kinky black hair. All the golden-WASP girls at my private school (what other venue for a NYC schoolteacher's daughter?)—where the only black was the janitor, boys and girls alike hailed from homes with three bathrooms, and the headmaster stressed that although his name was "Fisher" it lacked a "c"—were in love with Sandra Dee.

It has taken me half a lifetime to appreciate what my father himself had ceased to appreciate—what, for want of a better term, I know now is working-class authenticity. I have lived in two worlds: the pietistic one of academia, where the most vicious hatreds and the pettiest of quarrels are cloaked in politesse; and the hidden world of guilt, of shame, for my working-class father: that he picked his teeth, peppered his speech with curse words, and seemed, always, to be a few paces behind my mother when they walked the streets of conformist America. And that shame has all but choked my pride in him for believing, at one time, anyway, in social justice, in transcendent values, in Cliff, the hobo organizer.

Bildungsroman, in Brief

I. Closets

How was it that though we three lived more or less on top of one another in a flat meant for two, my mother and I lived a middle-class life and my father a working-class one? I'll begin with the closets, as good a place—or quartet of places, as it so happens—as any, for where we stored our respective possessions said as much about our divided economic affiliations as did the things themselves.

Even had she liked Jews, Virginia Woolf wouldn't have known what to do with my father's lack of lebensraum. Though he was by gender a member of the privileged patriarchy we hear so much about these days, he had no room of his own. He slept on the Castro in the living room. Because, for some reason, he slept with his balding head positioned at the foot of this makeshift bed, which, evidently of cheap design, sloped down to a bland, gray-carpeted floor, he chose to lie with his upper body closer to the ground. This oddity I observed nightly as I tried to move past him, sans noise, on my way to the bathroom. Invariably I woke him up; just as invariably he muttered a muted profanity; and, the curse in the darkened air, I steeled myself for being his second wakeup call when, a few minutes later, I had to step over him again on my way back to my room.

But I digress. If I had a little bedchamber, with swinging door and a nicely varnished wooden wardrobe, the poor man had none, no dresser, no dresser drawer, nada. Only, quite literally, a place to hang his hat: the hall closet. Actually it was one of two closets in the narrow entryway to the modest remainder of apartment 3J; in the other closet, just opposite, were stored linens and coats (his one topcoat, not bulky, was permitted to hang there, I recall). Like the denizens of J. Riis's *How the Other Half Lives,* Dan, though electing a closet over a steerage trunk, stowed away where he could his tatty collection of work shirts, scuffed shoes, slightly greasy Robert Hall ties, and single low-budget "good" suit for the odd family event (and, given the social tensions in the house, such trio gatherings were odd enough). He evidently accepted the fact that although he had made the transit from a bachelor-days Fourteenth Street tenement (where, come to think of it, he at least shared a room with an older brother, a less recent emigré), he was still living hard.

Mother and I lived easy. She had the large bedroom with the two windows, into which, at various times in her tenure there, she stuffed a mass of furniture, books, and office supplies—all that was needed, I guess, for a home away from home. Seeking escape, she had only to shut her bedroom door and turn on the classy three-speed desk lamp; the manual, later electric, typewriter; the motorized Barcalounger; the black-and-white, later color, television.

Or she could open her closet, filled with what to Riis's Jewish sewing machine operators might have seemed a healthy yearly output: dresses, jumpers, blouses, suit blouses, coats. The works, you know? And the appropriate trimmings in the shoe and boot department, all waiting to be thrust on top of a choice from the large chest of drawers in which reposed her white lingerie and on top of which lay three little jewel boxes, all in a row.

My choice was clear, if not noble: I sure didn't want to relive immigrant days on the Lower East Side. I wanted, and early on achieved, a closet with a room attached.

II. Two Educations

1. "Max Harris instructs," from Dan's novella

Max Harris [roving organizer] spoke for an hour, telling the men of various strikes and wage-cuts and how strikes had been won. He compared the conditions in organized industries and shops with those that were unorganized. He warned them of a wage-cut. He showed them a way out. He drove the idea of organization home to them. His slogan was "organize and fight against speed-up." The men applauded.

The chairman called for discussion. All seemed to agree. What could they add to the organizer's talk! "There is every bit of darned truth in it," they said to each other.

Cliff suddenly felt he had something to say. He had never heard anybody speak like that before. It made him see things differently.

"Folks, this fellow Harris put things pretty clear to us . . . ," he said halt-ingly. "Yes, what was I gonna say?" He lost the thread of his thought, and scratched his head. "Yes, I was gonna say, I thought it was Fred's fault that my buddy got sacked, and why we work like hell. But I can see now that it ain't him only. It's the company that makes us work like hell, while so many guys walk the streets. That ain't right, you know, folks. We got to do some-thing about it. And as the speaker said, we got to organize to do something about it."

There was rustle of applause. Cliff blushed, sitting down. . . . Harris had brought some light in the darkness in which Cliff was groping. He had never before met a fellow who knew so much. He wondered who this dark-haired Jewish boy was.

Even had I not taken a wad of literature courses (where the prole-tarian novel was noticeably absent from the syllabus), I would have known that my father's alter ego was not just Cliff, apprentice radical, but the more seasoned organizer, "this fellow Harris," who carries IWW luminary Bill Haywood's autobiography along with him on his travels and, who, toward the end of *Going East,* lends it to Cliff. For after my father came out of the army in 1943, well after the Moscow Trials, the Nazi–Soviet Pact, and his own renunciation of the CP and all of its works, Horwitz changed his last name to Harris to gain entry into non-Jewish-loving Plumber's Local No. 2. Whether the name choice was the last vestige of a firebrand consciousness, a bid for acculturation in the union "brotherhood," or a wry reminder that out of the ashes of a burnt-out idealism little but a "new" name could rise Phoenixlike, I do not know. I do know that when Dan finally took steady work, it was under the aegis of a union that found "reds" anathema. Was that just fine with him?

2. White Gloves and Castanets

In any case, whether he sang the "Internationale" anymore or not, Dan's day was spent in the blue-collar workmill, though he never referred to his daily activities, and, when pressed, told me to give "Heating Con-tractor" as his occupation (in case my preppy schoolmates asked). And I, too, was in a mill, though I punched my time card by aping my instructors and my only assembly line was acculturation. Compared to the unbroken jobtime my father served on the various high-rises and building lots of the city, mine was spent sweatlessly at the assimilation factory of the Garden School and, soon after, at the graduate school equivalents, the endless seminars on Henry James.

The Garden Country Day School in the borough of Queens (later, as if in a bid to come closer to the truth without sacrificing the snob appeal, rechristened simply the Garden School) was grounded in a kind of middle-class gentility that was the doing of its founder, Otis P. Flower. That venerable schoolmaster had gone to his heavenly reward for Christian uprightness by the time Garden opened its doors (and raised its fees for) the less-than-elect children and grandchildren of Irish and East European immigrants. In their younger days the Flowers no doubt were a part of the Protestant ascendancy in Jackson Heights, a neighborhood that lived down its Queens affiliation by boasting, in the blocks near Garden (though not near the soulless low-budget apartment houses in which my family dwelled), apartments into which private elevators opened. Cultivating the parents who owned these places, the Flowers flowered.

Given this sanctified clientele, what with my father's mysterious silence and my mother's nervous aspiration to respectability, I was so ill-equipped for Garden's mannered environment that even with her promptness in paying the bills—appreciated at a less-than-upper-crust private school in at best subway proximity to Manhattan—I doubt I could have gained entrance into the place had I not been enrolled in the first grade. There, as the sole behavior problem (I largely refused to sit down—was I looking for my father and the union meeting?) I became an interesting child, a challenge, and, not infrequently, the object of a scandalized "*Laura Harris!*" from long-suffering Miss Barry, my first-grade teacher.

By the time I was ten, and my father had been climbing up and down construction site high-rises without elevators for almost two decades, I had calmed down enough to attend the school's newly inaugurated white glove and castanet evenings. I still had no real concept of what he did for a living, although if I had troubled to take from the top shelf of his closet one of his many unpublished manuscripts, a passage like this would have instructed me: "He was beginning to feel the strain of the morning's work. He had a pain in his right shoulder, the veins in his left arm were blue as if they were about to burst, and he could feel them swell up. Sweat."

But I was far more aware of Otis P. Flower's widow, Linna, a wearer of silk suits, and, it seems in memory, flowered hats, who remained behind to instruct the majority of affluent and the few socially benighted like myself in a kind of etiquette. By the time I hit sixth grade, she had ironed out my rebellious soul, one commanding look from her squelching my slangy irreverence and the occasional "shut up!" I had often overheard from my father and used freely myself with classmates. As manageress more than classroom slavey, she directed the yearly operetta, in which, though I could hardly sing, I won a coveted role. All the grossly underpaid teachers held her in a kind of awe, to which she responded with the same mixture of hauteur and fairly kindly moral rectitude as she did in her tidy classroom.

Perhaps because Mrs. Flower suspected it would take more than a mannerly classroom, an operetta, and a girls' sewing class (she ran that too) to prepare some of her pupils for a berth in the middle classes, the school instituted a "white glove" mid-week dance evening for the preteeners around the time I was twelve or thirteen. I cannot recall having attended with much regularity, but I was there enough to learn the drill. We girls, in dresses and white gloves, sat primly on a row of chairs and gazed across the Arabia Deserta of the gymnasium floor at the equally white-gloved male adolescents headed unconvincingly our way, under the surveying eye of a wraithlike old dame (a college chum of Mrs. Flower's now in reduced circumstances?) wearing a fox head and some claws and, I now realize, anxiously determined to show that she had lost none of her breeding.

As a dozen constrained pairs negotiated the gym floor, our portly music teacher whipped up a waltz or a fox trot at the piano, wheeled in from a nearby classroom. Guided by Fox Fur's castanets and her fluty "*one*-two-three—yes!—*one*-two-three," we did our best to make careful conversation and in general imitate the little ladies and gentlemen of Victorian Christmas parties past in the knowledge that we were learning—what? What were we learning? Ostensibly, Social Dancing, a category of the great god Deportment. As I stared glassily at the face, or, more likely in this pre–high school stage, over the head of my partner, I may have had some sense that this charade was the first of many. What I do know is that my mother was in the parents' corner, where a few dentist and businessmen fathers chatted with their own or each other's wives; my father was not. Who needed a social flatfoot at the ball?

3. Totem and Taboo: Henry James and Theodore Dreiser

When I finally came to read my father's favorite author, Theodore Dreiser, that apostle of the inarticulate, the music was better, but the dance was much the same. There may have been Signet paperbacks of *Sister Carrie* and *An American Tragedy,* those classic defenses of the urban have-nots, in the college bookstores of the land or hidden away in the optional readings list for graduate exams, but no American author of his stature has ever been pelted with such a barrage of insults. If the 1960s was a time of storming the university barricades, where I was kept there were no shouts in the street; mostly I heard that feminist literary criticism was sociology, black studies self-indulgence, and *Jude the Obscure* (with its pitiable proletarian title character) a weaker Thomas Hardy novel than *The Mayor of Casterbridge*. And if one defied the dual prejudice against American literature in general and Dreiser in particular, it was like taking a job in some community college in South Dakota when one's sights were on the Ivy League; how to defend the suicidal choice not to be in what was then-fashion: parsing Marvell or gathering images in Shakespeare?

To backtrack, then: at college in a distinctly non–South Dakota milieu, I found Dreiser routinely vilified as a minor author of no learning or style (prose or otherwise); in graduate school, where I persisted in bringing up his name, I discovered his sin: he was not Henry James, dedicated to the so-called "true themes" of classic turn-of-the-century fiction: millionaires' aesthetic quests and moral crises, transatlantic marriages, the Upper Ten Thousand. Later, at my university affiliation, where the Jamesians still seemed to hold sway, allusions to him brought the same smirk that greeted Arthur Miller (*Death of a Salesman* lacked "tragic grandeur") or even George Gissing (he wasn't Dickens).

Around that time one of my future graduate professors, a Socialist éminence grise who had written widely on the big guns of European and American literature as well as on politics, immigrants, and labor, wondered in a widely-known essay why Dreiser had dropped out of the awareness of Americans. Good question. Here's another one: Why in this luminary's own courses in the early 1970s did we endlessly read Henry James, with not a word about Dreiser? It was as if we were to view our graduate education as a trip to Mount Olympus via the Modern Language Association, where we waited breathlessly for the approved mythology to manifest itself in Penguin paperbacks and conference sessions. Any writer of mere mortal status, who was less than a Dickens (though his star was only slowly rising again, as I recall) and presumed to write about the lower depths, was not in the godlike company before which we genuflected. And our worship, of course, took the form of glossing the text with virtually no attempt to locate a writer in the context of social class (my own advisor—himself viewed as declassé for his own interest in the subject—wrote a book on the Dreiser Era without mentioning the term), so that when I stubbornly came to write my dissertation on Dreiser and his contemporaries, my head was buzzing with literary devices and not much else. I doggedly produced a series of awful sentences such as: "The combination of the form of melodrama and the naturalist philosophy, however, create complexity of characterization impossible for a pure (and hence) sterile philosophy or for a hackneyed art form."

What was Dreiser's sin against (American) literature? Or, for that matter, that of Frank Norris, Jack London, Upton Sinclair? Not to mention Agnes Smedley or Anzia Yezierska? That he does not resurrect the Gothic with Hawthorne? Celebrate male bonding with Melville? Describe the American Princess with old Henry? No, it is that he shoves the noses of academics into what many of them may been in flight from themselves: the raw fact that to write about a shoe factory or transit strike may brand one as sympathetic to class struggle rather than "high art," whatever that is. And that allegiance might raise other questions: what were your origins? who were your forebears? And the academic milieu, at least until recently, was hardly receptive to such sympathies. Drenched in gentility, they were a gathering of aesthetes dedicated to proving that criticism is a science—a half-truth, I would add, that must be endlessly ratified by excluding from the MLA all who try to resurrect noncanonical texts. But who were these new scientist-aesthetes? The lesser universities in particular are peopled with the success stories of American higher education, those hard-working "good students" who may well have relished the fact that, whether children of the haute-, petite-, or sub-bourgeoisie, they had saved themselves from a high school teacher's trials or a middle-manager's anonymity. They were professors! And, until the recent revolution, for good or ill spawning terms like "multiculturalism" and "diversity" and, brought back from obscurity, "working-class literature," they were living proof that—as one of my graduate professors, with a wine cellar, a French wife (his second), a home in Scarsdale, and a penchant for the tennis court, told me—it did not matter what books we read as long as we all read the same books.

The same books. And thus I come full circle, back to my father, who, in our rare conversations, spoke of Dreiser with awe and yearned, no doubt, to write such passages as this, on the once-proud Hurstwood, variously a pillar of society, white-collar criminal, transit strike scab, and near-penniless Bowery vagabond, from *Sister Carrie*:

> "I can't stand much of this," said Hurstwood, whose legs ached him painfully, as he sat down on the miserable bunk in the small, lightless chamber allotted to him [in the Bowery lodging house]. "I've got to eat, or I'll die."

Or this, on Carrie's futile search for meaning in the female workplace:

Carrie turned her face to the west with a subdued heart. . . . She felt a slight relief, but it was only at her escape [after the long shoe-factory day]. She felt ashamed in the face of the better dressed girls who went by. She felt as though she should be better served, and her heart revolted.

Cliff and Max Harris would certainly have understood.

III. Coda

By the late 1980s, I had shaken off my (male) professors' Dreiser, but had not made my father's my own. I rejoiced that Dreiser critics, their ranks now growing, were beginning to combat the general (and their own) condescension, to rediscover Dreiser as the compassionate if careerist reporter who visited the sweatshops, toiled at menial jobs, and produced, but never finished, an autobiographical narrative called *An Amateur Laborer.* A scholarly edition, its lengthy preface not too remote from its topic, appeared in 1983, two years after some of the same scholars had, in the "restored" *Sister Carrie,* resurrected the "vulgarities" Dreiser's prudish wife and genteel editors had deleted. But I knew something remained for me to do: to carry on my first real conversation with Dan Horwitz, to offer his ghost, and anyone else who would listen, my own view. Mine, not his or the academy's, though I respected the one and accepted the other. For, unlike Dan in his prime, I was no 1930s denizen of the cheap all-night political cafeterias, where the superiority of *New Masses* to *Partisan Review,* or Mike Gold to Party fugitive James T. Farrell, was hashed out in the small hours. For better or worse, the (few) nights I had stayed up late were spent producing (later marking) papers, and meeting, as my diploma reads, "the requirements of the university for the degree of Doctor of Philosophy with all the ranks and privileges thereunto pertaining."

Because—and in spite of—the contrasting influences on my intellectual life, Dreiser today is my own. It is only now that I can argue with confidence that his vivid narratives concern the feminine work experience as much as, if not more than, the masculine one. I unearth his noisy, hapless, menial-job-holding sisters and recruit them for duty in my analysis of Carrie Meeber and, in *American Tragedy,* Roberta Alden. Mindful that the mass of Dreiser's contemporaries—whether labor union leaders, so-called philanthropists, mainstream apologists of the status quo, or proper matrons like Mrs. Frank Doubleday, who hated *Sister Carrie*—felt women could only be corrupted in (and corrupt) the workplace, I look for telltale signs in Theodore's own depictions, and, despite his humanity, often find them. I scour the period's many working-girl bestsellers, finding echoes of and challenges to them in his work. To illuminate his historical context I research—painstakingly, I hope—the rise of women's trade unions, female labor agitators (Dreiser interviewed Elizabeth Gurley Flynn), the Triangle Fire, statistics on types, wages, conditions, marital status, and the like, of women workers, from the 1890s (the beginning of the feminine mass entry into the workplace and of Carrie's escape from it) to the 1920s, time of Clyde Griffiths and the pathetic factory girl he victimizes, Roberta Alden. Haltingly, but with fascination, I apply the new feminist insights on "woman's work culture"—her combined response to her peers and her employer's strictures—to the experience of Carrie and her shopgirl coworkers that Dreiser so richly and skillfully delineates. I write an article, then a book.

I am not untrammeled by my past. But I do not slight fiction on women workers the way that American criticism has slighted the "working stiff" literature of my father's generation (and the nation, under business sway, continues to minimize the worker himself, as the many recent union defeats suggest). As I write on women wage earners, I hope I do not condescend, or almost as bad, idealize.

I am not free, because it is easier to reinvent Dreiser than to understand why my father had destroyed his past. I know too that in my young womanhood, I lacked a generous vision; I shared my father's ill-concealed shame at ethnicity and blue-collar roots, that scramble to throw out idealism with controversial affiliation, that so marred the 1950s. Primed by my success-driven but flawed schooling, I breathed the snobbish air of the academic Jamesians in what for others may have been the Freedom Riders' 1960s and the 1970s' Vietnam Vets Against the War. And mine was but a faint 1980s suspicion that Dreiser's greatness was his own comprehension, his own ambivalence aside, that for American writers one of the truest subjects is the outcast status of the working class.

If my father's tragedy was that he confused human decency with upward mobility and cultural and political assimilation, I hope that in the 1990s it will not be mine. In resurrecting him, I finally take pride in being the daughter of a worker-writer, for his sake and for mine.

Saul Slapikoff

I was born November 5, 1931, in Hunt's Point Hospital in the Bronx, New York. My father, David Slapikoff, was a presser in the dress industry, my mother, Fannie (Schmuckler) Slapikoff, a full-time housewife. When I was about a year old my father was laid off and my mother returned to work as a bookkeeper. When I was three years old, my parents—with loans from my father's brothers—bought a partnership in a grocery store in the Marine Park neighborhood of Brooklyn. In spite of the fact that the rest of my parents' lives were spent as shopkeepers, they never gave up the working-class consciousness of a just world, for everybody, that informed their politics. These ideals are their most important gift to me.

The photo shows (left to right) me and my sister, Pearl, my father and mother, and my maternal grandmother, Riva, and her brother, Zelig.

I attended PS 207, James Madison High School in Brooklyn. After graduating in 1952 from Brooklyn College, I worked as a milling machine operator until I was drafted into the U.S. Army in November 1952. Refusing to sign the Loyalty Oath and Affidavit after induction, I was discharged as a security risk in early 1954. Later that year I became an "industrial concentrator" for the Communist Party, holding a variety of jobs in the railroad industry in the New York City area. I quit the CP in 1956 after Khrushchev's speech to the 20th Party Congress detailing some of Stalin's crimes. I continued as a railroad worker until 1959. In 1960, at the age of thirty, I began graduate work in biochemistry at Tufts University Medical School. I received my Ph.D. in 1964 and spent two years as a postdoctoral fellow

in the Department of Biochemistry at Stanford University Medical School before becoming assistant professor of biology at Tufts in 1966.

Saul A. Slapikoff is an associate professor of biology and American studies at Tufts University and is currently director of the American Studies Program. His interests in biology are in environmental toxicology and he does occasional unpaid consulting for nonprofit environmental and occupational health groups such as the Massachusetts Association of Conservation Commissions and Massachusetts Coalition for Occupational Safety and Health. He has been a member of the editorial board of *Radical Teacher* for over fifteen years, has been involved in the movement for peace and justice in the Middle East since 1982, a member of the Boston Mobilization for Survival, and a supporter of a wide variety of peace and justice organizations. He is author of *Consider and Hear Me: Voices from Palestine and Israel* (Philadelphia: Temple University Press, 1993) and is currently writing short fiction and a memoir.

Saul Slapikoff

Inheritance

I grew up in a corner of Brooklyn as one of a very few Jews living in a neighborhood that was predominantly Roman Catholic. Many of my neighbors were followers of Father Coughlin, a priest from Detroit, I believe, who had a weekly radio program during which he filled the air with the peculiar blend of populism, anti-Semitic and anti-black rhetoric that characterized the "program" of the Christian Front that he headed. While my playmates were a mixed bunch including Jews, Catholics, and Protestants of various persuasions, I was daily confronted with expressions of anti-Semitism from name calling—"kike," "sheeny," "mocky," and "Jewboy" among others—to occasionally being physically assaulted. Thus, you might say that my identity as a Jew was hammered home by my external environment.

The most vivid and deeply lasting foundation of my personal and political identity I derived from my father. He came to this country from Russia as a teenager and immediately went to work, under dreadful conditions, as an operator of Schiffli embroidery machines and later as a presser in the dress industry. A unionist, he held fiercely independent socialist beliefs and was a part of the Jewish–Socialist immigrant community. His was a

This essay is adapted from the introduction to *Consider and Hear Me: Voices from Palestine and Israel* (Philadelphia: Temple University Press, 1993).

passionate commitment to social justice firmly rooted in his Jewish work-ing class consciousness.

If my father came from a poor background, my mother's was even poorer. Her father immigrated from White Russia first, sending for his wife and three surviving children after about a year. He supported his family of five doing fine hand-tailoring, at home, for Fifth Avenue clothiers. Living frugally, they managed to support the eldest child, a son, while he attended City College of New York to study accounting. My mother, the second child, initially was forced by her parents to go to work upon graduating from grammar school. From their point of view girls didn't need more edu-cation. My mother was saved by a truant officer. Since she was too young to work full-time legally, the educational authorities insisted that her par-ents send her to high school. After a term at a public high school, her par-ents insisted that she go to Hebrew Tech, an accelerated private school supported by the philanthropy of wealthy Jews, from which she could graduate in two and one half years rather than the four it would take at a public school. Upon graduation, she started working at the first of several jobs doing office work in the garment industry.

A major difference between my father and mother's families was that my father's family was secular, politically left, and avidly intellectual even though they barely managed to scrape out a living. My mother's family was religiously orthodox, and, within the family of her childhood, seemed con-cerned only with survival, family, and religion. In spite of the smallness of her parents' world my mother and her two brothers, especially her younger brother, developed broad intellectual interests and early on be-came secular Jews. So when my mother met my father—she was still in her teens—she was primed to absorb his political and social outlook even though she never quite developed the passion of his commitments.

During my growing up, I regularly heard stories about my parents, before and after their marriage, going to hear speeches by socialist mem-bers of the New York State Assembly. They attended these lectures even though neither of them were citizens at the time and thus they could not vote. Eventually, during the post–World War I Red scares, the socialists were purged from the Assembly.

My father's beliefs did not change when, during the Great Depression, after a year of unemployment, he became a shopkeeper, a partner in a gro-cery store. To become a shopkeeper was never his ambition—it was simply a way to survive. However, becoming a shopkeeper meant that he lost the venue of his political and trade union activities. Worse yet, he was afraid of alienating his far more conservative customers if he became publicly identified as a leftist—there were other grocery stores in the neighborhood.

My father was a deeply compassionate man who crafted his anger at being exploited as a worker and discriminated against as a Jew into the most exquisitely honed sense of fairness and humanitarianism that I have encountered. With his voracious appetite for news—he read three or four newspapers every day, from the *New York Times* to the *Daily Worker*— he was extremely knowledgeable about world and national affairs. Thus, even after his opportunities for political involvement were curtailed, our house was full of discussions of world events and of the triumphs (few) and defeats (many) of ordinary people in every corner of the globe as they struggled for a human life.

As a kid growing up in this atmosphere charged with social concern that made no distinctions among peoples, I identified the internationalist, humanitarian socialism of my father's vision as part of my Jewish working-class heritage. Thus, although neither of my parents had ever been members, I joined the Communist Party in 1948. I was still a high school senior—it was a few weeks after the presidential election in which Henry Wallace, for whom I had campaigned daily, had run on the Progressive Party ticket. My parents were concerned and disappointed in my decision: my father because he had long rejected the notion of democratic centralism, the ruling organizational doctrine of the Communist Party; my mother out of fears for possible future legal consequences for me. But for me, growing up in that family and looking at the world full of misery and promise, *doing* something to fulfill the dreams of progress, decency, and freedom for humankind was an existential necessity.

Following four stormy years at Brooklyn College as a party activist and a brief stint in the Army (I had been discharged early as a security risk), I decided to become an "industrial concentrator" for the Party. I worked at a series of jobs on the railroads in the New York City area. As an industrial concentrator, I was supposed to become a part of the working class, be active in the local union, and maintain a generally low but "progressive" political profile. After working a while as a freight handler, the Party and I agreed that I should seek work in the operating crafts—the elite jobs in the industry. The New York Central Railroad, Grand Central Division, became my center of work and operations.

Railroading was fun. The work was out of doors, just dangerous enough to be exciting, yet not scary enough to upset me. The men that

I worked with were varied, ranging from hopelessly depressed alcoholics to highly interesting self-educated working-class intellectuals. Since I worked as an "extra" most of the time, I had the opportunity of quickly getting to know nearly all of the switchtenders, brakemen, and conductors in the division. Given the men's diversity, the wide range in ages, the multiplicity of ethnic backgrounds, and wide variation in lifestyles, there was an unusually strong feeling of camaraderie and an amazing lack of nasty competitiveness.

The only elements in the work that seemed to lead to the sense of camaraderie I felt were the danger, and the almost constant battle to slow down the shrinkage of jobs: the railroads were being devastated by an avaricious and dishonest management, and a public policy favoring the auto and trucking industries.

The Grand Central Division may have been somewhat atypical among railroads. For example, during the Depression of the thirties the Division voluntarily went on a six-day work week to spread the available work around. When I began working there, every other railroad in the New York City area, indeed the vast majority in the country, was still working a seven-day week. The five-day week was not introduced until late 1955 or 1956.

I readily got into my work as an industrial concentrator. I had gone fishing and drinking with some of the other workmen, had become a regular at meetings of my Brotherhood of Railroad Trainmen lodge, and had been rewarded for my efforts by election to the post of chaplain—yes, chaplain!—of the lodge. The year was 1956.

Only a few months after my election my Party group received its copies of *For a Lasting Peace and a People's Democracy* (the Cominform newspaper), which, together with the *New York Times,* reprinted Nikita Khrushchev's speech to the 20th party Congress of the Communist Party of the USSR. The speech was a bombshell. It criticized "the cult of personality" which had been developed around Stalin. It even detailed some of the repressive horrors Stalin had perpetrated against dissenters within the CPUSSR. The effect on the CPUSA was swift and catastrophic. Many leaders and rank-and-file members quit the Party. Some, facing the criticisms the speech unleashed, opted for a more militant and dogmatic line and went on to form the Progressive Labor Party. Others, somehow, stayed on.

I found the speech devastating. For years I had led myself to believe that the things Khrushchev eventually detailed (only the tip of the iceberg, I'm sure) were lies concocted by the capitalist press. Any doubts I had I neatly interpreted as bourgeois weakness on my part. To discover that my "weakness" was really the exercise of rational critical judgment, that in fact I had been lying to myself and others, was crushing to me. Soon after the initial discussion of the speech by my cell of five, I decided to quit the Party. My disillusionment left me thoroughly demoralized. I became cynical about all political and ideological questions; I distrusted all movements. The thought of further discussing any part of Khrushchev's speech, or the feelings it released in me, seemed so thoroughly pointless that I wanted out as fast as possible.

Though I quit the Communist Party, I decided to remain a railroad worker. I enjoyed the work and the company of my fellow workers. Despite my being "furloughed" for about five months out of the year, my wages, supplemented by unemployment benefits, proved more than sufficient to meet my needs. That fall, however, I was laid off nearly a month earlier than usual, and was called back for only two or three weeks of the Thanksgiving–Christmas–New Year's rush period, rather than the usual six to eight weeks. I had gotten married before Thanksgiving and, given my changed circumstances, felt I had better plan some alternative to railroading, since my job might disappear altogether.

After a lot of thought and discussion with my wife, I decided to go back to college part-time to take courses in the sciences and math. I felt no conflict or guilt at giving up my earlier commitment to be a member of the working class. I had been a Sociology–Anthropology major before working on the railroad; I changed my mind. Now, the sciences seemed attractive to me. Although I had enjoyed my high school biology and chemistry, and had found my introductory biology and chemistry courses stimulating, I had majored in Sociology–Anthropology, rather than biology or chemistry. Being a science major would take too much time to allow me a full political life.

Given my cynical state of mind after quitting the Communist Party, the sciences seemed like the only direction for me. The social sciences were obviously value-loaded and ideologically challenging, while the sciences, it appeared, were relatively value free. I had my fill of ideologically loaded work and felt that I could not trust my own judgment in anything to do with ideology or politics: the mere thought of my years of self-deceit made it impossible for me to consider anything but the sciences.

I did recognize that the sciences were heavily in the service of industry. Therefore, I came to reject the notion of majoring in chemistry. I had read about the thrill of discovery in chemistry in Bernard Jaffee's book *Cru-*

cibles while in high school. But even from my relatively uninformed perspective, it was all too clear that chemists either worked in industry or trained other people to go into industry. The intent of the curricula approved by the American Chemical Society was too obvious to miss.

Biology seemed to be another case. As a field, it did not appear to have the same ties to the production of profit as chemistry. Biological research, I thought, was directed toward the improvement of the human condition through, for example, the enlargement of crop yields by plant geneticists, or the discoveries promising to improve medical care for the masses. In retrospect, I can only marvel, given my wariness of capitalist institutions derived from eight years in the Party, at the naivete that my science education, abetted by the reading of books like De Kruif's *Microbe Hunters,* had instilled in me.

In the spring of 1957 I went back to Brooklyn College to take one course in biology at night. Over the next two years I did work equal to more than half a B.S. degree, taking courses in math, physics, chemistry, and biology. For the next year and a half work on the railroad continued at a diminishing level. Finally, in the spring of 1959, I quit to become a research assistant on a cancer research project at Beth Israel Hospital in New York City. Not much later the hospital workers went on their first strike against New York's private hospitals. While I had quit the Party and had made a major change in the direction of my life, my fundamental values and commitments remained intact. Refusing to cross the picket line, I joined a small supporting picket line of professionals and was fired. Fortunately, one of the principal investigators of the grant paying my wages decided to protect me. He was on the Brooklyn College faculty, where in the forties he had been a stoolie for one of New York State's red hunts into the teaching profession. His conscience must have bothered him. Though he was angered by my action, he hired me to teach at a National Science Foundation Summer Institute for high school teachers, then got me back my job at Beth Israel that fall.

These were, for the most part, the most demanding years of my life. I worked thirty to forty hours a week on the railroad or on research; took four courses a semester whose contents took hours to master; and often needed to relearn material that I had not studied or used for seven or eight years. Meanwhile, my wife and I, trying to develop our relationship, did not see each for days on end, especially when I worked the night shift on the railroad. In spite of these demands, or possibly because of them, I thoroughly enjoyed those years. I was learning an awful lot very fast, and was getting ready for my next step—graduate school. Biochemistry, I decided, was the field I wanted to enter. It seemed to sit in a pivotal position between chemistry and biology, both of which I thoroughly enjoyed. Furthermore, biochemistry would provide an excellent foundation for movement into a wide variety of research areas.

Graduate school was not quite what I had expected. I was in the biochemistry department of a medical school with six or seven faculty members. The department was like a feudal kingdom, the chairman the feudal lord, the other faculty his vassals. The chairman's power derived from his success at grantsmanship and research. The signs of his power and success were everywhere to be seen. Forty to fifty percent of the graduate students, all of the postdoctoral fellows, and half of the research space were his; the department secretaries served his needs first, etc. Other faculty members had clear limits placed upon their ability to grow or increase their power within the department, since their space, facilities, number of graduate students, postdocs, and technicians were all limited. Research empires such as the chairman's were never to be theirs as long as they stayed on. On the other hand, as long as they produced something in research, and did some (not too much, to be sure) teaching, they could look forward to a degree of security and to protection from the chairman. The competition among them for the leavings was intense and often took the form of dumping on another faculty member's graduate students. None of these relationships were lost on the graduate students. In fact, we mimicked them by developing an obvious pecking order among ourselves. Since I worked hard, did well in my courses, had some luck in my research and quickly exploited it, and was a student of the second most powerful member of the department, I was able to complete the requirements for my Ph.D. in little over three and a half years. And so I went off to do postdoctoral research in one of the most prestigious departments of biochemistry in the world.

The department, chaired by a Nobel Laureate, was almost like a communal paradise—a marked contrast to the one I had graduated from. The faculty, postdocs, and graduate students showed mutual respect for and interest in each other's work; their willingness to cooperate was remarkable. Exceptions seemed to derive from personality traits rather than status. Even the support staff—secretaries, technicians, glassware washers—was treated with more respect than I have ever seen elsewhere. In that environment, where friendships and high-quality science flourished, I spent the happiest years of my career in science. It was not that the competitiveness and power-seeking that characterize most of capitalist science had been wholly eliminated from the department's lexicon; rather, their focus had been directed almost entirely outward. Here was a base from which the philosopher-kings could do battle with the world. The benefits of high status, memberships in study sections of the National Institutes of Health, editorial positions on leading journals, and so forth were constantly being exploited for the advantage of this elite. How could a scientist at Podunk U. ever hope to compete?

My postdoctoral fellowship came to an end in August 1966. I moved on to Tufts as an assistant professor of biology. During the almost ten years since I had quit the Communist Party I had done nothing politically. The civil rights movement, the beginnings of the New Left, and protests against the American involvement in Southeast Asia were occurring at a distance from my universe. I would read about them, feel a degree of sympathetic satisfaction, and guiltily send off a check responding to one or another appeal. But I could not allow myself to be personally engaged. The thought of becoming involved in a political organization or movement was so unsettling, I would not consider it. Instead, my energies had been devoted single-mindedly to mastering my field, and preparing myself for a career as an independent scientific researcher and teacher. It had been a lot of hard work. The rewards came from the satisfaction of participating in an exciting human endeavor, the deep pleasure in knowing I had helped to unravel some of the secrets of nature.

It was with a sense of eager anticipation that I assumed my new position. Upon arrival at Tufts I discovered that the lab I had been promised had not yet been built. Thus my first six months left me with more spare time than I had anticipated. By then a growing Students for a Democratic Society, the beginnings of a significant draft resistance, and a more vocal antiwar movement had begun to make greater demands on my conscience.

In the spring of 1967 the Fifth Avenue Parade Committee announced a major antiwar demonstration for New York City. When no publicity for it appeared on the Tufts campus, I felt compelled to do something. A young postdoc and I, fearing both financial and political disaster, decided to put up money for chartering a bus from Tufts to New York City. The response to our advertisement in the school paper proved great enough to allow us to charter a second bus. I was excited by the sheer size of the demonstration. However, I was moved at some deeper level by the sight of a group of young men sitting on the Sheep Meadow in Central Park tearing up or burning their draft cards. So, soon after, I signed the "Call to Resist Illegitimate Authority," pledging to support draft resistance and other forms of civil disobedience to the war. However, I could not bring myself to become involved with any organizations.

The completion of my lab in the spring of 1967 found me hard at work doing research and teaching. I felt challenged and excited by both. Preparing a biochemistry lecture course for the fall took much of my time. In the lab I often worked till midnight, enjoying the opportunity to do research on my own, sparing no effort to achieve some success.

There was to be a march on the Pentagon in the fall of 1967. When I heard that it was to be preceded, a day earlier, by a draft card turn-in at the Department of Justice, I felt a strong urge to attend. The Friday of the turn-in was one of the most unnerving days I have ever spent. From the time I boarded my plane in Boston, until I went to bed late that night, I spoke, with one brief exception, to no one.

A kind of controlled bedlam raged at the church where people gathered prior to the march. Functionaries, often near hysteria, their voices much too loud and nearly incomprehensible, tried to explain what was to happen and what we were to do. Outside, on the front lawn of the church, sat a group of draft resisters, sharing some bread, cheese, and milk. They talked with quiet animation, exuding a warmth toward each other that was truly moving. What a contrast to the mad scene inside the church! Throughout these preliminaries and the events that followed, I allowed myself to speak to no one, for to break my isolation would be to make some commitment to joining the movement, rather than just being there and observing.

That night I walked the streets of Washington feeling as alone and disconnected as a character in a Daliesque nightmare. I knew I would finally have to overcome the fears of ideological and political commitment I had carried since leaving the Communist Party in 1956. The next week I contacted an acquaintance working with Resist, a support organization for draft resisters. I returned to organizational political activity by raising money for Resist in the Boston area. Later I became active in the New University Conference (NUC), an association for radical academics. After NUC fell apart, I joined the editorial board of *Radical Teacher*, a socialist and feminist journal on the theory and practice of teaching. I also took part in the variety of meetings and demonstrations in the Greater Boston area around issues ranging from U.S. and Massachusetts domestic policy and U.S. policy in Latin America and South Africa.

The Israeli invasion of Lebanon in 1982, and the enormous toll in human suffering it caused, irresistibly drew me into Middle East work. I became a founding member of the Ad Hoc Lebanon Emergency Committee, an organization of Jews, Christians, and Arab-Americans that sought to carry on educational work in the Boston area on the background to the conflict and the U.S. aid to Israel that allowed it to carry out its campaign of destruction in Lebanon. We hoped through our work to bring to Americans information and history about the region and the conflict. Our aim was to change U.S. policy in the Middle East and specifically toward the Israeli–Palestinian conflict so as to assure peace in that region and in the world.

We became part of a coalition, the Campaign for Peace with Justice in the Middle East, that included the local American Friends Service Committee and the Boston Mobilization for Survival. Our coalition carried on educational programs of various sorts in the Boston area for several years. Once the drama of the war on Lebanon faded from the news, except for a regular audience of sympathetic and interested people, our efforts only succeeded in uncovering a deep vein of anti-Arab racism in ordinary citizens in the Cambridge and wider Boston area.

Thus, in the spring of 1989, a group of us felt that if we were ever to be able to influence U.S. foreign policy to be more even-handed and to recognize Palestinian human and national rights, we would have to help Americans overcome the anti-Arab racism we so regularly had to confront. To do so, we decided to organize what we came to call the Cambridge–Ramallah/El Bireh Sister City Campaign. Through the campaign to establish official sister city relationships between Cambridge and the neighboring West Bank cities of Ramallah and El Bireh, we hoped to develop an appreciation among Cambridge residents for the humanity of the Palestinians by providing access to information about Palestinian history, culture and views to the Cambridge community. An important part of our program was to make direct connections between Palestinians and Cambridge residents. To this end, among other activities, we sent two local groups (December 1989 and July 1990) to Ramallah/El Bireh to live with Palestinian families and to meet representatives of Palestinian community institutions.

I became a member of the second delegation and approached our trip with feelings of despair and frustration after eight years of political work on Middle East issues. If I was to find the political situation there as hopeless as I felt it was, I was ready to give up my commitment to Middle East work. Alternatively, I hoped that seeing the *intifada* up close, I might be able to stop seeing the Palestinians simply as victims and to gain energy and hope to continue my work from them.

I came away from the trip having realized neither of these alternatives. Profoundly moved by the stories I heard and for the first time seeing the Palestinians and Israelis I met as individuals, not political categories, I was impelled to write *Consider and Hear Me: Voices from Palestine and Israel.*

My mother, who had been widowed for fourteen years, was deeply pained by my writing the book. "Jews don't do things like that," she said after reading a chapter on life in Jalazon Refugee Camp that I observed while living with a Palestinian family in the camp. Had my father still been alive, I feel sure that he would have helped her resist her drift into becoming strongly pro-Zionist. In fact, I have come to feel that because of the circumstances of my life I was living out some of my father's dreams. Somehow his approval, even if only through my imagination and desire, is important to me, especially given my mother's anguish at my doing what I was raised to do. Thus, my initial reaction to my mother's response to my book was anger.

Even on her death bed in August 1991, my mother showed her upset with me when she expressed concern that any money that I might inherit from her would go to the Palestinians. Her last words though—truer to her lifelong beliefs—were "Gorbachev! The world's crazy—what do they think—that life will be better under capitalism? It's all crazy."

I have always found it easier to acknowledge those parts of me which I have derived—inherited—from my father, my patrimony, than those parts of me derived from my mother. I find it disturbing that there is in our language no word equivalent to 'patrimony' for that which we derive—inherit—from our mothers. Since her death, I have been trying to resolve the conflict between my anger and my feelings of loss. Thus, I have embarked on the project of writing down, in somewhat fictional form, the stories on which I grew up, and from which I learned who my parents were, my mother as well as father. These stories have helped to make me who I am. This story, "Take a Chance," is one such and is one of my early attempts to acknowledge that which I have inherited from my mother.

Take a Chance

"I'm beginning to wonder if I was that good for Dad. I don't know, I just don't know," Mom says as I rummage through the disorderly drawers of her still shiny mahogany dresser, part of the bedroom set she and Dad bought when I was about eight years old. I remember that as a child, when we lived in Brooklyn, the bottom two drawers held my socks, underwear, and shirts, all neatly folded as Mom had shown me. Mom, who still tries to keep her apartment neat and picked up, has stopped worrying about what cannot be seen, and although her clothes are sorted out, they no longer are folded and stacked neatly in the drawers.

"Do you want to take all of this underwear?" I ask, "Or do you want to go through them before I pack them?"

Impatient, Mom waves her right hand and says, "Oh, pack them all—just leave me enough until Pearl comes next week to take me."

It's New Years Day, 1991, and I'm in Mom's bedroom packing the clothes and other intimate belongings that she'll take with her in her move from Miami Beach to California to live with my sister, Pearl. The corner room, not large to begin with, is crowded with furniture: the mahogany dresser, a matching mahogany chest of drawers, a sewing machine, and a large upholstered armchair piled high with extra pillows and blankets. The double bed on which Mom sits is flanked by two night tables from the same mahogany set as the chest and dresser. Incongruously, the bed has an antiqued green headboard with a built-in bookshelf. What happened to the original mahogany headboard, I don't know. Above the headboard is a small shuttered opening that allows the circulation of air between the bedroom and living room. With the cartons and the suitcase into which I pack Mom's belongings scattered about on the floor, the bedroom is even more crowded than usual.

For the last several years Mom's world has been getting smaller and smaller as her friends die or become incapable of caring for themselves. And so, too, she has been shrinking—never much taller than five feet, she is now inches shorter. She's lost a lot of weight over the years—when I was a kid she weighed over two hundred pounds—and as if her skin remembers those days it now hangs on her as if it were two sizes too large. Mom's face doesn't show her eighty-eight years, though: the hair has lots of black among the silver and her eyes are still alert and clear. But her hands and knees, knobby and painful from arthritis, have failed her. It is harder and harder for her to care for herself: she depends on neighbors to shop for her, pays one to do her laundry and to cook for her occasionally when her arthritic pain is especially intense. But the help is hit or miss, and Mom stubbornly refuses to seek help from the Dade County agencies that provide support and services to the elderly. I can tell looking at her sitting on the bed in her faded cotton print house dress that it hasn't been washed in a while; the front of the dress is full of stains from the soups, tea, or coffee that she spills on herself every time she eats. Her hands shake so much that some of every meal ends up on her bosom or her lap.

My sister, Pearl, and I, unable to help from our distant homes in Orange County and Cambridge, pressured Mom to move, reluctantly, to California and live with Pearl and her husband, Pete, until a home for the elderly can be found for her to move into.

"Why do you question whether you were good for Dad?" I ask, as I carefully fold her slips, bloomers, and brassieres. "You've always told me how lucky people thought you and Dad were to have one another."

"That's true. I never had too much, but I had a lot when you come to think of it. Recently, cousin Hilda called and the first thing she says to me is, 'You know, your marriage was the best marriage I ever saw.' And people always used to feel that way about us. But now, I just don't know."

"But why, Mom?"

"Dad was afraid to cross me too much. He was always afraid to cross me, and that was bad for him."

You can say that again, I think. As long as I lived with you and Dad I never remember the two of you arguing.

"I don't know why, but maybe it's me, maybe it's my makeup. Actually whenever he stood his ground, I always gave in . . . I gave in to everything he wanted, actually. But he was always afraid to cross me. Don't forget when I met him he didn't know a word of English and he had very little to offer me but himself—which to me was the great thing. He never had confidence in himself. So I say, I don't know how good I was for him, because he needed more than he actually got from me. That's my opinion now when I look back."

Done packing Mom's intimate wear, I look over to the chest of drawers and the window blinds that keep rattling in the slight draft coming through the narrowly opened window. "Mom, what about the chest of drawers? Is there anything in it I should pack?" I ask.

"Nah," she says, shaking her head, "there's only linens that I'm leaving . . . the pictures we'll go through tomorrow. You can take what you want. The rest you'll put in another box I'll take with me," she says before going on as if I had not broken in on her narrative:

"But what could I expect of myself? You know what my life was like. Max, George, Mama and Papa, and me, we were all together. The damndest part is, as a girl I didn't count in the family. The boys slept in the dining room but there was no bed for them so we had to pull in a bed every night. Do you know, if I would be sitting out on the stoop, they would come out, 'Fannie, make the bed.' *They* didn't pull the bed, *I* had to pull the bed. It made me so angry inside, but I never said anything because this was the accepted thing to do. I had to do it, because Mama expected and made me do it. She didn't say to the boys, 'What is wrong with you doing it? It is your bed.' No, *I* had to do it. So, really I grew up with no confidence in myself at all. It's only that I was a bright student in class, so I was liked by the teachers. And then I met Dad very early and he really saved me."

"Mom," I interrupt, as I walk over to her large double-closet, once shared with my father, but which for the last fourteen years has known only her clothes—more and more of the clothes that she has sewn for herself to help to fill the time. "You'll have to get off the bed and sit in the chair so I can use your bed to fold your dresses. We'll have to sort through them and decide which you'll take—Pearl doesn't have enough closet space for *all* of them. I'll put the blankets in the living room."

"Yeah," she says. She gets off the bed and, forgoing her walker, hobbles unsteadily to the bedroom chair while I carry the pillows and blankets into the living room. When I return, she goes on: "So that was my youth. I was attractive, but I never knew how attractive or what I was, but people were attracted to me. I was liked—but I didn't like myself. I was made not to like myself. I was a nothing. How can you like a nothing? It isn't that my mother would have pride in me or that when I was skipped in school—it didn't mean anything to them. The boys yes, they also skipped. The boys were everything, especially Max. Not George, but Max. Max was perfection, her first creation, never to be equaled."

As we talk, I continue taking dresses, each carefully crafted from remnants of heavy-weight polyester bought in a nearby fabric store on Sixth Street. They come in a wild variety of colors: blue, pink, white, rose, lilac, yellow, pale green, mostly solids, a few in checkered patterns or polka dots.

Mom, sitting in the chair, signals me with the wave of a finger to consign each dress to the box to be given to neighbors or to Goodwill, or to the bed to be packed for shipment to California. Several that she wants to keep are so badly stained from food and coffee that I put them aside to take to the laundromat before I pack them. I notice the piles on the bed growing faster than the pile in the box, and I plead, "Mom, I know it's hard to part with so much, but Pearl really doesn't have much closet space since she and Pete moved to Leisure World. When they lived in Hacienda Heights, they had plenty of room but not anymore. So, please, try not to take so much."

"Yeah," she answers, shaking her head, "What do I need so much? When will I wear them all, anyway? Put the pink with white polka dots in the box.

"Y'know, Saul, even while I was a schoolgirl I was grown up already. I had to be because I had so much responsibility. My brothers never went to the buttonhole maker to deliver a coat; I was the one. I had to run all the errands for my father—I had to do all those things."

"Who made you? Your mother or your father?" I ask.

"My mother made me. My father didn't. He worked—I don't know how many hours—say twenty hours a day, so what could he do about it?

"At that time we still had gaslight. He did very fine hand tailoring. He worked for the so-called Fifth Avenue tailors and his stitching was so exact that he had to work like a horse just to make a bare living. He used to put a chair on the kitchen table so that he could be nearer the gaslight to see his work. That's how Papa worked, so what could he do? All that work for the miserable living he made.

"Mama worked hard too. She helped him with the linings of the garment. I don't blame Mama when I come to think of it. The way her life was, she didn't know any different. That's what it was, Saul. Of course, I was resentful for quite a few years, because I had it harder than the boys. I was never really given a chance."

While Mom is talking, my gaze falls on the window to the living room over Mom's bed and it brings back memories of my visits years earlier with Evie and our kids. Laura and Robbie would sleep around the corner at either Aunt Celia's or Cousin Idie's house and Evie and I would sleep in my parents' bed while they slept on the sofa bed in the living room. I have a picture in my mind of me making love with Evie under that window while my parents presumably were asleep in the sofa bed on the other side. Quiet as Evie and I were, a part of me secretly hoped that Mom and Dad would hear us.

"It's only that I was a bright student in class and was liked by the teachers . . . and then I met Dad very early and he really saved me. I was about sixteen. My brother George—he was still a kid—met him first. But I used to see Dad sitting in the alley reading the paper. He had come as an immigrant and didn't know a word of English. But he wanted to learn English. So he would come home and get washed—he did hard, dirty work. But you know Dad was so clean—and I would see a young man sitting there with a white shirt and clean. And you know, Dad attracted me.

"Well, once we met, Dad worshipped me; what can I say? In fact, we used to talk, talk, talk, first in Yiddish and then in English—he wanted so much to learn the language. We'd walk for blocks and blocks and talk, and I had so much to learn from him because he was bright and nice, and of course I fell in love with him.

"The whole family opposed my going with him. God, even Aunt Ida—she was still Max's girlfriend at the time—said, 'I'll kill you if you marry that Dave.' He offered me nothing. He had absolutely nothing, except himself. I appreciated him because he did something for me that money couldn't do. He gave me confidence in myself for the first time in my life."

Finished sorting and packing her dresses, I ask, "Mom, would you like some tea or coffee?"

"Yeah, I'd love a cup of coffee, but make it decaf."

"Okay, then why don't we go into the dining room—I'll do more packing tomorrow."

I go into the small galley-styled kitchen to heat some water for her coffee and my tea. Mom, leaning on her walker, charges into the dining room behind me. In spite of her arthritis and instability on her feet, she seems incapable of walking deliberately and I worry about her tripping on the throw rug in the hall between the bedroom and the dining room. The way she uses her walker reminds me of how I drive—with a heavy foot on the gas.

When we settle down at the dining table with our hot drinks, Mom goes on with her story as if uninterrupted.

"Mama and Papa threatened to bring men around. They wanted me married off immediately, because I was already going with Dad and nobody wanted him in the family. They knew I'd have a life of struggle and they didn't want it." Mom chuckles before continuing, "But I said, 'If you bring a man to me, you know what I'll do? I'm going to put on a pair of skates and I'm going to go skating. I'll even skate in the house if I have to. Don't you ever bring me any men in the house.' Because I was in love with Dad. I remember that like today. So, of course they knew that they couldn't win with me. One thing I learned finally was to be a rebel. When I was going with Dad, I used to speak up. I think after that I even stopped pulling in the bed. The boys started pulling in the bed.

"Well, anyway, after I met Dad a lot of the anger and resentment I felt toward my family was forgotten—because he gave me so *much*. He gave me the confidence I needed, and the family ended up really loving him. I think Mama liked him better than she did me. Later, Ida was crazy about him. Everybody liked Dad. Dad had something in him always that drew people to him.

"I remember as a young man he had a beautiful voice. He laid with me on the sofa we used to have—that was our living room furniture, a leather couch—and sang, and I'd join him in the singing. That I remember. Mama hugging me, *never*. I don't remember her ever showing me that kind of affection. That's why I say I was lucky that I met Dad."

It's funny, I think, I have no memory of ever seeing Mom and Dad hug or kiss each other. Walk hand-in-hand, yes; hug and kiss, no. I do remember though when I was maybe eleven poking through their night table and finding a box of condoms, and by then I knew what they were for. So why only hand-holding in public, I wonder.

"I don't know if you knew him as much as Pearl. She was close to him, you weren't. Were you that close to him? I don't remember, Saul."

"I got a lot from him," I say quietly. "I learned to care about the world—he taught me to care. Yes, I got a lot from him."

Yes, I think, I learned a lot from him, good and bad. Almost all of the values that I have, and which I cherish, came from him. He cared passionately about social justice, read four newspapers a day to learn all that he could about what was happening in the world, would analyze and argue with family and friends about all of the big issues of the day. But, oh my, how right Mom is that he never stood up to her.

I remember Dad only disagreeing with Mom once—and that was about me. He actually stuck up for me. The family was sitting around the kitchen table eating dinner. As usual my plate was piled high with meat, mashed potatoes, overcooked carrots and peas, and a big chunk of pumpernickel coated with a thick layer of butter. And I, as usual, tried to resist, somewhat, my mother's urgings, "Eat, Saul, eat darling, the *flanken* is good, eat." I sat silently, picked up the bread, which I liked, and began to eat. That finished, I slowly ate the mashed potatoes which were lumpy as usual. Mom, unhappy that I hadn't even begun the meat, repeated, "Eat, Saul, eat. The *flanken* is good."

"But Mom, I don't like *flanken,* I don't like meat," I whined.

"Eat," Mom insisted.

"He doesn't have to eat," my father said sharply. "Just *look* at him," he went on pointing at me in my size ten chubby clothes, "he doesn't have to eat."

That was it—the only time I ever heard my father disagree with my mother, during the twenty years I lived with them.

I hear Mom saying, "You did get a lot from him, because he was that type of person—he gave a lot. The only thing is that life was a hard struggle, I don't have to tell you what a struggle I had all the time, and a lot is because I didn't know anything. I was no manager of anything, and money—we're all the same. There was never any saving. I was always a giver, so things used to go through my hands.

"When I married him and we moved in with his family—they were running a laundry in Patchogue at that time—I knew nothing, Saul: I didn't know how to cook; I didn't know how to run a house; I didn't know a thing but I'm married and I'm supposed to be cooking for the whole family. Leon lived with us, Bernard, Dad, I and Grampa, five people, and I know nothing. So, of course, Grandpa had a lot to say about my inability to do things.

"Every Sunday when Dad's whole family would get together, Dad with them, I knew that they all talked about me. They were whispering about me and Dad was there and I really resented it, but I didn't say anything. In fact, Dad's brother Louie once went to Mama and complained about me, telling her everything Grandpa had told him about me 'Fannie can't cook, she doesn't even clean well, she knows nothing about keeping house.' I don't know what I was. So, Mama wrote me a letter (George wrote the letter at Mama's instigation) 'Move out of that house. If you haven't got for rent, we'll pay the rent, but don't stay with them.' They didn't want me to stay with Dad in that house. Not to leave Dad, but not to live with his family.

"Can you picture any girl, today, doing what I did? Getting married and moving with her husband's father and two brothers and having to cook and clean for them—and then to be whispered about? I can't. I just can't picture anything like it. What made me do it? You know, very often I ask myself, 'What is it in my character? Was it such an inferiority complex? What was it?' "

I think: Yeah, tell me about it—why do we *all* have inferiority complexes? Even me with my professional success. I live in constant fear of being discovered a fraud, that all I teach is bullshit, that the work that I've done is all wrong.

Mom continues, "When we left Patchogue we were broke. We came back to Mama. We had no money. We had nothing. I got a job immediately and Dad worked. There, too, I was stupid. I'm not the kind who can owe money and we owed Mama all the money that she lent us to go into the laundry business. On top of that one of Dad's brothers, Leon, once went to Mama against my wishes and borrowed money to buy another laundry. 'The machinery in the new laundry will be better,' Leon said. He did this even though I told him, 'Leon, you are going to New York, don't you dare go to my mother for money because I owe enough already.' But he did anyway, and Mama gave him the money and I ended up owing it. They never paid. Dad and I paid the money. So I paid and paid and paid, so I couldn't afford an apartment of our own.

"Others would say, 'The heck with it, I need an apartment' and go and live somewhere else. But not Fannie. I lived in that miserable place with Dad. 106th Street. I can't describe it. It was horrible. The windows were in an airshaft and we lived on the ground floor. All the dirt got in down there. There was no air, there was no nothing. Papa's shop was right near our room.

"Then I became pregnant. Pearl was born while we were living in that house on 106th Street. But of course it was impossible to live there. So Mama's sister, Aunt Celia, who didn't want to live in Harlem anymore said, 'You know what, we will get a big apartment in the Bronx and you will come and live with me.'

"We got a beautiful apartment and of course my standard of living went up immediately, but to say it was my home, it wasn't—it was always Aunt Celia's. Everything had to be the way she wanted it. It's not the same thing as when you are alone, so I think I lived that way about two years.

"It's a miracle that Dad and I stayed together, to tell you the truth. I think the only reason we did is that I had such an inferiority complex that I was always afraid to make a move of any kind, and Dad did too. I mean, I am not blaming . . . this is where I *do* blame Dad. He wouldn't put his foot down and say, 'Why are you so involved with your family? Why can't we have our own life?' He should have spoken up, but he never did. With another woman, Dad might have had a much better life than he had with me—being the person that he was."

"But he had responsibility for your relationship too. The two of you collaborated in making your relationship what it was," I say.

"How was I to you, as a mother? Were you afraid of me? Honestly."

"Afraid isn't the right word; I always felt judged."

"You always felt judged? Maybe. I am saying, I don't know," Mom replied, a puzzled expression on her face.

"I always felt that I never would be good enough," I say softly.

"Maybe, I don't know. I don't know what's in me that did it. I don't know."

"Well, your mother was so judgmental of you that you learned how to judge from the time you were born."

"That's true. We meant nothing. Only Max mattered. Once she kept telling me, 'I must see Max. I must see Max.' You know, Max was busy. I didn't bother him until finally she got on my nerves so, I called up Max and I said, 'Look, Max, Mama is bothering me. She must see you. I think it is about time you came to see her.' So, he did come, and what does she want him for?

"You know, she used to have a *pushke,* a can, she saved money in to contribute to charity. To contribute to charity is a righteous act. Of course, you buy your way into heaven with this kind of act. But she was worried about dying and wanted to leave her good deeds to Max. I didn't deserve it. I had all the work and all the trouble and everything else, but the good deeds went to Max. Well, Dad and I only smiled, and what could we do or say? There was nothing to say, because this was my life with her. I am sure she liked me, but I never felt the love. Dad gave love to me.

"In our younger days, my friends used to see how he looked at me and say, 'My God, that man must be crazy about you.' And he was—he really was. There was real love there between us. There is no question about it. I loved him, and there was no question that he loved me, but whether I was good for him or not is a different question. That's already a different question.

"He never disagreed with me. At the time when his sister, Esther, and Harry—they weren't married yet—wrote from Arizona that he'll buy an orange grove—if Dad will come, he'll give him full partnership. Without a penny—he knew we had no money. If Dad will only come, he'll buy it so then he'll settle there. I was so attached to my family. How do you leave the family? Which was stupid, utterly stupid, because the way Dad worked at that time—I never even went to the shop, I never even realized how he worked. Because if I had gone to the shop and seen, I might have changed my mind. But I never saw the way he worked. So, of course, how do I leave my mother and father? So Dad didn't accept the proposition.

"He never stood up for things. There once was a time he worked in the Schiffli embroidery. He was very well liked because he was a *mensch*, always. So the boss once told a mutual friend after the factory had moved to New Jersey he wanted to see Dad. Not for Dad to work for him, but he wanted to give him a proposition of some kind which would probably have been very good for us. How do you move to New Jersey? So he didn't go there. Do you know what I mean? He never stood up and that is what I resent *now*, because I feel guilty. About everything.

"He should have stood up that time with the orange grove and Jersey. He should have stood up. That was his job to stand up—but he was afraid."

"What about you, Mom, what were you so afraid of?" I ask.

"I was always afraid. All of my life it was pay, pay, pay. I didn't want you to have what I had in my life. Pay, pay, pay. That is all I had for years, because it took me years to pay back Mama, and I paid back every cent that she ever gave me. I never got anything for nothing. I didn't want it. I don't say it is her fault. I didn't want it.

"So, when Pearl wanted to marry Abe, I couldn't even tell her how I felt. When she asked me once, 'Why do you object to Abe?' I couldn't tell her the type of life she was going to lead. Which was so. That it was going to be as bad as mine and I didn't want that type of life for her. I couldn't tell her because I didn't want to cut Dad down. Wouldn't say a word to her. Until this day I never told her anything. I'm telling you, but I never told her."

"It sounds like you were ambivalent about the life you had with Dad even then . . ."

"There were times . . ."

"And that whatever you found in him, whatever he gave you, it wasn't enough," I go on.

"After a while . . . years later. You know you live that way. You're not happy with the decisions you've made in life. Don't forget until we bought the grocery store, I didn't know what it was to have peace of mind, to have a steady paycheck—and it works on you. I'm not a superhuman being, but yet I would never let Dad feel that, you know, that he's the one at fault.

"I think of it very often because at the end when he accused me of being in love and having an affair with his brother Morris I began to wonder, what is it? I gave my whole life to him, and this is what I get at the end.

I never loved Morris, and I was faithful to Dad all my life. Wouldn't *you* wonder if I was the right person for Dad? Wouldn't *you* think about it?"

"Sure I would," I reply, "but you must have some idea of why he accused you."

"I've thought about it for years but I don't know. Toward the end, the weaker he got the more jealous he got of me. If I spoke to a man on the bus when I was taking Dad to the doctor's office, Dad would get angry—he'd say I was flirting. You know me. Can I sit there and not answer someone on the bus if he talks to me? So I'd talk, and Dad would get furious.

"You know, we had never argued—but that last year before he died was hell. Anything I would say he would snap at me. I couldn't talk about anything, the urban renewal, the economy, the elections, the Russians, almost anything—he'd find something to snap at me about. It was hell.

"After all that I'd done for him, working side by side with him all those years after his heart attack, taking care of him. Something must have happened to his mind. How else could you explain it? To accuse me of being in love with Morris—of having an affair with him. And I never even *liked* Morris that much. Have sex with him—it was a joke."

"It sounds a little wacky to me, but why do you think he believed that about you and Morris?" I ask again.

Mom sits there a moment rocking slightly from side to side before she replies, "Well, he thought that once we stopped having sex after his heart attack that I must have been looking elsewhere."

Stunned, I finally say, "Mom, he lived for thirty years after his heart attack—he was still in his forties, so were you—why did you stop having sex with him?"

"When Dr. Baskin sent him home to bed for six weeks he said 'No sex' so we didn't have sex."

"But Mom, Dr. Baskin probably meant just while Dad was put to bed to recover."

"Sex—I've never cared for sex anyway. Who cared? I wanted to make sure Dad would be well. You know how I took care of him all those years. You know that when we had the children's clothing store, I wouldn't let him lift too much and how I made sure he took a nap in the back-room every day. If it wasn't for me he probably would have died years earlier."

Shocked by a secret I never wanted to know, I can't imagine what it was like for my father, who when he had his heart attack was younger than I am now. God, I think, that poor man—how could he live that way? I want to help Mom understand why he might have finally expressed anger that he had kept a tight lid on for years, but all I can say is, "But he was still a young man, you were both so young."

Mom, stunned by having shared her secret with me, sits there, her gaze averted from me. From the strange distant look on her face, I know she no longer wants to talk. We sit there silently in the gathering gloom, each deep in our own thoughts. Minutes pass and finally Mom breaks the silence, "What's the time?"

"About five to five. Do you want to get ready for dinner?" I ask.

"Yeah, I ought to cook some rice with mushrooms I have, and I have some veal, cooked veal. I don't know if you would like it or wouldn't like it, but take a chance."

Florence Howe

I was an unplanned baby born on March 17, 1929, nine months and one week after my penniless parents were married in Brooklyn, New York. My father had left school at age eight to work full-time in a hardware store to help support his Polish immigrant mother and two younger sisters. At the time of my birth, he was trying to eke a living from a pushcart of dry goods, but soon a fire ended that dream and he began to drive a taxi, which he did for the rest of his life. My mother's father had come from Palestine (via Scotland) and her mother from Jewish Russia. My orthodox Jewish grandfather was literate in four or five languages and made no effort to teach my illiterate

grandmother any of them. He refused to allow my talented mother to consider college, instead forcing her into a commercial high school course. She wanted to be a teacher. He wanted her to marry a rabbi of his choice. After working for five years as a bookkeeper, she married an uneducated man of her own choice and stayed in the marriage because of me, and then my brother. I owe especially to her some of the skills and attitudes that have helped me survive, even to flourish. She convinced me early that I was smart, and she taught me to value my mind, for I was to be the teacher that she could not be. Because of her, I learned the value of meaningful work, and the joy of achievement. I have always known that, set beside my mother's life, mine was immensely rewarding. I have not ever understood—perhaps I still do not completely understand—how much, still, I am my mother's daughter. Or perhaps I don't know how to be my mother's daughter.

Florence Howe is a professor of English at City College and the Graduate School, City University of New York, and Director of The Feminist Press at The City University of New York. She was one of the founders of The Feminist Press in 1970, and is the only person to have worked on its staff continuously since then. She was president of the Modern Language Association in 1973. An A.B.D. at the University of Wisconsin, she holds four honorary doctorates. Her most recent books are *Tradition and the Talents of Women* and *No More Masks! An Anthology of American Women Poets*. She is at work on a memoir and, with Mariam Chamberlain, on a history of women's studies worldwide.

Florence Howe

Am I Her Daughter?
Am I at Home?

One: The Bronx Jewish Home and Hospital, 1993

It's Sunday and I'm on the train to the Bronx, with a piece of the *New York Times* in my lap. But I can't read. I am trying not to stare at three people across the way, all dressed up in what I think of as "visiting best," though I assume that they've probably also been to church. What catches me is the banter between the two young daughters and then their mother's eye as she asks them to be "ladies" and "sit still." The mother wears a hat and carries gloves. The girls wear hose and shiny new shoes and pretty frocks, and they giggle as they try out the empty seats in the train.

It is the second summer of my mother's stay at Jewish Home and Hospital in the Bronx, but I don't think about that destination. I think instead of all the Sundays half a century ago that my mother and brother and I took the train from Brooklyn to the Bronx to visit my paternal grandmother and my aunt Rose. They lived together along with Uncle Sam and eventually Shelly, their son. But for many years I was Aunt Rose's pet, and I looked forward to those visits. Like the family I can see before me, my father was absent: if you drove a cab in the 1930s and 1940s, you took Monday off, not Sunday. My mother's day off was Sunday, since she worked in an airplane factory all week, and did housework and shopping on Saturday.

I don't think about the clothes, though I am sure we were not dressed like the trio across the way. But I remember my mother's eye as she urged my brother to sit still. I could read for the hour or more it took to get there, but he was restless, like the two girls changing seats in the empty train before me. And I wondered whether they, too, were going to visit their grandmother and doting Aunt.

On the short walk up the hill to the hospital, I stop in several shops and buy the grapes, watermelon, and plums my mother likes, and wonder whether I'll be able to find flowers today for her. It's not a neighborhood of florists. And I try to wait patiently as the coffee shop fixes the usual lean brisket sandwich, "on rye, with lettuce and mustard, no gravy." Sometimes I buy french fries. And always the coffee, this time iced, for me.

At the hospital, I sign in and say hello to the guard who nods a greeting and I walk to the Zweig elevators and take one to the third floor.

She is sitting in one of the blue chairs opposite the elevator. The other chairs are empty. "Hello, Mother," I say, and she offers a smile of recognition, the eyes crinkling. "Were you waiting for me?" She doesn't answer. She is struggling to rise from the chair and that takes concentration. She wants to help me with the packages and she wants to take my hand. We walk to her room, the second on the left. "Were you waiting for me? Did you know it was Sunday, that I was coming today?" I want an answer, but she can't give it, or she doesn't. The nurse tells me later that she sits opposite the elevator most days in the afternoon. I take it that she is waiting for me, though I come to visit only once a week, generally on Sunday, since that's the day there is often a concert, and she is able to enjoy music when there is a performer.

In her room, we begin to undo the packages. She wants the sandwich, I know, and I do that first, urging her to "Sit down and get comfortable." I have to say that several times, and eventually, she sits down, holding the sandwich I've safely placed into a paper towel. She focuses on eating. I bustle about the room, dropping the other packages around the sink, saying, "I'll fix the flowers and the fruit later. First, we'll have a little visit. O.K.?" I sit opposite in another chair, and we share the hospital tray at table level. I nibble at the other half of the sandwich, expecting that she will want at least some of it. But she also wants to see me eating. I put my straw into the iced coffee and take a sip. Her eyes tell me she sees all that I do and that it is as it should be.

But I am desperate for speech. "Is it good, Mother? Is the sandwich delicious?" I say the words slowly, pronouncing each one carefully. But I must say it all again before she says "Yes." She then offers a few other words, but I don't understand them, though I think I've heard the name "Sara" in the midst of her sentence, and I repeat the name. "Sara?" There's a question in my voice. "Your mother, Sara?" More words from her now, again not clear to me. But I am willing to guess: "She didn't have enough to eat? Is that what you are saying? She was hungry?" "Yes," she says. And I must be content with that.

She continues eating and I fix the flowers, emptying the old ones into the wastebasket, breaking the stems of the new ones, washing the vase, and arranging red, pink, and white carnations in the middle of green fern. I move the filled vase to the nightstand beside her bed. "Do you like these flowers, Mother?" She tries to turn her head, perhaps only to see where my voice is coming from, but the medicine she has been taking for years has done some damage to her neck muscles, and so I pick up the flowers again and take them closer to her so that she can see them. "Pretty," she says, glancing up for a second, and returns to her eating, this time it's the watermelon. She is carefully removing the pits, then eating the chunks with her fingers.

I begin to wash the grapes and plums, arranging them in the plastic boxes and dishes I have left fruit in the week before. I am busy at the sink, but I carry a handful of grapes over to her, and she begins to eat them. She has closed up the watermelon for the moment.

Before I sit down again, I go through her chest of drawers, seeing whether the socks are holding up, locking them together in pairs, and pulling the folded dresses out of the drawers to put them on hangers in the closet. She looks at the dresses as though they were new to her, and when I say, "Isn't that a pretty one?" she says, "No."

On her birthday in March this year, I gave away all her former clothes—blouses, trousers, skirts—which she had refused to wear almost from the moment she entered the nursing home in Florida. But I brought them to New York anyway, and hung some of them in this closet, some in my own apartment closet. The only clothing she will accept now are dresses not unlike the button-down-the-front "house dresses" she wore when we were children, only now they are made with snaps and called "breakfast coats." They are, of course, easier for the nurses to dress her in, and I've stopped mourning about her clothes, brought up from Florida so that she would have familiar things around her.

I sit down and say, "Shall we go for a walk in the garden? Would you like to hear music?" She looks interested, but goes on eating. I stand up, move the tray/table, and put a few pieces of fruit into a plastic bag. "Why don't you stand up, Mother, and we'll take a walk?" She grips the two sides of the chair—she really doesn't need my help to rise. I offer her one of the new sweaters from the closet, bought to match the dresses, but now quite shrunken by many hospital launderings. She accepts the sweater, but insists on buttoning it, though it is too small for that, and I am impatient to get going. "No," I say, "It's just for your shoulders, in case you feel chilly." But the buttoning continues, and I wait.

We walk to the elevator, holding hands, and I press the down button. She presses the up and grins. We enter and I press "B" for basement, and say it all aloud. We watch the numbers and I read them out loud and she echoes me: "Three, two, one, and B for basement." We walk down the hall towards the doors that lead to the gardens, opened by pressing a huge, square "button" that reads "press here to enter." She likes that, and presses it. We walk through the small garden once around, and I remind her of how, last summer, we sat here and ate our sandwich and fed the birds. We don't stop, but walk back to the hall and press the other button to walk the larger garden, a walk that concludes in an ice cream for her. This time she wants a piece of Danish too. I buy them both, and we take them out to a table on the pretty patio. She breaks off a piece of the Danish for me, and I say, "Thank you," and eat it. She then begins to scoop ice cream onto her napkin, carefully. I realize that she is giving me some of her ice cream. She finishes dividing the ice cream, and I say, "Thank you, but it's all for you. I don't eat ice cream." She accepts that and eats the portion she has placed on the napkin, carefully covering the remaining portion, and then removing the cover.

When she is finished, she folds the napkin neatly into the ice cream cup and collects the plate and spoon. And she rises on her own and begins to look around. I watch her, but say nothing. She walks toward the hospital door, enters, still looking, but then she seems to forget her mission and heads for the open elevator. I grab her hand before she gets in, turn her around, and say, "Let's look for a 'Pitch In.'" We walk out to the gardens again, and find the one she passed on her way in. "Here," I say, "Here is the 'Pitch In.' Pitch it in." "All?" she asks. "Yes," I say. But she carefully removes the fork and the spoon, places them in her dress pocket, and then pitches in the rest.

On some days, we go to a concert, where I try to get her a seat right in front. If the music is not to her liking, she will say, "Shall we go now?" quite loudly. And sometimes we do. When she first entered this hospital, she sang along in her lovely musical voice, and with all the words, as though she were her self. Once last year, when there was lively Jewish music, and some dancing up front, she too danced, and when I got up to dance as well, her eyes glowed with joy. We were both dancing! The singing has turned now into an annoying sound she makes far back in her throat, toneless, and when loud enough, distracting for others around her. But now and then, especially when the song is "God Bless America," she will know the words, and try to sing along.

On rainy days, I sit down and ask, "Shall we play cards now?" "No," she says. But I get the cards, and say, "Let's play our game." I place one of each of the thirteen cards face up on the table and hand her the rest of the pack. "Now it's your turn." If she's forgotten what to do with the pack, I hold it and hand her one card at a time. She can still place the cards correctly on top of other cards, often making no mistakes at all. And sometimes, she wants to do this again and again. Other times she will simply push the tray/table away and stand up and leave the room, walking down the long hall to the common room/dining room at the end, as though I were not there. When I follow her to say good-bye, she will get up again and take my hand and walk down the hall with me, as though I had just arrived. When I tell her I have to leave now, "to go to work," she will walk me to the elevator, and wave good-bye to me. Once she said something that sounded like "Have a nice day."

She never asks to come with me. She never asks where she is. In Florida, she liked to take a ride with me in the car I rented each time I came to visit. Sometimes, she'd want to go back to her room almost as soon as we began to move. Other times, she seemed interested especially in reading aloud all the signs she could see. In those days, she was still reading signs, though not books or magazines, nor was she watching television. I had borrowed a small television set for her room. She insisted on having it turned on but with a blank screen and no sound. And she forgot quickly how to turn it on and off.

These days, when I don't see her in front of the elevator, I find her in the common room, beside the television set, either dozing or intently looking at it. She never sits in her room unless I am there, perhaps because of the painting and the carving of "MOM" I put on her bulletin board when I moved her into this room. When she sits with me, she can look past me at the painting of herself made in Hawaii on one of her many travels in 1980. I hung it there because she used to have it in her Florida bedroom. She also gave me a copy of it. The "MOM" was a carving I found among her things, and I brought it along to New York, where it fit on top of the bulletin board, over and a bit to the right of the large painting.

Once, when we were playing cards, I said, to make conversation, and because I was worried about her declining memory: "Who is that?" pointing to the painting. I expected to hear her usual reply, "That's a beautiful lady."

"When I have time, I'm going to kill her." Her words were clear, precise.

"But why? You used to say she was a beautiful lady."

"No," she said, "She's a mom."

"But that's Frances," I said, "That's you, you're a mom."

"She's a bad mom, and I have to kill her."

"Do you want me to take the painting away?" I went to move it, but it was clear that that was not what she wanted.

What did she want? Once, very early in her illness, when she was still at home and petulant, angry, weepy, unhappy—all at once, I stamped my foot, and said, in frustration because I hadn't been able to figure out what she wanted, "What *do* you want, Mother?" She looked up at me and said, her voice firm, "I want to be my self."

Two: Brooklyn, the Late 1930s, Early 1940s

It is Sunday, and I am sitting on the large deck of an exquisite East Hampton house, in the midst of oak woods. I am polishing my nails, and thinking of my mother a hundred miles away. My friend Joanne is in Italy and I am minding the house and cat. I haven't been to the hospital in ten days. The last time I brought my polish to the hospital and offered to file and polish her nails, she refused.

As I polished my nails, she stared at hers, turning them over and over again, as though searching for some defect. She stroked one hand with the other. She straightened her rings, one of which she had picked up somewhere in the hospital—a thin band with two small green stones mounted on it, the third one missing—is loose and needs straightening often. When I finally understood that only rings interested her—she had lost her hearing aid, her glasses, her watch, even the Jewish star she had worn for many months—I gave her several rings, most of which also disappeared. But she retained two: a Mexican, broad band of silver cut so that it twinkles; and a fake diamond ring from her own junk jewelry.

She looks at her hands as she does not look at her face or her body. Her hands are smaller than mine, and white—no age spots at all, no calluses, burns, no redness from the decades of great tubs of laundry she scrubbed on a board, never wearing rubber gloves. To look at her hands, one would not know that for six years those hands came home etched in the grease of an airplane factory where she was known as "Rosie the Riveter" long before that phrase became famous, the "Rosie" for her last name, Rosenfeld.

Long before I was ten, as soon as I could handle an iron, we did the laundry together. She said she didn't mind the washing; it was the ironing she hated. And so I learned to iron the sheets, removed very carefully from the clothesline outside the bedroom window so that they were folded correctly for ironing; my father's dress shirts, the shoulders and collar ironed first, the sleeves next, and the body of the shirt last. I loved most of all the handkerchiefs, which were ironed wet, wrung right out of my mother's washtub, placed one over another, and rolled into a long tube. All the other things were taken off the line and sprinkled at the sink. The clothes were piled on a small white deal table that stood next to the double sink. I stood in front of the table facing the ironing board, and my mother was to my left at the double sink, working at some new laundry. The radio was tuned to one of mother's programs, "The Shadow," perhaps, or "I Love a Mystery," or some other evening serial. My brother was playing and my father was at work.

My mother loved working in the factory. For the first time in her life, she had real money of her own. She could pay the rent on time, and send the laundry out. She could even buy a decent winter coat for herself. She could own a raincoat. But when the war ended, like thousands of patriotic women, she left that well-paying job without a murmur, and worked as a bookkeeper, as she had before she married. My father's objections to her going to work at all had been overruled by the income she had brought in during the war. Now her salary was cut by more than two-thirds, for there was no overtime. She kept the financial records and did payroll for a junk dealership in Astoria whose earnings were more than a million dollars a year. She was paid $80.00 a week, and when she left that job twenty years later to move to Florida, she was earning $125 a week. She loved her "bosses," for, as she said, "They are wonderful people—they treat me right."

When I went off to high school at thirteen, the huge L. C. Smith typewriter she had bought secondhand the year before was rolled into the kitchen on its typing table, where the overhead light was bright enough for work. I outlined fifty pages of world history each night directly onto the typewriter, while the radio continued to play my mother's programs. She reminded me often that, if I was to get through high school and go to college, it would be on my typing. And she didn't mean schoolwork—that was "extra." She meant I would have to earn my way.

Even before I began Hunter College, I could no longer manage doing my homework with the radio on and with my mother doing her evening chores and talking with my younger brother. By then, he went to sleep in the tiny bedroom off the kitchen that still held two small cots, and I was sleeping in the living room, still badly lit for study, on a couch that was really a daybed. I began my homework when my mother turned off the radio and went to bed. Then I had the kitchen table, though I couldn't type until I was sure that everyone was asleep. My father would come home between three and four in the morning. We would talk for a bit, but he was usually too exhausted to do more than tell me to go to bed.

Three: Hunter College in the Late 1940s

When I think about Hunter College, I think about a beloved special place, my true home. For the new building on 68th Street and Park Avenue was just that. I arrived early in the morning and left when the building closed, and returned to my parents' house in Brooklyn only at midnight. By the end of my first year I had been elected Chair of the Elections Committee, a position that entitled me to a space in the suite of student offices on the ground floor of Hunter's sparkling seventeen-story building. There I had my own space, a desk, a lamp, a closet, and a bulletin board. There I could leave my things in the morning. I did not have to carry all my books and my coat, gym suit and sneakers, and other articles of clothing from class to class. I could also afford, having this office, to take classes whenever I chose through the day, for I could use my office in between classes for homework or for haven, as well as for the extracurricular work I had to do. From that office I could go to my paying job for two or three hours each day, again leaving my books and other personal things behind in my office. After work I would return to Hunter, see other students, gather up my things, and then finally leave for Brooklyn.

Hunter also meant people to me—what Kate Simon has called "the wider world." My introduction to that world through three years at Hunter College High School had not been auspicious. My experience in the two institutions mirrors the two buildings: the tiny, fortresslike high school, and the expansive, grand modern college building that had been completed in 1939, and that I entered as a freshman in 1946. In the high school, I had been acutely conscious of my social and intellectual ignorance, my cultural inferiority, though I could not have expressed my feelings in those words. The high school experience had terrified me into more of the stillness that my orthodox Jewish childhood had demanded. I became an observer and a listener. But silent. I who had always been an "A" student, who had skipped two years of school despite a year in hospital, and months of illness besides, was a low "B" at best, and in physics, almost a "D." What had happened? Partly it was the trauma of becoming aware of class differences, the unconscious kind of trauma that still grips students coming into Hunter today.

I was not conscious of being Jewish, for I had been born and bred inside a ghetto in Brooklyn, and the fact of my Jewishness did not seem important to me in high school. But I was conscious of my poverty, an immediate sign of which was that I "talked funny." I was sent to speech therapy on the first day of school and there declared "defective." I was handed a mirror to practice with and told to report to the clinic two or three times a week, after classes had ended. I remember practicing at home, showing my mother what I was doing with that mirror, as I tried to watch my tongue move up to an unfamiliar place in my mouth to make the series of "t, t, t" and "d, d, d" sounds required by the exercise. Of course I could hear that no one in my classes sounded as I did. And so I was silent. Even after my speech patterns had been declared "satisfactory," I was silent.

And though Hunter College became my home, and I was not silent in my "office," I continued to be silent in classes. Perhaps one closing piece of high school experience was also partly responsible for my classroom behavior. Miss Brubaker, my senior English teacher, was the faculty advisor to *Annals,* the yearbook and literary magazine. I was the Literary Editor; Cynthia Ozick was the Editor—which meant that Cynthia contributed a piece of creative writing, and I put the publication together. Miss Brubaker was fond of me, and fond of telling me that I was "the perfect 'B' student." What did that mean? She told me one day: "You don't have a creative bone in your body," she said in admiration, "you are reliable, accurate, and I can depend on you."

I treasured the praise so highly that when I was placed into Creative Writing, after having earned an "A" in Freshman English, I petitioned in writing to be allowed to take the regular second semester Freshman English, quoting Miss Brubaker's assessment of my missing creative talents.

Despite my high grades and extracurricular work, I never remember asking or volunteering an answer to a question in class. I spoke if called upon—a rare occurrence, since classes were large enough to hide in, and since lecturing was the most common mode of instruction. I recall only one teacher who insisted that I speak, and that was in German. Frau Hathaway wanted German conversation in class, and would call upon students to respond in German. I would always respond in English, and explain that I couldn't respond in German. Since my examinations were usually perfect, as was my homework, she was not pleased by my responses. So she assigned "Der Erlkönig"—I was to memorize the long poem and then recite it to the class. It was not only a punishment for what she saw as stubborn behavior; it was also meant to assure me that I could, in fact, speak German. I memorized with ease; it was a faculty I had under strong control. And my German accent was at least satisfactory. The recitation went off without a flaw, and Frau Hathaway beamed throughout. But when she asked me a question somewhat later in the hour, I answered as before, in English, and with humble apologies. I was not being stubborn, I tried to explain, I simply could not speak German. I didn't understand why I couldn't. I simply couldn't.

Only a decade later, in psychoanalysis, did I remember an initiating experience that might account for my unwillingness to speak German in class. I went to kindergarten at five bilingual, having learned to speak both Yiddish and English in a household in which my maternal immigrant grandmother, Sara Stilly, spoke no English. In kindergarten, I saw children struck with a ruler for speaking Yiddish, and heard the teacher say, "We talk only English in school." I left that first day of school with the teacher's admonition fixed in my soul, for when my beloved grandmother addressed me in Yiddish that afternoon as she fixed milk and cookies for me, I told her that she was to "talk to me in English, that's what the teacher said. I will talk only English." No one admonished me that day for rudeness to my grandmother. I was the first grandchild to go to school, and nothing that teachers and schools demanded could be wrong. My grandmother would learn to understand English, if that was what I needed, even if she could not speak it.

That I could simply cease being bilingual astonishes me, but only when I began to dream in Yiddish, at age twenty-seven, did I discover that I had been bilingual from the start, that my grandmother Sara, whom I called Baba, had been one of the main persons to care for me. In my dream, I was speaking Yiddish, not simply understanding it.

When my Baba died, I was seven. I remember that my younger brother and I had been locked up all morning in the very tiny bedroom we shared, told to "be quiet." I remember we were standing in front of the only window and laughing at something when my father opened the door, shouting at us to "Stop laughing, Baba is dead. This is no time for laughing." My father never shouted at us. My father never had so red a face. Frightened, we crept out of the bedroom into the kitchen where my father had gone to sit in the chair next to the icebox. His head was in his hands and he was making strange sounds. I knew he was crying. I felt terribly embarrassed that I had been laughing.

My grandmother, I came to understand only many years later, had died that morning because she had glaucoma and had opened the wrong door, one that did not lead to the back of the grocery store closed on Saturdays, but to a sheer drop onto the cement cellar floor. Her death changed my life in particular, since my grandfather—fifteen years older than his wife—came to live with us and not with his rich sons whose middle-class wives did not want him.

During those last three years of his life, Zaida taught me to read and write Yiddish and Hebrew. Why did that man, Max Stilly, teach me? Why did he bother to teach me when he hadn't taught his illiterate wife to read or write in any of the several languages he could use? Why, when he never taught my mother, and insisted that she could not take the pre-college course her teachers had recommended, but instead forced her into a commercial course of stenography and bookkeeping, into which she sneaked the Spanish she had hoped to be able to teach?

This was not a joyous activity for either of us. I did what I was told; he did what he felt he had to do before his death—teach a grandchild, and I was the only one old enough to be taught. I was seven when the lessons began, and ten when they ceased. No one thought to continue the lessons he had begun. They were clearly for him, not for me.

He was the only person in my childhood experience who cared for books, though they were books I couldn't read. My grandfather's Hebrew books were given away in the beautiful glass-doored bookcase housing them. Or were they sold? He, they, and the clock he used to wind each afternoon before the lesson vanished from my daily life, though not from my young consciousness. And I can't help wondering now what he would have thought of my years at Hunter High and Hunter College. Had he lived, would I have had his blessing? Do I want it still?

The relief I might have felt, the freedom to play after school I might have begun to enjoy again, was short-lived. For my mother chose that moment to defy my father and find a wartime factory job. Instead of lessons with my grandfather, I began to do the housework so that my mother could come from her new factory job to find the beds made, the dishes washed, the clothes picked up, and her children doing their homework on the kitchen table. Sometimes I also had to do a bit of shopping, or peel potatoes. But my mother preferred to cook alone. Things in her kitchen had to be done exactly her way.

And so I never learned to cook at home where I remained the clean-up person I am today in my friends' homes. Or the salad-maker: I am good at chopping things to order. And of course, in direct reaction to my mother's temperament, I am easy with others in my kitchen, undemanding and with no compulsions about the placement of objects or the handling of instruments.

My success in school, the ease with which I learned anything, must have cut two ways for my mother. She had to be pleased by a child who learned, as she had instructed her, *to be like the teacher.* Here was her child following in the steps she had wanted to walk. Here was her child becoming a teacher. But of course, there is always the risk attendant on crossing the gulf between the wish, the dream, and the reality of behavior. During my first year of high school, for example, I learned to speak sounds entirely foreign to my family's speech patterns. "How now, brown cow" was a litany I practiced nightly along with efforts to disappear all evidence of glottal stops and dentalized t's and d's. How did that make my mother feel? How did I feel? In the beginning, I was mocked at home for being "hoity-toity." Later on, when my different speech patterns had ceased to be even a cause for family comedy at my expense, other issues forced some quarrels and some compromises.

Somehow, I knew, even when still in junior high school, that to hate or fear "Negroes" was wrong. My parents' phobic view of the non-Jewish, non-white world first troubled, then embarrassed me. At Hunter, even before I had the extraordinary experience of taking a course with Mary Diggs, the only African-American on the sociology faculty, I insisted that Harriette Kilpatrick was going to spend a night with me in Brooklyn, and I was going to spend a night with her in Harlem. Our apartments, we had discovered, were duplicates. Each of us slept in the living room, and we could pull out a spare cot for the other. Her parents were as furious with her as mine were with me—but we triumphed.

I was somewhat more malleable on the subject of my postgraduate future. When my academic success in the English department led Professor Hoxie Neale Fairchild and President George Shuster to recommend that I apply for graduate school scholarships, I discussed the idea with my mother. "You'll never make it," my mother spoke, remembering her own life. "You must continue the education courses, just in case." I couldn't do that, I explained, since student teaching would take up much of a whole semester, and I needed the time for more advanced English courses. "Well, then," she looked very unhappy, "you'll have to take stenography." I was horrified, but she explained that, since I was an excellent typist, when rejected by all those graduate schools, I could "fall back on secretarial work," and, she added, "Secretaries are always needed."

I couldn't shake her conviction that I needed an alternative plan, "just in case." Though the year of stenography lowered my grade point average, the skill was ultimately useful in graduate school.

I don't remember how I first met Dean Anthony. She was the Dean of Students, and I suppose that, because I was active in student government, I got to meet her early in my second year. I remember her spacious, quiet office, and the leather couch that stood against the wall opposite her desk. She never sat behind her desk when you came into her office. She rose and came to meet you, a trim figure, of medium height, with short gray hair and a quick and gracious smile. Perhaps her nose was long; perhaps her smile was a bit too wide. To me, she was beautiful. And immeasurably kind. For one thing she listened, and she understood more than any adult I had ever known.

I sat on the couch and she sat on a chair to my left, her back to the window, and it was the beginning of my final term at Hunter. I had been President of Student Government the previous year, elected while I had been a junior, and now I held no college office. I was also a married woman, had married the returning soldier I had corresponded with during almost the whole of my college years, but whom I had spent almost no time with. And I had walked out on that marriage the night before, less than three months since its beginning. I had walked out in the middle of the night, leaving the sleeping man and all my things, even my wrist watch and rings, except my school books. I had taken the train at one A.M. back to my parents' apartment.

Mother was clearly shocked to see me. I was feeling lightheaded and almost happy. "Mother," I was fairly shouting, "I've left Jerry, and I'm not going back." I didn't say why I had left, and she didn't try to question me. She assumed we had quarreled, and I didn't correct her.

"You can stay the night," she said, "but in the morning you go back to your husband." "I can't do that," I said, "and besides, I have to go to school in the morning."

"Well, after school you go back to your husband."

"I can't go. I'm never going back." My mother opened her mouth as if to speak, then shut it again. I was silent too.

"When you were two, I wanted to leave Daddy, but I didn't. I stayed." She stopped. "I stayed because of you." She stopped again. I waited for the rest of the story. But she was finished.

"But there is no baby, there is only me. It's different, and I don't have to stay." I sounded defiant, but I felt frightened.

"You made your bed and you'll have to lie in it," she responded, a sentence I had heard often, and I took it that the conversation was concluded. That was the way my mother thought, in absolutes, unchanging absolutes.

On Dean Anthony's couch, I told her about the evening before, in more detail than I could tell my mother. I told her also that I could not go back to my parents' apartment, that I would not go back to my husband. She did not need to be told that I was desperate—she heard my feelings, the grief and the fear beneath the confusion, and the strength that had allowed me to walk out. She was wise enough not to try to untangle all the strands that had landed me married at nineteen in the first place. She accepted as given that I wanted to be out of the marriage, and she said she would help me. She knew that I wanted to finish college, and that my academic record, including election to Phi Beta Kappa as a junior, qualified me for graduate school.

And so she proceeded to do the practical things that Hunter deans in those days could do. She telephoned the "Y" and arranged for me to have a room for a week until, she said, she could help me to find a job that would also give me housing. I was numb with gratitude, and remember feeling only that I was in the presence of magic. A job and housing. And then she gave me money and said, feeling my embarrassment, "Consider it a loan."

I remember that "Y" closet of a room, the first I had ever had of my own. It seemed a palace to me—of freedom and peace. Of course, having acted in my behalf, Dean Anthony was thereby "involved." I don't remember how my mother found me, but she did, and eventually both she and my husband had quiet conversations with Dean Anthony, and they were persuaded to let me go my own way. The marriage was annulled shortly thereafter.

I don't remember ever thanking her enough for what she did for me. I did try to stay in touch with her through graduate school and afterward, but she retired and traveled, and I moved around a great deal as graduate students and young faculty members are wont to do. And I remember that I learned of her death only years after it had occurred, and that I felt miserable for weeks afterward that I hadn't seen her again to tell her once more how much she still meant to me.

Four: Manhattan, Work, The Feminist Press

That tension, unresolved between my mother and me the night I left my marriage and returned home, continues to shape my life and my work. Am I my mother's daughter, locked fatally into a bed I never made? Or am I a new creature, sprung from her thwarted ambitions and the accident of her father's teaching? Perhaps my father caught the future in a few words, when he told me how proud he was that I had been awarded a full scholarship for a year's graduate study at Smith College, but how concerned also that I "would never lead a normal life." I don't think he was thinking of class conflict: but he sensed that I was leaving forever the Jewish working-class world in which successful young women became elementary school teachers, then married and had babies.

I tried marriage more times than was good for me, chiefly because I wanted those babies I was never able to have, and that I know my mother longed for as well. She never ceased to give up hope that I would one day tell her I was pregnant. I knew her coded question: no matter what news I had for her—my book was about to appear, an important article had been accepted, I was invited to speak at Yale—she would say, "And what else is new?" "Nothing," I would say, "there is nothing to tell you."

In so many ways I disappointed her. We were not easy friends; we did not like the same things. She had never been to a museum, a ballet, an opera, regarded these as "not for her." She didn't understand the books I was writing, the peripatetic life I was leading as an academic. She didn't understand the series of marriages. She couldn't understand why I didn't become pregnant as easily as she had. And we could rarely talk about any of these matters. Hers was not a talking spirit, at least not with me.

But we could eat together and chat about the food, about the trips she was planning, the bingo game she had won, or the troubles her neighbors were having. After she moved to Florida, my annual or semi-annual visits were marked by at least one festive meal of Maine lobster, hours long, which would begin with her "virgin mary" and my scotch, and conclude with her urging me to taste the cherry cheese cake she ordered for dessert.

More than anything throughout my life, I feared looking like my mother, losing my teeth as she had at twenty-nine, and, at her most obese, unable even to tie her own shoes. These days she weighs twenty pounds less than I do, and I can make her smile, and sometimes laugh heartily, when I call her "my skinny mother." For the first time ever, in this terrible illness, she is able to enjoy eating without guilt and without the punishing obesity of the past.

More than our bodies, more than our eating habits, our hands connect us fast, for I remember how I could stop smoking only when I began knitting through every faculty meeting, every conference with students, every bit of time when I was not using my hands. I caught on to the fact that smoking was not for oral gratification, when I noted that I didn't smoke when typing or ironing or gardening, or taking minutes at a meeting, activities that demanded the use of my hands. In order to stop smoking, I began to knit even in the movies, even when reading. It worked.

My mother's hands were always occupied, if not with the housework, or her work as a bookkeeper, then with knitting, or mending clothes, or sewing curtains, or crocheting doilies. In addition she was a volunteer worker for the Palestinian soup kitchen that my grandfather had helped to found. And at certain periods, we'd go to work in a dusty, strange-smelling office on the lower east side, where a white-bearded rabbi presided, and where we would stuff thousands of envelopes for a major "appeal." The process of stuffing and sealing envelopes quickly and effectively, a skill I learned from my mother before I was ten, is one I've been teaching staff for two decades. In her best Florida days, when my mother came to New York for her annual upstate meeting, she'd also visit for a few days with me and want some "work" to do. If we were in the midst of a mailing, she'd join the staff and immediately set to rearranging and correcting their stuffing and sealing styles.

Later, in my teen years, we also used to take on the typing of envelopes for some tiny pay, and we'd take turns banging away at the big L. C.

Smith in the kitchen. When she retired and moved to Florida, I feared for her loss of work. How could she live without the dailiness of work? I meant, of course, though I couldn't have stated it this way, work with her hands. "Don't worry," she said, "Every day is Sunday, and I just love it this way." I felt better when she told me she had found a typing job for the first five days of each month and that she would arrange her travel plans around those days. When that job ended, several years before the acute phase of her illness came into view, I should have seen it as a clue to what was coming. It wasn't that she didn't want to do the typing: she wasn't able to do it well anymore, and somehow she and the people she worked for knew it and ended the arrangement.

For many years she kept the household books for the women with whom she had bought a small house, wrote all checks, and kept a meticulous checkbook for herself. When she came to New York, she found all the errors in my checkbook, and insisted on bringing it into exact line with the bank's report, finding my resolutions incredibly sloppy. When she became ill, I found her checkbook confused, and worse, I found that, instead of saving for the travel vacations that were her annual treat, she was spending all of her income on every charity that wrote to her, sometimes writing to the same cause as many as six checks a year, each for $20.00, and this on an income of $700 a month. Taking away her checkbook was like taking away her life, she said, when I proposed doing that three years ago. And so I left her checkbook, with instructions to the bank not to honor any checks, and moved her remaining $2,000 into a CD where she could not spend it.

Once in the Florida nursing home, she never asked for her checkbook, she never mentioned money, she couldn't read or watch television. So I brought her knitting. She had recently made me a gargantuan gray sweater, unlike anything else she had ever done, for it was twice the size it should have been, and the complex pattern had not been worked out properly so that the fronts and the back were unmatched. But I thought a scarf would be simple—she could make the kinds of scarves I now make for friends. And I had brought some of the mohair I use and the needles, in the event that I needed to knit. But even three years ago that was an activity that her hands and her brain could no longer manage. When I realized that she had forgotten how to knit, I brought envelopes for her to stuff. She managed that, but lost interest very quickly and told me, "You can finish it."

And how do I finish it? What deep layers of guilt do I bear for not being the daughter she wanted? I ask the question with the clear understanding that, to begin with, and through much of my childhood, she didn't want a daughter at all. She wanted to be the person she had dreamed of becoming. And then I was to be that person for her. But I was not.

And yet in so many countless ways, especially now that she is no longer the self she was, I remind myself of her. It is hard for me, to take one example, to sit still and "enjoy myself" as guest in a friend's house, or at a party. Invariably, I will take up duties in the kitchen unasked, dicing vegetables or cleaning up after the cook. I won't watch television without ironing or crosswords or other kinds of busywork in my hands. And though I don't do this much anymore, when The Feminist Press first began, what I loved best after a morning of reading or editing manuscripts, typing letters and grant proposals, was to pack books and rearrange inventory in the afternoon. My idea of a vacation is to write in the morning and swim or walk (or both) in the afternoon, and to do silly busywork—even the sorting of a year's receipts for the income tax report—in the evening. It is impossible for me to consider "doing nothing." At a very minimum, I would have to be knitting or reading a mystery.

Not surprisingly, given the story I've told, the work of The Feminist Press is at the center of my life, replacing even the teaching I loved for thirty years, and competing only with my private dream of "writing." My own commitment to social change cannot be ascribed simply to one root cause. Unlike my "red diaper" working-class friends, I had no theoretical lessons in class struggle. I was not a precocious teenage reader of Marx. But I experienced daily the simple angers of injustice in my own family, not only for my own life, but, again and again, for the immovable mindset of my mother's life. Long before I had gone to Mississippi and experienced firsthand the racist underpinnings of U.S. culture and politics, long before I was shocked into an awareness of sexism, long before I had met Tillie and Jack Olsen and began to place the roots of my own life in some political perspective, I knew that my mother should have had the opportunities I was having.

So it is not surprising to me now, looking back at the nearly twenty-five years of The Feminist Press, to note how strong has been our allegiance to working-class literature, black and white, and increasingly, Hispanic and Asian-American. It is more surprising to me that, over the past decade, I have become The Press's financial manager, able to write both a cash and an accrual budget, to check or critique the accountant's quarterly reports, and to cost out new projects and printings, as well as to transact sales of foreign rights. My own checkbook may still be sloppy, but at work I am truly my mother's daughter.

Like her, but only from time to time, I know that never-being-satisfied feeling, that feeling of being thwarted at every turn. Like her, I can be critical, demanding, even on occasion, rigid, though I try to laugh at myself more than she was able to. But I have not had her difficult life. And I know that her persuading me that I was smart, that I could learn anything, continues to feed me. If only it could have also fed her.

When The Feminist Press began to publish books in the early 1970s, my mother had moved to Florida, and I sent a copy of each book to her. She read them in between her fat pulpy novels usually telling me that "the story was good." We never talked about the differences between the characters in Kate Chopin's stories and those in Agnes Smedley's novel. We never talked about the growing proportion of working-class stories The Press was publishing.

Indeed, I never stopped in any conscious way to connect my early life with The Feminist Press's publishing mandate. It always seemed obvious that The Press ought to do what trade and university presses would not or could not. And social class was both a denied and an invisible element in the world of publishing. Yet, of course, as a reader, the books that mattered to my life, that I chose to write about, were *Daughter of Earth* and *The Maimie Papers* in the seventies, and, more recently, Jo Sinclair's memoir, *The Seasons.*

As I look back at the more than sixty years, the pain and the pleasure inextricably intermingle, the patterns writ large. I learned embarrassment early—about my self, my behavior, and my voice, and about my family. My dear father told me when I first went off to junior high school never to say that he was a taxi-driver. If asked "What does your father do?" I was to say, "He's in the transportation business." Only halfway through my life did I understand that who I had been was more than something to be ashamed of. Only then could I connect my new feminist understanding with my gut-level hatred of racism and other forms of prejudice and with the painful experience of class bias I had lived through and learned, in part, to perpetuate. I used to describe my public life as a "success," especially, I would add, the work of helping to establish women's studies as a significant area of knowledge, and helping to found and build The Feminist Press into a viable institution dedicated to publishing for social change. At the same time, focusing on my marriages and childlessness, I described my private life as a "failure."

I know better now. Like many other women of my class, and of varying cultural and racial backgrounds, I have come to know, I have begun to understand the potential strengths of that underclass position. Building on Joan Kelly's notion that feminist women can see the world through a "double vision," I can claim a "third" sight. I have also begun to understand the special privileges I had within my family, as well as at the schools and colleges I attended, that allowed my talents to grow. And yet, I can't forget that the awakening to consciousness came only after I had lived more than half my life. All through school, college, and more than the first decade and a half of teaching, I had missed having a cultural and historical home and a political sense of the world. I certainly knew early that the world was an "unfair" place, but nowhere had I learned about the possibilities of change, despite the ironies of my own life's changes. Perhaps that is why the work of women's studies and African-American studies, and other ethnic studies programs, has seemed to me of special importance. I have seen new generations of women and men begin to feel culturally and historically at home in classrooms, and to take those feelings out into the world. Perhaps ultimately such work will help future generations to feel at home from the start—in the culture that continues to bring grandparents and parents to these shores.

Julie Olsen Edwards

I was born in 1938, just as Spain was falling to Franco's forces, and was named for a man who died there fighting for democracy as a member of the Abraham Lincoln Brigade. My parents, Jack and Tillie Olsen, raised four daughters, and home and family seemed to me to be the one safe haven in a world of wars, persecution, hatred.

Despite that harsh reality, my parents held out the continual message that the world could be made safe, made to be a place where humans flourished, and they lived their lives in an ongoing effort to bring about social change and justice. It was a class-"conscious" childhood and one I remember as rich and full despite economic deprivation and the real dangers and betrayals of Nazism, McCarthyism, racism.

I married young, to my high school boyfriend, and over the next fourteen years we struggled to put each other through college while raising our Rebekah and Tobias. We settled in Santa Cruz, where we both teach at the local community college.

This snapshot (left) was taken when I was three. It's an unusual shot because none of my sisters are in it with me. Mom is dressed up because she is leaving for a national CIO convention. (I still remember the hat.) Dad died in 1988. I miss him every day, and I am still grieving.

The recent photo (below) is one of my favorites because I'm with kids, I'm reading a book I made with the children, I'm teaching, and just after this was taken, we all collapsed in gales of laughter.

I have written this piece in fragments and brief moments, a terrifying and wondrous process. It is a love song to my parents and although it is incomplete and flawed, I offer it as a gift to my children and my students.

Julie Olsen Edwards directs the Department of Early Childhood and Family Life Education at Cabrillo Community College in Santa Cruz, California. Her short story "Mother Oath" was

published by The Feminist Press and she is the editor of *Embracing Diversity: Teachers' Voices from California Classrooms*, published by California Tomorrow. She appears regularly on various radio talk shows on issues regarding children, parents, and schools.

Julie Olsen Edwards

Class Notes from the Lecture Hall

Incident: It is the first week of the Child Development class. The room is quiet as students sit filling out a personal information form I have handed them. Name. Which classes this semester. Number of hours employed. What is it about children that particularly interests them. Something about the family in which they grew up including their class background.

One student raises her hand and asks "What's a class background?"

Later that day as I read the forms I discover that almost all the students, those raised by truck drivers, secretaries, beauticians, schoolteachers, salesclerks, mail carriers, almost all of them list their answer as middle class.

I always knew I was a working-class child. A Mission District San Franciscan. Jack and Tillie's kid (the second of four daughters). And a union kid. A worker's kid. Proud of being a worker's kid.

There are all the other layers that flavored and formed. As a child growing up through the war years, the Holocaust years, what parts of this story are shaped by my parents Russian/Jewish immigrant history? What did it mean to be the child of unionists, Communists, activists through the McCarthy years? What differences did it make to be a girl child in a family of girls? It was an urban, political, intellectual childhood, profoundly shaped by the economics and lack of entitlement that still today define class.

Today, at fifty-five, I am a Community College teacher, head of department, mother, foster mother, wife, writer, editor. I have helped build a program with a national reputation, am much sought after as a speaker for radio and public forums. I am seen as a leader on my campus, in my union, my community, my state. And still, I know myself as a working-class woman, recognize that all I do, all I say or write, is based in that particular class-conscious childhood. And yet, just as my students have no language to name their class experience, I find I have only fragments of memory to describe mine. Looking for, listening for memory, I find only sporadic incidents, or entire fabric with no detail. In a world that denies class existence, I am just now learning to speak of my legacy.

Memory: I am about twelve years old. A music school has been set up in our neighborhood to provide low-cost lessons for children of "needy families." My two younger sisters are enrolled, one on the violin, one on the piano. A patron of the school donates a packet of opera tickets for the students and I am invited to attend with my sisters. Dressed in our best clothes we go to the Opera House, hear Carmen. I am transfixed. Amazed. In love. More than anything I want to be able to sing like the women I have heard that day. At home I beg my parents to get me tickets to attend again, and watch the pain on their faces as they tell me we cannot afford it. "It is wrong," my Mother says, "for wonderful music to be only the province of the wealthy." "When you are older," she says, "when you are older, I will help you find a way to usher so you can go as often as you want." "Someday," my Father says, "someday, all working people will have music, good music. Everyone will have music lessons if they want them, be able to use their gifts and talents." "Really?" I ask. "Yes," they both say. "And you will help make that happen."

We were a family who loved to talk.
All issues had moral overtones. Was it good for humanity or bad for humanity? What were the implications of my behavior on my sisters? On my family?
Righteous indignation was cherished and fostered.
Words and ideas and intense discussion were the keys to finding truth, to changing the world, to deciding how to take action, to make it *better*.

Consider: Last week I was watching television. *Homefront* was portraying a union meeting and I watched with amazement and tenderness—and with a hollow sense of loss as I realized that this all so familiar event—working people, on their own precious out-of-work time, meeting together to figure out what was going on, and how to handle it—this common day experience is never (rarely) portrayed, spoken of, included in our movies, books, telly shows. (Why is it that we don't notice what is invisible until someone makes it visible however briefly?)

So I watch the show, and the union meeting is hot and angry—and I am paying less attention to the content then to the pleasure of familiarity with the clothes, the tired faces, the sense of intensity and directness—when suddenly I am betrayed. The screen erupts with a yelling fist fight, chairs flying through the air, big men slugging and mauling. What I read as directness, argument to seek information, state a clearer or different view has been constructed to be thoughtless, angry, dumb brutish men (and silent women)—and the screen gives no resolution to the issue at hand because the fight is the expected, necessary outcome.

Memory: Two weeks ago at a faculty meeting. The Dean is discussing "downsizing" as a result of the budget cuts from the State. Everyone sits about listening, speaking code words I never quite learn. Disgusted (heartsick) I finally say "What you mean is firing. You are talking about firing people from their jobs." I sense the whole room tensing and recognize that my language is too direct, my hurt and anger somehow impolite. I am flooded with an old familiar shame that I do not know the language, the gestures, the correct decibel. I feel my colleagues (never described as my fellow workers) stiffen in their seats, look away, drop their eyes.

(It would be bad enough coming from a male—it is worse coming from someone who clearly does not know how to be a lady.)

In my head the shame struggles with a memory of adults leaning across the table in my childhood house—their faces alive with caring, seeking the right words, caught up in a search for a better world, for a deeper truth—trying to convince and to understand. I know that in this setting my language is "wrong," my intensity foreign, that I am again a stranger. Yet I know to keep silent is impossible.

Sometimes all those words serve me well. I am known on campus for delivering powerful speeches, for moving people, for being persuasive. People listen when I talk and expect me to bring a new perspective. I am respected—but my fellow workers/colleagues are uneasy, discomforted. They are, I realize, waiting for the fist fight, the flying chairs, the sense that violence stands next to direct, straight words.

(It is so hard for me to remember that "we'll take it under advisement" means "I am saying no.")

Above my desk hangs a sign "Silence is the Voice of Complicity."

Work.
What did I learn about work during that Mission District childhood?

Work was what you did in life.

Everyone worked.

Survival meant you worked.

I have yet to get over the privilege of not punching a time clock. I acknowledge that it's a sixty-hour work week. Acknowledge that the job exhausts, and consumes. Acknowledge that classes must be met, meetings attended. Still I revel in the knowledge that I do not ask permission to eat lunch at 11:00 or at 3:00, that I can decide to work until midnight in order to go see the kids in a school play. It seems unbelievable luxury to prepare for class at my kitchen table and not walk through the doors at work until mid-morning. The freedom from that time clock still makes me feel slightly naughty, like a kid playing hooky or forging an excuse slip from a parent.

It also makes me slightly anxious—and I find myself explaining to the department secretary (who must come in by 8:00) that I have spent the morning working even if I was not in the building.

I presume I am here on this planet to work hard. It is what one does. But this does not make me distinct from my friends who were raised in middle-class families. Most of the people I know work intensely, are driven, wearied from their work. At the college, most of us also get great satisfaction from our work, feel we are among the privileged. I am always somewhat surprised that I get a paycheck (yes, I know, it's supposed to be referred to as "salary") for talking about, reading about, getting others to talk and read about, things I care about.

When I was a child Mom and Dad went to work so we could live. They had jobs—not careers. The pleasures I saw them derive came not from the work itself (although there was pride over work well done) but from friends and from their political lives.

They worked hard, and there was always anxiety over whether there would be enough work, or if it would pay enough.

Whatever else might be going on—one went to work.

You left the sick child home alone, you took aspirin to dull the headache or force the fever down, you ignored the aching feet, the hurting back—and you went to work.

Consider: I became seriously ill five years ago. I am one of the lucky ones with good sick-leave benefits. (It is no accident—it exists because of my working-class parents and their generation's willingness to put their bodies on the line, to organize and demand.) And so, I have sick leave—a paycheck will continue if I am out due to illness. But month after month I dragged myself to work getting sicker with each day. Finally I became bedridden, and for a long year I had no work. I stayed at home, I did physical therapy, I lay in bed. And I had no work.

What was amazing to me was the sense of shame.

If I wasn't working I had no excuse to be taking up space.

What was amazing to me was the sense of responsibility and guilt.

My being out sick made the job harder for every one of my colleagues in our understaffed, overworked program.

What was amazing to me was the sense that somehow it was a moral issue. That I ought to be able to *will* myself up out of that bed and onto the bosses' time.

Memory: I am little. Three women are talking; one is my Mother. Someone says with sorrow and great admiration, "He broke his wrist on the line, but he kept working until the shift was over." My Mother interjects with words about the right to Workers' Comp., the injustice of the price the man has paid. But I am struck with the solemnity of the first speaker's voice as if some great courageous act has taken place.

Memory: My Mother, face lined and exhausted from nursing my little sister through a long night of an asthma attack. I, too, am sick and she sets me up on the couch with a chair pulled close. She has draped a towel over the chair, pinned a paper bag for Kleenex to the blanket, left me a glass of ginger ale (a treat reserved for sick children). She walks to the stair carrying my sister who will be taken to a neighbor, cautioning me about the day, promising me she will call during every one of her breaks . . . and she goes to work.

There is this about work. One goes.

Work, rather than defining life, consumes life.

Memory with my Grandfather: We are getting on to a bus in Santa Monica (maybe going to the library). The bus driver is rude and snarls at an elderly woman who is very slow in getting up the high step onto the bus. Grandpa, sensing how troubled I am (did I say anything?), takes my hand and with great seriousness says "He (the bus driver) does not know how important his work is. It is his work that lets people get to their jobs, takes us to the library, Grandma to the groceries. Without his work, all of our lives would be so much harder. But people treat him as if he is just part of the bus, and his bosses just tell him to hurry hurry hurry—so he doesn't know how important his work really is. That's why he is so rude to people who are slow."

Memory with my Father: It is Labor Day. The parade is down Market Street.

Daddy is driving the union's car (a wood-sided station wagon) with loudspeakers mounted on the roof. Peter (my classmate) and I are permitted to ride on the open rear door, legs dangling, holding American flags.

As the parade moves up Market I can see all the way back to the Embarcadero—a solid path of men and women marching with banners, hats covered with union buttons, laughing, some singing.

It is an era of racial separation and discrimination (we didn't yet know the word racism) but our union, ILWU, is proudly integrated and the faces marching behind the slow moving station wagon are browns and golds and pinks and very beautiful to my nine-year-old eyes.

As far as I can see, today working people own Market Street.

I wave my flag and am very proud to be an American, very proud to be union, fully believing my Father's voice on the loudspeaker

"We do the work of the world."

Memory with my Mother: It is 1949, the year of the big strike.

Mom and I stand with another woman from the union outside of a large grocery store. We have a barrel in which we are collecting donations of food for families of strikers.

Mom and the other woman are laughing as they try to predict who will donate and who will not.

Well-dressed, "well-heeled" folks will pass us by. "Working folk," tired-looking women, women hauling a passel of kids—they will contribute.

Their predictions are accurate.

I stand with them trying to figure out what they are seeing, trying to figure out why the few exceptions to their predictions. I feel very proud to be collecting the food and (although too shy to do so) want to hug each person who puts cans into our barrel.

They are on our side.

The college is divided into certificated staff (teachers) and classified staff (office, clean up, support, etc.). The work of the classified staff is mostly rendered visible only when it does not get done, and then is the target of annoyance and frustration.

I always see the work. When I walk down the corridors my years as housewife notice the swept floors, the clean windows, the repaired screen. Every form we use, every phone call, every schedule that the students pore over—all speak to me of someone's work.

It often irritates my colleagues that I always suggest each committee send notes of appreciation to our various fellow workers who make our jobs doable.

They think it's an ok idea, but must it be done every time?

Yes.

Every semester on the first day of class I welcome the students.

Special welcomes to those who are immigrants—my awe at the task they have taken on to learn in a new culture, a new language—my hope they will teach us some of what they know from their original home, that they will gift us with a bigger understanding of our world. Special welcomes to the reentry students, and to the "first in family" to come to college. I talk about pioneering—finding new paths to travel, new languages, new ways of thinking and doing—that it takes courage, effort. "Remember," I tell them, "that you know a lot already. Each of you knows many things I do not. Take what you hear in this class and weigh it against your own lives and experiences—and if you do not understand how to do something, or say something—remember it is not your failure, but mine—and I rely upon you to help me become a better teacher by letting me know what has not been clear, has not worked."

Why do I write this here? Why does this seem so closely allied to having a working-class/left identity?

Memory: sitting in the second grade. New child in class. Chinese. The teacher stumbles over her name, then says in loud and exaggerated clipped syllables "That is not an American name. Your name in this school will be Wendy." Not knowing why, I feel a sweep of embarrassment, discomfort, shame. It is somehow very important that I go up to her at recess and try to play. She only stays in the class a few months and I never learn her real name.

Memory: Valentine's Day. It is my turn to pass out the cookies and milk for snack time. I have laboriously figured out the calendar and have been wait-

ing for this day. The cookies will be heart shaped. I go to the front of the room and get the box from the teacher who suddenly frowns and takes my hands. Her face is tight with disapproval. "Look at those disgusting nails! Don't you ever wash? Someone else will have to hand out the snack." She goes on talking, someone else is given the box of cookies. I remember looking at my hands as if they belonged to someone else. It had never occurred to me that there was an underside to nails, that one was supposed to do something to them.

Recent memories: I still carefully clean under my nails before any faculty meeting, interview, speech, conference. It is a source of great frustration to me that I cannot grow long nails. (Once I went to a manicurist and had pretend nails put on. As I left she said to me "now remember—these are jewels not tools.")

Frequently I can identify the urban working-class faculty at the college in the first few minutes of conversation. We speak differently, and frequently think differently about the work than the raised middle-class faculty. For one thing, we know we are employees. We presume we will see the work differently than the administration and that our interests may well not be the same. We recognize that when the president says, "We must reduce the number of faculty but we will not compromise on serving all our students"—we recognize he is talking about a speed-up in our work lives, and that the students' experience will indeed be compromised.

Another way my class background appears on the campus is that I often break taboos I do not know exist by asking about, talking about, things that are "private." I am baffled by the sense of privacy, of all the things that the middle-class faculty aren't supposed to or don't talk about.

"Taboos I do not know exist"—that may be the central description of the foreigner's experience.

In my childhood neighborhood we all knew who were the alcoholics, who was "broke," who was out of work, who was fighting. We also knew whose houses kids could always go into for an invitation to eat, to play, for comfort. There wasn't much opportunity to pretend everything was fine. And keeping a smooth exterior never became a goal worth pursuing.

The notion that one struggles with one's work seems as obvious to me as does the need to connect with others doing the same work. I still speak easily about what goes wrong in my classes, blowing it in a committee meeting. (Many of my academic coworkers are made nervous by my self-revelation and yet are attracted by it. They perceive my interest in teaching, in students, in my own learning process as an aspect of my femaleness which gives them permission to dismiss it.) I recognize that traditional academics are not supposed to acknowledge what they don't know or discuss their teaching as if it was central.

Most of us on the college faculty were educated in traditional academic programs where the emphasis was on success through isolation. We were encouraged to listen to each other solely for the purpose of finding out what was wrong in the other person's thinking. Under the guise of learning critical thinking skills, attack on our colleagues was respected and rewarded. Now we each teach in our own rooms, isolated from one another's experience, and are encouraged to think of our teaching as an individual effort unrelated to any one else's classes. Our struggles become individualized, personalized, and private. It is no accident that the drive to organize the faculty union came first from those of us who had lived working-class lives that taught us we were smarter in the amalgam than in isolation, taught us that those of us closest to the task are the ones who understand it best and should make the decisions about the tasks, taught us to always consider, and talk about, the conditions under which work is done.

Not only do I talk about the conditions of our work, I also talk about that most taboo of all subjects—money.

Growing up poor, or on the edge, or broke (which is a lot better than poor), you grow up with a strange sense of money. When there isn't enough money to go around—and little chance that there can be enough—it seems to me that you either become totally anxious and focused on being secure and knowing where every penny is, or you presume it is something that is beyond your capacities to think about. I fall into the category of folks who grew up with little hope that there would ever be enough money to go around no matter how hard you worked. The idea of saving, or of planning, was ludicrous. How do you plan for the future if there is not enough to get by right now! It skews the way I think about money today. I still tend to spend whatever is available and presume I will find extra work to cover whatever emergencies may arrive. I also give away a lot of money. Anytime I am confronted with someone's (or some group's) need, I find I cannot say no. I give money to scholarships, to send students to conferences, to social action groups, to community service groups. I loan money to students. I pay for their books. It does not occur to me to say no. There are so many memories of the times that ten dollars would have made a difference—of times that someone helped and made hope possible.

Memory: The semester it looked like Rob would finally get his B.A. after eight years of struggling. I was pregnant with our second child and became seriously anemic and had to stop operating the Day Care Home that was covering our rent. It looked as if (again) Rob would have to drop out. We shopped regularly in a little corner grocery owned by Vince Bell, a Korean immigrant. On the day that Rob and I had decided he would have to drop out I waddled into the store. Vince (noticing my tear-swollen face) asked what was wrong. I told him. And he said. "He must not stop going to school. Education is what matters. That baby needs a father with an education. You charge your groceries for as long as you need. Someday you will pay me. But don't let Robert stop going to college." And for almost eight months we charged everything we ate, and it took us four years to pay Vince back. But we did. And Rob did graduate.

Memory: I am working as a cashier on the weekends when Rob can be home with the babies. It is Rebekah's birthday and we are completely broke. Two of the waitresses come up to me after their shift and hand me their tip money. "Get the little girl something really pretty." "It's important to have a birthday party." I take the money and Bekah has a birthday.

Memory: Rob is driving truck days, going to school nights. He studies on his lunch break and when waiting around the warehouse for loads to be calculated. The guys tease him, call him Professor. Still, they tell him about the loan fund the Union has set up for students. It's supposed to be for kids of the truckers, but "Hey, maybe if you go down to the credit union and tell 'em you work here now, they'll bend the rules for you." The shop steward adds "I'll give 'em a call." Rob, whose father was not a trucker—but dirt farmed each year in Oklahoma until the crop failed, then worked the mines in Colorado, the shipyards in California, and then headed back to Oklahoma to try again, year after year—Rob gets the loan and starts graduate school.

Another factor for me and for most of my working-class friends is that money does not carry the moral message that it does for middle-class families. The notion that somehow "good" people are rewarded by having lots of money was proved incorrect in our childhoods. We all have memories of hardworking, intelligent, caring, good people who could barely scrape by. Being financial stable does not equate with being virtuous, and "prudent" is not a word of glowing esteem.

It is not that the raised working-class faculty are all alike. Some of my colleagues feel they are among the lucky, or the talented, or the special, who were able to escape and who measure their success by the gulf between them and their working-class students. Others use the memory of their own struggles as a bridge, a connection.

Memory: Staff training day. A workshop on "Retaining Students," a codeword title for figuring out how to teach to/with the students of color, the working-class students, those for whom English is their second language. I am one of five panelists, all of us talking about our search for ways to help students find their own unique voices, helping them see they have something important to say. We talk about shaping the curriculum so that it reflects the world that the students came from, helping the students to believe they are intelligent, capable, creating an environment which makes it more likely they will be able to do well. Two doors down, another workshop is going on entitled "Working with the Difficult Student." Here the conversation is different. "If they show up late, lock the door." "Remember, you've got to have standards." "What you need is to be absolutely objective, and if people don't cut it they're out." The message is that there is a fixed amount of preselected knowledge, and that the true job of the teacher is to present this data which students will either learn or they won't. It is the information itself that is primary. And it is the faculty's task to protect the information rather than the student.

Unspoken, but agreed upon, is the notion that some students are smart and some are not.

Mission High School was one of the schools on the wrong side of Market Street. The school was about one third central American, one third African American, and one third a mix of Anglo, Filipino, and Samoan. (We would have described the mix as Spanish, Negro, and White. So much for the language of the 1950s.) Out of my graduating class of six hundred, five of us went on to college.

Classes were tracked in those days, and I was in the high track, destined for better things than most of my classmates. There were X classes for good students, regular classes for ordinary students, and R classes for poor students. How severe the tracking was wasn't clear to me until one semester when I had to take "regular" English rather than X English. State law decreed that we were to read *The Count of Monte Cristo*. Instead of the book, the teacher handed out the Classic Comic Book. (I was asked to stay after class and told confidentially that if I wanted to I could read the abridged edition because I was one of the "smart ones.")

Despite being in the X track, during my senior year I went onto 4/4, a system where one attended classes in the morning and worked for money in the afternoon. I think that was when I was at Woolworth's, maybe it was the American Can Company. The schedule meant I didn't take language or science classes. No one, at home or at school, said anything or seemed to have any objections to my schedule. Almost all the kids I knew worked, and we all paid for our own clothes, books, entertainment. Many of us contributed our earnings to our families and for some of my friends, their income was key to the family survival. College was something that other people did.

(I am awestruck these days as I watch my friends preparing their kids to go to college before the kids are even out of elementary school. A six-year-old friend told me recently "I'm going to be a famous scientist when I grow up. But I have to go to a really good college to be a really good scientist.")

Recent memory: Last week, my daughter-in-law asked me, "When Rebekah was a little one, what did you think she would 'be' when she grew up?" I was somewhat startled and heard myself answer "We didn't think in those terms then. I thought about who she was, but I presumed she would grow up and work, not grow up and have a profession." Later I wondered at my response—certainly we had treasured and nourished her gift of language and love of books. Certainly we delighted in the thoughtful analytic way she examined the world. We took her to the library, to the aquarium. But I had no idea how to prepare her for college, aim her at a good profession. The most I hoped for from her schools was that she would not be injured.

My parents believed in education. They, and the Left community in San Francisco, treated kids as if we were intelligent, capable. We were listened to, included, encouraged. Our house was filled with books, records, artwork. Still, no one at home knew to check out my high school course work, to shape and focus me toward college. Whatever my parents' dreams were about me and college, they (and I) had no idea how to go about considering any option other than City College. And at sixteen I wasn't sure I wanted to go at all.

Two things changed that scenario.

First, I had been working since I was fourteen. I had had enough of being a sales clerk, a waitress, holding lousy jobs, on my feet, trying to please foremen and supervisors. Anything was better than working at the Emporium, even college.

Second, there was the chance encounter—a counselor at the summer camp I had attended thanks to camperships from the Guardsmen. She was a college student. Furthermore she was a college student at Mills College, a small liberal arts "girls" college. I had a marvelous crush on her and she had been very interested in me. She suggested I apply to Mills, and went so far as to invite me over to the campus and introduce me to an admissions officer.

So I applied, was accepted, and received a scholarship which made it cheaper for me to attend Mills than to support myself going to City College.

I remember someone asking me why I was going to college and their shock and disdain when I said "to get a better job."

(Today it is fashionable and politically expedient to "train" working-class kids for jobs and to presume that education is a privilege for the few. It is strange for me to find myself in the position of fighting the "Vocational-Education-is-all-you-need" wave and being a continual voice for the rights of all students to read and write and think.)

Memory: Mills is surrounded by trees, literally fenced off from the city that surrounds it. I am completely lost. My classmates move differently, use words differently, stand further apart, laugh over jokes I do not understand. It is the fifties. There is no social analysis available for me to figure out what is going on. My two years there changes my life—gives me tools that I still use today—makes much of what is good in my life possible. And injures me so profoundly that thirty years later I cannot bring myself to attend a conference that is held on the college grounds.

Like most working-class kids I have few skills that would enable me to succeed in the academic world. Study habits imply a quiet space to work, one's own room (or at least one's own desk). At my high school, standards were low, expectations low. Quick and verbal, I had gotten good grades without ever having to rewrite or rethink anything I did. My first paper at Mills receives a F, my second a D−, the third D, the fourth D+. Painfully, slowly, I struggle with how to construct a paragraph, support an argument, document information, shape an essay. In class I am lost. I have no idea how to take notes, what is and what isn't significant. It is clear to me that something is wrong. My roommate's notes flow down the page. She has little cards she writes on and shuffles in some magic manner to create her papers. Through some alchemy that I have not participated in she not only knows what to write but which kinds of comments in class are acceptable and which are irrelevant.

It's not just that I make mistakes, but that I do not even recognize they are mistakes. I become nerve-ending sensitive to subtle clues that tell me I am "wrong," "foreign." Much of my energy goes into reading the professor's body language, the other students' tones, the slightly lifted eyebrow, the barest step backward, the pitying smile, the widened eyes of outrage. There is not much left over for paying attention to content although I hunger for the content and am in awe of how much everyone else knows. I wear my lack of student skills as a brand, labeling my "otherness," my sense of failure. At the end of the year when I finally receive an A on a paper it is not a cause of delight, only fatigue and anxiety that I will not be able to do it again, as I am still not sure why this paper is acceptable and the earlier ones were not.

My students (almost exclusively working class or poor although most of them think they are middle class) cannot imagine that they have a right to have it easier than they do. It does not occur to them that working thirty or forty hours a week, raising children, and carrying twelve units is inherently too difficult. The issue in their mind is that they are not smart enough.

It is a continual struggle for me how to counsel students who come in to me with their lives in overload. They must work to eat, to have a roof, to feed their kids. They fall further and further behind in school. If they drop down to one or two classes, they lose their lousy financial aid, and they feel as if getting through, getting done, is impossibly far away and inaccessible. And in the meantime, there is no one with the emotional slack to respond to, care for, nurture their children.

I work with them on their papers, have elastic deadlines, permit indefinite rewrites, encourage use of all the support services, tutorials, accept papers in any language I can find someone to read them, provide crisis counseling on abortions, divorces, custody, housing, food stamps, and occasionally on transfer to four-year programs.

And I sometimes counsel them to drop out for a while—to take fewer classes—and it feels like such a betrayal of their hopes (and rights)—and often—like the only hope for their children and their personal lives.

I often go home in tears.

Memory: Mills College. There is a television in the dorm sitting room and students are watching Sir Laurence Olivier in Hamlet. *It is being shown in two segments on consecutive nights. I am enthralled and the next day mention to Dr. P., the head of the English Department, that I can hardly wait to find out how the story ends. She is amazed. Have I never read the play? Have I never read any Shakespeare? Now she is enthralled. "I always wanted to teach Shakespeare to someone who came to the plays fresh! Who hasn't been pretaught what is and isn't supposed to be significant." Mixed with surprise, her voice is tinged with shock, and pity, and worst of all, amusement. I turn and walk away and am too embarrassed to watch the second half of the program.*

Memory revised: In the years that follow I make up a story. In my mind Dr. P. invites me into her Shakespeare seminar and offers to tutor me to make up my deficit in background. I imagine myself sitting in her office, or in the living room of her campus home, showing her my notes, listening to her explain all those terms other students write down with comprehension, "anecdote, essay format, Elizabethan, documented statement, Globe theater, T. S. Eliot, Thoreau (Oh well, him I know. He served time in jail for civil disobedience). In my fantasy she recognizes what I don't know (it doesn't occur to me to imagine she might be interested in what I do know) and helps me to discriminate what is appropriate, what is significant, what is merely filler.

I cannot remember when this story took life in my memory, at what point my longing and need created this myth of what should have been. But I do recognize how quickly my most at risk students take offense, how sensitive they are to the slightest patronization, impatience, or amusement I might betray. I recognize that only those untouched by a specific exclusion have the luxury of presuming that a person is being super sensitive about that exclusion, injustice, humiliation.

How vulnerable the foreigner.

How thin the coat of pride, and what a poor garment against the unknown.

Memory: There is another footnote to the Hamlet *story. I do not get into the Shakespeare seminar (I don't even try). However, partly from humiliation, partly from hunger, I start reading Shakespeare and am so swept up in the language that I memorize phrases, passages, whole sections. The second semester of my sophomore year I write a special project paper in which Shakespeare is on trial for misrepresentation of history; and he defends himself by saying that history too is fiction, written to tell a chosen story. It is the first academic writing I do that has any connection to me and to which I feel a sense of pride. This paper, on which I receive only a B, I send home to my parents, and keep for years.*

Outside the classroom where I now teach there is a long bulletin board in the hall. Once a semester I instigate a collective display designed to include our students' lives and thinking.

For International Women's Week I ask students to bring in snapshots of their mothers, aunts, women friends, daughters and to pin them on the board with short written comments about how these women have influenced and impacted their lives—about why they love and admire them.

Sometimes we have done displays about grandparents—what kinds of lives they lived, how our lives are different, the ways in which they shaped us.

Sometimes we do a "concimientos" with huge sheets of paper on which everyone answers a series of questions about who in their family had how much schooling, why they are in school, how many hours do they work outside their homes, who did what kinds of work in their childhood home, who does it now, what is wonderful/hard about being a student, what three things would they most like to change to make being in college easier for their children someday in the future.

I want my students to be connected to the college. I want their homes, their lives, their histories to be visible, welcome. And then I want them to feel committed to the larger world. It is clear to me that the reason I teach is to help my students find the legitimacy of their own voices, to convince them that the world can be changed and that they can be the change makers.

(I can't always feel it—but I always believe it).

Memory: When the war was over.

Daddy came home. Daddy came home. Daddy came home.

Karla was thirteen, I was seven, Kathie was two. Daddy had left when Kathie was a few weeks old and she had no idea who this Daddy man we were waiting for could possibly be.

I remember we cut letters out of Momma's typing paper, and spelled WELCOME along the wall over the banister of the stairwell.

I remembered him, had longed for his presence, can still feel his arms around me as he came up the stairs.

Daddy was home and now for a short while

Momma was home.

Mom was able to leave her job, and with the GI bill we bought a house, and Mom was home after school, and my beloved sister Laurie was born.

A time of hope.

Dad and Mom talked a lot about the world that could be.

We were going to build a world with no hatred, no "prejudice," no national boundaries. There would be education for all, health care for all.

We were going to build a world without war.

If we worked together we could change things. We would change things.

Our union brought the Kaiser Health plan into San Francisco. We each had our own card. (I still remember my number.) And that card meant we could get whatever care we needed, whatever medication we needed. No more going to the clinic and waiting to see if they would see you. No more charity case treatment.

Memory: I am probably seven years old. I have taken the bus, by myself, across the city to Mt. Zion Hospital to the dentistry clinic. I am not too frightened. Mom has told me it is to have my teeth cleaned and checked and that I will not be given a shot or have any drilling.

Once I am in the chair, the dentist decides I have a cavity that must be filled immediately and as he tells the young woman assistant to get tools ready I begin to cry and call for my mother. He turns to me and snarls "Behave yourself or I'll pull all your teeth out!"

I am terrified, try to get down out of the chair.

Another dentist is called in, and a nurse, and the two of them hold me down as the first dentist administers the Novocaine.

I capitulate, and sit still in the chair as the dentist berates my mother for sending me alone, and comments to the nurse "Hasn't anyone ever taught her how to behave?"

Humiliated and frightened, I sit still in the chair. Profoundly ashamed, I do not defend my mother, and guilt-ridden, I do not tell her what happened when I arrive home.

I realize that if she reads this, it will be her first knowledge of the event.

I teach classes about children, about families, about institutions which do (and don't) support the emergence of strength and learning in human beings. Some of my students are headed for the universities. Most of my students are parents, child-care workers, foster parents, group home staffs. I love the teaching. (I love how much they teach me.) My students come to class after working all day on understaffed jobs caring for children whose needs are greater than there are resources available to meet. Many of them work weekends waiting tables to earn enough money to support their "habit" of working with little ones. Anything I discuss in class they are putting into practice the next day. If I have generalized, glossed over, simplified—I hear about it in the next class. "It didn't work." "It is important." "Try again."

I insist upon these students' right to literature. I insist upon their right to ideas, critical thinking, the world of the mind. I will not ghettoize them into being Vocational students who only need to be taught the particular skills that a specific employer requires.

(". . . hearts starve as well as bodies, give us bread but give us roses")

In all of my classes we read short stories, poetry, essays. I encourage them to write about their own lives, their own experiences, and whenever possible I "publish" their writing in books we distribute to the rest of the class. I assign them the task of looking for literature that reflects their parents' lives, their own work, the work they dream of.

Every textbook is used as a tool for critical questioning. Who were the people who wrote it? Who did the research? Who was the research focused upon? What assumptions do the illustrations make about the nature of the world? (For that matter, we discuss the outrageous prices they are charged for textbooks and the nature of the publishing industry in the United States.)

I expect each of my students to write clearly, mindfully, accurately. And I consider it part of my job to see that they are able to meet my expectations. We set up study groups and writing groups. I work with each student on setting up a study schedule, walk them through the library, take them personally to the college tutors if necessary.

These students are doing some of the most difficult work of our world, and are the lowest paid professionals in the country. Every class, every semester I work at connecting them to the bigger social picture and showing them tools to changing their circumstances. I use an idea of my father's and have a media watch where students bring in clippings from the paper that speak to the issues in the class. I teach collaboration skills, organizing skills. My department sends students to conferences, workshops, to testify in front of legislative committees. We teach them how to write letters to the editor, to speak in public. I assign essays in which I ask them what the world would look like if it were good for children. And then, what are four steps they can take with others to move the world in that direction? In every way I can think of I tell them, people make history. People like you make history.

Memory: December 1991—I attend a Modern Language Association conference in San Francisco in order to hear my mother speak on a panel titled "Working-Class Literature." One of the speakers, a brilliant writer, a Chicana, says of herself with great sorrow, "I am a member of a University faculty. I have such privilege now. I am no longer working class." And my mother, almost in tears, replies, "Oh no. You embody the working class in all you do. You are the working class that your working-class parents fought into being, believed could be. To call education a privilege, to call development of self, of capacity—to call those the province of the middle class is a distortion of history. You are the first generation of your family to be able to claim this birthright. You have not left your family behind, you carry them with you. You are committed to the true potentiality of your students. You are doing your work serving and honoring the working class."

Classes started last week. A new semester. I love working registration. I get heady on the hope, excited by the energy. As in most schools in California, our students represent the entire planet. I have students in my class who are immigrants from eleven different countries—the new Californians, the new citizens. They are the embodiment of my parents' prophecy—all one people—no race but the human race. Within the walls of the classroom, the fears, misinformation, tensions between them are tentatively put aside as they wait to see what I have to offer. I have the privilege of orchestrating our dance together. I tap into their hope and offer them mine. "Your families and mine," I tell them, "do the work of the world. We already know about being strong and enduring. You already have great intelligence. We have it in our power to make a world in which all people's work is respected, all humans flourish. If not today, then tomorrow. And you will be among those who make it happen."

Tillie Olsen, the second eldest of six children, was born in 1912 and raised in Nebraska. Her Socialist, Russian-Jewish parents immigrated there after the failed Russian Revolution of 1905. Her father, who worked with his hands all his life, was Nebraska State Secretary of the Socialist Party for many years. Public libraries were her college. She wrote as a girl, but the necessity of raising and supporting four daughters through "everyday jobs," and her activism, kept her from writing for many years. She is the author of *Tell Me A Riddle; Yonnondio: From the Thirties;* and *Silences.* Her work has been translated into thirteen languages, and anthologized over 130 times. She is a longtime San Franciscan.

Tillie Olsen

> What they came into by virtue of their birth, we have had to earn at the cost of years and our youth.
>
> —Anton Chekhov

> However, it was my poverty and not my will that consented to be beaten. It takes two or three generations to do what I tried to do in one.
>
> —Hardy's *Jude the Obscure*

from *Silences*

Of the first generation . . .

A phenomenon of our time, the increasingly significant number of first (or second) generation of our people to aspire to the kinds of uses of capacity possible through the centuries only for few human beings of privilege—among these, to write.

Marginal. Against complex odds. Exhausting (though exhilarating) achievement.

Tillie Olsen, *Silences* (New York: Delta/Dell, 1979).

This the barest of indications as to vulnerabilities, balks, blights; reasons for lessenings and silencings:*

The education, most often gotten part-time, over years and with difficulty; seldom full-time for absorption in it. Often inferiority of it. Intimidations.**

Anxieties, shamings. "Hidden injuries of class." Prevailing attitudes toward our people as "lower class," "losers," (they just didn't have it); contempt for their lives and the work they do ("the manure theory of social organization" is what W.E.B. Du Bois called it).

The blood struggle for means: one's own development so often at the cost of others giving themselves up for us or of our own inability to help our kin. "Love, tenderness, responsibility, would only have meant pain, suffering, defeat, the repetition of my mother's life for another generation" (Agnes Smedley).

Likelihood of part-time, part-self writing. Having to support self by means other than writing. Problems of getting to writing at all. Problems of roots; ties; separation.

Camus's "loving with despair"; sense of possibilities not come to; knowledge of the latent, the unfulfilled, the gargoyled, in our kin.

Coercions to "pass"; to write with the attitude of, and/or in the manner of, the dominant. Little to validate our different sense of reality, to help raise one's own truths, voice, against the prevalent.

Problems of what Chekhov (a first generation) called "squeezing the serf out of one's soul."

Meagerest of indications only.

Class—economic circumstance; problems of being in the first generation of one's family to come to writing—its relationship to works of literature: the great unexamined.

---

*Some of what has been written here of the writer-woman is parallel; clues (and many writer-women are first generation of their families, women or men, to write).

**Little teaching of writing as process to fortify against measuring one's earlier work against that of established writers. (No anthology of the work that admired writers were doing *their* earlier years.) Little reinforcement to the V. Woolf conception that if writing "explains much and tells much" it is valid. Little to rouse confident sense of one's own source material—the importance of what one has to bring into literature that is not there now, and one's right to say it.

Selected References

Albrecht, Lisa and Rose M. Brewer, ed. *Bridges of Power: Women's Multicultural Alliances.* Philadelphia: New Society Publishers, 1990.

Amott, Teresa L. and Julia A. Matthaei. *Race, Gender & Work.* Boston: South End Press, 1991.

Anzaldúa, Gloria. *Borderlands/La Frontera.* San Francisco: Spinsters/Aunt Lute, 1987.

———. *Making Face, Making Soul.* San Francisco: Aunt Lute Foundation Books, 1990.

Aptheker, Bettina. *Tapestries of Life.* Amherst: University of Massachusetts Press, 1989.

———. *Woman's Legacy: Essays on Race, Sex, and Class in American History.* Amherst: University of Massachusetts, 1987.

Arac, Jonathan, ed. *After Foucault: Humanistic Knowledge, Postmodern Challenges.* New Brunswick: Rutgers University Press, 1988.

———. *Critical Genealogies: Historical Situations for Postmodern Literary Studies.* New York: Columbia University Press, 1987.

Aronowitz, Stanley. *The Politics of Identity: Class, Culture, Social Movements.* New York: Routledge, 1992.

Bakhtin, M. M. *The Dialogic Imagination.* Edited by Michael Holquist. Translated by Caryl Emerson and Michael Holquist. Austin: University of Texas Press, 1981.

———. *Speech Genres.* Edited by Caryl Emerson. Minneapolis: University of Minnesota Press, 1964.

Barlett, Donald L. and James B. Steele. *America: What Went Wrong?* Kansas City: Andrews and McMeel, 1992.

Baron, Ava, ed. *Work Engendered: Toward a New History of American Labor.* Ithaca: Cornell University Press, 1991.

Bauer, Dale M. and S. Jaret McKinstry, eds. *Feminism, Bakhtin and the Dialogic.* Albany: State University of New York Press, 1991.

Belsey, Catherine. *Critical Practice.* London: Methuen, 1980.

Benn, Tony, ed. *Writings on the Wall: A Radical and Socialist Anthology 1215–1984.* London: Faber and Faber, 1984.

Bennett, Tony. *Outside Literature.* New York: Routledge, 1990.

Berger, John. *The Sense of Sight.* New York: Pantheon, 1985.

——— and Jean Mohr. *A Seventh Man.* New York: Penguin, 1975.

Bernstein, Basil. *Class, Codes and Control.* Vol. 1. London: Routledge and Kegan Paul, 1971.

Blake, Casey Nelson. *The Beloved Community: The Cultural Criticism of Randolph Bourne, Van Wyck Brooks, Waldo Frank and Lewis Mumford.* Chapel Hill: University of North Carolina Press, 1990.

Bluestone, Barry and Bennett Harrison. *The Deindustrialization of America.* New York: Basic Books, 1982.

Bourdieu, Pierre. *Distinction.* Translated by Richard Nice. Cambridge: Harvard University Press, 1984.

————. *Outline of a Theory of Practice.* Translated by Richard Nice. New York: Columbia University Press, 1977.

Braverman, Harry. *Labor and Monopoly Capital.* New York: Monthly Review Press, 1974.

Bromley, Roger. *Lost Narratives: Popular Fictions, Politics, and Recent History.* New York: Routledge, 1988.

Buss, Fran Leeper. *Dignity: Lower Income Women Tell of Their Lives and Struggles.* Ann Arbor: The University of Michigan Press, 1985.

Butler, Judith and Joan W. Scott, eds. *Feminists Theorize the Political.* New York: Routledge, 1992.

Calderon, Hector and José David Saldivar, eds. *Criticism in the Borderlands: Studies in Chicano Literature, Culture, and Ideology.* Durham: Duke University Press, 1991.

Churchill, Ward and Elisabeth R. Lloyd. *Culture versus Economism.* Denver: University of Colorado, 1984.

Clifford, James and George E. Marcus, eds. *Writing Culture.* Berkeley: University of California Press, 1986.

Coiner, Constance. *Better Red: The Writing and Resistance of Tillie Olsen and Meridel Le Sueur.* New York: Oxford University Press, 1995.

Collins, Patricia Hill. *Black Feminist Thought: Knowledge, Consciousness, and the Politics of Empowerment.* New York: Routledge, 1990.

Davis, Lennard J. *Resisting Novels: Ideology and Fiction.* New York: Methuen, 1987.

Davis, Mike. *City of Quartz.* New York: Vintage, 1992.

————. *Prisoners of the American Dream.* New York: Verso, 1986.

Dawley, Alan. *Class and Community.* Cambridge: Harvard University Press, 1976.

deCerteau, Michel. *Heterologies: Discourse on the Other.* Translated by Brian Massumi. Minneapolis: University of Minnesota Press, 1986.

Denning, Michael. *Mechanic Accents.* London: Verso, 1987.

Du Bois, Ellen Carol and Vicki L. Ruiz, eds. *Unequal Sisters.* New York: Routledge, 1990.

Du Bois, W.E.B. *The Souls of Black Folk.* New York: New American Library, 1969.

Edwards, Richard. *Contested Terrain: The Transformation of the Workplace in the Twentieth Century.* New York: Basic Books, 1979.

Fanon, Frantz. *The Wretched of the Earth.* New York: Grove, 1963.

Felski, Rita. *Beyond Feminist Aesthetics: Feminist Literature and Social Change.* Cambridge: Harvard University Press, 1989.

Forché, Carolyn, ed. *Against Forgetting: Twentieth-Century Poetry of Witness.* New York: Norton, 1993.

Forgacs, David, ed. *An Antonio Gramsci Reader: Selected Writings 1916.* 1935 rpt. New York: Schocken, 1988.

Foster, Hal. *The Anti-Aesthetic.* Port Townsend, Wash.: Bay Press, 1983.

Freire, Paulo. *Pedagogy of the Oppressed.* New York: The Seabury Press, 1973.

————. *The Politics of Education: Culture, Power and Liberation.* South Hadley, Mass.: Bergin & Garvey, 1985.

Frisch, Michael. *A Shared Authority: Essays on the Craft and Meanings of Oral and Public History.* Albany: State University of New York Press, 1990.

———— and Daniel Walkowitz, eds. *Working Class America: Essays on Labor, Community and American Society.* Urbana: University of Illinois Press, 1983.

Fusco, Coco. "About Locating Ourselves and Our Representations" in *Framework 36: Theory and the Politics of Location.* London: Sankofa Film and Video, 1989.

Garson, Barbara. *The Electronic Sweatshop.* New York: Penguin, 1988.

Geertz, Clifford. *Local Knowledge: Further Essays in Interpretive Anthropology.* New York: Basic Books, 1983.

Giroux, Henry A. *Border Crossings: Cultural Workers and the Politics of Education.* New York: Routledge, 1992.

———. *Teachers as Intellectuals: Toward a Critical Pedagogy of Learning.* South Hadley, Mass.: Bergin & Garvey, 1988.

Goldman, Emma. *Living My Life.* 2 vols. 1931. Reprint (2 vols. in 1). New York: Dover, 1970.

Gorz, Andre. *Farewell to the Working Class.* Translated by Mike Sonenscher. Boston: South End Press, 1982.

Graff, Gerald. *Professing Literature.* Chicago: The University of Chicago Press, 1989.

Gramsci, Antonio. *The Modern Prince and other Writings.* Reprint. New York: International Publishers, 1987.

———. *Selections from the Prison Notebooks.* Edited and translated by Quentin Hoare and Geoffrey Howell Smith. New York: International Publishers, 1971.

Grossberg, Lawrence, Cary Nelson, and Paula Treicher, eds. *Cultural Studies.* New York: Routledge, 1992.

Gutman, Herbert. *Power and Culture: Essays on the American Working Class.* Edited by Ira Berlin. New York: Pantheon, 1987.

Hamilton, Roberta and Michele Barrett, eds. *The Politics of Diversity: Feminism, Marxism and Nationalism.* London: Verso, 1986.

Hansen, Karen V. and Ilene J. Philipson, eds. *Women, Class, and the Feminist Imagination.* Philadelphia: Temple, 1990.

Hapke, Laura. *Tales of the Working Girl.* New York: Twayne, 1992.

Haraway, Donna J. *Simians, Cyborgs, and Women: The Reinvention of Nature.* New York: Routledge, 1991.

Harlow, Barbara. *Resistance Literature.* New York: Methuen, 1987.

Harrington, Michael. *Socialism.* New York: Saturday Review Press, 1970.

Hennessy, Rosemary. *Materialist Feminism and the Politics of Discourse.* New York: Routledge, 1993.

Hitchcock, Peter. *Dialogics of the Oppressed.* Minnesota: University of Minnesota Press, 1993.

———. *Working-Class Fiction in Theory and Practice: A Reading of Alan Sillitoe.* Ann Arbor: UMI Research Press, 1989.

Hobsbawm, Eric. *Workers: Worlds of Labor.* New York: Pantheon, 1984.

Hoerder, Dirk, ed. *"Struggle a Hard Battle": Essays on Working-Class Immigrants.* DeKalb: Northern Illinois University Press, 1986.

Hoggart, Richard. *The Uses of Literacy.* Hammondsworth: Penguin, 1958.

hooks, bell. *Feminist Theory: From Margin to Center.* Boston: South End Press, 1984.

——— and Cornel West. *Breaking Bread: Insurgent Black Intellectual Life.* Boston: South End, 1991.

Howe, Florence. *Myths of Coeducation.* Bloomington: Indiana University Press, 1984.

———, ed. *Tradition and the Talents of Women.* Urbana: University of Illinois Press, 1991.

Katznelson, Ira and Aristide R. Zolberg, eds. *Working-Class Formation: Nineteenth-Century Patterns in Western Europe and the United States.* Princeton: Princeton University Press, 1986.

Kaye, Harvey J. and Keith McClelland. *E. P. Thompson: Critical Perspectives.* Philadelphia: Temple University Press, 1990.

Kecht, Maria-Regina, ed. *Pedagogy is Politics: Literary Theory and Critical Teaching.* Urbana: University of Illinois, 1992.

Kessler-Harris, Alice. *Out to Work: A History of Wage-Earning Women in the United States.* New York: Oxford University Press, 1982.

Kingsolver, Barbara. *Holding the Line: Women in the Great Arizona Mine Strike of 1983.* Ithaca: ILR Press, 1989.

Klaus, H. Gustav. *The Literature of Labor.* New York: St. Martin's Press, 1985.

Kuczynski, Jurgen. *The Rise of the Working Class.* Translated by C.T.A. Ray. 1967. Reprint. New York: McGraw-Hill, 1971.

Lang, Berel and Forrest Williams, eds. *Marxism and Art.* New York: David McKay, 1972.

Lauter, Paul. *Canons and Contexts.* New York: Oxford University Press, 1991.

———. "Working-Class Women's Literature: An Introduction to Study." *Radical Teacher,* no. 15 (1980): 16–26.

Lerner, Gerda. *The Majority Finds its Past: Placing Women in History.* New York: Oxford University Press, 1973.

Lesy, Michael. *Bearing Witness: A Photographic Chronicle of American Life 1860–1945.* New York: Pantheon, 1982.

Levine, Lawrence. *Highbrow/Lowbrow: The Emergence of Cultural Hierarchy in America.* Cambridge: Harvard University Press, 1988.

Levison, Andrew. *The Working-Class Majority.* New York: Penguin, 1975.

Luria, A. R. *The Mind of a Mnemonist.* Translated by Lynn Solotaroff. Cambridge: Harvard University Press, 1968.

Marable, Manning. *The Crisis of Color and Democracy.* Monroe, Maine: Common Courage Press, 1992.

———. *How Capitalism Underdeveloped Black America.* Boston: South End Press, 1983.

Mariani, Philomena, ed. *Critical Fictions: The Politics of Imaginative Writing.* Seattle: Bay Press, 1991.

Marx, Karl, et al. *The Marxist Reader.* New York: Avenel Books, 1982. [With commentary and notes by Emile Burns]

Matthaei, Julie A. *An Economic History of Women in America.* New York: Schocken Books, 1982.

McLellan, David. *Utopian Pessimist: The Life and Thought of Simone Weil.* New York: Poseidon Press, 1990.

Merod, Jim. *The Political Responsibility of the Critic.* Ithaca: Cornell University Press, 1987.

Miami Theory Collective, eds. *Community at Loose Ends.* Minneapolis: University of Minnesota Press, 1991.

Miller, Nancy K. *Getting Personal.* New York: Routledge, 1991.

Minh-ha, Trin T. *Woman, Native, Other: Writing, Postcoloniality and Feminism.* Bloomington: Indiana University Press, 1989.

Mirabella, M. Bella and Lennard Davis, eds. *Left Politics and the Literary Profession.* New York: Columbia University Press, 1991.

Moraga, Cherríe and Gloria Anzaldúa. *This Bridge Called My Back: Writings by Radical Women of Color.* 1981. Reprint. Latham, N.Y.: Kitchen Table/Women of Color, 1984.

Morley, Dave and Ken Worpole, eds. *The Republic of Letters: Working Class Writing and Local Publishing.* London: Comedia Publishing Group, 1982.

Myerhoff, Barbara. *Number Our Days.* New York: Touchstone/Simon and Schuster, 1978.

Nekola, Charlotte and Paula Rabinowitz, eds. *Writing Red.* New York: The Feminist Press, 1987.

Nelson, Cary and Lawrence Grossberg, eds. *Marxism and the Interpretation of Culture.* Urbana: University of Illinois Press, 1988.

Newton, Judith and Deborah Rosenfelt, eds. *Feminist Criticism and Social Change.* New York: Methuen, 1985.

Ohmann, Richard. *English in America.* New York: Oxford, 1976.

———. *Politics of Letters*. Middletown, Conn.: Wesleyan University Press, 1987.

Ollman, Bertell. *Dialectical Investigations*. New York: Routledge, 1993.

Olsen, Tillie. *Silences*. New York: Dell, 1978.

———. *Tell Me a Riddle*. New York: Dell, 1971.

———. *Yonnondio: From the Thirties*. New York: Dell, 1975.

Ong, Walter J. *Orality and Literacy*. New York: Routledge, 1982.

Palmer, Bryan D. *Descent into Discourse: The Reification of Language and the Writing of Social History*. Philadelphia: Temple University Press, 1990.

Poulantzas, Nicos. *Classes in Contemporary Capitalism*. Translated by David Fernbach. London: NLB, 1975.

Portelli, Alessandro. *The Death of Luigi Trastulli and Other Stories*. Albany: State University of New York Press, 1991.

Rabinow, Paul, ed. *The Foucault Reader*. New York: Pantheon, 1984.

Rabinowitz, Paula. *Labor and Desire: Women's Revolutionary Fiction in Depression America*. Chapel Hill: North Carolina University Press, 1991.

Robbins, Bruce. *The Servant's Hand*. New York: Columbia University Press, 1986.

Robinson, Lillian. *Sex, Class, and Culture*. Bloomington: Indiana University Press, 1978.

Roediger, David R. *The Wages of Whiteness*. New York: Verso, 1991.

Rogovin, Milton and Michael Frisch. *Portraits in Steel*. Ithaca: Cornell University Press, 1993.

Romero, Mary. *Maid in the U.S.A.* New York: Routledge, 1992.

Rose, Mike. *Lives on the Boundary*. New York: Penguin, 1986.

Rosner, David and Gerald Markowitz. *Dying for Work: Workers' Safety and Health in Twentieth-Century America*. Bloomington: Indiana University Press, 1989.

Rothenberg, Paula, ed. *Race, Class, and Gender in the United States*. St. Martin's Press, 1992.

Ruddick, Sara and Pamela Daniels, eds. *Working It Out*. New York: Pantheon, 1978.

Said, Edward W. *The World, The Text, The Critic*. Cambridge: Harvard University Press, 1983.

Scott, Joan Wallach. *Gender and the Politics of History*. New York: Columbia University Press, 1988.

Scully, James. *Line Break: Poetry as Social Practice*. Seattle: Bay Press, 1988.

Sennett, Richard and Jonathan Cobb. *The Hidden Injuries of Class*. New York: Alfred A. Knopf, 1972.

Shloss, Carol. *In Visible Light: Photography and the American Writer: 1840–1940*. New York: Oxford University Press, 1987.

Shulman, Alix Kates, ed. *Red Emma Speaks: Selected Writings and Speeches of Emma Goldman*. New York: Random House, Vintage, 1972.

Slapikoff, Saul. *Consider and Hear Me*. Philadelphia: Temple University Press, 1993.

Soelle, Dorothee. *Suffering*. Translated by Everett R. Kalin. Philadelphia: Fortress Press, 1975.

———.with Shirley A. Cloyes. *To Work and To Love: A Theology of Creation*. Philadelphia: Fortress Press, 1984.

Stedman-Jones, Gareth. *The Languages of Class*. Cambridge: Cambridge University Press, 1983.

Steedman, Carolyn. *Landscape for a Good Woman*. New Brunswick: Rutgers University Press, 1987.

Thompson, E. P. *The Making of the English Working Class*. New York: Vintage, 1966.

Tressell, Robert. *The Ragged Trousered Philanthropists*. 1914. Reprint. London: Lawrence and Wishart, 1955.

Vanneman, Reeve and Lynn Weber Cannon. *The American Perception of Class.* Philadelphia: Temple University Press, 1987.

Vogel, Lisa. *Marxism and the Oppression of Women.* New Brunswick: Rutgers University Press, 1987.

Ward, Kathryn, ed. *Women Workers and Global Restructuring.* Ithaca: ILR Press, 1990.

Warhol, Robyn R. and Diane Price Herndl. *Feminisms.* New Brunswick: Rutgers University Press, 1991.

Weis, Lois. *Working Class Without Work.* New York: Routledge, 1990.

Welch, Sharon D. *Communities of Resistance and Solidarity.* Maryknoll, New York: Orbis Books, 1985.

———. *A Feminist Ethic of Risk.* Minneapolis: Fortress Press, 1990.

Wilentz, Sean. *Chants Democratic.* New York: Oxford University Press, 1976.

Williams, Raymond. *Border Country.* London: Chatto and Windus, 1960.

———. *Keywords.* Revised edition. New York: Oxford University Press, 1976.

———. *The Long Revolution.* New York: Columbia University Press, 1961.

———. *Marxism and Literature.* Oxford: Oxford University Press, 1977.

———. *The Politics of Modernism.* London: Verso, 1989.

———. *Resources of Hope.* Edited by Robin Gable. London: Verso, 1989.

Willis, Paul. *Learning to Labor.* New York: Columbia University Press, 1977.

Zandy, Janet, ed. *Calling Home: Working-Class Women's Writings.* New Brunswick: Rutgers University Press, 1990.

Zinn, Howard. *A People's History of the United States.* New York: Harper Perennial, 1990.